Sing Me a Story!
Tell Me a Song!

Sing Me a Story! Tell Me a Song!

Creative Curriculum Activities for Teachers of Young Children

Hilda L. Jackman

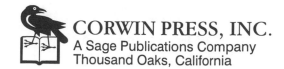

CORWIN PRESS, INC.
A Sage Publications Company
Thousand Oaks, California

Copyright © 1999 by Hilda L. Jackman

For information address:

Corwin Press, Inc.
A Sage Publications Company
2455 Teller Road
Thousand Oaks, California 91320
E-mail: order@corwinpress.com

SAGE Publications Ltd.
6 Bonhill Street
London EC2A 4PU
United Kingdom

SAGE Publications India Pvt. Ltd.
M-32 Market
Greater Kailash I
New Delhi 110 048 India

Printed in the United States of America

Library of Congress Cataloging-in-Publication Data

Jackman, Hilda L.
   Sing me a story! Tell me a song!: Creative curriculum activities for teachers of young children / Hilda L. Jackman.
     p. cm.
Includes bibliographical references.
   ISBN 0-8039-6797-7 (pbk.: acid-free paper)
   1. Early childhood education — Activity programs — United States — Handbooks, manuals, etc. 2. Curriculum planning — United States — Handbooks, manuals, etc. 3. Project method in teaching — United States — Handbooks, manuals, etc. I. Title.
   LB1139.35A37 J33 1999
   372.13 — dc21

                                                                98-40278

This book is printed on acid-free paper.

99 00 01 02 03 04 05 10 9 8 7 6 5 4 3 2 1

Typesetter: Publisher's Studio
Cover Designer: Michelle Lee

Contents

Preface

When teachers of young children get together at conferences, workshops, and staff development meetings, they like to exchange ideas and activities. This book is intended to be like a newly found "teaching friend" that will offer creative curriculum activities to help new teachers, teachers already practicing in early childhood education, administrators, supervisors, college educators, and students.

The easy-to-follow format uses themes to integrate the curriculum for young children from **infancy through eight years of age**. Theme teaching involves creating many activities around a central idea. These activities are blended into every part of the curriculum within a flexible time frame, ranging from several days to a few weeks. The activities are designed for the classroom teacher to select and combine as needed in order to meet the needs and interests of the children.

The basic concepts of this teaching resource emphasize the following:

1. Themes and activities reflect the philosophy suggested by the National Association for the Education of Young Children (NAEYC) for Developmentally Appropriate Practice in Early Childhood Programs (DAP), such as:
   - the critical role of teachers in understanding and supporting children's development and learning,
   - the concept of classrooms or groups of children as communities of learners,
   - the importance of each child in the group, and
   - the significant role of families in early childhood education.

2. Themes and activities take into consideration the age, stage of development, and experiences of young children.

3. Themes and activities emphasize and integrate different aspects of development and learning:
   - visual
   - auditory
   - tactile
   - olfactory
   - taste
   - creativity
   - language
   - critical thinking
   - problem-solving
   - social and emotional development
   - cultural development
   - coordination
   - motor development

4. Themes and activities are developmentally appropriate, and they underscore the importance of individual differences and cultural diversity among young children. This allows children to learn at their own pace and style.

5. Themes and activities encourage the development of positive self-esteem and a sense of "I can do it" in young children.

6. Activities have been "child-tested." They are easily adaptable to large group, small group, or individual instruction.

The Text

SECTIONS AND THEMES

This book is divided into six broad **sections**, with individual **themes** comprising each section. The thematic approach introduces children to activities that require active exploration, problem-solving, and the acquisition of specific concepts or skills. Each theme is designed to merge play with child-initiated and teacher-created experiences. Thirty themes are identified in this text.

THEMATIC WEBS

The curriculum **web** diagram for each theme assists in categorizing thoughts and determining what needs to be emphasized in each theme. The process of webbing is a form of brainstorming that explores and organizes connections between ideas. The web at the beginning of each theme is a starting place, to which you can add your own ideas, topics, and activities to meet the needs of your children. Creating webs helps you remain flexible.

THEME GOALS

Goals for each theme are written in a *developmentally sequenced* listing to aid your planning for the ongoing development of children as they grow and learn.

Additionally, teachers should be aware that the goals and concepts children achieve in association with a particular theme do not end when the unit is over. Children continue to explore and apply their knowledge within succeeding themes.

VOCABULARY

Vocabulary development is not done in isolation. It is a part of language development and progresses from the repetition of words to the understanding and acquisition of words. The **vocabulary** words included in each theme are only suggestions. Vocabulary should be an outgrowth of teacher and children sharing experiences relating to the theme. Review what children *know,* continue with what children *want to find out,* and conclude with what children *have learned.*

BULLETIN BOARDS

The children-created **bulletin board** featured in each theme should come from ideas suggested by the children, as should the process of creating the final product. The bulletin board ideas in this book are only recommendations. The bulletin board should be a visual extension of what is happening in your classroom. Remember to place bulletin boards at a child's eye level.

THEMATIC ACTIVITIES

Selecting developmentally appropriate **activities** begins with what the teacher knows about each child in the classroom. Understanding the developmental changes that may occur in the years from infancy through middle childhood is critical in making curriculum decisions. The **developmentally appropriate materials and supplies charts** on the inside covers of this book can assist you in making such determinations.

The activities presented in each of the themes provide for all areas of a child's development: physical, cognitive, social, emotional, cultural, language, aesthetic, and creative. At the same time, these learning activities enable children to achieve curriculum goals, skills, and concepts through:

- fingerplays, poems, and flannelboard stories
- dramatic and puppet play
- music and movement
- creative food experiences
- sensory art
- math
- science
- social studies
- children's books

Each activity is introduced by an illustrated **icon** that suggests its appropriateness for specific ages:

Note: In no case was any activity, chant, fingerplay, song, or poem of known authorship used without credits. The vast majority of these have been shared with me by young children, teachers, and students I have taught in my college courses. Other material is either from old folk songs, traditional games, or is completely original content.

BOOKS

A selected bibliography of **children's books** is included with each theme. Books are an essential part of curriculum development. Children's interests should motivate selection of children's literature, a vital part of early childhood learning. Learning is basically the process of associating that which is new with what is already known, and stories can be a powerful tool to accomplish this for young children. Interactions with children through books help us enfold literature into language and literacy development.

PARENT LETTERS

Special letters sent home on a periodic basis help promote trust and a partnership between teachers, parents, and young children. These letters also can help develop open communication between home and school by sharing opportunities for learning experiences that parents need to help their children develop and grow.

This book contains thirty letters, one for each theme, plus a special one (on CD-ROM) for parents of infants. These can be personalized to fit the group of children and parents in your classroom. Messages are more effective if they are personal and specific to your program.

The letters:

- encourage parents to share with you what they know about their children and what is important to them as parents.

- encourage parents to keep in touch with you so that you can answer any questions or concerns mentioned in the letter.

- contain general early childhood information.

- discuss the theme the children are exploring and offer activities parents can do with children at home to extend or emphasize classroom experiences.

- encourage parent involvement in events and activities, thereby strengthening teamwork between parents and teachers.

Appendix

The Appendix at the back of this volume contains full-page enlargements of music presented in various themes. These may be photocopied for ease of use and for sharing.

CD-ROM

The CD-ROM (Windows and Mac compatible) that accompanies this book contains the following teaching tools: a detailed table of contents, thematic outlines, lesson plans, parent letters, and the collection of rebus charts and patterns from the text. Including the rebus charts and patterns on the CD-ROM allows for reproducing in 8½-by-11-inch format. The parent letters, which also appear in the text, are included here to make producing and personalizing them easier for teachers. The letters are in four categories for parents of toddlers, of preschool children, of school-age children, and a special letter for parents of infants, which is included only on the CD-ROM. Letters are written for each theme. They are suggestions and intended to be personalized with what is

happening in *your* classroom. The lesson plans and thematic outlines are additional tools included on the CD-ROM.

THEMATIC OUTLINES

The outlines on the CD-ROM are a complete list of each theme and activity contained in the text. The outlines are intended as an additional guide for your theme and activity selection.

LESSON PLANS

After theme selection, webbing, and activity choices, the process of **lesson planning** is the next step in curriculum development. Lesson plans should be based on the developmental stages, learning styles, abilities, and interests of the children.

The three examples of lesson plans offer ways to:

- apply the theme across the curriculum.

- support theme-related and nonrelated activities.

- integrate thematic instruction with other required program elements.

The activities included in the lesson plans for infants, toddlers, preschool, and kindergarten through third-grade children are selected from several of the themes suggested in this resource book. Both completed and blank lesson plan forms are included on the CD-ROM.

Get Ready to Play, Explore, Learn, and Sing

There was a time when the world was a song, and the song was exciting.
Les Miserables, the musical

That time *is* early child hood. Young children entering early childhood programs are eager to sing, play, explore, and learn about themselves and their world. A developmentally appropriate classroom should give the children a multitude of opportunities to select activities from a variety of curriculum areas. This thematic curriculum resource book is designed to help you offer appropriate experiences and activities for each child in your care.

I hope you and the children experience as much enjoyment, exploration, and discovery from these creative learning experiences as I did!

Acknowledgments

A book is always a collaboration of many ideas and experiences. A sincere and heartfelt *thank you* goes out to the numerous children, teachers, parents, college students, and colleagues with whom developmentally appropriate themes and activities were shared over many years.

Special recognition and thanks must go to:

Laurent Linn, my son, whose amazing illustrations demonstrate the exuberance of early childhood. He expresses with his pen to paper what I try to say with words.

Philip Jackman, my husband, who was always there with a rhyming word, an original fingerplay or poem, and continuous patience, encouragement, and love.

Jo Eklof, my friend and colleague, whose charming songs reflect the affection and respect she feels for the children and the world we live in.

Janet Galantay, **Connie Prince**, **Roberta Robinson**, **Nita May Tannebaum** and **Bea Wolf**, my friends, exceptional teachers of young children who contributed their activities and expertise that added so much to this book.

Stephen Linn, my son, whose additional support and encouragement always came at the right moment during this project.

Jared Cohen, my nephew, who continues to tell me what kids like to do, even though he has grown beyond the early childhood years.

Jay Whitney, my editor and friend, who was *always* there! Many thanks for your reassurance, support, and commitment to young children and their teachers.

To the **Publisher's Studio Staff**, Mary Robinson, Linda Ayres-DeMasi, and Bruce Sherwin — thank you for all your support.

And to my reviewers, from all points of the compass, a special thanks for all their help:

Marietta Lamberson
Education Program Specialist
BCMW
Head Start
Mt. Vernon, IL

Joan Cobb
Professor
Baltimore City Community College/Johns Hopkins University/Salisbury State

Deb Barron
Early Childhood/Special Education Educator
Brandywine School District
Wilmington, DE

Dr. Eileen Donahue Brittain
Assistant Professor of Child Development
Harry S. Truman College
Chicago, IL

Allyson Goldberg, Teacher
Head Start
Elkton, MD

Dr. Nancy Yost
Assistant Professor
Indiana University of PA
Indiana, PA

Kathy Mohney
The Children's Place
Western Michigan University
Kalamazoo, MI

Adrianne L. Rose
Founder, A Learning Center for Children, Covina, CA
and
Julie Titus, Teacher
A Learning Center for Children

Dr. Gayle Mindes
School of Education
DePaul University
Chicago, IL

Susan Whatley
Philips Shore Elementary School
Tampa, FL

Keith L. Pentz
Assistant Professor
Gordon College
Wenham, MA

Kristin Perrone
Education Coordinator
ABC Child Development Center
Rochester, NY

About the Author

My professional life has been a growing and changing collage of education and experiences with young children. With the writing of *Sing Me a Story! Tell Me a Song!*, I have added one of the most meaningful pieces to my collage. My undergraduate degree in theatre and television from Texas Christian University led to an early career as an actor and director in children's theater, and later as puppeteer and writer/producer of children's programs for three Dallas-Fort Worth television stations. Underlying all this was a love of and commitment to young children, a passion which eventually motivated me to earn a master's degree in early childhood education at the University of North Texas.

I then went on to become first a teacher of young children two years through kindergarten and then Director of Early Childhood at the Dallas Jewish Community Center. Later, I was selected to create and direct the child development program when Brookhaven College (Dallas County Community College District) was opened in 1978. There, I served as Coordinator/Professor of the Parent-Child Study Center and Child Development Program until retiring in 1994.

Since retiring, I have kept busy as an author. Prior to writing *Sing Me a Story! Tell Me a Song!*, I wrote *Early Childhood Curriculum: A Child's Connection to the World* (Delmar Publishers, 1997). In addition, I conduct numerous workshops and staff development seminars, and am an early childhood consultant.

Like a child's collage, mine is still under construction.

SECTION I

All About Me!

The *children* are at the center of all we do in early childhood education. Developmentally appropriate curriculum is based on knowledge about how children develop and learn. Their age and experience also should be taken into consideration.

With this in mind, select thematic activities from this section, realizing that not all of the children in your class have to do the specific activity at the same time. Let *their* individual differences, abilities, and interests guide you. The activities are designed to meet the diversity of your children.

The following themes are included in Section I — All About Me!:

Theme 1   —   My Body

Theme 2   —   My Friends

Theme 3   —   My Family

Theme 4   —   My Self

Theme 5   —   My Home

Theme 6   —   My Community

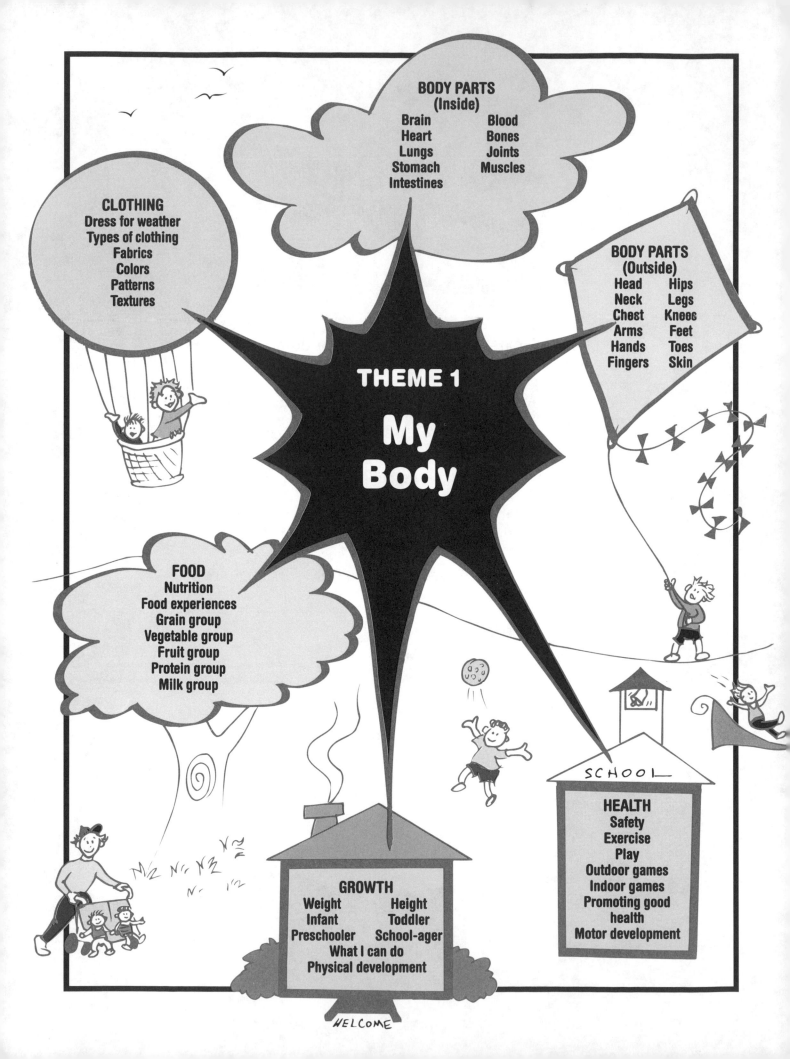

THEME GOALS

To provide opportunities for children to learn:

1. Every person is special.
2. Everyone has a body with many parts.
3. The body can move in many ways and do many things.
4. Food, exercise, and sleep help our bodies grow.
5. Eating fruits and vegetables and drinking milk keeps our bodies healthy.

Children-Created Bulletin Board

This bulletin board allows each child to draw her face on a paper plate. There is no right or wrong way to do this. A new "face" can be drawn to replace the one being displayed. Each child's "face" may change several times during the course of the theme.

✳ Use large-size paper plates for older infants and toddlers to scribble and draw on with crayons.
✳ For older children, add additional materials to the paper plates, such as markers, paints, construction paper, buttons, yarn, and pipe cleaners.
✳ To get children started, have them look into a mirror and describe what they see, such as the color of their eyes, hair, and skin. This helps children to draw self-portraits.

Vocabulary Starters

Let the children add additional words. Include pictures where appropriate.

heart — a muscle in the chest that pumps blood to all parts of the body.

stethoscope — an instrument doctors use to hear your heart beat in your chest.

lungs — two balloonlike sacks inside the chest that fill up with air when we breathe in and empty when we breathe out.

stomach — a special sack inside our body that catches the food we chew and swallow.

brain — a place inside our head that helps us think, remember, and learn new things.

weight — how heavy the body is.

height — the distance between the top of the head to the feet when standing.

Language Experiences

FINGERPLAY: Two Little Fingers

Two little fingers crawling up your arm,
   (crawl two fingers up child's arm)
Now they're on your shoulder trying to stay warm.
   (crawl fingers up to shoulder and "snuggle" them
   between shoulder and neck)
Two little fingers crawl into your hair,
   (crawl fingers into child's hair)
Cover your ears because they're almost there.
   (crawl fingers down to ears)
Two little fingers jump on your knee,
   (jump two fingers to child's knee)
See how they get there as fast as can be.
   Now they jump up to your eye,
   (two fingers jump up to eye)
And it's time to wave bye-bye.
   (wave bye-bye with two fingers)

POEM: "Looking In the Mirror"

When I look in my mirror
I'm happy to see
Someone I like
And that someone is me.
When you look in your mirror

It really is true
There's someone to like
And that someone is you.

Philip Jackman

Introduce a full-length nonbreakable mirror or small hand mirror to explore individual characteristics, such as eyes, skin, hair, mouth, nose, and clothing.

ALL ABOUT ME BOOK

This is a book the child starts at the beginning of the school year and adds to throughout the year. Simplify this project for younger children by including only those items toddlers can do developmentally. The book could contain:

✳ hand-, foot-, finger-, or thumbprints

✳ chart of weight and height

✳ pasted pictures from magazines, or drawn pictures of favorite foods, colors, and shapes

✳ any dictated story

✳ a picture of the child, family members, and friends

✳ address, phone number, birthdate

✳ what he likes to do

STORY STARTER: "When I Was a Baby"

With younger children:

✳ Let them tell you a story about themselves as babies.

✳ Later you can put the stories into each child's *All About Me* book.

With older children:

✳ Let them dictate story sentences about when they were babies. Put these on sentence strip paper.

✳ Mix the sentences up and have the children read each line and put them in the correct sequence.

✳ This activity can be extended by the children. They can make a book of the story and illustrate each line.

TIME FOR A RHYME

With the children, make a list of words that rhyme with body parts. For example:

✳ heart (smart, chart)
✳ head (bed, red)
✳ hand (band, stand)
✳ feet (seat, treat)

Dramatic Play

DOLL CORNER

✳ Select sock or soft dolls that depict different cultures and are easy to wash.
✳ The clothing on the dolls should be washable.
✳ The clothes should be easy to take off and put on.

BATHE THE BABY

✳ Provide dolls and a plastic tub with one or two inches of water.
✳ Children add tear-free baby shampoo and bathe the baby dolls.
✳ Older toddlers can squeeze a few drops of liquid soap into the tub. Encourage them to beat the soap into suds with an eggbeater.
✳ Preschoolers like using washcloths and small bars of soap.
✳ Have several towels ready for drying the baby.

CLOTHING STORE

✳ Set up the dramatic play center with boxes of clothing and related items, such as coats, shirts, skirts, gloves, hats, purses, sunglasses.
✳ Divide the space into two "dressing rooms," one for girls and one for boys.
✳ Have a nonbreakable mirror available for the children to see how the clothes look on them.

SUPERMARKET/GROCERY STORE/MERCADO/FARMER'S MARKET

✳ With the children's help, set up and extend the dramatic play area.
✳ Provide the following:

cash register
calculator
play money or money the children make
price tags
markers, pens, and colored pencils
sales slip pad
empty food containers, some with print in different languages on them to represent foods from diverse cultures

artificial fruits and vegetables
grocery sacks
coupon pages and scissors
shopping lists with words and pictures of items
telephone
signs in several languages with pictures to explain what is for sale

Puppet Play

THUMB FACE PUPPET

✳ Use a ballpoint pen to draw eyes and a mouth on the child's thumb.
✳ This becomes a very personal puppet.
✳ Play can be extended if a child wants to make all fingers into puppets.
✳ Finger face puppets can also personalize fingerplays.

CHILD STICK PUPPET

- ✳ This puppet can be made out of cardboard, tagboard, or construction paper.
- ✳ Attach puppet to a craft stick or dowel rod.
- ✳ Younger children can make a smaller child and attach a straw instead of a stick.
- ✳ Encourage children to add eyes, a nose, a mouth, ears, hair, clothes, and shoes.
- ✳ Provide crayons, markers, paints, and construction paper. Be sure to include a variety of colors that can be used to depict different skin tones.
- ✳ Include many colors of yarn for hair and clothing decoration.
- ✳ This activity promotes self-awareness and positive self-esteem.

Music

MUSICAL BEAT ACTIVITY: "Everybody Do This"

The teacher does the motions first, then asks for suggestions from children.

Everybody do this, do this, do this
Everybody do this, just like me.
Everybody clap hands, clap hands, clap hands
Everybody clap hands, just like me.
Everybody wiggle fingers, wiggle fingers, wiggle fingers
Everybody wiggle fingers, just like me.
Everybody bend knees, bend knees, bend knees
Everybody bend knees, just like me.
     (Stamp feet, shake shoulders, nod head, etc.)

SONG: "Body Rap"

C'mon, girls and boys, do the body rap.
If you think you can do it just clap-clap-clap.
Now, first you bend over and touch your toes,
And then you stand up and pat your nose.
Put your two hands down and lean on your knees.
Then turn around, turn around as nice as you please.
Now stand up straight, put your arms out wide,
And swing your hips from side to side.
Put your hands on your waist, stick your elbows out
     straight,
And twist back and forth like you open a gate.
Now point to your eyes and blink-blink-blink.
Make your mouth big and wide like you're taking a drink.
Put your hands on your head, put them right on top.
Now bend both your legs and go hop-hop-hop.
Stop where you are, stand up straight again.
Put your hands on your ears, and stick out your chin.
The last thing you do is to clap-clap-clap,
And that's the way you do the body rap.

Philip Jackman

Movement

OBSTACLE COURSE

- ✳ Set up a simple mini-obstacle course indoors for infants and toddlers to crawl through (cloth tunnels), climb over (large pillows), crawl under (sheets draped over small tables), and walk over (small sturdy stairs).

* For older children, set up an obstacle course outdoors with cardboard boxes, hollow blocks, balance beams, hoops, and cloth tunnels.

* Encourage children to crawl or walk through the course slowly, walk sideways or backwards around the course, or any other way they can think of. Verbalize their position in space by saying, "You are under the table" or, "You are on top of the pillows."

* Encourage older children to change the course or create a new one after the first one is mastered.

* Set up several short courses or have another activity going on at the same time so children do not have to wait a long time between turns.

BASIC MOVEMENTS

Children need to become aware of the many ways they can move, as well as understand the flexibility of their bodies.

* Make your body as tall as you can by stretching high.

* Make your body as small as you can by curling into a ball.

* Move across the room as if you are ice skating.

* Move across the room fast. Move slowly.

* Walk across the room on your heels. Walk on your toes.

* Walk across the room taking big steps. Take small steps.

* Swim across the room.

* Swing your arms back and forth, over and around, and side to side.

* Twist and turn like a washing machine.

* Pull an imaginary wagon across the room.

* Shake like jello.

* For younger children, simplify the movements, and demonstrate what you want them to do. Continue to do the movements with them.

WALK THE LINE

* Place an eight-to-ten-foot strip of masking tape on the floor.

* Children can crawl; walk forward, backward, sideways, or heel to toe; or jump along the line.

* This is a great way for children to learn balance and coordination safely.

Sensory Art

DRAW A CHILD

* A favorite activity of toddlers is for the teacher to draw around them while they are lying on a large piece of brown wrapping paper or butcher paper.

* An older child can choose a partner, and they can draw around each other.

* Each child then adds eyes, nose, mouth, ears, hair, and clothing with materials from the art scrap box.

* Place the drawings around the room.

FINGERPRINTS AND FOOTPRINTS

Fingerprints

* Spread pieces of construction paper or butcher paper on the table in the art center.

* Set out ink pads and magnifying glasses.

* Children make thumb and fingerprints by placing individual fingers first on ink pads and then on the paper.

* Place a plastic tub with soapy water and paper towels nearby for children to wash their hands when they are finished using ink pads.

* Children can then examine their fingerprints with a magnifying glass.

* They can look at each other's prints and discuss the similarities and differences they see.

* To extend this activity, encourage children to use the magnifying glass to look at the skin on their hands and arms. Compare the skin with their fingerprints. Examine several strands of hair with the magnifying glass.

* This activity encourages children to investigate and experiment with a magnifying glass while providing a sensory experience. The children also discover more about their bodies.

Footprints

* Next, encourage the children to make footprints. Begin by covering the floor or outdoor sidewalk with newspaper, and then place long pieces of brown wrapping paper or butcher paper over the newspaper. Tape the corners so that the paper will stay in place.

* The children remove their shoes and socks and then stand at one end of the paper.
* Help them step into tubs or containers to which you have added enough tempera paint to coat their feet without dripping. Paint is slippery, so you may need to assist some children as they walk on the paper.
* At the other end of the paper, place a tub of warm, soapy water and some towels. The children will end the activity by stepping into the tub of water.
* This special "feet painting mural" can be placed anywhere in the room or school to show what's happening in your classroom.

WEAVING

* Collect enough plastic strawberry baskets for each child to have one to work with. Ask parents to help you collect these.
* Children select lengths of brightly colored yarn.
* Dip one end of the yarn in glue, which will work as a weaving needle when it hardens.
* Encourage children to weave the yarn in and out of the holes in the basket until the basket is covered.
* This activity helps children develop small muscle skills.

Creative Food Experiences

LET'S MAKE CRACKER FACES

Toddlers need some guidance in spreading the peanut butter. The main purpose of this activity is to give the children an opportunity to try.

You will need:

> round crackers (such as Ritz crackers)
> peanut butter (or cream cheese or margarine for children who are allergic to peanut butter)
> raisins
> miniature marshmallows

1. Wash hands.
2. Spread the peanut butter on crackers.
3. Add raisins and marshmallows to make a face.
4. Eat!

LET'S MAKE CRACKER FACES!

Wash hands.

Spread some peanut butter on round crackers.

Then add raisins and marshmallows

to make a face!

EAT!

HEALTHY SNACKS

* celery sticks spread with peanut butter or pimiento cheese
* apple wedges or slices, which can be dipped in honey
* strawberries or pineapple chunks
* dried fruits: apples, raisins, apricots
* juice popsicles
* gelatin, made by the children in the morning and eaten in the afternoon

Math

MATCH THE SOCKS

Younger children enjoy this activity. They can play this with you, with another child, or by themselves. Toddlers sometimes need more assistance.

* Ask parents to send you pairs of old socks of all sizes.
* Place the socks in a colorful basket.
* Ask the children to match the socks according to color, size, pairs, and texture.

LOOK HOW I'VE GROWN

* Have children bring baby pictures from home.
* Take individual pictures of the children when they first come into your class.
* Take a current picture of each child.
* Put all the pictures up to create a special wall in the classroom. Children can show each other how they have grown.
* During circle or individual time, have each child tell about how she has grown. For example: "I can help serve and clean up at snack, I am taller, my feet are bigger, I can take turns and share."
* Demonstrate to the toddlers how they have grown. Show them their baby pictures. Have them look in a mirror to see how they have changed. Talk to them about all the things they can do now.
* Measure and weigh the children at different times during the year to show how they have grown.
* Children enjoy knowing how tall they are and how much they weigh. Even though they may not understand what the numbers mean, children seem to gain a sense of self-identification from them.

LET'S MEASURE

Older children enjoy doing this activity.

* Make different size footprints, right and left.
* Cut them out and laminate.
* Discuss the dimensions of the footprints with the children. Which is the smallest? Which is the largest? Which ones are right feet? Which ones are left feet? How can you tell?
* Line them up from smallest to largest or any other way the children decide. They can even create a pattern.
* The children can measure their own feet and shoes.

Science

EXPLORING SHADOWS

* Read Asch's *Bear Shadow,* Dodd's *Footprints and Shadows,* or Hoban's *Shadows and Reflections.* All are listed in the books section of this theme.

* What is a shadow? Let the children discover the answer.
* By experimenting with different objects in the room, children can discover which ones cast shadows and which ones do not.
* They will discover that shade is a dark place that light cannot reach. A shadow is the shape cast by whatever is in front of the light.
* It is fun for the children to outline their shadows on the sidewalk with chalk. They can help each other do this. They can also measure how long or how short their shadows are. Try this at different times during the day. Do the shadows change?
* Show toddlers exactly where their shadows are. Move their arms to help them find their shadows. "Wave your arms. See the shadow's arms wave?"
* What happens when the children dance or wiggle?

FOOD, HEALTHY FOOD

Together, you and the children cut food pictures from old magazines that you and the parents have collected. Ask for the magazines several months before you do this activity so you will have plenty available.

* From the cut-out pictures, create a food group chart. This opens up an opportunity for the class to discuss healthy foods.
* If the children cannot find their favorite foods among the pictures, they can draw them and put them on the chart in the appropriate place.

CLOTHING FABRICS ARE ALL WET

This activity develops problem-solving and observation skills.

✳ Collect all kinds of fabric scraps: corduroy, wool, flannel, satin, nylon, vinyl, plastic, and cotton.

✳ In small groups, the children take turns using an eyedropper to drop water on each piece of fabric. Then they sort the fabric into two categories: those that absorb water and those that repel water. Ask the children which fabrics they would wear as outer clothing during a rain storm?

Social Studies

WE ARE ALIKE, WE ARE DIFFERENT

✳ Select several books relating to similarities and differences, and read them to the children. Choose from the list of suggested books at the end of this theme.

✳ While reading the book to younger children, it is helpful to point to the different parts of the face and body on each child.

✳ Next, ask the child to point to her own nose, eyes, mouth, etc.

✳ After reading the books to older children, provide supplies and materials they can use to create their own "alike" and "different" pictures.

✳ Place the books in the book center and put the pictures around the room or on the bulletin board.

PUZZLING FACES

✳ Collect many large pictures of children's faces from catalogs, magazines, newspapers, and posters. If you prefer, collect pictures of the entire child, not just faces.

✳ Glue each picture to a piece of cardboard or foam sheet, and let dry.

✳ With light pencil marks, mark the photo into puzzle pieces.

✳ Cut into puzzle pieces.

✳ Put each puzzle into an eight-by-ten envelope or resealable plastic bag.

✳ Introduce these to the children with emphasis on placement of the eyes, nose, mouth, ears, and hair. With older children, discuss position, such as top and bottom, left and right.

✳ Discuss similarities and differences. If the puzzles are of the entire child, talk about the different body parts.

✳ Place the puzzles in the manipulative center.

Children's Books

Aliki. (1992). *I'm Growing.* New York: HarperCollins.

Aliki. (1990). *My Feet.* New York: Crowell.

Aliki. (1990). *My Hands.* New York: Crowell.

Aliki. (1987). *The Story of Johnny Appleseed.* Upper Saddle River, NJ: Prentice Hall.

Asch, Frank. (1988). *Bear Shadow.* New York: Aladdin.

Brown, Tricia. (1984). *Someone Special Just Like Me.* Photographs by Fran Ortiz. New York: Henry Holt.

Cisneros, Sandra. (1994). *Hairs — Pelitos: A Story in English and Spanish.* Illustrated by Terry Ybanez. New York: Alfred A. Knopf.

Danziger, Paula. (1994). *Amber Brown Is Not a Crayon.* New York: G. P. Putnam's Sons.

Dodd, Anne W. (1994). *Footprints and Shadows.* New York: Aladdin.

Heide, Florence P., and Judith H. Gilliland. (1990). *The Day of Ahmed's Secret.* Illustrated by Ted Lewin. New York: Lothrop, Lee & Shepard.

Hoban, Tana. (1990). *Shadows and Reflections.* New York: Greenwillow.

Hoffman, Mary. (1991). *Amazing Grace.* New York: Dial.

Hudson, Cheryl W., and Bernette G. Ford. (1990). *Bright Eyes, Brown Skin.* Illustrated by George Ford. Orange, NJ: Just Us Books.

Kates, Bobbi Jane. (1992). *Sesame Street's We're Different, We're the Same.* Illustrated by Joe Mathieu. New York: Random House.

Kissinger, Katie. (1994). *All the Colors We Are: Todos los Colores de Nuestra Piel.* Photographs by Wernher Krutein. St. Paul, MN: Redleaf Press.

Martin, Bill, Jr., and John Archambault. (1987). *Here Are My Hands.* Illustrated by Ted Rand. New York: Henry Holt.

Morris, Ann. (1993). *Bread, Bread, Bread.* Photographs by Ken Heyman. New York: Mulberry.

Rogers, Fred. (1986). *Going to the Potty.* Photographs by Jim Judkis. New York: G.P. Putnam's Sons.

Sabin, F. (1985). *Human Body.* Mahwah, NJ: Troll.

Spier, Peter. (1980). *People.* New York: Doubleday.

Steptoe, John. (1988). *Baby Says.* New York: Lothrop, Lee & Shepard.

Winter, Susan. (1994). *A Baby Just Like Me.* New York: Dorling Kindersley.

Parent Letter (Preschool)

Dear Parents,

Our theme is My Body. We will provide opportunities for the children to learn:

- Every person is special.
- Everyone has a body with many parts.
- Our bodies can move in many ways and do many things.
- Food, exercise, and sleep help our bodies grow.
- Fruits, vegetables, and milk keep our bodies healthy.

We will be talking about:

- inside body parts
- outside body parts
- growth
- health and safety
- food
- clothing

To reinforce the concepts we are working on at school, here are some things to do at home with your child:

- Talk with your child about when he or she was a baby and how he or she has grown.
- Take "time for a rhyme." Rhyme words with names of body parts. This is a good activity for you and your child to do on the ride home.
- Let your child help you match socks on laundry day.
- Take a walk or exercise together.
- Start a growth chart. If you already have one, talk about it together.

Join us for parent participation opportunities at school:

- Help measure and weigh children.
- Help when we make "paint footprints."
- Come take snapshots.

Date _____ Time _____
Date _____ Time _____
Date _____ Time _____

The wish list for this theme includes:

empty food boxes for our dramatic play grocery store

grocery sacks

plastic berry baskets

old magazines

fabric scraps

yarn scraps

pairs of old, clean socks

Thank you for sharing your child with us.

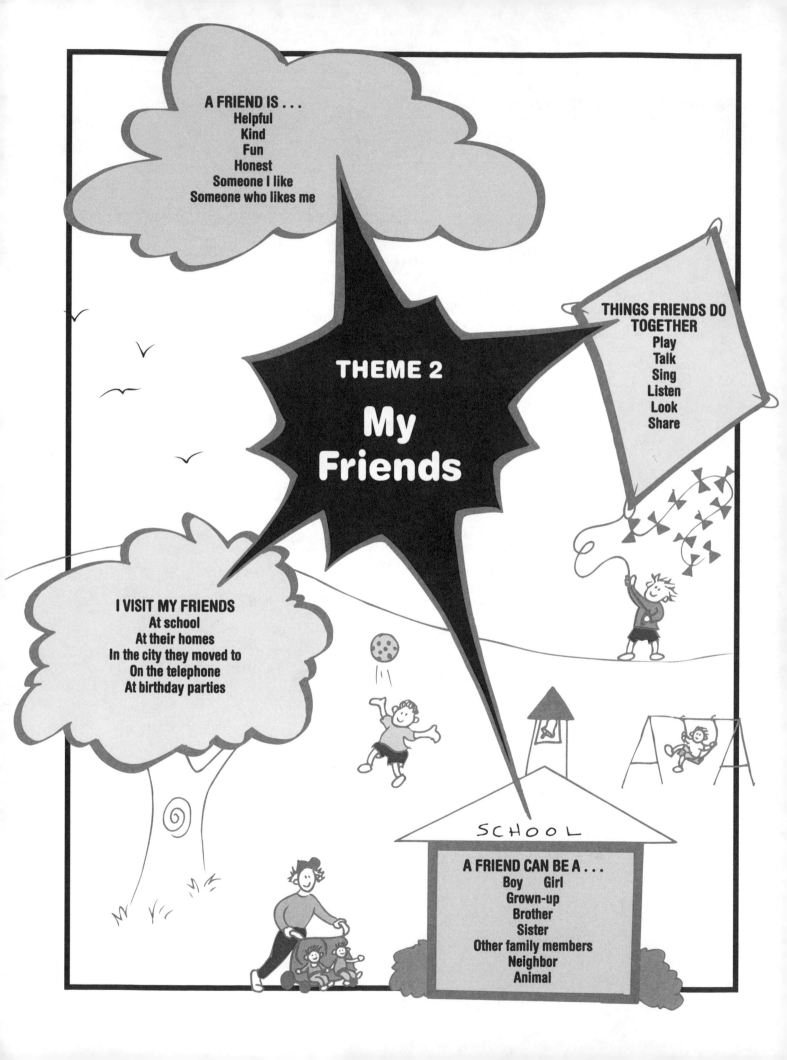

THEME GOALS

To provide opportunities for children to learn:

1. Everyone can be a friend and have a friend at the same time.
2. Friends can be people or animals.
3. Friends can be family or other people outside the family.
4. Friends are like you in some ways and different from you in some ways.
5. Friends show they are friendly in many ways, such as sharing, helping, listening, talking, and playing together.

Children-Created Bulletin Board

This bulletin board offers an opportunity for children to work together cooperatively, to develop respect for each other's creativity, and to care about what they are accomplishing together.

* Discuss what a quilt is. Invite a quiltmaker or family member to visit the class and show the children examples of quilts.
* Read Flourney's *The Patchwork Quilt,* Johnston and De Paola's *The Quilt Story,* or Polacco's *The Keeping Quilt.* All are listed in the books section of this theme.
* Provide precut, assorted colored or white squares of paper.
* Older children can cut other papers into desired shapes and glue them onto the squares of paper.
* The children select <u>fabric</u> crayons or markers and create designs on the paper squares.
* Each individual crayon drawing on paper can then be ironed onto an individual small fabric square by an adult.
* Sew these together to make the friendship quilt.

Vocabulary Starters

Let the children add additional words.

friend — a person you like and who likes you.

share — letting someone use what you have.

helpful — to do friendly things that make someone else's play or work easier.

thoughtful — to pay attention to what someone else feels or wants.

listen — to pay attention and hear what someone else is saying.

neighbor — someone who lives near you.

Language Experiences

POEM: "I Have A Friend"

I have a friend and
My friend has me.
We're great friends,
As you can see.
We play together
In the rain and sun,
Come join us and have some fun.

FINGERPLAY: Friends

Two houses, clean and neat
    (hold up two fists facing each other)
Open doors wide, so friends can meet.
    (open fists and hold up all the fingers)
"Hello" to you, and "hi" to you,
    (all fingers wave "hello" to each other)
Let's decide what we will do.
    (fingers face each other)
It's sunny so let's run and play.
    (fingers run and play)
Friends have fun every day.
    (hands clasp together)

POEM: "One Little Friend"

Based on the traditional folk song, "Five Little Ducks," this can be used as a transition activity to move the children from inside to outside play.

One little friend went out to play

On the playground one fine day.
He (she) was having so much fun
He (she) called another friend to come.
Two little friends went out to play
On the playground one fine day.
They were having so much fun
They called another friend to come.

Repeat until all the children in the classroom have been counted.

TODDLER TELEPHONE TALK

This activity promotes language development for young toddlers.

✳ Encourage two children on individual telephones (toy or discarded real ones) to talk to each other.

✳ Guide them by saying, for example:
    "I like to call my friend on the telephone."
    "You can call your friend on the telephone."
    "Hello, friend."
    "How are you today?"
    "Good-bye, friend."

✳ Then, step back and let the children talk to each other.

✳ You may have to repeat this on several days before the children begin to pick up the phones and "talk" to their friend.

Dramatic Play

ANIMAL FRIENDS

The following activity is designed to integrate several curriculum areas. The activity can be extended over the entire time that the My Friends theme is emphasized.

✳ Ask the children to bring a favorite stuffed animal "friend" to class.

✳ At group time invite each child to introduce her friend to the other children.

✳ Encourage several children at a time to go to the dramatic play or housekeeping center and plan a pretend birthday party for their stuffed animals or for each other.

✳ With older children, talk about friendship, acceptance, and belonging.

✳ Begin to read the book *The Velveteen Rabbit* or another book from the list at the end of this theme. Continue reading the book over several days.

Puppet Play

BANANA PUPPET

Older infants and toddlers enjoy this activity. It is best to do this right before snack time.

✳ On an unpeeled banana, draw two eyes and a mouth.

✳ Make several banana puppets.

✳ Have one banana "talk" to the children. Add a second banana.

✳ After a few minutes, peel the bananas, cut them into small pieces, and serve as a snack with milk.

✳ Older toddlers can peel the banana and cut it in two with a plastic knife. They can share with their friends.

SOCK PUPPET

✳ Have children bring some of their old socks from home in the colors of tan, beige, cream, brown, peach, or white. Child-sized socks fit their hands better than adult-sized socks.

✳ Guide them to make a sock puppet that is like their own skin colors.

✳ Suggest making a puppet with a partner.

✳ Have felt scraps, yarn, fabric scraps, markers, and glue set up at the art table.

✳ Older children could sew on buttons using dull-pointed needles and thick thread.

✳ This activity promotes hand-eye coordination, small muscle development, creativity, and language development.

Music

SONG: "Name Song" by Bea Wolf

Reproduced by permission of B. Wolf - 1995
Copyright B. Wolf - 1993

(See page 297 for enlargement.)

SONG: "It's So Good to Be with Friends" by Jo Eklof

Additional verses:

It's fun in the snow with friends in cold and snowy weather.
We could shiver and play all through the day. We love to be together.

It's fun to swim with friends in warm and sunny weather.
We could splash and play all through the day. We love to be together.

© 1998 by Jo Eklof. All rights reserved. Used with permission.

(See page 297 for enlargement.)

SONG STICKS

This activity is designed for older children.

✳ Each time the children learn a new song, print the title of the song on a craft stick or tongue depressor.

✳ Add a sticker or small picture to help the children read the song stick.

✳ Place the sticks in a decorated can or box.

✳ Have the children close their eyes and take turns drawing a song stick.

✳ Next, the class sings the song picked.

✳ Let the children tell you when it is time to stop this activity. Some children will want to drop out earlier than others.

✳ Continue with children who want to proceed, and let the others choose another activity center.

Movement

TODDLERS TOGETHER

✳ To encourage parallel play outdoors, have a wagon available. This invites two children to share.

✳ One child rides and the other child pulls.

✳ They can then take turns riding and pulling.

✳ You may need to help the children get started. Give them a lot of praise when they take turns.

THE FRIENDS GO MARCHING

This is a variation of a traditional activity, "The Ants Go Marching." It can be both a movement/music and a transition activity.

The friends go marching two by two,
Hurrah, hurrah.
The friends go marching two by two,
Hurrah, hurrah.
The friends go marching two by two,
It's the greatest thing to do.
As we all go marching around the room,
Boom, boom — boom, boom.

✳ Expand this activity by adding extra verses, such as: friends go jumping, stomping, skipping, tiptoeing, and walking.

✳ Add musical instruments to emphasize the beat.

I'M A RAG DOLL

This activity can be done inside or outside, with or without music. Simplify it for younger children.

✳ Have a rag doll to show to the children. This will help the children understand the concept.

✳ Ask the children to stand up straight and tall, with feet together, head erect.

✳ Place arms stiff at their sides, tummy in, chest out.

✳ Inhale, exhale, and relax body.

✳ Now become a rag doll. Bend at the waist. Hang your head down and sway it from side to side.

✳ Bend the knees and swing from side to side.

✳ Drop to the floor, still relaxed.

✳ Then, reverse the process until all are standing up straight and tall.

✳ Become a rag doll again.

✳ See if any of the children want to give the rag doll any directions of what to do.

FOLLOW A FRIEND

This activity is similar to "Follow the Leader," but with this exercise each child has a partner.

✳ Have the children form two circles, one inside the other. The inner circle faces the outer circle. This gives each child a partner.

✳ Start by having the outer circle of children do an action, such as patting the head. The inner circle repeats the action.

✳ Each child selects an action that his partner follows. The children can speed up and slow down various rhythmic exercises.

✳ After a few minutes, the inner circle changes places with the outer circle and decides on the action to be followed.

✳ Older children can expand this activity. One child becomes a mirror that reflects all she sees her partner do. For example, the children could pretend to put on clown makeup, do exercises, or become distorted mirrors like those found in amusement parks.

Sensory Art

PARTNER PAINTING

This activity promotes taking turns and sharing for young children.

* Set up the easel with two brushes and two colors of paint.
* Have the children paint their picture standing side by side.
* At first you may want to closely supervise the children.
* Encourage them to "use their words" if there is a disagreement. Model appropriate behavior, if necessary.

THREE-DIMENSIONAL FRIENDS

This activity is designed to help children listen, follow directions, and create a three-dimensional picture.

* Place skin-toned construction paper (black, brown, tan, peach, and cream), scissors, rulers, and glue in the art center.
* Guide the children, two or three at a time, into the activity.
* Use one sheet of paper for the background.
* Cut other paper into strips about one inch wide.

* Fold, curl, or pleat the paper strips for hair, nose, and other features. You may need to help some children with curling and pleating.
* Glue the pieces onto the background sheet.
* Allow glue to dry.
* The children can play with and display their three-dimensional pictures of their friends and themselves.

RAINBOW OF FRIENDS

This activity encourages group participation and problem-solving.

* Provide a prism (a triangular piece of glass that breaks up a ray of light into a color spectrum) for the children to experiment with.
* Talk about the colors of the rainbow.
* Cut a large sheet of butcher paper into the shape of a rainbow arc. Older children can work together to cut the rainbow.
* Have the children create the rainbow. They decide what colors to use and the placement of the colors.
* They decide if they want to use crayons, markers, water colors, or tempera paint.
* Let the mural dry.
* Later, the children can create "self-portraits" of themselves to add to the rainbow.

FRIENDSHIP HEART

This is an activity for two or three children to do together to encourage cooperation and sharing with friends.

* Cut a medium-size heart out of cardboard or posterboard for each group of children.
* Place the hearts, strips of colored tissue paper, two or three small plastic dishes of diluted white glue, cotton swabs, and scissors on the art center table.
* Encourage the children to tear off small pieces of tissue paper.
* Glue them onto the heart, using swabs to help spread the glue.
* Older children can draw a heart design and cut the heart out themselves.

✳ They may also like to make small tissue paper balls to glue on the heart.

✳ When each heart is complete, ask the children to tell you what they learned about friendship while making the heart.

Creative Food Experiences

CINNAMON TOAST

You will need:

> 1 teaspoon cinnamon
>
> 3 tablespoons sugar
>
> 4 tablespoons butter or margarine
>
> 4 slices of bread

Heat oven to 375 degrees.

1. Wash hands.
2. Mix cinnamon and sugar.
3. Add softened butter or margarine, and mix well. Spread on pieces of bread. Bake 5 minutes or until light brown.
4. Eat!

✳ For toddlers, give each child a plate with a piece of toast on it.

✳ Guide them in spreading some soft butter or margarine on the toast using a plastic knife. Model the appropriate way to use knives.

✳ Mix cinnamon with sugar in several salt shakers, and let the children sprinkle the cinnamon-sugar on their buttered toast.

FROSTED GRAHAM CRACKERS

You will need:

> 1 cup powdered sugar
>
> 1/4 cup margarine
>
> food coloring
>
> 1 teaspoon vanilla extract
>
> 1 box graham crackers
>
> nuts or shredded coconut
>
> 1 tablespoon milk

FROSTED GRAHAM CRACKERS

Wash hands.

Mix sugar, margarine, and 2 to 3 drops of

food coloring. Mix vanilla and milk. Slowly add

vanilla-milk flavoring, a drop or 2 at a time.

Spread over graham crackers. Decorate with

chopped nuts and/or shredded coconut.

YUM! Eat and enjoy!

1. Wash hands.
2. Make this recipe several times with different small groups of children.
3. Mix sugar, margarine, and two to three drops of food coloring.
4. Mix vanilla and milk.
5. Slowly add vanilla-milk flavoring, a drop or two at a time, until you have a spreading consistency. Spread over graham crackers. Decorate with chopped nuts or shredded coconut. Enjoy!

Math

FAVORITE FOODS

✳ During circle time, ask about favorite foods of the children. Place the emphasis on what children and their friends *like*. It won't be necessary to ask about foods they dislike; they will tell you during the discussion.

✳ Take the information, and with the children make a favorite food graph. See Theme 10 for an example of a simple graph.

✳ To extend this activity, review the food groups with the children and make a graph of favorite foods within each food group. Older children can make a food pyramid.

FIND A FRIEND FOLDER GAME

✳ Take an ordinary file folder, open it, and draw a maze on the right page.

✳ Place "Start" and "Stop" on the maze.

✳ At the stop point, have an illustration, picture, or sticker of a child.

✳ On the cover of the file folder, write "Find a Friend."

✳ Laminate the folder.

✳ Provide a rub-off crayon or washable marker.

✳ The child playing the game begins at "Start" and marks a path to the friend at "Stop."

✳ To simplify the activity, place numerals 1 through 10 at places in the maze to guide the child.

WHAT'S MISSING?

✳ Fill a picnic basket full of picnic items.

✳ Place all the items on a cloth napkin for the children to see and name.

✳ To simplify for younger children, use only a few items.

✳ Have children close their eyes while you take an object away.

✳ Have them guess which item is missing.

✳ Continue this with several items.

✳ To extend, let the children, two at a time, take the picnic basket to the manipulative center and play the What's Missing game.

✳ To further extend, play a What's Missing game by grouping several related items together.

Science

THE FRIENDLY GARDEN

✳ Before planting a garden, explain the process of a seed growing into a plant, using a flannelboard to illustrate. The pieces can be handled easily by the children.

✳ Let the children select which flower seeds they want to plant. This emphasizes that a class of friends can plant and grow a garden together.

✳ Talk about how plants need water, warmth, and sunlight to grow and live. Ask older children open-ended questions so they can tell you what the plants will need in order to grow.

✳ With the children's help, prepare an area in one corner of the playground for a garden. Or, take the sand and water table outside, and fill it with potting soil.

✳ Have the children drop the flower seeds into the soil and cover them with more soil.

✳ Use a stick and the seed package picture to make a sign for identification of the plant.

✳ Watch the garden each day and water as needed. With your help, the older children can pull weeds as necessary.

A FRIENDLY RAINBOW

This activity extends and integrates with the sensory art activities. This is a great activity to do outside in the bright sunshine.

✳ Place several shallow bowls of water in the sun.

✳ Place a drop or two of oil on the surface of each bowl of water. Use eyedroppers if you want the children to drop the oil on the water.

✳ Ask the children open-ended questions, such as, "How many colors do you see?" "Do the colors you see match the colors in the rainbow?" "When did you see a rainbow?" "If you stir the water with a stick, do the colors change? Try it and see."

Social Studies

FRIENDS ARE SPECIAL PARTY

This activity integrates all of the curriculum areas. Begin by telling the children, "We are a class of friends, so let's have a Friends Are Special Party!"

* The children choose a day and time for the party.

* They write invitations to the party and post them on a special bulletin board for the parents and the children in the class to see.

* Children make a list of what they will need for the party and how much it will cost.

* Give them suggestions for what they can make or bake for the party, such as the frosted graham crackers recipe in the cooking portion of this theme.

* The list is given to the teacher or to a parent who has volunteered to purchase the party supplies.

* Place construction paper in the art center for the children to use in making party hats.

* Have children select the music they want to play and the songs they want to sing.

* Then it's party time!

* To expand this party idea, the children can visit a class of younger children and bring the party to them. This extends the concept of friendship.

PUZZLE PIECES

* Select puzzles depicting children from other countries. The younger the child, the fewer pieces there should be in the puzzle.

* Introduce the puzzles during group time. Talk about the country where the children in the puzzle live. Show the places on a globe or map.

* Invite two or three children to work as friends to put the puzzle together.

* Encourage the children to talk about what the children are doing in the puzzle. Ask open-ended questions.

Children's Books

Aliki. (1995). *Best Friends Together Again.* New York: Greenwillow.

Aliki. (1982). *We Are Best Friends.* New York: Mulberry.

Bunnett, Rochelle. (1992). *Friends in the Park.* Photographs by Carl Sahlhoff. New York: Checkerboard Press.

Cheltenham Elementary School Kindergartners. (1991). *We Are All Alike . . . We Are All Different.* New York: Scholastic.

Elhert, Lois. (1988). *Planting a Rainbow.* San Diego, CA: Harcourt Brace.

Flournoy, Valerie. (1985). *The Patchwork Quilt.* Illustrated by Jerry Pinkney. New York: Dial Books.

Freeman, Don. (1976). *Corduroy.* New York: Puffin Books.

Greenfield, Eloise. (1991). *Big Friend, Little Friend.* New York: Black Butterfly Board Books for Children.

Greenfield, Eloise. (1991). *My Doll Keshia.* Illustrated by Jan S. Gilchrist. New York: Black Butterfly Board Books for Children.

Gross, Theodore F. (1990). *Everyone Asked About You.* Illustrated by Sheila W. Samton. New York: Philomel.

Isadora, Rachel. (1990). *Friends.* New York: Greenwillow.

Johnston, Tony, and Tomie De Paola. (1985). *The Quilt Story.* New York: G.P. Putnam's Sons.

Kellogg, Steven. (1990). *Best Friends.* New York: Dial.

Marxhausen, Joanne. (1990). *Some of My Best Friends Are Trees.* St. Louis, MO: Concordia.

Moore, Inga. (1991). *Little Dog Lost.* New York: Macmillan.

Morris, Ann. (1990). *Loving.* Photographs by Ken Heyman. New York: Lothrop, Lee & Shepard.

Newman, Nanette. (1990). *Sharing.* New York: Doubleday and Company, Inc.

Oxenbury, Helen. (1981). *Friends.* (Board book). New York: Simon & Schuster.

Palacco, Patricia. (1992). *Mrs. Katz and Tush.* New York: Bantam Books.

Palacco, Patricia. (1988). *The Keeping Quilt.* New York: Simon & Schuster.

Roberts, Sarah. (1981). *Ernie's Big Mess.* Illustrated by Joe Mathieu. New York: Random House.

Rogers, Fred. (1987). *Making Friends.* New York: G.P. Putnam's Sons.

Williams, Margery. (1991). *The Velveteen Rabbit.* New York: Doubleday and Company, Inc.

Parent Letter (Toddler)

Dear Parents,

We will be talking about friendship as we begin our theme My Friends. We will provide opportunities for the children to learn:

- Everyone can be a friend and have a friend at the same time.
- Friends can be people or animals.
- Friends can be family or other people outside the family.
- Friends are alike in some ways and different in some ways.
- Friends show they are friendly in many ways, such as by sharing, helping, listening, talking, and playing together.

We will be talking about:

- qualities of friendship
- who can be a friend
- things friends do together
- where I visit my friends

Things to do at home with your young child include:

- You are your child's first friend. Spend time talking and playing together.
- Invite another child over to play.
- Help your child have "gentle hands" with a tame family pet or stuffed animal.
- Read stories about friends and friendship.
- Make friends with a friendly puppet. For example, use a sock, or draw a face on a banana.

Parent participation opportunities at the center will be to:

- Come anytime for some quality rocking chair time.
- Come for a toddler and friend picnic.
  Date _____ Time _____
- Send snapshots of baby's friends and family to put on the wall by the crib (to be covered in clear contact paper).

Our wish list for this theme:

pictures of friends together

stuffed toy friends

picture books about friends

nonworking, real telephones

Thank you for your special friendship.

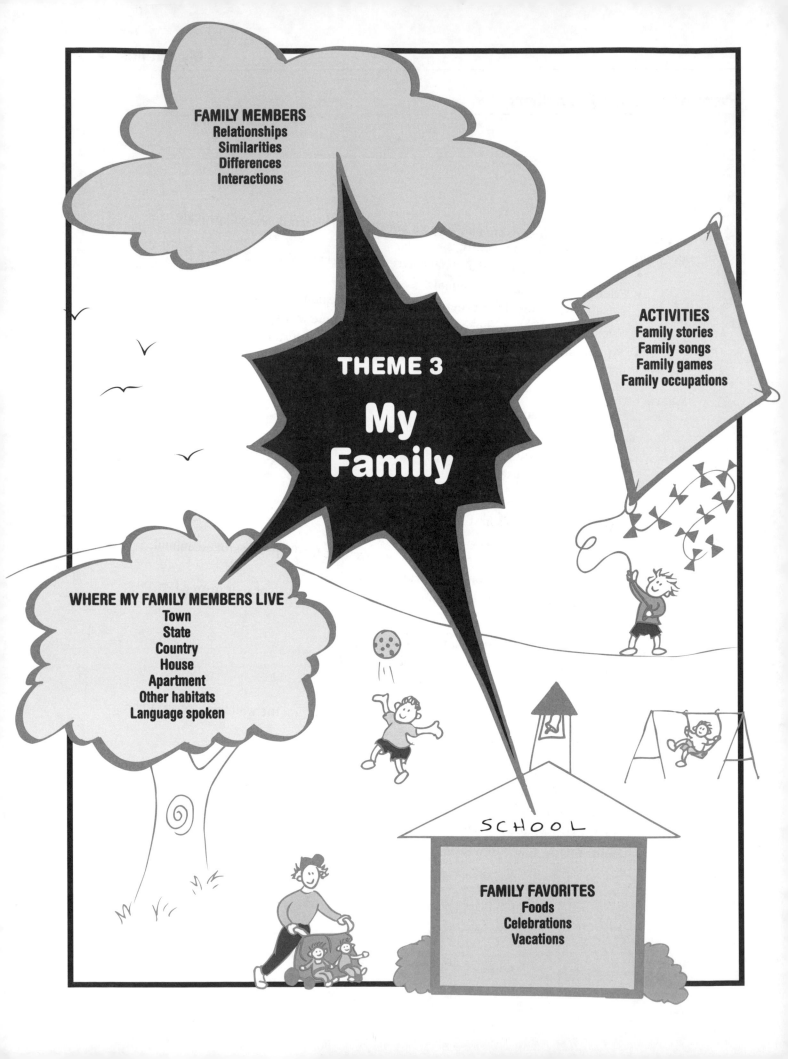

FAMILY MEMBERS
Relationships
Similarities
Differences
Interactions

ACTIVITIES
Family stories
Family songs
Family games
Family occupations

THEME 3

My Family

WHERE MY FAMILY MEMBERS LIVE
Town
State
Country
House
Apartment
Other habitats
Language spoken

SCHOOL

FAMILY FAVORITES
Foods
Celebrations
Vacations

THEME GOALS

To provide opportunities for children to learn:

1. A family is two or more people who are connected by love or kinship.
2. Families may have relatives other than those who live together, such as grandmothers, grandfathers, aunts, uncles, and cousins. Some people are part of more than one family.
3. Each member of a family is important and special.
4. Families live all over the world.
5. Family members are alike in some ways and different in others.
6. Members of a family work, play, and learn together. They also help each other.
7. Some families have special foods that they eat and certain days they celebrate together.
8. Some families have and care for pets.

Children-Created Bulletin Board

This bulletin board encourages children to think about all the members of their families and to understand and be accepting of the family units of their friends.

* You and the children make a family tree out of brown paper bags or brown wrapping paper.
* The paper can be crumpled and crushed to add texture.
* Staple to a bulletin board to form a tree shape.
* Take a walk outside to look at the leaves on the trees. The leaves the children will make should reflect the colors currently on the trees outside, depending on the season in which you use this theme.
* Children cut out leaf shapes for the tree.
* Children write their names on some leaves and family members on others.
* If the children bring family photos to display, let them place these all around the tree.

Vocabulary Starters

Let the children add additional words.

relatives — people who belong to your family or to the families of your grandmothers, grandfathers, aunts, and uncles.

son — a child of a father and mother who can be a boy or a man.

daughter — a child of a father and mother who can be a girl or a woman.

tradition — something that has been done or said over and over again in a family, such as special holidays, foods, songs, and stories.

occupation — what people do to earn money for themselves and their families.

vacation — a special time when people do things or go places to have fun.

Language Experiences

FINGERPLAY:
Grandpa's Glasses

These are grandpa's glasses,
  (make two circles with the thumbs and index fingers, and put them in front of your eyes like glasses)
This is grandpa's hat,
  (put both hands over your head in a point to make a hat)
This is how he folds his arms,
  (place one arm over the other arm)
Just like that.
These are grandma's glasses,
  (repeat gesture and make glasses)
This is grandma's hat,
  (repeat hat gesture with both hands)
This is how she folds her hands,
  (clasp hands together)
And puts them in her lap.

FAMILY MEMBER BINGO

This activity is designed for older children, especially those who are just starting to read. It can be played with the entire class or with two or three children at a time.

✳ Make enough bingo cards for each child to have one card.

✳ Write the names of family member relationships on each card (see the pattern sample).

✳ Each card should have the relationship names in a different order. On a few of the cards write the same names twice, while leaving one or two names off so that each card will be different.

✳ Laminate each card.

✳ Write the family relationship names on individual sentence strip paper or on large cards. Laminate. The printing should be large enough for the children to see and match on their cards.

✳ Give the children enough large buttons or large plastic circles to cover all the family names on their cards.

✳ Then play the game just like bingo. Call out the name you hold up, and have the children match it on their cards. The first child to cover all the names on his card wins the game.

✳ To extend this activity, make and laminate matching name pieces to be placed on an individual board. Place the card and the pieces in the language or manipulative center for one child to play.

ASK QUESTIONS

Read the book *A Chair for My Mother,* by Vera Williams. Ask the children open-ended questions, such as:

— Have you ever been furniture shopping?

— Whom did you go with?

— Do you save money?

— Where do you put the money you save?

— What are you going to do with your money?

— Should we save pennies to buy something for the classroom?

✳ Vote on what to buy. This relates to the math activity in this theme.

✳ Place *A Chair for My Mother* in the book center for the children.

Dramatic Play

TODDLER PRETEND PLAY

It's easy and fun to play "let's put the baby to bed" with a toddler and a doll. This can be an activity for the teacher to do with one child.

✳ Start by saying, "You be the mommy, and I'll be the daddy. This box can be the baby's bed, and here is the baby's blanket."

✳ Continue to talk through the activity, guiding the child through the step-by-step process of putting the baby to bed, covering the baby, and kissing it good night.

✳ Other children may want to do the same thing, so have enough dolls, boxes, and blankets for two or three children. Use washcloths or hand towels as doll blankets.

✳ This activity helps toddlers role-play what happens at home. It also emphasizes an example of caring relationships that develop within a family.

HOME LIVING CENTER

From time to time, take an inventory of the home living center. You will probably want to replace or add new items.

✳ What about aprons, bibs, tablecloths, artificial flowers, newspapers, magazines, cookbooks, dustpans, brooms, mops, and dusters?

✳ In addition, ask the children to bring one item from home that they would like to add to the center.

FAMILY VACATION

✳ Expand the home living/dramatic play center to be about three times its usual size. You can close another center to have room for this.

✳ Take one part of the expanded area and make it the "getting ready to go on vacation" space.

✳ In this area, place suitcases, clothes to pack, shoes, toy or discarded cameras, sunglasses, sunhats, scarves, backpacks, maps or road atlases, envelopes, picture postcards, travel brochures, and travel posters.

✳ For younger children's "luggage," use small suitcases, camera cases, briefcases, or backpacks.

✳ In another area, arrange chairs in rows with two or three chairs side by side to form seats in a car, bus, train, or plane.

✳ The children can start in the home living center for the planning stage of the vacation. They can even make lists of what to take and what to do on the vacation.

✳ They then move to the suitcase area to pack for the trip.

✳ Finally, they move to the transportation area where their "vehicle" is ready to go.

✳ This activity encourages planning together as a family does, sequencing, placing things in order, problem-solving, sharing, taking turns, and creativity.

Puppet Play

PAPER CUP FAMILY POP-UPS

✳ You will need Styrofoam or paper cups, craft sticks, yarn, construction paper, fabric scraps, markers, glue, and tagboard, cardboard, or posterboard.

✳ Cut posterboard or tagboard circles sized to fit vertically inside the cup. Let older children cut the circles themselves.

✳ The children create faces on the circles. They can add hair and hats. Suggest they make it look like a family member.

✳ Glue a circle to a craft stick, and let dry.

✳ Push the end of the stick gently through the bottom of the cup.

✳ Pull the stick down to hide the family member's face.

✳ Push the stick up to make the person pop up.

Music

SONG: "I Am a Member of My Family" by Jo Eklof

Additional verses:
We love each other...........
We're kind to each other...........
We laugh with each other...........
We take care of each other...........
We play with each other...........
We smile at each other...........
We hug each other...........
We cheer up each other...........

© 1998 by Jo Eklof. All rights reserved. Used with permission

(See page 298 for enlargement.)

"MAMA'S COOKIES" CHANT

✳ Use a simple clapping pattern or a patting-the-knee pattern.

✳ Infants enjoy having you hold their hands and clap them together.

✳ Older children can vary the clapping patterns from simple to complex. Add clap — pat — clap — pat or clap — pat — snap/clap — pat — snap, for example.

✳ Add musical instruments to emphasize the beat.

✳ After repeating the chant several times, let the older children try to do the chant by themselves. Then, one child takes a line, then another, and try to go from one child to the next without any interruption. Children can add to the chant by supplying other family names.

Here is the chant, adapted from an American traditional game:

Mama baked some cookies for the cookie jar.
  (Children repeat the line.)
I ate a cookie from the cookie jar.
  (Children repeat the line.)
Brother ate a cookie from the cookie jar.
  (Children repeat the line.)
Sister ate a cookie from the cookie jar.
  (Children repeat the line.)
Daddy ate a cookie from the cookie jar.
  (Children repeat the line.)
We all love the cookies from the cookie jar.
  (Children repeat the line.)

"HUSH LITTLE BABY"

This traditional song, which has been passed down through several generations, can be sung or chanted, or told like a story. Vary the song by using papa, grandma, or grandpa instead of mama some of the time. Add flannelboard characters or stick puppets to help illustrate it for younger children.

Hush, little baby, don't say a word,
Mama's going to buy you a mockingbird.
If that mockingbird won't sing,
Mama's going to buy you a diamond ring.
If that diamond ring turns to brass,
Mama's going to buy you a looking glass.
If that looking glass gets broke,
Mama's going to buy you a billy goat.
If that billy goat won't pull,
Mama's going to buy you a cart and bull.
If that cart and bull turn over,
Mama's going to buy you a dog named Rover.
If that dog named Rover won't bark,
Mama's going to buy you a horse and cart.
If that horse and cart break down,
You'll be the sweetest little baby in town.

Movement

MUSICAL SHEET

Share this movement idea with the parents. It is fun to do at school and at home. Ask parents to send old bedsheets or small blankets from home to use as "parachutes." Younger children may use a lightweight blanket instead of a sheet.

This is a great outdoor activity, one the children can do at school with their friends or at home.

✳ Form a circle with the children, holding the outer edges of the sheet.

✳ Put on a record, tape, or CD. Use music of different cultures, styles, and tempos.

✳ Have the children breathe deeply as they raise and lower their arms, making the sheet seem to move with the music.

✳ After the children can raise and lower their arms comfortably, have them run up and back, still holding onto the edges of the sheet.

✳ To vary this activity place assorted sizes of soft, lightweight balls on top of the sheet.

BEANBAG TOSS

This activity promotes large muscle development.

✳ Place a large plastic laundry basket outside or a large box with a hole cut out of the side. Children enjoy decorating the basket or box.

✳ Older children can paint a smiling face on the box with the hole becoming a big red mouth.

✳ Have beanbags of all shapes, sizes, and colors available. Every beanbag should be different, so each child can identify her own.

✳ You and the children can make up different games to play with the beanbags. For example, start with the throw line close to the basket or box so the children can more easily hit the opening. Slowly move the line further away from the opening. Continue this until the children tell you to stop!

✳ Some children like to try throwing the beanbags with both hands, first with the right, then with the left.

FOLLOW THE HULA HOOPS

Place several hula hoops or tires around the playground. Arrange them in a pattern that will make it easy for the children to progress from one hoop to the next. This exercise promotes cooperative play, group problem-solving, and physical development.

✳ Each child selects a beanbag.

✳ Set up a starting line. Each child tries to throw the beanbag into the first hoop. If she misses, she takes a second throw from the spot where her

beanbag landed, continuing until the beanbag lands in the hoop.

✳ The child then stands inside the first hoop and throws the beanbag into the second hoop.

✳ The children continue through the hoops, going from one hoop to the next, until they reach the finish line.

✳ After the children have played this, they can make up their own rules and move the hoops into different configurations.

Sensory Art

FAMILY LACING MATS

This activity is fun for older toddlers and young preschoolers. It promotes hand-eye coordination and small muscle development.

✳ Using a pencil, draw several different sizes of heads and faces on foam sheets or the back of placemats.

✳ Cut out the faces.

✳ Punch large holes just inside the edges of the faces.

✳ Draw eyes, nose, and smiling mouth on each face.

✳ You will need ten-to-fifteen-inch cotton shoelaces.

✳ Tie one end of the lace to the face shape and show the child how to push the string through the holes.

FAMILY BOOK

✳ Have children draw pictures of each family member, pets included.

✳ If any child does not want to draw, have him cut family pictures from magazines.

✳ Suggest that children draw family members together on the last page of the book.

✳ Children can dictate or write something for each page. This will encourage children to read their books.

✳ Older children can draw a picture of the family doing something or going somewhere, then tell the story in writing.

✳ Provide wrapping paper, wallpaper scraps, and fabric pieces to make the front and back book covers.

FAMILY CULTURAL YARN ARTISTRY

Place a world globe or map in your classroom. Throughout the year you can guide the children to discover the countries their family members come from or where they now live. If you use a map, mark each country with a pushpin for visual effect.

Invite the parents to share their cultures with the children. This will reinforce the concept that the class is a family.

Mexican Yarn Pictures

✳ Invite the children to select pieces of brightly colored yarn and a piece of cardboard for each picture they plan to make.

✳ Place glue at different places on the cardboard to make a design.

✳ Then, press the yarn into the glue, coiling it or making rows to create the designs. Sometimes it is helpful to use a craft stick to move the yarn into place.

✳ Let them dry.

✳ Display these creative art pieces around the classroom.

Huichol Indians of Mexico: "Ojo de Dios" (God's Eye)

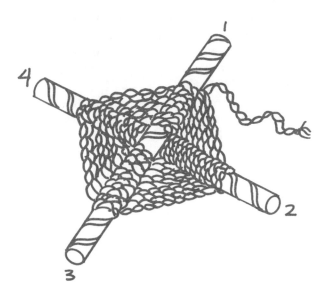

This weaving activity is designed for older children.

✳ Provide pieces of brightly colored yarn, glue, pencils, and two craft sticks, tongue depressors, or straws for each child.

✳ Suggest that the children cross the two sticks in the middle and glue them together. Allow sticks to dry.

✳ Lightly mark in pencil the ends of the sticks with numbers 1, 2, 3, 4.

✳ Tie the yarn around stick near the center. Then wind the yarn once around stick 2. Continue winding around sticks 3 and 4.

✳ Proceed in this manner until you reach the ends of the sticks.

✳ Tie the end of the yarn and tuck it into the woven design.

Creative Food Experiences

CHINESE EGG DROP SOUP

You will need:

    1 egg

    3 cups clear chicken broth

    1 tablespoon cornstarch

    2 tablespoons cold water

1. Wash hands.
2. Pour broth into a saucepan. Bring to a boil.
3. Measure water and cornstarch into a container with a lid, and shake energetically.
4. Pour cornstarch mixture from the container into the broth. Stir with a fork until smooth.
5. Break an egg into a small bowl and beat with a fork.

6. Slowly pour the beaten egg into the broth.
7. Stir until all the egg has been added and cooked.
8. Remove from heat, and serve.
9. This recipe serves 4. Make it several times with small groups of children.

Let the children see what happens when the egg cooks in shreds as it is dropped into the broth.

FAMILY SNACK

You will need:

    peanuts or small pecan pieces

    sunflower seeds

    pumpkin seeds

    raisins

    dried apricot, pineapple, apple, or peach pieces

    shredded coconut

    chocolate or butterscotch chips

    dry cereal pieces

1. Wash hands.
2. Mix ingredients together.
3. Eat!
4. Place remaining snack mix in a closed plastic container.

FAMILY RECIPE BOOK

✳ Have each parent send in a simple recipe that her child enjoys at home.

✳ Plan to try each recipe on a different day. This could extend over several weeks or months.

✳ From these recipes create a class cookbook, and add to it throughout the year.

✳ Each child's recipe becomes a page in his Family Book. (See sensory art Family Book in this theme.)

CHINESE EGG DROP SOUP

Wash hands.

Pour 3 cups clear chicken broth into a saucepan and

bring to a boil. Measure 2 tablespoons cold water and

1 tablespoon cornstarch into a container with a lid

and shake. Pour cornstarch mixture into

the broth. Stir with a fork until smooth. Break an egg

into a small bowl and beat with a fork. Slowly pour the beaten egg into the broth. Stir until all the egg has been added and cooked. Remove from heat and serve!

Math

PENNIES IN A JAR

This activity ties in with the book *A Chair for My Mother,* as discussed in the language experiences part of this theme.

✳ Collect pennies in a large, unbreakable jar. The jar should be small enough to be filled in a reasonably short time.

✳ The pennies can be collected by you, other teachers, parents, and the children.

✳ Have the children guess how many pennies will be in the jar when it is $\frac{1}{4}$ full, $\frac{1}{2}$ full, and full.

✳ Measure and mark the jar.

✳ Some children may want to use the pennies to see how far they can count. This is fine, as long as they put the pennies back in the jar.

WHO IS MISSING?

✳ Provide pictures of different family members cut from magazines or use real photos sent from home.

✳ Include a variety of ages, cultures, clothing.

✳ Place three or more pictures on a table or on the floor where all the children can see them. The number of pictures you use will vary according to the developmental abilities of the children.

✳ Ask the children to close their eyes while you remove one of the pictures.

✳ Let the children tell you which picture is missing.

✳ Then, allow the children to take turns removing one picture, so that the other children can guess which one is missing.

✳ To make it more difficult for older children, keep adding additional pictures.

MATCH THE STICKS

✳ Using ten craft sticks or tongue depressors, number each stick from one to ten.

✳ Make a duplicate set of sticks.

✳ Using stickers of faces, birds, butterflies, etc., or dots of colored glue, add the corresponding number of stickers or dots on each numbered stick.

✳ The children then match the two sets of sticks.

✳ To expand the activity, select one set of numbered sticks, and invite the children to arrange the sticks in order from one to ten, or backward from ten to one.

✳ Older children can put two or more sticks together and add the number of sticker objects on the combined sticks.

Science

LET'S SEE WHAT WE CAN SEE

✳ On a partly cloudy day, spread out several blankets on the grassy area of your playground.

✳ Have the children lie on their stomachs and explore what they can see from that position.

✳ Next, have them turn over on their backs and explore what they see up above. This is a great time to talk about cloud formations.

✳ Introduce Shaw's book *It Looked Like Spilt Milk,* listed in the books section of this theme.

✳ You can learn a lot about how the children see and think about their world.

✳ Parents can do this activity at home, giving them special time with their children in a way they might not have thought about.

ARE ROCKS ALIKE OR ARE THEY DIFFERENT?

✳ Collect all kinds of rocks. Have the children and their families help you.

✳ Save egg cartons, old muffin tins, paper plates, and margarine tubs for sorting and grouping the rocks.

✳ Encourage small groups of children to sort rocks that are alike in some way and put them in various containers.

✳ This usually stimulates a lot of discussion about the color, size, shape, texture, and pattern of rocks.

* The children continue with their discovery of rocks and bring in new ones from home once this activity is introduced in class.

* Older children can experiment with ways to tell which rocks are hard and which are soft. For example, try a simple scratch test with a penny. Which rocks can be scratched by a penny? Which ones cannot?

* Make books available to assist with rock identification.

* Place the rocks in the science center, and let the children keep going back to find new ways to classify rocks.

* Before placing rocks in science center, discuss appropriate use of rocks and safety factors.

Social Studies

The following curriculum suggestions are built on activities presented in this theme.

POT LUCK FAMILY FEAST

This can be a culminating class project at the conclusion of the family theme.

* Ask each family to bring a favorite family dish, or one that represents their culture.

* Have them also bring the recipe to be included in the class cookbook.

* The feast can be at lunch or dinner.

* A variation can be to have a breakfast feast and bring only breakfast dishes.

POSTCARDS

* Have parents ask relatives who travel or live in other cities or countries to send postcards to the children.

* You and the children can then place the cards on the map of the world in the classroom.

* You may get so many that you will have to rotate the cards. When they are not on the map, put them in boxes labeled with the city or country name.

FAMILY TREE

* Have the children and their parents make a family tree showing their family members.

* Encourage the parents to share their family trees with the class.

FIND THE COUNTRY

* Books included in the last part of this theme offer insights into families from many countries.

* On a map or globe find Africa, China, England, Israel, Japan, Mexico, Puerto Rico, Russia, Taiwan, and the United States.

Children's Books

Berenstain, Stan, and Jan Berenstain. (1984). *The Berenstain Bears and Mama's New Job.* New York: Random House.

Chanin, Michael. (1994). *Grandfather Four Winds and Rising Moon.* Illustrated by Sally J. Smith. Tiburon, CA: H.J. Kramer Inc.

Cooney, Barbara. (1985). *Miss Rumphius.* New York: Puffin Books.

Dorris, Arthur. (1991). *Abuela.* Illustrated by Elisa Kleven. New York: Dutton Children's Books.

Flournoy, Valerie. (1985). *The Patchwork Quilt.* Illustrated by Jerry Pinkney. New York: Dial Books for Young Readers.

Friedman, Ina R. (1984). *How My Parents Learned to Eat.* Illustrated by Allen Say. Boston: Houghton Mifflin.

Garza, Carmen Lomas. (1990). *Family Pictures, Cuadros de Familia.* San Francisco, CA: Children's Book Press.

Greenfield, Eloise. (1991). *Daddy and I.* Illustrated by Jan A. Gilchrist. New York: Black Butterfly Board Books for Children.

Hazen, Barbara Shook. (1992). *Mommie's Office.* Illustrated by David Soman. New York: Macmillan.

Hudson, Wade. (1993). *I Love My Family.* New York: Scholastic.

Johnston, Tony, and Tomie De Paola. (1985). *The Quilt Story.* New York: G.P. Putnam's Sons.

Joose, Barbara M. (1991). *Mama Do You Love Me?* New York: Chronicle Books.

Keats, Ezra Jack. (1967). *Peter's Chair.* New York: Harper & Row.

Kulkin Susan. (1992). *How My Family Lives in America.* New York: Bradbury Press.

Ostarch, Judy, and Anthony Nex. (1993). *My Family.* (Board book). Los Angeles: Price Stern Sloan Inc.

Polacco, Patricia. (1988). *The Keeping Quilt.* New York: Simon & Schuster Books for Young Readers.

Say, Allen. (1997). *Allison.* Boston: Houghton Mifflin.

Scott, Ann Herbert. (1992). *On Mother's Lap.* Illustrated by Glo Coalson. New York: Clarion Books.

Sonneborn, Ruth A. (1987). *Friday Night Is Papa Night.* Illustrated by Emily A. McCully. New York: Puffin Books.

Williams, Vera B. (1982). *A Chair for My Mother.* New York: Mulberry Books.

Parent Letter (School-age)

Dear Parents,

We are very excited to begin our new theme, My Family. The children will have opportunities to learn:

- A family is two or more people who are connected by love or kinship.
- Families may have members other than those living together.
- Each family member is important and special.
- Family members can be alike or different.
- Family members work, play, learn together, and help each other.
- Some families eat special foods and have celebrations.
- Some families include pets.

We will be talking about:

- relationships of family members
- where our family members live
- family activities
- family favorite songs, books, etc.

Try some of these things to do at home with your child:

- Look through family photo albums together.
- Talk about things you did when you were a child, such as games, songs, activities.
- Find special ways to include your child in preparing for family celebrations.
- Plan a family night of stories, songs, and games with no TV.
- Rent a video of one of your favorite childhood movies, and watch it with your child.

Parent participation opportunities at school include:

- Send in family snapshots to share.
- Ask out-of-town relatives to send postcards to the class.
- Take part in the family feast.

6

Date ———— Time ————

- Help to create a cookbook from recipes turned in by other families in the class.
- Share the family tree that you and your family made.

Wish list for this theme:

road maps
postcards
rocks of all kinds
old luggage (small and medium)
nonworking cameras

paper sacks
paper plates
postage stamps
envelopes
stationery

Thank you for being part of our class family.

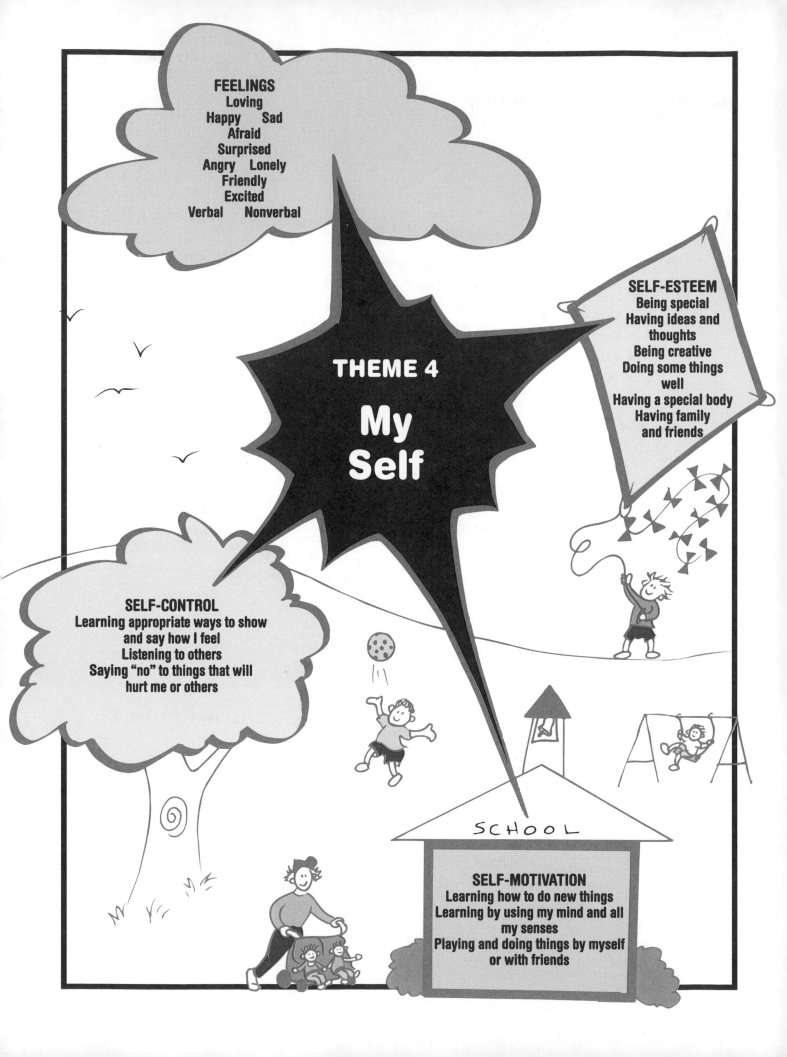

THEME GOALS

To provide opportunities for children to learn:

1. I am special because I am **me.** There is no one else just like me.
2. I am still discovering how to do new things.
3. I can use my mind and my senses to accomplish many things.
4. I can play and do things by myself or with friends and family.
5. I can show my emotions and say how I feel without hurting others.
6. I can say "no" to things that will hurt me or others.

Children-Created Bulletin Board

This bulletin board gives children an opportunity to express how they feel about themselves. Throughout the theme, the bulletin board changes as the children learn more about feelings, self-esteem, self-motivation, and self-control.

* ✳ Cut white posterboard cards in various shapes, such as circles, squares, rectangles, and triangles.
* ✳ Have each child select one card in his favorite shape.
* ✳ Write, or have the children write, the following (fill in the appropriate word):

"Special Recipe for (Child's Name)"

Two big (color) eyes,
One great smile,
(Long, short — color) hair,
Smooth (color) skin,
One cup of niceness,
Two cups of laughter.

✳ Children add anything they want about themselves. Give a few examples to get them started: "Add one cup of books. Stir in puzzles. Mix together and discover (child's name)."

✳ You may find it easier to do this with each child individually.

✳ Put the finished recipes on the bulletin board.

✳ Have the children add photos of themselves or pictures they draw of themselves.

✳ As they learn to do more things during this theme, they can add to the original recipe.

✳ Drawings that express feelings also can be added.

✳ Adding new items will make this an interactive bulletin board.

Vocabulary Starters

Let the children add additional words.

self — whatever is just about you and nobody else.

feelings — what you mean when you talk about or show being happy, sad, afraid, angry, or surprised.

thoughts — what happens when you get ideas and decide to do things.

creative — discovering new ways of doing things.

learn — to know and understand something you did not know or understand before.

Language Experiences

BALL NAME GAME

All you need for this activity are the children and a large ball. This is a good transition activity. When a child's name is called, she can choose a learning center and go to it.

✳ Everyone sits on the floor in a circle.

✳ Talk about how special everyone's name is.

✳ Roll the ball to a child, and everyone says the child's first name.

✳ Ask the toddler to roll or bring the ball back to you. Continue rolling the ball and saying each child's name.

✳ The preschooler can roll the ball to someone else and everyone says that child's name. The ball passes from one child to another until each child's name is called and repeated.

✳ Extend this activity by rolling the ball to a child and saying the child's last name.

✳ Continue until each child's last name has been called.

WHOSE VOICE IS THIS?

Use a tape recorder to tape each child's conversational voice, giggling, laughing, or singing.

✳ Record each child privately, away from the other children. If they do not know what to say, help them say something with you. This way you are recording your voice too.

✳ Next, play back what each child recorded and have the other children guess whose voice they hear.

✳ Talk about how each person's voice is unique.

✳ Place the tape recorder in the music center. The children can listen to the voices whenever they wish.

LET'S SHARE

✳ Read Hutchins' *The Doorbell Rang,* listed in the books section of this theme.

✳ Discuss the concept of sharing as a way of showing someone you care about him.

✳ Ask open-ended questions: "What have you shared?" "Whom did you share it with?" "Why do you need to share?" "How do you feel when someone shares with you?" "What are some things we could share in the classroom?"

✳ *The Doorbell Rang* is about sharing cookies. Buy or bake a giant cookie, and let the children find ways to share.

Dramatic Play

I AM HAPPY

This activity can be done indoors or outdoors.

✳ Give the children opportunities to show emotions (happy, sad, angry, afraid, and surprised) by the way they run, walk, hop, throw a ball, or move their bodies.

✳ Role-play appropriate ways to handle situations.

✳ Ask children to share what makes them feel happy, sad, etc.

✳ This could be repeated throughout the year to help children deal with their feelings.

PANTOMIME TIME

✳ Read Carle's *The Mixed-Up Chameleon,* see the books section of this theme.

✳ Ask open-ended questions, such as: "Why do you think the chameleon was feeling unhappy?" "What feelings do you have about the chameleon?"

✳ Help the children decide which "chameleon character" they want to pantomime. Act without using words. One child can even be the sun and another the fly.

✳ Then, read the story again.

✳ The children pantomime their roles as the story unfolds.

✳ To extend this activity, have the children create paper costumes of the different "chameleon characters."

✳ The children can also draw their own chameleons.

Puppet Play

TENNIS BALL PUPPET FRIEND

Let the children name this puppet. For the purpose of describing this activity, we will call the tennis ball puppet "Happy." This activity promotes positive self-esteem, self-motivation, and self-control.

✳ To make Happy, an adult should cut a slit in the middle of the ball across from one seam to the

next. (See the illustration for clarification.) **Caution:** Be careful when cutting. A tennis ball is difficult to cut. It is hard to hold without slipping.

✳ Use markers or "puff paint" to make eyes, eyebrows, nose, and mouth.

✳ To make Happy "talk," press the sides of the ball.

✳ Use a box to make a special home for the puppet.

✳ Let a different child take Happy home each day after school and bring him back the next day.

✳ Happy reports on his overnight (or weekend) adventure at the child's home.

✳ This gives the child an opportunity to develop a voice for the puppet and tell about what happened.

✳ You and the children can write in a special book about what happens to Happy. Where did he go? What did he eat? Whom did he see? Where did he sleep?

✳ The children can also illustrate their books.

✳ They vote on who gets to take Happy home.

✳ Next, you and the children can make a calendar and count the days until Happy goes home with the next child.

FEELINGS

Children of all ages enjoy this activity.

✳ Put tongue depressors, crayons, and markers out for the children to use.

✳ Encourage the children to make a set of "feelings" puppets.

✳ They can draw faces on the tongue depressors that show happy, sad, fearful, angry, and surprised expressions.

✳ Give the children envelopes in which to put their "feelings." They place the envelopes in their individual cubbies. When the children want to express how they feel, they can pull out their "feelings" puppet.

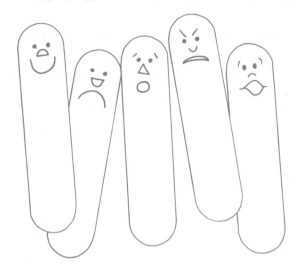

Music

SONG:
"Hello, Hello"

The following song is a *musical beat* activity. It also can be chanted.

Hello, hello,
We sing in many ways.
Hello, hello,
Let's sing it now today.

In the following verses of this Hello chant, a simple method of indicating the beat is used. Though the Hello chant is original, the system of indicating the beat is adapted from Sally Moomaw's *More Than Singing,* published by Redleaf Press.

   Use a drum or other musical instrument to reinforce the beat. A vertical line (|) above a syllable means that it is accented. An asterisk (*) indicates a pause (or "rest," as in music) in the phrasing. In addition, phonetic pronunciations are provided under the foreign words.

English

*Hel-lo * hel-lo **
*We sing in ma-ny ways **
*Hel-lo * hel-lo **
*Let's sing it now to-day **

Spanish

*Ho-la * ho-la **
(oh-la oh-la)
*We sing in ma-ny ways **
*Ho-la * ho-la **
*Let's sing it now to-day **

French

*Bon-jour * bon-jour **
(bone-zhoor bone-zhoor)
*We sing in ma-ny ways **
*Bon-jour * bon-jour **
*Let's sing it now to-day **

German

Gu-ten tag gu-ten tag
(goo-ten tog goo-ten tog)

Italian

*Ci-a-o * Ci-a-o **
(chee-ah-oh chee-ah-oh)

Japanese

Kon-ni-chi- wa Kon-ni-chi-wa
(koh-nee-chee-wah koh-nee-chee-wah)

Chinese

*Ni-hao * ni-hao **
(nee-how nee-how)

Korean

*An nung * an nung **
(ahn nyong ahn nyong)

Vietnamese

*Chao * Chao **
(Chow Chow)

Hebrew

*Sha-lom * sha-lom ***
(sha-lome sha-lome)

Arabic

*Mar-h-ba * mar-h-ba ***
(mar-hah-bah mar-hah-bah)

Movement

EXERCISES FOR OLDER INFANTS AND TODDLERS

* **Push the chair:** to practice walking.
  Have the infant on his feet holding onto the back of a low, sturdy child's chair. Help him push the chair while practicing walking.

* **In and Out of the Box:** for coordination.
  Use a heavy cardboard box or tub, and place the baby inside. Encourage her to climb in and out.

* **The Rocking Chair:** for fun and to strengthen muscles.
  Have the infant sit on the floor next to you. Bring your knees up, and rock back and forth. Encourage the child to do the same.

* **Pop-Up:** for upper body and stomach strength.
  Do this exercise together. Have the baby sit on the floor and bend over. Quickly have him straighten his legs while sitting upright and stretching his arms up high. Hold for two seconds, then quickly return to bent-over position. Repeat.

LET'S WAVE, WOBBLE, AND WIGGLE

Do this activity with or without recorded music, or try it using the traditional tune "The Bear Went Over the Mountain."

My thumbs, my thumbs want to pop up.
My thumbs, my thumbs want to pop up.
My thumbs, my thumbs want to pop up.
That's what they like to do.

Continue the pattern with the following changes:

My hands, my hands want to shake . . .
My arms, my arms want to wave . . .
My head, my head wants to wobble . . .
(That's what *it* likes to do.)

My legs, my legs want to wiggle . . .
My feet, my feet want to dance . . .
Now all of me wants to jump . . .
(That's what *I* like to do.)

End with:

Oh, I am starting to giggle,
I am starting to giggle,
I am starting to giggle,
I think I'll just sit down!

I'M THE LEADER

* Everyone forms a big circle. Select one of the children to be the leader.
* Suggest that she hop, jump, or crawl and say, "Do it just like me."
* The other children then try to do what she does.
* Continue with the children taking turns.
* This is one of those quick activities that can be used anytime.

RIGHT, LEFT, RIGHT, STOP!

This movement activity helps with recognition of left and right.

* Let the children help you come up with other ideas.
* Older children like to combine several body movements at one time.
* Children like to do this at home with family members, too.

March with feet	Sway with upper body
Left, right,	Right, left,
Left, right,	Right, left
Left, right,	Right, left,
Stop!	Stop!

Raise arms	Move head
Left, right,	Right, left,
Left, right,	Right, left,
Left, right,	Right, left,
Stop!	Stop!

Sensory Art

EXPRESSING FEELINGS

To ease the times a child may feel frustrated, angry, or full of energy (and "using his words" won't help), bring out the clay or play dough. Many types and textures are available. Recipes for play dough are provided in Themes 6 and 10.

✳ Set up a special space for the child to have some alone time with the clay or play dough.

✳ For a toddler, a special place to pound on the plastic pounding bench can help defuse some feelings.

MAKE AN "I'M SPECIAL" VEST

Do this is project with each child individually, if possible.

✳ Take a large paper grocery sack and invert it, with the bottom of the sack now at the top.

✳ Cut straight up the center of one of the wide sides to where the bottom creases.

✳ Here, cut a large round circle out of the bottom of the sack.

✳ On each narrow side of the sack, cut a vertical oval that starts at the bottom crease and descends about eight inches.

✳ The child puts the vest on by placing his head through the large round opening, with the long vertical slit to the front, and arms through the two side ovals.

✳ Have each child decorate the "I'm Special" vest with crayons, markers, felt and fabric scraps, construction paper, feathers, cotton balls, all kinds of shapes, stickers, and buttons.

✳ Put magazines and catalogs out as well, and suggest that they cut out pictures of what they like and glue these to the vest.

TWO-DIMENSIONAL ART GALLERY

In a school hallway, walkway, or entrance area, display some of the children's art along with posters or pictures of famous paintings.

✳ Mat and attractively exhibit all the art, so that the children's creativity is treated the same as that of well-known artists.

✳ Let the children help you mount the exhibition.

✳ This is a good way to introduce the children to great works of art and the painters who created the works.

✳ There are also many children's books on art available to share with the children. For example: *Getting to Know the World's Greatest Artists Series,* published by Children's Press, and *New York's Metropolitan Museum of Art Series,* published by Viking.

Creative Food Experiences

HAPPY FACES

You will need:
    a loaf of bread
    cream cheese
    peanut butter
    apple jelly
    raisins
    nuts

HAPPY FACES!

Wash hands.

Cut circles from bread with a round cookie cutter.

Spread bread with cream cheese, peanut butter,

or apple jelly. Use raisins and nuts to make

eyes, nose, and mouth.

ENJOY!

1. Let the children cut circles from bread with a round cookie cutter.
2. Spread bread with cream cheese, peanut butter, or apple jelly. Children sometimes use all three.
3. Use raisins and nuts to make eyes, nose, and mouth. Enjoy!

LET'S MAKE A CAKE

This recipe is easy for the children to do and can give them a sense of accomplishment. It is also a fun one to pass on to the parents.

1. Wash hands.
2. Put one can of fruit, with the juice, into a buttered nine-by-thirteen inch metal or glass pan.
3. Dump 1 box of white or yellow cake mix over the fruit.
4. Cut one stick of butter or margarine into small pieces.
5. Dump shortening pieces on top of the cake mix.
6. Bake at 350 degrees for 30–40 minutes.
7. Then, eat!

Math

THE LANGUAGES OF MATH

This activity encourages learning to count from one to five in many languages. It also helps to build self-esteem for children of other cultures.

Numbers

English	Spanish	French	German	Italian
one	uno	un	eins	uno
	(oō-no)	(oŏn)	(īnes)	(oō-no)
two	dos	deux	zwei	due
	(dose)	(doŏ)	([ts]vye)	(doō-eh)
three	tres	trois	drei	tre
	(trais)	(t(r)wah)	(dry)	(treh)
four	cuatro	quatre	vier	quattro
	(kwáh-tro)	(ká-tra)	(fear)	(kwáh-tro)
five	cinco	cinq	funf	cinque
	(seén-ko)	(sank)	(toŏnt)	(cheen-kay)

English	Chinese	Japanese	Hebrew	Arabic
one	yi	ichi	achat	wahid
	(yee)	(ée-chee)	(a-(h)áht)	(wáh-hid)
two	er	ni	shta'yim	ithinin
	(uhr)	(nee)	(shtah-yéem)	(ith-nín)
three	san	san	shalosh	thalatha
	(sahn)	(sahn)	(shah-lŏśh)	(ta-lá-ta)
four	si	shi	arba	arba'a
	(suh)	(shee)	(ar-báh)	(ar-báh)
five	wu	go	hamesh	kamisa
	(woo)	(go)	([h]ah-meśh)	(k(h)ahm-sa)

MATH COOKIES

Relate this activity to Hutchins' book *The Doorbell Rang*. See the language experience activity in this theme. This activity promotes problem-solving, one-to-one correspondence, and cooperation.

✳ You and the children make three dozen "cardboard cookies." These can be made easily out of heavy cardboard or posterboard cut into circles.

✳ Decorate the cookies with markers and crayons.

✳ Some of the cookies should be alike.

✳ Then, make up math games that can be played with the cardboard cookies.

✳ Younger children can sort the cookie circles by color or by the number of "chocolate chip dots" on the cookies. They can also practice making a straight line with the cookies.

✳ Older children can practice counting and sorting the cookies into pairs, as well as figuring out how many children are in the class, whether they can share the cookies equally, and what they have to do to share the cookies equally.

Science

FIXING THINGS

✳ Collect broken toys, torn books, or anything that can be fixed with masking tape, clear tape, or glue.

✳ You and the children decide how to repair the broken or torn items.

✳ Children may work together in partnership with another child to figure out how the broken pieces might fit together again.

MY BODY IS MADE OF HINGES

This project has many levels. The beginning levels are appropriate and interesting for preschoolers. The entire procedure is fascinating for older children. To introduce this activity, have a variety of hinges in a box.

✳ Demonstrate how the hinges work, and allow the children to experiment with them for several days.

✳ Next, talk about hinges in the room, and then show how their bodies have hinges.

✳ Let them bend fingers, wrists, knees, etc., to music.

✳ Introduce silhouette pieces: head, neck, trunk, arms, hands, legs, and feet. These can be made from black construction paper or shiny, lightweight black art paper.

✳ Have a prepared figure put together with brads to show how the body moves.

✳ Prepare the silhouette body parts for each child and place the pieces in individual envelopes.

✳ Go through magazines and catalogs for action poses.

✳ Encourage each child to select one picture and, using glue sticks, glue it on one-half of an 8½-by-11-inch piece of white paper.

✳ On the side of the page opposite the picture, have the child position the silhouette body parts in the same position. They will need your watchful eye to do this.

✳ When each child is satisfied with the pose, she glues the parts, one at a time, onto the paper.

✳ Place all the finished silhouette pictures on the bulletin board.

Social Studies

CELEBRATING BIRTHDAYS AND SPECIAL MONTHS

Birthdays are special days for children. Help them celebrate by setting up a big classroom calendar that you and the children design.

✳ Have each child write his name and birthdate on the calendar.

✳ Since some cultures and religions do not emphasize birthdays, also include on the calendar special events that happen each month in your community or nationally.

✳ You can celebrate birthdays and other special days at the same time.

✳ Play special recorded music, eat a new snack, or read a new book to celebrate the birthday.

Here are some suggestions for special events to celebrate. You and the children can decide how you will observe the day.

September: Monarch Butterfly Migration Month
Good Neighbor Day (4th week)

October: Popcorn Month
Apple Month
Teddy Bear Day (Oct. 27)

November: National Children's Book Week (3rd week)
Homemade Bread Day (Nov. 17)

December: Birds in the Snow Week (4th week)
Poinsettia Day (Dec. 12)

January: National Soup Month
New Year's Day in 123 nations (Jan. 1)

February: Black History Month
Presidents' Day (2nd week)

March: National Nutrition Month
Children's Poetry Day (March 21)

April: Week of the Young Child (Consult the
National Association for the Education
of Young Children for specific dates:
1-800/424-2460.)
Earth Day (April 22)

May: Be Kind to Animals Month
National Safe Kids Week (2nd week)

June: Children's Day (2nd week)
Flag Day (June 14)

July: Blueberry Month
National Ice Cream Day (3rd week)

August: National Clown Week (1st week)
Family Day (2nd week)

PRIMARY-GRADE

NEW NAME GAME

This activity is designed for older children. It emphasizes the importance of a child's name and the feelings connected to her name. It helps children recognize the importance of a name as part of one's identity. The Ball Name Game in the language experiences part of this theme is a similar activity for younger children.

✳ Give each child in your class a new name, just for this project. Do not give any reasons why. This will be explained later.

✳ Throughout the morning, you use only the new name. If a child gets upset, **stop,** and explain that it is only a game.

✳ In the afternoon, gather the children together and talk about how they felt about having their names changed. Ask open-ended questions. "How did you feel when I changed your name?" "What were your feelings when I wouldn't answer why I changed your name?" "How do you think other children feel when someone doesn't say their name right?"

Children's Books

Aliki. (1984). *Feelings.* New York: Greenwillow.

Allen, Constance. (1997). *Chelli, Be Mine.* Illustrated by Laurent Linn. New York: Golden Books Publishing Company, Inc. and Children's Television Workshop.

Carle, Eric. (1996). *The Grouchy Ladybug.* New York: HarperCollins Juvenile Books.

Carle, Eric. (1984). *The Mixed-Up Chameleon.* New York: HarperTrophy.

Christopher, Matt. (1993). *The Lucky Baseball Bat.* Illustrated by Dee Derosa. New York: Little Brown & Company.

Hayward, Linda, Children's Television Workshop, and Norman Gorbaty. (1997). *Mine: A Sesame Street Book About Sharing.* (Board edition). New York: Random House.

Howe, James, and E. Young. (1987). *I Wish I Were a Butterfly.* San Diego, CA: Harcourt Brace.

Hutchins, Pat. (1989). *The Doorbell Rang.* New York: Mulberry Books.

Lebrun, Claude. (1997). *Little Brown Bear Is Growing Up.* Chicago, IL: Children's Press.

Lopshire, Robert. (1986). *I Want to Be Somebody New!* New York: Random House.

MacCarone, Grace. (1995). *The Lunch Box Surprise.* New York: Cartwheel Books.

Mayer, Mercer. (1995). *I Am Sharing.* New York: Random House.

Merriam, Eve. (1994). *Poems: Higgle Wiggle, Happy Rhymes.* Illustrated by Hans Wilhelm. New York: Mulberry Press.

Reiser, Lynn, Rebecca Hart, and Corazones Valientes Organization. (1998). *Tortillas and Lullabies/Tortillas Y Cancioncitas.* New York: Greenwillow.

Viorst, Judith. (1972). *Alexander and the Terrible, Horrible, No Good, Very Bad Day.* Illustrated by Ray Cruz. New York: Macmillan.

Wells, Rosemary. (1997). *Noisy Nora.* New York: Dial Books.

Weninger, Brigette. (1998). *What's the Matter, Davy?* Illustrated by Eve Tharlet. New York: North South Books.

Wood, Audrey. (1990). *Quick as a Cricket.* New York: Child's Play International.

Zolotow, Charlotte. (1985). *William's Doll.* Illustrated by William Pene DeBois. New York: HarperTrophy.

Parent Letter (Preschool)

Dear Parents,

We are starting another theme this week, My Self. We will provide opportunities for the children to learn:

- I am special because I am **me.** There is no one else like me.
- I am still discovering how to do new things.
- I can use my mind and my senses to accomplish many things.
- I can play and do things by myself or with friends and family.
- I can show emotions and say how I feel without hurting others.
- I can say "no" to things that will hurt me or others.

We will be talking about:

- feelings
- verbal expression
- nonverbal expression
- self-esteem
- self-motivation
- self-control

Things you can do at home with your preschool child are:

- Welcome "Happy" (the tennis ball puppet) when it comes home with your child. It will be in the box it "lives in," but "Happy" enjoys getting out sometimes. "Happy" should be included in family activities, such as going where your child goes and sleeping in the room with your child.
- Sing songs with your child and record them on a tape recorder. This gives the family a special musical cassette.
- Make cookies or a cake with your child.
- Let your child help you repair things around the house.

Parent participation opportunities at school will be to:

- Help us make "I'm Special" vests.
  Date _____ Time _____
- Come visit the children's art gallery.
- Help us make silhouettes.
  Date _____ Time _____

This is our wish list for this theme:

magazines and catalogs

posters of famous paintings

tennis balls

large paper sacks

heavy cardboard

Thank you for sharing your child with us.

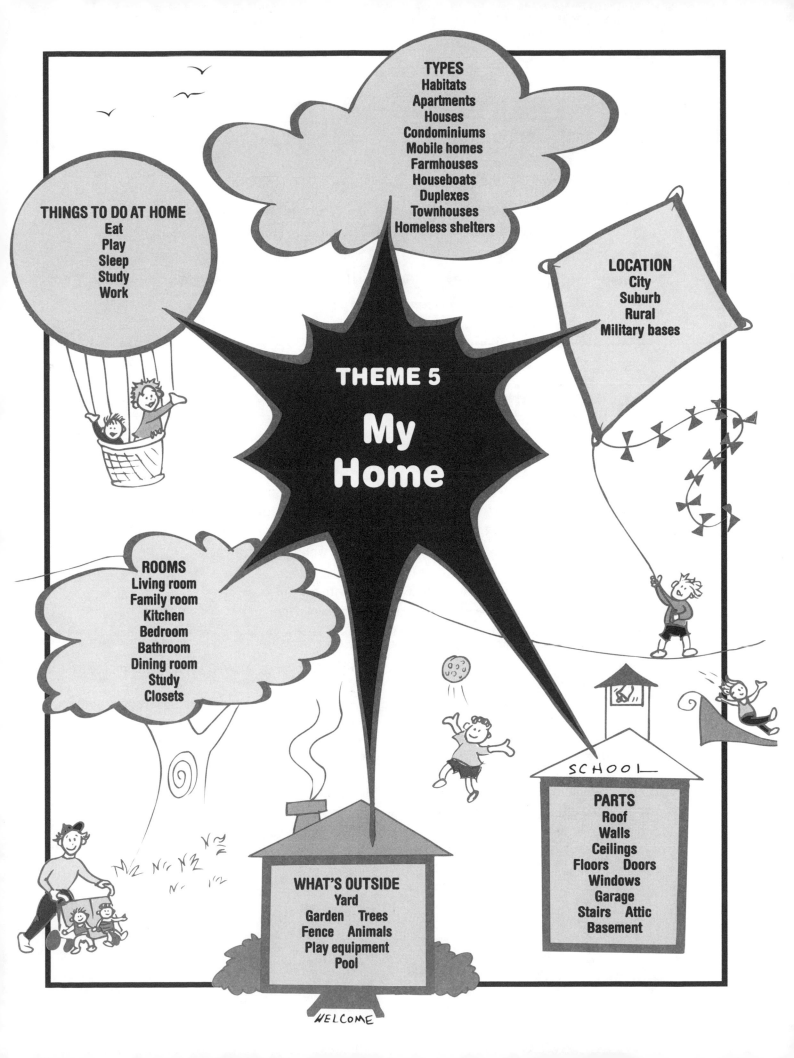

TYPES
Habitats
Apartments
Houses
Condominiums
Mobile homes
Farmhouses
Houseboats
Duplexes
Townhouses
Homeless shelters

THINGS TO DO AT HOME
Eat
Play
Sleep
Study
Work

LOCATION
City
Suburb
Rural
Military bases

THEME 5

My Home

ROOMS
Living room
Family room
Kitchen
Bedroom
Bathroom
Dining room
Study
Closets

SCHOOL

PARTS
Roof
Walls
Ceilings
Floors   Doors
Windows
Garage
Stairs   Attic
Basement

WHAT'S OUTSIDE
Yard
Garden   Trees
Fence   Animals
Play equipment
Pool

WELCOME

THEME GOALS

To provide opportunities for children to learn:

1. A home is a place where you live, sleep, eat, work, and play.
2. A home can be built from brick, stone, wood, metal, cement, mud, and straw.
3. Homes come in many types, sizes, and shapes.
4. Homes can be found in many locations, such as cities, rural areas, and suburbs.
5. Homes are different in different parts of the world.

Children-Created Bulletin Board

This bulletin board of a house-shaped book encourages children to recall and classify the rooms in their homes and the furnishings, objects, and activities located in each room. If the majority of the children in your class live in apartments, mobile homes, or on the farm, make the shape of the home correspond to this.

* Cover the bulletin board with butcher paper or wrapping paper.
* Cut a large house-shaped front and back cover for the book out of posterboard.
* Leave the covers blank so the children can draw windows, doors, and doorknobs on them.
* Using the cover for a pattern, cut pages for the book from white butcher paper.
* Cut a page to represent each room in the home.
* With the help of the children, title and label each page with a room name.
* Punch three holes on the left side of each page and the book covers.
* After assembling the book pages, attach loose-leaf rings, ribbons, yarn, or pipe cleaners twisted together to form rings through the holes.
* Ask the children to select a title for their Big Book. While the children are watching, print it on the front cover, and say the words as you write.
* Let the children help you number the pages. Many times, the children will think of this without you suggesting it.
* Throughout the duration of the My Home theme, have the children cut and paste pictures of objects and furnishings that belong in each room. These can be cut from magazines and catalogs, or drawn by the children.
* Continue to personalize the book whenever the children have a suggestion.
* "Read" the book often with the children.
* Expanding this activity can integrate many areas of curriculum. The children may want to make their own *little* house book.

COVER

Vocabulary Starters

Let the children add additional words.

shelter or habitat — a structure that protects you from the weather and keeps you safe.

home — a place where you live.

apartment — a building that has many homes inside.

duplex — a house that is divided into two homes.

mobile home — a home that can be moved from one place to another.

houseboat — a home made to float on the water like a boat.

farmhouse or ranch house — a house in the country where a farmer or rancher and her family live.

Languages Experiences

FINGERPLAY:
Houses

Here's a nest for Robin Redbreast.
   (cup hands with palms up)
Here's a hive for Busy Bee.
   (hands cupped together with fingers up)
Here's a hole for Bunny Rabbit.
   (make a circle with thumbs and index fingers)
And here's a house for me.
   (tips of fingers touching, palms apart)

POEM:
"My House"

My house, my house is very tall.
It has a ceiling and a wall.
It has a window and a door.
It has a carpet on the floor.
My house, my house is clean and bright.
It has a lamp that I can light.
It has a table and a chair.
It has a closet with clothes to wear.
My house, my house, it is the best.
It has a bedroom where I rest.
It has a kitchen with food to eat.
It has a stove and oven to heat.
My house, my house, it has a hall.
It has some pictures on the wall.
It has a bookcase filled with books.
It has a coatrack with some hooks.
My house, my house is very fine.
It's warm and snug and it is MINE!

Philip Jackman

WHAT'S THAT SOUND?

This activity helps children develop listening skills, and creative and abstract thinking. For younger children:

✳ Record on a tape recorder simple sounds around the house, such as a faucet running, a telephone ringing, a timer going off, and music playing.

✳ Play the tape and ask the children to identify what is making the sound. Use pictures to help younger preschoolers with the identification of what makes each sound.

✳ Record additional sounds with the children's help.

✳ Go outside and listen for new sounds to record.

For older children:

✳ Record more complex sounds, such as a washing machine, a dishwasher, a toilet flushing, a toaster popping up, a clock ticking and its alarm ringing, a doorbell sounding, someone knocking on a door, a garage door opening, and a closet door opening and closing.

✳ Go through the same process: play the sounds, have the children guess what is making the sound, and record additional indoor and outdoor sounds.

✳ Have the children identify which room in the house the sound came from.

✳ Extend this activity by having the children pretend to be the object and act out what it does while making the sound.

Dramatic Play

THE NAPPING HOUSE

This activity promotes paying attention to what the author and the illustrator were saying, the sequencing of events, and using dramatic play to express what was happening.

✳ After reading Wood's *The Napping House* (see books in this theme), have the children first make the sounds of each character asleep, then the sounds each character makes when awakening.

✳ Ask open-ended questions about the book, such as, "What did you see happening to the colors of the illustrations of the book?" "Were the colors at the beginning different than from those at the end of the book?" "Why were those colors used?" "What was happening outside the house?" "What was happening inside the house?"

✳ To broaden this activity, make materials available for the children to paint their own illustrations of *The Napping House.*

LET'S GO CAMPING

✳ Change and expand the home living/dramatic play area into a campground.

✳ Pitch a tent, either indoors or outdoors, and put cots or mats inside.

✳ Add camping equipment, such as blankets, paper cups, plates, plastic knives, forks, spoons, and flashlights.

✳ Ask parents to send one item they might use when camping.

✳ This activity extends the concept that even when a family goes on a camping vacation the tent becomes a home.

✳ Talk about other times and places when people lived in tents.

LET'S BUILD A HOUSE WITH BOXES AND BLOCKS

✳ Put pictures of all types of houses in the block center.

✳ Place unit and hollow blocks, sanded pieces of wood, varied sizes and shapes of boxes, and milk carton blocks in the area.

✳ Add multiethnic family figures, small animals, and small cars and trucks.

✳ Encourage the children to build homes.

✳ Have the children label the rooms in each home.

✳ Arrange the houses into neighborhoods, and add streets for the cars and trucks.

✳ Extend this for older children by placing boxes of various sizes in the block center. The children can color or paint the boxes, draw windows, and glue several together to make an apartment building.

✳ Using masking tape, make a street down the center of the building site.

✳ Children may decide to add buildings, such as a school, child care center, grocery store, or hospital.

✳ Keep the center like this for several days or weeks. The children will help you decide.

✳ Another way to keep the children involved is to take the house building outdoors.

✳ Fill the sand and water table or a plastic tub with water and dirt.

✳ Let the children build mud houses.

Puppet Play

KITCHEN GADGET PUPPETS

This is an activity for older children. This activity promotes cooperation, problem-solving, creativity, literacy, and language development.

✳ Collect wooden spoons, new dishwashing sponges with handles, splatter shields (shields that fit on pans to prevent splattering while cooking), and large sieves. Ask parents to send in one kitchen gadget with their child.

✳ Talk about how puppets can be made from many things. Show them the selection of gadgets. What would they do to make these into puppets?

✳ Guide them to the table where you have already set up glue, markers, felt, yarn, craft moveable eyes, and construction paper.

✳ Place yourself nearby with the hot glue gun to help with fast gluing.

✳ Then, step back and let the children create puppets.

✳ To extend this activity, suggest to the children that they could write a short puppet play and use their newly made characters to bring the play "to life."

Music

KITCHEN BAND

✳ Collect pots, pans, spoons, empty plastic bottles, empty oatmeal containers, and rhythm sticks.

✳ The children select their "instruments" and make a circle or a line.

✳ Put on a record, audio tape, or CD of marching music, such as "76 Trombones" from *The Music Man* or a John Philip Sousa march.

✳ That's all you need to have a children's marching band.

PLAY THE PIANO

This activity is designed for older toddlers and young preschoolers to promote listening skills and small muscle development.

✳ Gather the children around the tables in the classroom.

✳ Ask them to pretend that the table in front of them is a *piano*. "Hold your fingers on your table as if you are playing the piano."

✳ "First, we'll play some very soft music." Demonstrate moving your fingers lightly, touching the fingertips gently to the table.

✳ "Now let's play some very loud music." Demonstrate moving your fingers, touching your fingertips to the table with a very heavy, firm touch.

✳ Next, play slow, then fast music.

✳ Guide the children into moving all fingers up and down independently from each other. This exercises individual finger muscles.

✳ Once the children have the general idea of what to do, play some recorded piano music.

✳ Ask the children to follow along with the music and play softly, loudly, slowly, and fast when the music does so.

SONG: "Here's the Way We . . ."

Sing these verses to the tune of "Here We Go 'Round the Mulberry Bush."

Here's the way we get out of bed,
Get out of bed, get out of bed,
Here's the way we get out of bed,
So early in the morning.
Here's the way we wash our face,
Wash our face, wash our face,
Here's the way we wash our face,
So early in the morning.

Continue with:

Here's the way we brush our teeth.
Here's the way we drink our milk.
Here's the way we eat with a spoon.
Here's the way we open the door.
Here's the way we play outside.

Sing about the rooms in a house:

Here's the way we walk to the kitchen.
Here's the way we sleep in the bedroom.
Here's the way we play in the family room.

The children will help you add more verses.

Movement

JACK-AND-JILL-IN-THE-BOX

Jack-in-the-box, (child stands)
Push Jack in. (child crouches down)
Turn the handle,
See Jack again. (child jumps up)
   Jill-in-the-box, (child sits down)
   Sits so still.
   Won't you come out?
   Yes I will. (child jumps up)
Jack-in-the-box,
Close the top. (child squats down)
Turn the handle,
And up Jack pops. (child jumps up)
   Jill-in-the-box,
   Where is she? (child sits down)
   Open the lid,
   And there she'll be. (child jumps up)

JOHNNY BUILDS WITH ONE HAMMER

"Hammer" with a pretend hammer in the right hand as you begin to sing.

Johnny builds with one hammer, one hammer, one hammer,
Johnny builds with one hammer all day long.
   (hammer with pretend hammers in the right and left hands)
Johnny builds with two hammers, two hammers, two hammers,
Johnny builds with two hammers all day long.
   (hammer with pretend hammers in the right and left hands and with the right foot "hammering" on the floor)
Johnny builds with three hammers, three hammers, three hammers,
Johnny builds with three hammers all day long.
   (hammer with pretend hammers in the right and left hands and with the right foot and left foot hammering on the floor)
Johnny builds with four hammers, four hammers, four hammers,
Johnny builds with four hammers all day long.
   (hammer the same as above and add the head going up and down like a hammer)
Johnny builds with five hammers, five hammers, five hammers,

Johnny builds with five hammers all day long.
  (reverse the process and end up with no hammers)
Johnny builds with no hammers, no hammers, no
  hammers,
Johnny builds with no hammers all day long.

Sensory Art

MAKE MILK CARTON BLOCKS

✳ With the children's help, cut off the tops of two milk cartons, and push the open end of one carton into another carton to make a sturdy block.

✳ Ask the children to cover the blocks with wallpaper scraps, construction paper, or contact paper.

✳ Older children can color or draw brick designs on the blocks.

✳ For toddlers, make the blocks and let them decorate, or give some of the blocks made by the older children to the younger children.

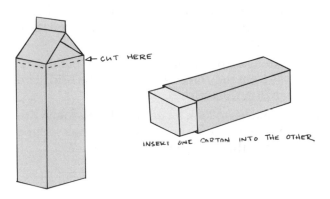

CUT HERE

INSERT ONE CARTON INTO THE OTHER

CONSTRUCT A HOUSE

✳ Place construction paper, craft sticks, and glue at a table.

✳ Suggest to the children that they build the shape of a house, apartment house, or any other type of house with the craft sticks and glue.

✳ After the glue dries, they can add windows and doors.

✳ The children may build several structures or create original designs of craft sticks placed on the paper. It is the process that's important!

A DIAGRAM OF MY HOUSE

Older children enjoy this activity. It stimulates abstract thinking, recall, and language development.

✳ Before you begin this project, show the children examples of several room diagrams or maps.

✳ Then, place different sizes of paper, rulers, pencils, markers, and crayons on a table.

✳ Ask each child to draw a diagram or map of the inside of her house.

✳ To further develop this concept, have the parents help measure the child's room. Note the doors and windows, as well as the furniture in the room. Have the child draw the room on graph paper.

✳ Prepare a place in the classroom to display the finished drawings.

DESIGN A ROOM

Children enjoy doing this with a partner.

✳ Collect small- to medium-sized boxes with lids.

✳ Supply glue, scissors, fabric and wallpaper scraps, construction paper, markers, crayons, and tagboard.

✳ Guide children into designing a room inside a box. The lid becomes the ceiling.

✳ Let them decide which room it will be.

✳ They can wallpaper the sides of the box (walls of the room), cut out windows and doors, make curtains for the windows, and construct simple furniture.

Creative Food Experiences

A SANDWICH TREAT

You will need:

    1/4 cup undiluted frozen orange juice

    1/2 cup peanut butter

    8 slices of bread

1. Wash hands.
2. Mix concentrated orange juice and peanut butter.
3. Spread on bread that is plain or toasted.
4. Cut into small pieces.
5. Enjoy!

BANANA MILK SHAKE

You will need:

    1 cup of ripe banana, sliced

    1/2 teaspoon vanilla

    1 cup liquid nonfat milk

1. Wash hands.
2. Beat banana until creamy.
3. Add vanilla.
4. Mix.
5. Stir in milk.
6. Chill and serve. Makes 1 pint.

SKILL DEVELOPMENT IN THE KITCHEN

These ideas can be done at the center, school, or home. Pass them on to the parents.

✳ Try a tasty way to develop finger-thumb ability by putting a pinch of grated cheese on a cracker.

✳ Motivate a child to place a raisin in the middle of a round cookie or cracker, and you are watching eye-hand coordination.

stir   pour   peel

squeeze   beat   scrub

roll   spread   snap

shake   tear   compare

Here are more ways to help a child begin to master skills through learning experiences in the kitchen:

stir (spoon)	roll (rolling pin)
pour (measuring cup)	spread (plastic knife)
peel (a hard boiled egg)	snap (green beans)
squeeze (orange)	shake (salt)
beat (milk or egg)	tear (lettuce)
scrub (potato)	compare (apples)

Math

MATH SETS OF THREE

✳ Select several books or poems to read to the children that include the number *three,* such as *The Three Little Pigs,* "The Three Kittens," and *Three Billy Goats Gruff.*

✳ Talk about the concept of three, and use flannelboard pieces of the characters in the stories to demonstrate this.

✳ Then place the flannelboard activities in the manipulative center for the children to tell the stories again.

✳ An extension of this is for children to build the house from the *Three Little Pigs* or the bridge from *Three Billy Goats Gruff.*

✳ Ask children to look for sets of three around the room, such as three crayons, three chairs, three windows, three people, and three blocks.

SORT KEYS

✳ Collect keys of all sizes.

✳ Place them in the math center for the children to sort or place in order from smallest to largest or largest to smallest.

✳ Draw large outlines of the keys on paper or tagboard. Then make patterns for the children to use in a matching game.

BUILD WITH GRAHAM CRACKERS

* To introduce this activity, talk or read about how a house is built. See the books listed in this theme for some suggestions.
* Show pictures of houses being built.
* Guide the children to where you have set up graham crackers, peanut butter, and frosting.
* Wash hands.
* Everyone starts with a square graham cracker placed on a piece of wax paper.
* The children spread a thin layer of peanut butter or frosting (for children allergic to peanut butter) along all the edges of the graham cracker.
* Next, place another graham cracker standing up on one edge of the flat cracker. Younger children can "build" onto a one-pint milk or juice carton with graham crackers. This provides a framework for their small hands.
* Continue this process to build a structure that looks like a room of a house.
* Place another flat graham cracker to make a ceiling, forming a cube, or place two crackers "cemented" with peanut butter at the top to form a peaked roof.
* To complete this activity, the children can eat their graham cracker room.

Science

PLEASE TOUCH

* Set up a science table in your room filled with safe objects that stimulate a child to explore, experiment, and discover.

What Floats and What Sinks

* Place a small plastic tub with water on the table.
* Nearby have objects for the children to test which ones sink and which ones float.
* Talk about why some things sink and some float.
* Suggestions for items are objects found around the house: a plastic measuring spoon, a wooden spoon, keys, straws, nails, several pennies, a crumpled foil ball, a rock, a shell, corks, and a sponge.

Magnets

* Put all sizes of magnets on the science table.
* For younger children, nonaluminum baking sheets work well for putting on and taking off the magnets.
* Metal popcorn or cookie tins work well, and they provide storage space inside for the magnets.
* Give each older child a single magnet to experiment with. Let them discover which objects are attracted to the magnet and which are not. Have assorted items available.

Discovery with Plastic Bottles

* Fill one clean plastic bottle half full of water and replace the top.
* In a second clean plastic bottle, place some sand.
* Place each bottle in the water-filled tub.
* Which sinks? Which floats?
* How much water is needed for that bottle to float? How much sand is needed for that bottle to sink or float?

Social Studies

SHELTERS AND HABITATS

This plan of instruction familiarizes children with pictures of homes, shelters, and habitats around the world. It promotes observation, problem-solving, creative thinking, and small-muscle skills. Ann Morris's *Houses and Homes* and *National Geographic* magazine are good resources. The books section of this theme offers additional resources.

✳ Temporary habitats include tents, RVs, igloos, teepees, and caves.

✳ Permanent habitats are homes, apartments, condominiums, mobile homes, adobes, duplexes, townhouses, and farmhouses.

✳ Ask open-ended questions, such as, "How are the houses alike?" "How do they differ?" "Who usually lives in these habitats?" "Are any of these homes the same as where you live?" "Are they different?" "Why can't we live outside all of the time like some animals do?" "Why do people live in homes?"

✳ Next, have large sheets of paper, crayons, markers, craft sticks, fabric and paper scraps, glue, tape, and Styrofoam pieces accessible.

✳ Encourage the children to create the type of temporary habitat they would live in if they lived in a very hot climate, or the type of habitat they would want if the weather were extremely cold.

✳ Give the children plenty of time to finish this project. It could take several days.

✳ Take pictures of their structures to put on the bulletin board.

Children's Books

Ackerman, Karen. (1992). *This Old House.* New York: Macmillan Children's Book Group.

Angelou, Maya. (1994). *My Painted House, My Friendly Chicken.* Photographs by Margaret C. Clarke. New York: Clarkson N. Potter, Inc.

Barton, Byron. (1990). *Building a House.* New York: Greenwillow.

Brown, Margaret Wise. (1989). *Big Red Barn.* New York: Harper & Row.

Bunting, Eva. (1996). *Going Home.* Illustrated by David Diaz. New York: HarperCollins.

Dorros, Arthur. (1992). *This Is MY House.* New York: Scholastic.

Emberly, Rebecca. (1990). *My House, Mi Casa: A Book in Two Languages.* New York: Little Brown and Co.

Gibbons, Gail. (1990). *How a House Is Built.* New York: Scholastic.

Hoberman, Mary Ann. (1978). *A House Is a House for Me.* New York: Viking.

Jackson, Thomas C. (1994). *Hammers, Nails, Planks, and Paint: How a House Is Built.* New York: Scholastic.

Marzollo, Jean and Ashley Wolff. (1998). *Home Sweet Home.* New York: HarperTrophy.

Morris, Ann. (1994). *Houses and Homes.* Photographs by Ken Heyman. New York: A Mulberry Paperback Book.

Pinkney, Gloria Jean. (1992). *Back Home.* Illustrated by Jerry Pinkney. New York: Dial Books for Young Readers.

Pinkwater, D. Manus. (1993). *The Big Orange Splot.* New York: Scholastic.

Reasoner, Charles. (1995). *Whose House Is This?* (Board book). New York: Price Stern Sloan.

Rockwell, Anne. (1991). *In Our House.* New York: HarperCollins Children's Books.

Rowe, Julian, and Molly Perham. (1994). *Build It Strong.* Chicago: Children's Press.

Soya, Kijoshi. (1986). *A House of Leaves.* New York: Philomel.

Stevens, Janet. (1985). *The House that Jack Built.* New York: Holiday House.

Wood, Audrey. (1984). *The Napping House.* Illustrated by Don Wood. San Diego, CA: Harcourt Brace Publishers.

Parent Letter (Preschool)

Dear Parents,

Our theme is My Home. We will provide opportunities for children to learn:

- A home is a place where you live, sleep, eat, work, and play.
- A home can be built from many different materials.
- Homes come in various types, sizes, and shapes.
- Homes can be found in numerous locations.
- Homes are different in different parts of the world.

We will be talking about:

- types of homes
- location of homes
- what's outside
- parts of a house
- rooms in a house
- things to do at home

Things to do at home with your preschool child are:

- Identify sounds around the house, such as a clock ticking, a doorbell ringing, the washing machine, and the dryer.
- Put up a tent in the backyard or the family room, and camp out with your child.
- Using pots, pans, spoons, empty oatmeal containers, and plastic bottles, make a "kitchen band" and play music.
- Help your child make a diagram of the house or your child's room.
- Take a walk around the neighborhood. Talk about the kinds of homes you see. Are there any houses being built in the neighborhood? Talk about how a house is built.

Parent participation opportunities at school will include:

- Read books to the children.
  Date_____ Time_____
- Help when we make our big book bulletin board.
  Date_____ Time_____
- Help when we build graham cracker houses.
  Date_____ Time _____

Our wish list for this theme includes:

all sizes and types of boxes and milk cartons

empty, clean plastic bottles with caps

empty oatmeal containers

all sizes of keys

camping items, such as flashlights and camping dishes

kitchen gadgets, such as wooden spoons, new dishwashing sponges with handles, and large sieves

Thank you for your continued support.

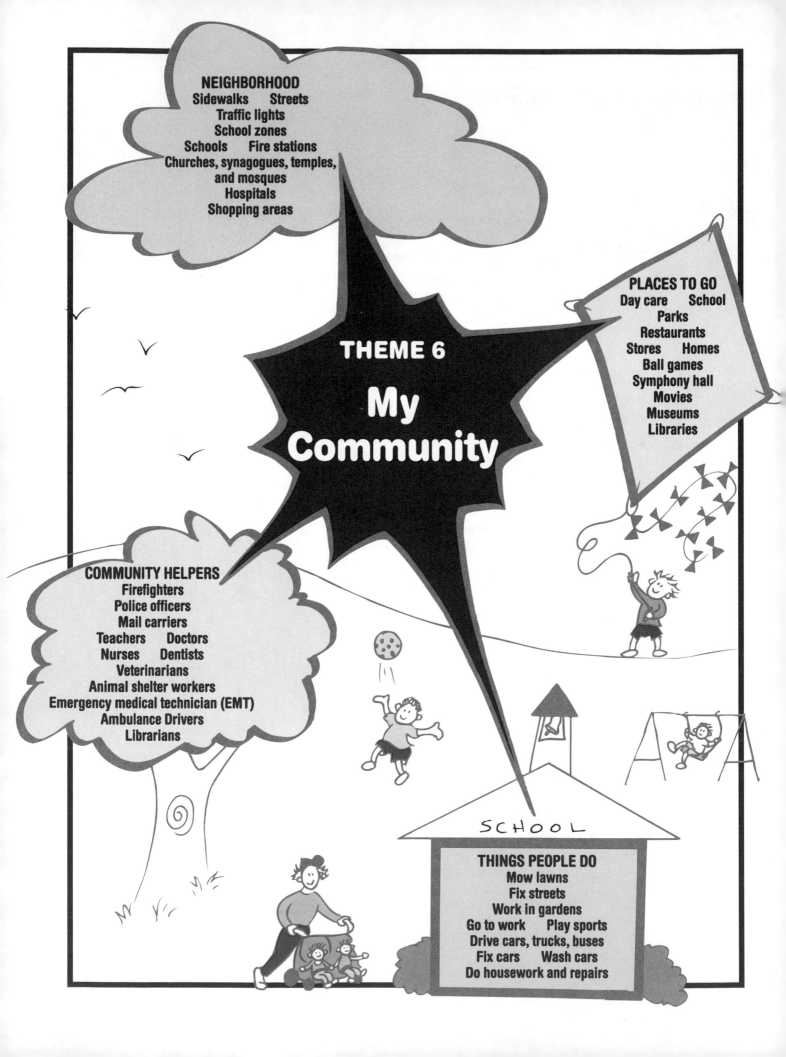

NEIGHBORHOOD
Sidewalks   Streets
Traffic lights
School zones
Schools   Fire stations
Churches, synagogues, temples,
and mosques
Hospitals
Shopping areas

THEME 6

My Community

PLACES TO GO
Day care   School
Parks
Restaurants
Stores   Homes
Ball games
Symphony hall
Movies
Museums
Libraries

COMMUNITY HELPERS
Firefighters
Police officers
Mail carriers
Teachers   Doctors
Nurses   Dentists
Veterinarians
Animal shelter workers
Emergency medical technician (EMT)
Ambulance Drivers
Librarians

SCHOOL

THINGS PEOPLE DO
Mow lawns
Fix streets
Work in gardens
Go to work   Play sports
Drive cars, trucks, buses
Fix cars   Wash cars
Do housework and repairs

THEME GOALS

To provide opportunities for children to learn:

1. We all live in a community that is made up of many people.

2. Members of a community work in many different places, such as stores, offices, homes, schools, indoors, and outdoors.

3. Some people wear special clothes or uniforms when they work and use special tools or machines.

4. Family members need to work in the community to buy what the family needs, such as housing, food, clothing, and transportation.

5. We should respect and get along with community members who may think, dress, and act differently than we do.

Children-Created Bulletin Board

This bulletin board will keep changing during the time that the My Community theme is emphasized. Creating the bulletin board fulfills several purposes: keeping the children interested in their community; offering a space where they can put their drawings, comments, and thank-you notes; and keeping the parents aware of the ongoing community involvement of their children.

✳ Divide the bulletin board into two sections.

✳ One area will be for photographs that you and the children take of people from the community who visit the school and for photos you take of community helpers working at their jobs.

✳ The other section will be for photocopies of the thank-you letters the children send to community helpers and the drawings they create.

✳ Change the bulletin board every time a new community person is introduced to the children.

Vocabulary Starters

Let the children add additional words.

community — a place where a group of many people live, work, and play together.

neighbors — people who live or work close to your house.

job or occupation — what a person does to earn a living for herself and her family.

community helpers — a man or woman who works at a job that helps the people who live in the community.

respect — treating other people with kindness and understanding.

Language Experiences

MAILBOXES

✳ Collect and make mailboxes out of shoe boxes or milk cartons.

✳ Have each child make one for himself. Include a box for the teachers.

✳ Have each child write his name on a box or place on it a photograph for those children who are not yet recognizing their names.

✳ Provide envelopes and "stamps" (stickers, Easter Seal stamps, magazine coupon stamps, for example) in the writing center.

✳ The children can write letters or draw pictures and "send" them to their classmates by placing them in the appropriate classroom mailboxes.

WRITE THANK-YOU LETTERS

✳ Have the children write thank-you letters or notes to community members who visit the class and to those visited during field trips.

✳ Younger children can draw pictures to accompany the thank-you note you write.

✳ Suggestions for people to visit or invite include: firefighter, nurse, doctor, veterinarian, animal caretaker from the zoo, storyteller from the library, museum staff member, doll collector, dance teacher, member of the orchestra, square dance group, and a bell choir.

LETTERS OR GREETING CARDS TO THE FAMILY:

✳ It is fun for the children to write letters or make greeting cards to send to family members.

✳ Mail them or take a field trip to the post office to mail them.

✳ Have the children keep track of how long (how many days) it takes mail to get to their houses. Was the family member surprised?

Dramatic Play

PROP BOXES

✳ In a sturdy box, collect authentic items that represent a certain job or occupation.

✳ Label each box clearly for identification.

painter — several sizes of brushes, roller, bucket, sandpaper, masking tape, paint-stirring sticks, cap, gloves, old clothes, and a smock or apron. Let younger children paint on boxes with water. Older children can paint with tempera.

baker/chef — hat, apron, spoons, rolling pin, dough, flour, and sifter. See sensory art activities in this theme for a play dough recipe.

firefighter — hats, several pieces of garden hose, raincoats, boots, and gloves.

gardener or florist — plastic flowers, pots with dirt, watering can, garden gloves, and hand shovel.

post office worker or letter carrier — play money (children can make their own with crayons, markers, and scrap construction paper), rubber stamps and stamp pad, postmarked stamps or stickers, envelopes, mail bag (large purse), hat, scrap paper, markers, pencils, and tape.

TELEPHONE DIRECTORY

✳ In the dramatic play/home living area, set up a special place with a small table, a nonworking telephone, a phone message pad and pencil, and a telephone book.

✳ Make a class telephone directory by having each child write her name, address, and telephone number on a blank piece of paper in a small loose-leaf notebook.

✳ Add telephone numbers for community services, such as the library, grocery store, and zoo.

✳ Place this directory by the telephone.

✳ Suggest to the children that they begin writing down telephone messages and numbers when they "answer the phone" in the dramatic play area.

✳ An extension of this activity could be to set up a "telephone space" made from a refrigerator box.

✳ Place another copy of the class telephone directory in the booth along with an actual telephone book or yellow pages.

MY TOWN — MY NEIGHBORHOOD

This activity encourages creativity, observation, problem-solving, cooperation, and spatial awareness skills.

✳ Take a walk around the neighborhood surrounding your center or school.

✳ Point out buildings, businesses, houses, street names, and roads. In some communities it may be necessary to walk a wider area to find any buildings or businesses.

✳ For this activity you will need to close some of the centers in the room and expand the dramatic play area.

✳ Using boxes of varying sizes, construct a community.

✳ Talk about which buildings are needed, such as houses, apartments, stores, fire and police stations, hospitals, banks, churches, shopping malls, airports, movie theaters, and schools.

✳ On a large piece of cardboard place the buildings as they are located in your community.

✳ With the children, name and label the buildings and the streets.

✳ If you have enough room on your playground, use larger boxes, and make a town that includes cars, buses, and trucks.

✳ See math activities in this theme for a further extension of this project.

Puppet Play

COMMUNITY HELPER PUPPETS

✳ Cut cardboard circles eight to ten inches in diameter or use large paper plates.

✳ For infants and young toddlers, draw large simple facial features on the cardboard circle.

✳ Attach a stick, such as a paint stirring stick or tongue depressor, to make a puppet.

✳ Play peekaboo by placing the face in front of an adult's or baby's face.

✳ Let older children make a set of stick puppet faces by themselves.

✳ They can add construction paper hats that represent community helpers, such as firefighters, police officers, letter carriers, and construction workers.

Music

THE ORCHESTRA

Introduce the children to the concept of a community orchestra. Start with Rubin and Daniel's book, *The Orchestra,* listed in the books section of this theme.

✳ Play several classical music selections, such as Britten's *A Young Person's Guide to the Orchestra,* Prokofiev's *Peter and the Wolf,* and Saint-Saëns's *Carnival of the Animals.* Choose short excerpts of these to play at any one time.

✳ Visit your local library for these selections and to find children's books to accompany the music.

✳ To further develop this activity, add puppets, flannelboard characters, or musical instruments as the children become familiar with the music.

MAKE MUSICAL INSTRUMENTS

✳ Collect bathroom tissue rolls, paper towel tubes, waxed paper, rubber bands, new combs, aluminum pie plates, paper plates and cups, and cereal and oatmeal boxes.

✳ Guide the children into making and decorating:

drums — from oatmeal boxes.

plate shakers — with clothespins or birdseed placed between two aluminum pie plates or paper plates tied together with yarn.

cup shakers — with dried beans inside two paper cups taped together with masking tape.

flutes — from paper towel tubes. Punch a line of several holes to about two inches from the end. Cover the end with a square of wax paper held in place with a rubber band.

rhythm sticks — from dowel sticks cut to specification at the hardware store.

humming combs — with wax paper loosely wrapped around a comb, place to the lips and hum.

Movement

LET'S DANCE

Infants enjoy all kinds of music. Toddlers enjoy dancing to lively music, especially when you tie bells to their shoestrings. Tie some on your shoes, too.

✳ Place the infant on his back, hold his ankles, and move the child's feet to the rhythm of the music you are singing or playing.

✳ Take the baby's hands and move his arms up and down or clap his hands together as the music plays.

ACT OUT A STORY WITH DANCE

✳ Read a story or poem to the children, such as Stecher's *Max, the Music Maker,* listed in the books section of this theme.

✳ Let the children be the orchestra. They can play rhythm instruments or the ones they made as you read the book.

✳ Have the children dance or act out the story by walking quickly and slowly, running in place, tapping along, or moving with scarves or crepe paper streamers.

✳ Try having half the class be the orchestra while the other half dances.

MORE DANCING

✳ Take a field trip to a dance studio or have a dancer visit your class.

✳ The children enjoy watching a dancer in ballet or tap shoes.

✳ Have the dance teacher or dancer show the children and you how to do some simple steps.

✳ Give the children opportunities to repeat these steps over and over again. Try it with different kinds of music.

Sensory Art

MAKE PLAY DOUGH

You will need:

    1 cup flour

    1/2 cup salt

    1 cup water

    1 tablespoon cooking oil

    2 teaspoons cream of tartar

    vanilla, peppermint, or almond extract

1. Wash hands.

2. Mix all ingredients.

3. Stir over low heat until the mixture forms a ball.

4. Remove from heat, and wrap in wax paper to cool.

5. Store in an air-tight container.

6. The play dough will last much longer if kept in the refrigerator.

7. You and the children can add food coloring before cooking or wait until after cooking, so the children can see the change from white, to marbled, to the final color.

8. Fragrant extracts, such as vanilla, peppermint, or almond, may be added to the play dough.

Theme 10 has the recipe for *uncooked* play dough.

COMMUNITY TELEPHONES

✳ To make a set of telephones, you will need two empty tin cans, a long piece of string, two toothpicks or nails, and a hammer.

✳ Punch a hole in the bottom of each can with a hammer and nail.

✳ Thread ends of string through the holes.

✳ Tie the string around the toothpicks to keep them from coming out of the cans.

✳ Two children hold the tin can "telephones" and pull the string tight.

✳ The children then take turns talking and listening.

✳ For variation, add more phones and create a "community party line."

WOODWORKING

This activity encourages positive self-esteem, self-motivation, problem-solving, large and small muscle development, hand-eye coordination, and creativity.

✳ Visit a community hardware store with the children before setting up the woodworking area. This gives the children a firsthand experience seeing many different types of nails, screws, washers, bolts, hammers, screwdrivers, and wood.

✳ Introduce the children to the woodworking center with its materials, tools, and pictures of houses and buildings under construction at various construction sites.

✳ Children should be closely supervised, with only two at a time using the tools.

✳ Collect real tools and materials, such as small claw hammers (eight to twelve ounces), assorted nails, safety goggles (children's swimming masks work well), clamps, a hand drill, wood glue, sandpaper, rulers, pencils, and paper.

✳ For older children add a cross-cut saw (approximately eighteen inches long), screws, and screwdrivers.

✳ Obtain inexpensive grades of wood from carpenter shops, lumber yards, and do-it-yourself discount stores, or ask parents to contribute.

✳ In the beginning, children enjoy sanding and gluing the pieces of wood. Add hammering, sawing, and nailing later.

Creative Food Experiences

EAT RICE WITH CHOPSTICKS

✳ Begin this project by reading Dooley's *Everybody Cooks Rice,* listed in the books section of this theme.

✳ Introduce the children to how food connects one neighbor to others in the neighborhood. Recipes using rice are included at the end of this book.

1. Bring broth to a boil.
2. Add chicken and rice.
3. Reheat and eat.

This recipe serves 8.

Math

PARTNER TOWER BUILDING

Tower building promotes math skill development, such as problem-solving, exploration of spatial relationships, and experimentation with weight and balance. Socialization and cooperation are also emphasized.

✳ In the block center have one child build a tower or shape, and another child duplicate it.

✳ Let the children continue this activity until they tire of it.

✳ To vary the activity, have a small group of children build a tower.

✳ The first child puts a block in place. Each child in the group takes a turn stacking a block on the top of what has been built. Continue taking turns until the tower falls over.

✳ The children can discuss why they think the tower fell over.

✳ They may want to experiment with stacking blocks another way.

✳ To further develop the understanding of other cultures, introduce the use of chopsticks to eat rice.

✳ Chopsticks are useful tools that are part of Chinese, Japanese, Korean, and Vietnamese cultures.

✳ Cook rice according to the instructions on the package.

✳ Give each child a new pair of chopsticks that she can take home after using. Many Asian restaurants give sets of new chopsticks to teachers for the asking.

✳ Demonstrate to the children how to hold the chopsticks by the thicker end.

✳ Put one chopstick at the base of the thumb, and hold the other between the thumb, index, and middle fingers. Move only the finger-held chopstick to pick up rice or small pieces of food.

✳ Many young children find the task easier by holding the chopsticks closer to the end where they are picking up food.

✳ Explain to the children that it is rude to point with chopsticks. Avoid licking the chopsticks or spearing food with them.

MIXED-UP PEOPLE

Older children like to draw pictures of people, such as firefighters, bakers, nurses, cowboys, ballet dancers, and farmers.

CHICKEN SOUP WITH RICE

Here is another way to connect language, literacy, and cooking. Read Sendak's *Chicken Soup with Rice*, listed in the books section of this theme.

You will need:

6 cups chicken broth

1 cup chicken, cooked and diced

3/4 cup cooked rice

* Supply plenty of paper, crayons, markers, and scissors for children to use to make pictures of people.
* Suggest that they cut pictures they have made in three pieces, dividing the picture into body, head, and legs.
* Put the body of one, the head of another, and the legs of another together to make a mixed-up person.
* Leave this activity available throughout the theme. Children come back to draw mixed-up people often.

SHAPE CITY

* Provide the children with colorful construction paper, scissors, and glue.
* Demonstrate how to cut out all sizes of different shapes. Precut the shapes for younger children.
* The children glue the shapes on a piece of paper to make designs of homes, buildings, vehicles, and people. Younger children enjoy just gluing the shapes everywhere on the page, with no specific design in mind.
* An extension of this activity is for the children to create a shape city on a long piece of butcher paper.

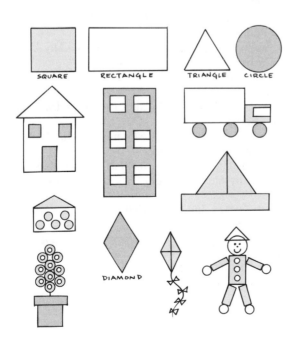

Science

FIRE PREVENTION

* After visiting a fire station or having a firefighter visit the school, reinforce the experience.
* Try STOP (don't run — freeze), DROP (fall to the ground), and ROLL (over and over until the fire is out) to put out fire on clothing.
* Practice what to do to escape from a smoky room. Crawl to the nearest exit. Stay low, since smoke and hot air rise.
* Another vital rule is: If the DOOR is HOT, don't open it! Ask the children what it means if the door is hot.
* Start a list of fire-safety rules on a large sheet of paper or posterboard.
* Ask children to contribute rules you have discussed or ones they learned at home.
* Continue to add to the list. Post it at the children's eye level.

PULLEYS

* Ask open-ended questions relating to children's experiences with tall buildings and apartment houses.
* How do the people get from one floor to another?
* Introduce the concept of pulleys and elevators.
* Next, let the children see you set up two chairs to support the ends of a wooden dowel or broomstick.
* Tie heavy string to the handle of a small basket filled with toy animals and people figures from the block center.
* Loop the string over the dowel.

✳ Ask a child to pull the string down on one side of the dowel. This illustrates how a pulley lifts the basket with toys on the other side.

✳ Let the children experiment with the pulley.

✳ Provide materials, and encourage them to make other pulleys.

✳ Guide them into adding pulleys into the block area with their buildings.

Social Studies

COMMUNITY BUILDINGS

✳ Show pictures of all kinds of buildings in communities around the world.

✳ Obtain the pictures from travel agents, airlines, travel brochures, and magazines such as *National Geographic.* You may want to take some photos as well.

✳ With the children, compare the similarities and differences of the buildings.

✳ Ask open-ended questions, such as, "Who do you think works in this building?" "What is her job?" "Why do you think the building is so tall?" "Why is this building so small?" "What country do you think this building is in?" "What city?"

✳ This discussion can be combined with the Shape City activity in the math section of this theme.

COMMUNITY MAP

✳ With older children, use a map of your community to show them where their school is. Mark the spot on the map.

✳ Find some of the streets, roads, houses, and buildings in the neighborhood, and mark these.

✳ Let the children make a large floor map of the neighborhood and city.

✳ Provide a large piece of butcher paper, masking tape, construction paper, crayons, and markers. Egg cartons make interesting structures, and paper towel tubes make great tunnels.

Children's Books

Bauer, Judith. (1990). *What's It Like to Be a Doctor?* Mahway, NJ: Troll Associates.

Bauer, Judith. (1990). *What's It Like to Be a Nurse?* Mahway, NJ: Troll Associates.

Borden, L. (1990). *The Neighborhood Trucker.* New York: Scholastic.

Butterworth, Nick. (1992). *Busy People.* Cambridge, MA: Candlewick Press.

Darling, David. (1992). *Spiderwebs to Skyscrapers.* New York: Dillon Press.

Dooley, Norah. (1991). *Everybody Cooks Rice.* Illustrated by Peter J. Thornton. Minneapolis, MN: Carolrhoda Books.

Flanagan, Alice K., and Christine Osinski. (1998). *Mrs. Murphy Fights Fires.* San Francisco, CA: Children's Press.

Friend, David. (1992). *Baseball, Football, Daddy, and Me.* New York: Puffin Books.

Henderson, Kathy. (1991). *I Can Be a Basketball Player.* Chicago, IL: Children's Press.

Kuklin, Susan. (1989). *Going to My Ballet Class.* New York: Macmillan.

Merriam, Eve. (1989). *Mommies at Work.* New York: Simon & Schuster.

Muntean, Michaela. (1993). *Sesame Street's I Want to Be President.* Illustrated by Tom Brannon. New York: Western Publishing Company and Children's Television Workshop.

Patrick, Denise L. (1993). *The Car Washing Street.* Illustrated by John Ward. New York: Scholastic.

Powers, M. E. (1992). *Our Teacher's in a Wheelchair.* Chicago, IL: Whitman.

Pringle, Laurence. (1989). *Jesse Builds a Road.* New York: Macmillan.

Rogers, Fred. (1989). *Going to the Dentist.* New York: Putnam Publishing Group.

Rubin, Mark. (1995). *The Orchestra.* Illustrated by Alan, Daniel. Buffalo, New York: Firefly Books.

Sendak, Maurice. (1962). *Chicken Soup with Rice.* New York: Scholastic.

Seymour, Peter. (1990). *Firefighters.* New York: Dutton Children's Books.

Skurzynski, Gloria. (1992). *Here Comes the Mail.* New York: Macmillan Children's Books.

Stecher, Miriam. (1990). *Max, the Music Maker.* Photographs by Alex Meyboom. New York: Lothrop, Lee & Shepard Books.

Tasky, Sue. (1997). *The Busy Building Book.* New York: G. P. Putnam's Sons.

Van Laan, Nancy. (1992). *People, People, Everywhere.* New York: Knopf.

Ziefert, Harriet. (1991). *City Shapes.* Illustrated by Susan Baum. New York: HarperCollins.

Parent Letter (School-age)

Dear Parents,

We are beginning our new theme, My Community. The children will have opportunities to learn:

- We live in a community made up of many people.
- Members of a community work in many different places.
- Some people wear special clothes or uniforms when they work and use special tools or machines.
- Family members work in the community to buy what the family needs, such as housing, food, clothing, and transportation.
- We should respect and get along with community members who may think, dress, and act differently than we do.

We will be talking about:

- our neighborhood, and who lives and works there
- community helpers
- things that people do
- places to go in the community

Things to do in the community with your child:

- Take a walk around your neighborhood. Let your child point out things that relate to what he is doing in school.
- Look at ongoing construction sites of homes and buildings.
- Ask about what she is building at school.
- Discuss how specific community helpers have helped your family.
- Eat a dinner using chopsticks, if you have not done so. Let your child show you how.
- Visit a museum, see a play, cheer at a ball game, and enjoy the symphony orchestra in your community.

Come join us for parent participation opportunities at school:

- Visit the class and share your occupation with the children.
  Date _____ Time _____
- Join us on our neighborhood walk.
  Date _____ Time _____
- Help us in the woodworking center.
  Date _____ Time _____

On our wish list for this theme are:

nonpostal stamps	milk cartons
envelopes	aluminum pie plates
all sizes of boxes	magazines and catalogs
paper cups and plates	empty oatmeal boxes
tubes from paper towels	

Thank you for your interest and participation in your child's class.

SECTION II

The Senses

Young children learn through their five senses. Beginning in infancy, children first learn about their world through seeing, hearing, tasting, smelling, and touching. Because of this, it is important to include curriculum that offers many sensory experiences.

The thematic activities in this section suggest how to interconnect the senses with each other and with the total curriculum. They are designed to meet the individual differences, abilities, and interests of the children in your class. Encourage the children to make choices. Be supportive of the activity choices they make.

The following themes are included in Section II — The Senses:

WHAT WE SEE
Our world and what's in it
Colors
Shapes
Patterns
Designs
Sizes

EYES
Two eyes move
Different shapes
Different colors of iris
Pupils
Cornea   Retina
Eyelids open and close
Blink   Wink
Eyelashes
Eyebrows

THEME 7
Seeing

HOW WE TAKE CARE OF OUR EYES
Glasses and contact lenses
Sunglasses
Safety goggles
Eye checkups

SCHOOL

WHAT SEEING HELPS US DO
Read   Write
Locate objects
Warns us of danger
Identify things in our world
Enjoy people, nature, and art

THEME GOALS

To provide opportunities for children to learn:

1. The importance of the five senses, with this theme's emphasis on the sense of sight.
2. The eyes are the part of the body used to see and help us learn.
3. We should take good care of our eyes.
4. Some people cannot see at all or cannot see objects clearly.
5. Humans cannot see in the dark; we need light to see.

Children-Created Bulletin Board

This bulletin board provides opportunities for interactive discovery. It will change during the time the five senses are being studied. Encourage the children to think of things to put on the bulletin board and to discover what you have added.

* Cover the bulletin board with burlap to give the area a new texture as you begin the interconnecting theme of the senses.
* In one corner of the bulletin board place an unbreakable mirror. This allows the children to look closely at the parts of their faces at times throughout the day.
* For the theme Seeing, arrange big cutouts of two eyes at the top of the bulletin board.
* Under the eyes, put the words, "Look What I See!"
* The children place pictures they have drawn or cut out on the board. They can write or dictate sentences about what they see and put these up.
* It is also fun for the children to make faces with eyes the color of their own eyes and add these to the collection.
* More objects can be placed on the bulletin board as the children become involved with activities relating to this theme.

mirror

Vocabulary Starters

Let the children add additional words.

eye — the part of the body with which we see.

iris — the colored part of the eye.

pupil — the black spot in the middle of the iris.

eyelashes — the hairs on the eyelids that help protect the eyes from dust particles.

eyebrows — the hair that grows in an arch pattern above the eyes.

eyelids — the skin that opens and closes over the eyes.

vision — being able to see things.

Language Experiences

WHERE ARE YOU?

The very young infant will watch the movements of an adult.

✳ Move to different parts of the room and call the baby's name.

✳ When the infant turns his head to look for you, give the baby hugs and verbal praise.

✳ Change positions of the baby, from the back, to the stomach, or sitting up. This gives the child an opportunity to use different kinds of movement when looking for the adult.

POEM:
"Looking at the World"

When I wake up
What do I do?
I open my eyes
Just like you.
  When I get up
  What do I see?
  I see my bedroom.
  It's all around me.
I go to the window
And look outside.
I see the world
So big and wide.
  It's filled with wonderful
  Things to see.
  Like the sun and flowers,
  Like grass and trees.

Like cars on the street,
Like clouds in the sky.
I love to watch
The world with my eyes.

Philip Jackman

CHILDREN'S POETRY

Most children enjoy making up poems. Using the fives senses is a way to get them started.

✳ When it is raining, go outside and sit under a safe, covered area.

✳ Have the children *look* at the rain and describe it in one or more words. Write the dictation exactly as each child says it.

✳ Next, have them close their eyes and *listen* to the rain. Describe this.

✳ Have children stick out their tongues, *taste* the rain, and describe it.

✳ Then, they *feel* the rain on their hands and describe what that feels like.

✳ What does the rain *smell* like? Have them describe the odor.

✳ For older children, thunder and lightning add to the poetry writing experience.

✳ Follow up by placing the poems on the bulletin board.

SEEING THE WORLD DIFFERENTLY

✳ When the children are outside, encourage them to look all around them and talk about what they see.

✳ What do they see to their right? To the left? In front? In back?

✳ What do they see when they hang their heads between their legs? Does the world look different upside down?

✳ How does everything look when they crawl through the outdoor play tunnel?

✳ Follow this up by having the children look at the classroom from different points of view.

Dramatic Play

MIRRORS, MIRRORS EVERYWHERE!

* Place mirrors of many shapes and sizes throughout the room. These should be well-secured wall mirrors, unbreakable, and with rounded edges.
* Put them in unexpected places, such as the manipulative center and the music center.
* Place them at eye, floor, and knee level.
* These mirrors are props that can extend impromptu dramatic play. Observe what the children do when they look in the mirror.
* This activity opens up the entire room and offers the children additional ways to see themselves.
* As an alternative to mirrors, place foil or other reflecting objects around the room.

LET'S PAINT

* Set up a dramatic play area outdoors for the children to role-play being a house painter.
* Supply clean quart and gallon paint cans full of water, brushes of various sizes, painter's hats, smocks, and dropcloths.
* The children can paint the building, the playground equipment, and other objects.

LET'S LOOK

Turn the dramatic play center into an optometrist's office or eyewear store.

* Collect an assortment of old plastic eyeglass frames (regular eyeglasses with lenses removed), and place them into several little baskets.
* Near the baskets, place an unbreakable stand-up or wall mirror.
* Encourage the children to try on the different glasses to see how they look.
* Add eye charts, pictures of people wearing glasses, posters, a cash register, and play money.

Puppet Play

THE "SEEING" PEOPLE PUPPET

To make this puppet you will need a paper plate about nine inches wide, a tongue depressor or large craft stick, and colored cellophane.

* Cut two eye-holes slightly above the middle of the plate. They must be large but can be round, oval, or other shapes.
* The rounded side of the plate may be colored by the child with crayons to look like the child or the child's favorite animal.
* Then, on the other side of the plate, glue or tape a piece of cellophane a little larger than both eye-holes.
* Finally, tape the stick to the back side, allowing enough stick showing below the plate to use as a handle for the child to hold.
* Have each child look at classmates, the room, pictures, books, or other colored surfaces.
* Ask them to notice how, for example, the yellow cellophane "eyes" make blue things look black, or yellow things look white. A complementary or opposite color always looks black, while the same color disappears.
* Have the children go outside and see how different trees and buildings look through their colored "eyes."

STEP 1   STEP 2   STEP 3

Music

MONKEY SEE, MONKEY DO

This is a traditional song with a beat. Use a simple clapping–patting–stamping pattern to emphasize the beat.

✳ Infants enjoy having you hold their hands and clap them together.

✳ For older children, let them take turns being the leader that others follow. The children enjoy acting like monkeys.

Monkey see, monkey do,
Clap, clap, clap your hands.
Monkey does the same as you,
Clap, clap, clap your hands.
Monkey see, monkey do,
Pat, pat, pat your knees.
Monkey does the same as you,
Pat, pat, pat your knees.
Monkey see, monkey do,
Stamp, stamp, stamp your feet.
Monkey does the same as you,
Stamp, stamp, stamp your feet.

✳ You and the children can add other actions, such as "shake, shake, shake your head," "wiggle, wiggle, wiggle your body," or "sniff, sniff, sniff your nose."

Movement

INFANT CRAWL

Babies want to reach and touch everything in sight. When they begin to crawl, give them something to crawl to.

✳ Cover paper towel rolls with brightly colored paper.

✳ Then, place clear contact paper over the roll to strengthen it and make the tube easy to wipe off.

✳ These can be pushed and rolled.

✳ You can make a pull toy from the rolls as well. Just tie several together on a string.

✳ Other ways to encourage infants to crawl are: knock the ends out of large cardboard boxes for a crawl tunnel, or pile large cushions on the floor for them to crawl under, over, and around.

LETTER HOP

This activity promotes the practice of motor skills, sight recognition of the letters, and listening skills.

✳ To highlight the letters emphasized during this theme, make big letters and place them on the floor with masking tape.

✳ Have the children outline the letters by walking forward, backward, and sideways, or hopping, skipping, tiptoeing, and marching.

✳ Play music that tells them how fast or slow to move around the letters.

Sensory Art

IT'S FAR AWAY; NO, IT'S NEAR

✳ Show the children a flower in a vase.

✳ Ask them to look at it closely.

✳ Then, move the flower and vase across the room.

✳ Ask the children, "Has the flower changed?" "Does the vase look different or the same?"

✳ Talk about how something looks when it is near you and how its look changes when it is far away.

✳ Next, place sheets of paper, pencils, and crayons in the art center.

✳ Also include pictures of birds, airplanes, trees, flowers, and people. These should show how an object, such as an airplane, looks when it is far away and when it is near.

✳ Ask the children to draw two pictures; i.e., one showing an object far away, and another showing the same object up close.

✳ Talk about the pictures.

LETTERS AND NUMBERS

✳ With the children's assistance, make upper and lower case letters and numbers out of different grades of sandpaper, sponges, pipe cleaners, burlap, and velvet.

✳ The children can sort the letters by shape and size, spell their names, differentiate between letters and numbers, and integrate the senses of sight and touch.

ART CAN CATCH THE SUN

✳ Give each child a square sheet of wax paper.

✳ Let them cover it with glue. For gluing, use small squeeze bottles with long tips to strengthen small muscles.

* Completely cover the glue with colorful tissue paper.
* Next, the children cover the paper with another layer of glue.
* Place another sheet of wax paper on top.
* Let dry for several days.
* Then, peel the wax paper off.
* Have the children gently punch one or two holes in the glue/tissue art.
* Put a string in the top.
* Hang the suncatchers where they receive the full sun. Discover the patterns they make and see what the sun does to the colored tissue.
* Encourage the children to experiment with other ways to make suncatchers. These should not all be the same. Promote creativity.

Creative Food Experiences

FORGOTTEN COOKIES

Doing this type of cooking activity with the children will help them understand, in a positive way, that they cannot always have instant gratification. This is a recipe the children want to do again. It is a good one to share with the parents, too.

You will need:

2 eggs (only the whites are needed)

2/3 cup of sugar

1 teaspoon of vanilla

6-ounce package of chocolate bits

1. Wash hands.
2. Preheat oven to 350 degrees.
3. Beat two egg whites until stiff peaks are formed. Add the sugar while beating.
4. When the egg whites are stiff, add the chocolate bits and vanilla.
5. Drop by spoonfuls onto a greased cookie sheet.
6. Put into the oven. TURN THE OVEN **OFF**.
7. Forget the cookies for at least 2 hours.
8. Then, remember what's in the oven and enjoy!
9. Talk about how the egg whites look before and after beating.
10. Discuss how the cookies look before and after baking them.

BREAD PUDDING FOR ALL

This is a great activity to do when you have a large block of time available. The recipe will take about an hour for you and the children to prepare. It makes enough for 20 servings.

You will need:

12 slices of white bread

8 eggs

2 cups of sugar

4 tablespoons margarine

6 cups of milk

2 teaspoons of vanilla

2 teaspoons of cinnamon

1/2 cup of raisins

BREAD PUDDING FOR ALL

Wash hands. Preheat oven to 400 degrees.

Break 12 slices of white bread into small pieces and place in 2 long baking dishes. Beat 8 eggs and 2 cups sugar together in a bowl. Add 2 teaspoons of vanilla and 6 cups milk to the egg mixture and pour over the bread. Put small pieces of margarine on top.

Add 1/2 cup raisins and sprinkle cinnamon over the top.

Bake in oven for 30 minutes. Cool and eat. YUM!

1. Wash hands.
2. Preheat oven to 400 degrees.
3. Break bread into small pieces and place in two long baking dishes.
4. Beat the eggs and sugar together in a bowl.
5. Add vanilla and milk to the egg mixture and pour over the bread.
6. Put small pieces of margarine on top.

7. Add raisins, and sprinkle cinnamon over the top.

8. Bake in oven for 30 minutes.

9. Cool and eat. Yum!

Math

MATCH THE FRUITS AND VEGETABLES

✳ Make a folder matching game of fruits and vegetables.

✳ Use duplicate pictures from magazines, stickers, or draw and color them yourself.

✳ For younger children, use fewer fruit and vegetable pictures.

✳ Open up a file folder. On one side paste pictures of fruits. On the other side paste pictures of vegetables. Double-sided sticky tape can be used to secure the pictures in place.

✳ Print in lower case the name of each fruit and vegetable.

✳ Make a set of matching cards with duplicate fruits and vegetables.

✳ Laminate the folder and each card.

✳ Label the front of the folder with two of the pictures and the words "Fruits and Vegetables."

✳ Glue an envelope or locking plastic bag on the back of the folder. Place the card pieces in this.

✳ Place the folder game in the math center for the children.

SORTING IDEAS

✳ Collect sample cards of paint colors from hardware and paint stores.

✳ Put the samples in an open box, basket, or plastic container in the math center.

✳ Have the children sort the paint cards by color.

✳ In another container, place fabric and wallpaper squares. Make these available for the children to sort by patterns.

✳ This stimulates the children to look around their homes. What colors do they see in their environment? Which surfaces are painted, and which are wallpapered? What patterns are on the fabric of their furniture? Parents can be included in this activity.

Science

WATCH MY EYES

✳ Give each child a partner.

✳ Have each pair sit where they can look at each other's eyes.

✳ Look at the iris, the colored part of the eye.

✳ Look at the pupil, the black spot in the middle of the iris.

✳ Turn the lights off in the classroom for a few minutes.

✳ Then, turn the lights back on. Ask the children to observe their partners' pupils again. Do they look the same? Are they different?

✳ Explain that the pupils get larger (open up) in the dark to let more light enter the eye. This helps the eyes to see.

✳ In bright light, such as sunshine, the pupils get smaller (contract) to let less light enter the eyes.

✳ The children may want to do this again. Repetition is important to reinforce learning.

LOOK FOR THE DOTS

✳ Put several magnifying glasses out on the science table with a group of black-and-white pictures cut from the newspaper.

✳ The children can do this activity in groups of two or three.

✳ Ask the children to look through a magnifying glass at the newspaper picture. "What do you see?"

✳ They will see that each picture is made up of lots of black dots. The dots are largest in the dark areas.

✳ The children will want to share their discovery with their parents.

Social Studies

SPECIAL COLLECTIONS

✳ Invite a family or community member to visit the class and share their special collection with the children. Perhaps someone has collected items from all over the world, such as dolls, stamps, or shells.

✳ Each item collected usually has an interesting story connected to it.

✳ The children can ask questions to find out more about how and when the individual started collecting.

✳ Locate all the countries, states, and cities on maps or globe of the world. This will help the children "see" where the objects came from.

✳ A natural follow-up is for the children to bring their collection of toys, stamps, sport cards, or stuffed animals to share with their classmates.

✳ What about your special collection? You can share, too.

Children's Books

Aliki. (1989). *My Five Senses*. New York: HarperTrophy.

Carle, Eric. (1973). *I See a Song*. New York: Scholastic.

Cousins, Lucy. (1997). *What Can Pinky See?: A-Lift-the-Flap-Book*. Cambridge, MA: Candlewick Press.

De Paola, Tomie. (1996). *The Bubble Factory*. New York: Grosset & Dunlap.

Dr. Seuss. (1997). *And to Think that I Saw It on Mulberry Street*. New York: Random House.

Dr. Seuss. (1968). *The Eye Book*. New York: Random House.

Hoban, Tana. (1997). *Look Book*. New York: Greenwillow.

Hoban, Tana. (1988). *Look! Look! Look!* New York: Greenwillow.

Johnson, Neil. (1997). *A Field of Sunflowers*. New York: Cartwheel Books.

Martin, Bill, Jr. (1983). *Brown Bear, Brown Bear, What Do You See?* Illustrated by Eric Carle. New York: Henry Holt.

Noll, Sally. (1990). *Watch Where You Go*. New York: Greenwillow.

Oppenheim, Joanne. (1986). *Have You Seen the Birds?* Illustrated by Barbara Reid. New York: Scholastic.

Oxenbury, Helen. (1995). *I See*. (Board book). Cambridge, MA: Candlewick Press.

Shaw, Charles G. (1947). *It Looked Like Spilt Milk*. New York: HarperTrophy.

Showers, Paul. (1992). *Look at Your Eyes*. New York: HarperCollins.

Snape, Juliet and Charles Snape. (1987). *The Boy with Square Eyes, a Tale of Televisionitis*. New York: Simon and Schuster.

Ward, Leila. (1992). *I Am Eyes — Ni Mac Ho*. New York: Scholastic.

Winch, John. (1997). *The Old Woman Who Loved to Read*. New York: Holiday House.

Worthy, Judith. (1988). *Eyes*. New York: Doubleday.

Parent Letter (Toddler)

Dear Parents,

We are beginning to talk about the Five Senses. Our first theme is Seeing. The children will learn:

- About the five senses, starting with the sense of sight.
- The eyes are the part of the body used to see.
- We should take good care of our eyes.
- Some people cannot see at all.
- We cannot see in the dark; we need light to see.

We will be talking about:

- our eyes
- the color of our eyes
- what seeing helps us do
- how we can take care of our eyes
- what we see in our world

Here are some things to do at home with your toddler:

- Spend time with your child talking about what each of you see, both indoors and outdoors.
- Look in the mirror with your child, and point out the color of the eye, the eyelashes, eyebrows, and the eyelid that winks and blinks.
- Sort laundry with your child. Look for colors, patterns, and sizes.
- Read books with your child.

Parent participation opportunities at school will include:

- Come visit us and share our classroom experiences.
  Date _____   Time _____
- Share your special collection of stamps, dolls, shells, or other objects with the children.
  Date _____   Time _____

Wish list for this theme:

colored cellophane sheets

colored tissue paper sheets

wallpaper or fabric pieces

paper towel rolls

paper plates

paper cups

Thank you for sharing your child with us.

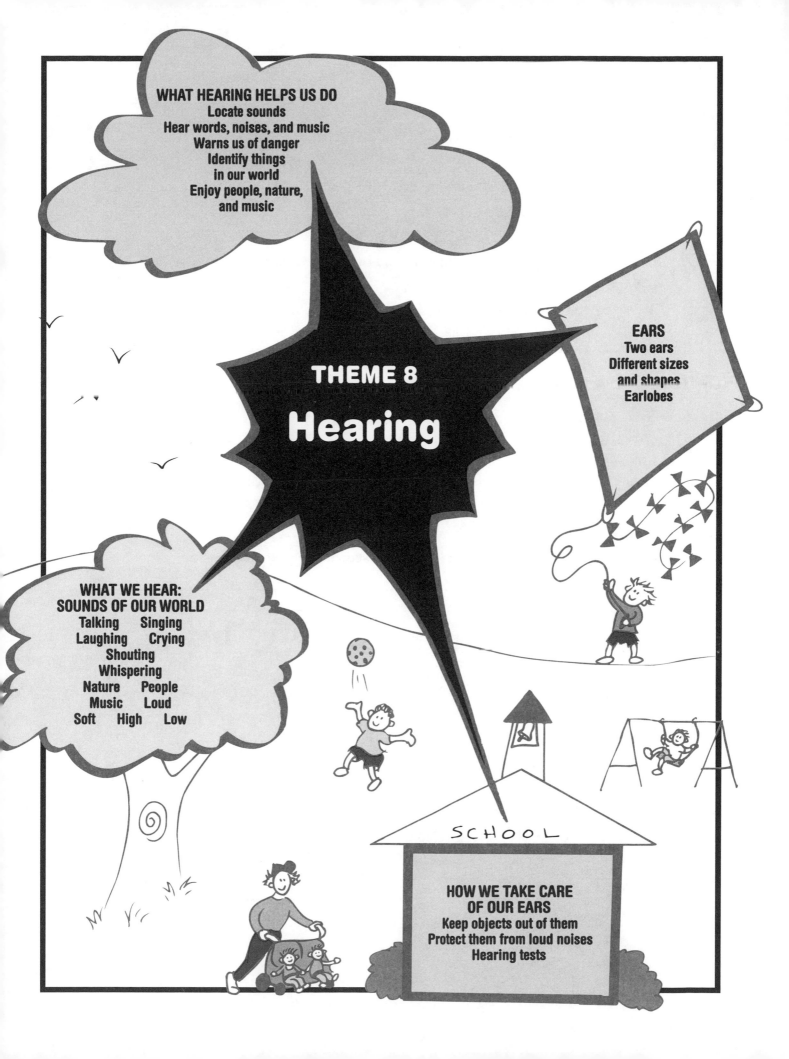

WHAT HEARING HELPS US DO
Locate sounds
Hear words, noises, and music
Warns us of danger
Identify things
in our world
Enjoy people, nature,
and music

THEME 8
Hearing

EARS
Two ears
Different sizes
and shapes
Earlobes

WHAT WE HEAR:
SOUNDS OF OUR WORLD
Talking   Singing
Laughing   Crying
Shouting
Whispering
Nature   People
Music   Loud
Soft   High   Low

SCHOOL

HOW WE TAKE CARE
OF OUR EARS
Keep objects out of them
Protect them from loud noises
Hearing tests

THEME GOALS

To provide opportunities for children to learn:

1. How the five senses are used.
2. The ears are the part of the body used to hear.
3. We listen to hear many sounds and find out many things.
4. We should take good care of our ears.
5. Some people cannot hear at all, or cannot hear well.

Children-Created Bulletin Board

This bulletin board is a continuation of the one started in Theme 7, Seeing.

✳ Place two oversized ears on the sides of the bulletin board. Leave the "eyes" in place.
✳ Add the word "Listen!"
✳ During the theme Hearing, the children place pictures and words of what they hear.
✳ They create new faces with ears to add to the board.
✳ Add small bells on strings or colored ribbon to hang from the bulletin board. The children enjoy making these "jingle."
✳ Add more items as the children become busy with activities related to this theme.

Vocabulary Starters

Let the children add additional words.

ear — the part of the body with which we hear.

hearing — the ability to notice sounds with the ears.

earlobe — the soft skin at the bottom of the ear.

sound — what we hear with our ears.

listen — to pay attention to what we are hearing.

Language Experiences

HEAR A SOUND, MAKE A SOUND

Infants enjoy making sounds, hearing sounds around them, and responding to what they hear.

✳ Shake rattles, bells, and tambourines for the babies to see and hear.

✳ They will answer the sounds by watching and cooing.

✳ Repeat the sounds many times.

✳ Shake–coo. Shake–coo. A kind of rhythm will occur.

✳ Try many different kinds of sound-making toys and musical instruments.

✳ Let the infant play with the rattle or appropriate toy, and watch how she plays with it.

FINGERPLAY:
My Little Ears

I have two little ears.
  (point to ears)
They belong to me.
  (point to yourself)
They help me hear.
  (put hand behind ears)
Don't you see?
  (place hands above eyes)
My two little ears
  (point to ears)
Go everywhere I go,
When I'm way up high
  (point up to the ceiling)
Or when I'm way down low.
  (point down to the floor)
My two little ears
  (point to ears)
Love the beat of a drum,
  (pretend to beat a drum)

Or the roar of an airplane
  (make your arms fly like an airplane)
Or a bumble bee's hum-m-m-m.
  (fingers together, fly like a bee)
I have two little ears.
  (point to ears)
They belong to me.
  (point to yourself)
They help me hear.
  (place hands behind ears)
Don't you see?
  (place hands above eyes)

Philip Jackman

Dramatic Play

FIND WHAT'S NEW

✳ To introduce children to the new items you have added to the dramatic play/home living area, hide a ticking kitchen timer or alarm clock there. See if the children can find it without any clues.

✳ After they find the timer, ask the children to point out what other new items have been added.

✳ Suggestions of objects to add to the area are: bongo drums, bells, maracas, rain sticks, cymbals, autoharp, kitchen pots and pans, wooden spoons, rhythm sticks, tambourines, and a washboard.

✳ The children can explore the different musical instruments and the sounds they make.

✳ The more they hear, the more they learn about their environment.

✳ For younger children, place a "jack-in-the box" somewhere in the room.

✳ See if the children can find where the music is coming from before it pops open.

✳ Introduce the toy to the children before you hide it in the room so that they will expect the "pop-up."

SCARVES, STREAMERS,
AND TAMBOURINES

This activity can be done indoors or outdoors. You will need a large space so the children can move around.

✳ Have the children select scarves, crepe paper streamers, or tambourines that you have made available for them.

✳ Play a variety of music for them to "act out" what the music is "telling" them to do.

✳ Suggestions for musical selections available in libraries or stores under many different labels and performing artists are:

Composer	Selection
Copeland	*Rodeo*
Dukas	*The Sorcerer's Apprentice*
Grofé	*Grand Canyon Suite*
Rimski-Korsakov	*Flight of the Bumble Bee*
Rossini	*William Tell Overture*
Saint-Saëns	*Carnival of the Animals*
Tchaikovsky	*The Nutcracker Suite*

Puppet Play

RABBIT EARS

For this activity, the children will need small, six-inch, white paper plates, small craft sticks, yarn, pipe cleaners, crayons, and markers.

✳ Help the children cut two ear holes about an inch from one edge of a paper plate.

✳ The children will put their index and middle fingers through these holes to be the rabbit's ears.

✳ Ask the children to draw a rabbit face on one side of the plate. Yarn or pipe cleaners can be used for whiskers.

✳ At the bottom of the face on the opposite side of the plate, tape or glue the craft stick so that it projects down far enough to serve as a handle.

✳ The children may want to make more than one rabbit puppet, so have plenty of plates and sticks available.

✳ By holding the handle with one hand and using the two fingers of the other hand as wiggly ears, the puppets are ready for lots of imaginative play.

Music

SONG: "I Have Two Ears" by Jo Eklof

(See page 299 for enlargement.)

TEACHER'S TURN

✳ Place a box of musical instruments in the center of the circle.

✳ Explain to the children that you are going to close your eyes while each child selects an instrument from the box.

✳ The children put their instruments behind their backs.

✳ Your eyes stay closed while one child plays an instrument and you try to guess which instrument it is.

✳ After the instrument is played and you guess, then open your eyes. Were you right or wrong? It is important for you to guess wrong some of the time.

✳ Continue playing until all the children have had a turn.

LISTEN!

After reading Martin and Archambault's book *Listen to the Rain,* listed in the books section of this theme, give each child a musical instrument to play.

✳ Some of the instruments can be ones the children made (see Theme 6, music section). Others can be pots, pans, wooden spoons, maracas, rain sticks, cymbals, triangles, tambourines, and drums.

✳ Ask the children to listen to the book again and add the musical sounds to match the sound of the rain. Here is an example of the delightful language of the book:

> Listen to the rain,
> the whisper of the rain,
> the slow soft sprinkle,
> the drip-drop tinkle.
> . . . the lightning-flashing,
> thunder-crashing,
> sounding pounding roaring rain

✳ For follow-up activities, older children can write their own poems about rain or take the poems they created in Theme 7 and add musical sounds.

✳ Endicott's imaginative illustrations in *Listen to the Rain* may stimulate the children to create their own drawings for their poems.

Movement

FREEZE

This game is easy for children to understand. It helps them develop bodily control and balance, and can be done either indoors or outdoors.

✳ Have the children evenly scattered in a large play area with their personal space clearly defined.

✳ Tell them that when you say "go," they are to move around easily and flowingly, as though they are floating through the air or water.

✳ Encourage them to let their head, arms, hands, and legs move loosely "every which way."

✳ Then, tell them that when you say "freeze" they are to follow directions and "freeze" in whatever position they are in at that moment.

✳ They are to stay motionless until you say "unfreeze." Then, they are to resume moving around.

✳ Do this "freeze" and "unfreeze" three or four times. Let the children take turns being the one to say "freeze" and "unfreeze."

✳ To make this activity successful, the children should be careful not to bump each other and avoid moving so fast that they lose their balance and fall.

GO IN AND OUT THE WINDOW

This activity is designed to help children coordinate words with actions, follow oral directions, and develop spatial awareness.

Go in and out the window,
Go in and out the window,
Go in and out the window,
Hi, ho, hi, ho, hi, ho.

March in and out the window,
March in and out the window,
March in and out the window,
Hi, ho, hi, ho, hi, ho.

✳ Arrange the children's chairs in a circle. Leave enough "window" space between each chair for the children to pass through.

✳ When they sing the traditional song "Go In and Out the Window," the children move through the circle of chairs.

✳ Moving into the circle of chairs they are moving "in the window." Moving out of the circle they are moving "out the window." The children weave in and out of the circle all in the same direction. You may want to lead the line the first time the song is sung.

✳ Change the words and the movement by marching or tiptoeing, or in other ways the children think of.

Sensory Art

INFANT WIND CHIME

✳ Collect lightweight items, such as foil pie tins, metal lids from jars, chimes, and anything else that will make fascinating sounds when the wind blows.

✳ Make sure they are safe and will not scratch or cut fingers when touched.

✳ Tie these with strings or yarn to a tree limb or clothing hangers so that the wind can move them.

✳ Carry the infants to the wind chime to listen to the sounds it makes.

✳ Talk about the sounds.

✳ Let the babies touch the safe chime pieces if they want to do so.

POPPING BUBBLE PRINTS

✳ Prepare a solution of equal parts water and dish detergent. Put the liquid in several small containers.

✳ Add food coloring or tempera to create desired colors.

✳ Place the containers in a pan.

✳ Have the children blow with a straw into the container until bubbles reach the top of the container. To prevent the children from "drinking" the solution, cut a little hole near the top of each straw.

✳ Make a print by lightly touching plain or manilla construction paper to the bubbles. The bubbles will stick to the paper, then pop! This will leave a colorful imprint on the paper.

✳ Let the paper dry.

✳ This is a special way to create class stationery, gift wrap, or unusual art prints.

Creative Food Experiences

CRUNCHY SALAD

You will need:

2 carrots	1 teaspoon lemon juice
1 stalk of celery	1/4 teaspoon salt (optional)
2 apples	1/2 cup yogurt or sour cream
1/2 cup raisins	lettuce

1. Wash hands.
2. Wash carrots, celery, and apples.
3. Cut off ends of carrots, peel, then grate. Put in large mixing bowl.
4. Cut out core of apples, and cut the apples into small, bite-size pieces. Add to the mixing bowl.

5. Cut celery into small pieces and put in bowl.
6. Add raisins.
7. Sprinkle with lemon juice and salt.
8. Stir in yogurt or sour cream.
9. Precut all the ingredients for younger children. They can help you mix the salad.

CRUNCHY SALAD

Wash hands.

Wash 2 carrots, 1 stalk celery, and 2 apples.

Cut off ends of carrots, peel, then grate.

Put in large mixing bowl. Cut out apple cores.

Cut the apples and celery into small bite-size pieces

and add to the mixing bowl. Add 1/2 cup raisins.

Sprinkle with lemon juice and salt.

Stir in 1/2 cup yogurt or sour cream. Mix and eat!

CRUNCHY GRANOLA

You will need:

> 1/2 cup chopped unsalted peanuts (the more nuts you add, the crunchier the granola gets)
>
> 1/4 cup hulled sunflower seeds
>
> 1/2 cup coconut
>
> 1/2 cup chopped dried fruit (the more fruit you add, the chewier the granola gets)
>
> 1 teaspoon cinnamon
>
> 1/4 teaspoon nutmeg
>
> 1/2 cup honey (the more honey you add, the sweeter the granola gets)

1. Wash hands.
2. Mix all of the dry ingredients with the honey.

3. Store in an airtight container.

This recipe serves enough for a group of eight children to have one-half cup per child.

Math

ONE-BEAT, TWO-BEAT, THREE-BEAT RHYTHM

This activity helps develop an awareness of sound patterns in mathematical terms.

* Give each child a rhythm stick. To make a sound, have the child strike a solid object, such as a box, table, or the floor.
* You should also have a rhythm stick to lead them. Ask them to follow what you do.
* First, start a one-beat rhythm, counting "one" on each beat: one–pause/one–pause/one–pause/one, etc. Stop.
* Second, do a two-beat rhythm: one–two—long pause/one–two—long pause/one–two—long pause, etc. Stop.
* Third, do a three-beat rhythm: one–two–three—pause/one–two–three—pause/one–two–three—pause, etc. Stop.
* Fourth, do a four-beat rhythm with no pauses: one–two–three–four/one–two–three–four/one–two–three–four, etc. Stop.
* Then, ask one child to volunteer to lead the group doing the one-beat rhythm, after first reviewing it.
* Next, have another child lead the two-beat rhythm, a third child lead the three-beat rhythm, and a fourth lead the four-beat rhythm.

Science

MATCH THE SOUNDS

* Collect small plastic, 35 mm film containers. If you have been collecting for several years, you may have some of the old metal film cans. They work very well.
* Divide the film containers into pairs. Partly fill one pair with bird seed. Replace the cap.
* Continue this process using dried beans, salt, rice, coffee grounds, medium-size screws, metal washers, paper clips, and macaroni.
* Be sure that each set of containers sounds the same when you shake them.

* Put all of the containers together.
* Have the children, one at a time, pick up and shake the containers until they have found a pair that makes a sound match.
* It sometimes works better to do this activity in small groups.
* For younger children, start with fewer pairs of containers.
* The children will want to see what's making the sounds inside the containers. Closely supervise the younger children while they explore.

BOTTLE SOUNDS

* Save five glass bottles that are all the same. Wash them thoroughly. Drinking glasses may be used instead of bottles. They will make different sounds.
* Place a few drops of food coloring into a pitcher of water.
* Pour different amounts of the water into the bottles.
* To get a good range of notes, vary the amount of water in each bottle.
* Put the bottles on a table in a row.
* Let the children, one at a time, tap each bottle gently above the water line with a spoon or wooden stick. This will create different musical sounds for the children to hear.
* Guide the children into sequencing the sounds from lowest to the highest.

Note: When the children strike the bottles or glasses, the glass and the air vibrate. It is the vibration the children hear. The different amounts of water combined with the vibration produces the musical sounds of different pitches.

Social Studies

FIELD TRIP

Children enjoy taking field trips. Visit a neighborhood ear, nose, and throat doctor (otolaryngologist) or audiologist. If a field trip is not possible, ask a doctor, audiologist, or nurse to visit the class.

✳ Ask the professional to show the children a plastic ear and explain the parts of the ear.

✳ Using the ear model, have the doctor demonstrate what is done during an ear examination, and talk to the children about hearing safety.

✳ Follow up in the classroom by having the children write a thank-you note to the doctor or audiologist. They can draw pictures too.

✳ Place a copy of the note and the drawings on the bulletin board.

WHISPER GAME

This game is designed to show older children that what they think they hear is not necessarily what someone has said.

✳ Have the children sit in a circle. This works better if there are at least six to eight children playing.

✳ To get them started, you will whisper a statement into one child's ear, such as, "I have a brown dog that has a white spot on his back, but my kitty is black and has white fur on her paws."

✳ Tell the child to whisper the same words into the ear of the child to the left, and for this child to pass on the message exactly as she heard it to the next child on her left.

✳ This continues until all the children have done so. The exception will be the last child, who will tell aloud to the whole group what he heard.

✳ Next, you say exactly what you did say to begin the game.

✳ Usually the message gets jumbled in the telling and hardly resembles the original statement.

✳ Explain to the children that this is how false things are said about people. What is said can even be hurtful and dangerous.

✳ Remind them that it is important to listen carefully and be sure they understand what someone says before repeating their words to others.

THE ABC'S OF SIGN LANGUAGE

✳ Introduce the children to sign language. Explain that it is a special language for people who cannot hear the spoken word.

✳ Sesame Street's book, *Sign Language ABC with Linda Bove,* listed in the books section of this theme, is one way to acquaint the children with sign language for the deaf.

✳ Ask someone from the local Association for the Deaf or the American Speech-Language-Hearing Association to visit your classroom and share American Sign Language (ASL) with the children. Perhaps a relative of a child in the class knows ASL and will come visit.

Children's Books

Berger, Melvin. (1994). *All About Sounds.* New York: Scholastic.

Brown, Craig. (1992). *City Sounds.* New York: Greenwillow.

Cousins, Lucy. (1997). *What Can Pinky Hear?: A Lift-the-Flap-Book.* Cambridge, MA: Candlewick Press.

De Zutter, Hank. (1993). *Who Says a Dog Goes Bow-Wow?* Illustrated by Suse MacDonald. New York: Bantam Doubleday Dell Books for Young Readers.

Dr. Seuss. (1995). *Learn About the Sound of B and Other Stuff.* New York: Random House.

Dr. Seuss. (1987). *Horton Hears a Who.* New York: Random House.

Dr. Seuss. (1968). *The Ear Book.* New York: Random House.

Martin, Bill, Jr. (1997). *Polar Bear, Polar Bear, What Do You Hear?* (Board book). Illustrated by Eric Carle. New York: Henry Holt.

Martin, Bill, Jr., and John Archambault. (1987). *Listen to the Rain.* Illustrated by James Endicott. New York: Henry Holt.

Miller, Margaret. (1994). *My Five Senses.* New York: Simon and Schuster.

Moncure, Jane B. (1982). *Sounds All Around.* San Francisco, CA: Children's Press.

Oxenbury, Helen. (1995). *I Hear.* Cambridge, MA: Candlewick Press.

Palmer, Hap. (1991). *Homemade Band.* New York: Crown.

Pettigrew, Mark. (1987). *Music and Sound.* New York: Gloucester.

Sesame Street. (1985). *Sign Language ABC with Linda Bove.* New York: Random House/Children's Television Workshop.

Showers, Paul. (1991). *The Listening Walk.* New York: HarperCollins.

Showers, Paul. (1990). *Ears Are for Hearing.* New York: HarperCollins.

Wells, Rosemary. (1994). *The Night Sounds, Morning Colors.* New York: Dial Books.

Van Kampen, Vlasta. (1990). *Orchestranimals.* New York: Scholastic.

Parent Letter (Preschool)

Dear Parents,

We are continuing to study the Five Senses. Our theme is Hearing. We will provide opportunities for the children to learn:

- How the five senses are used.
- The ears are the part of the body used to hear.
- We listen to hear many sounds and find out many things.
- We should take good care of our ears.
- Some people cannot hear at all or cannot hear well.

We will be talking about:

- our ears
- what hearing helps us do
- how we take care of our ears
- the sounds we hear in our world

Try some of these things to do at home with your preschool child:

- Play music at home. Share all types of music with your child.
- Read books with your child. Use different voices for the characters.
- Talk about and listen to the sounds you hear every day.

Parent participation opportunities for you at school will include:

- Help us make a crunchy salad.
  Date ————— Time —————
- Go with us on our field trip to the ear, nose, and throat doctor or audiologist.
  Date ————— Time —————
- If you know of anyone who could introduce the children to American Sign Language (ASL), please tell us about him or her.

Our wish list for this theme includes:

drinking straws

35 mm film containers

foil pie tins

metal lids from jars

Thank you for your continued support.

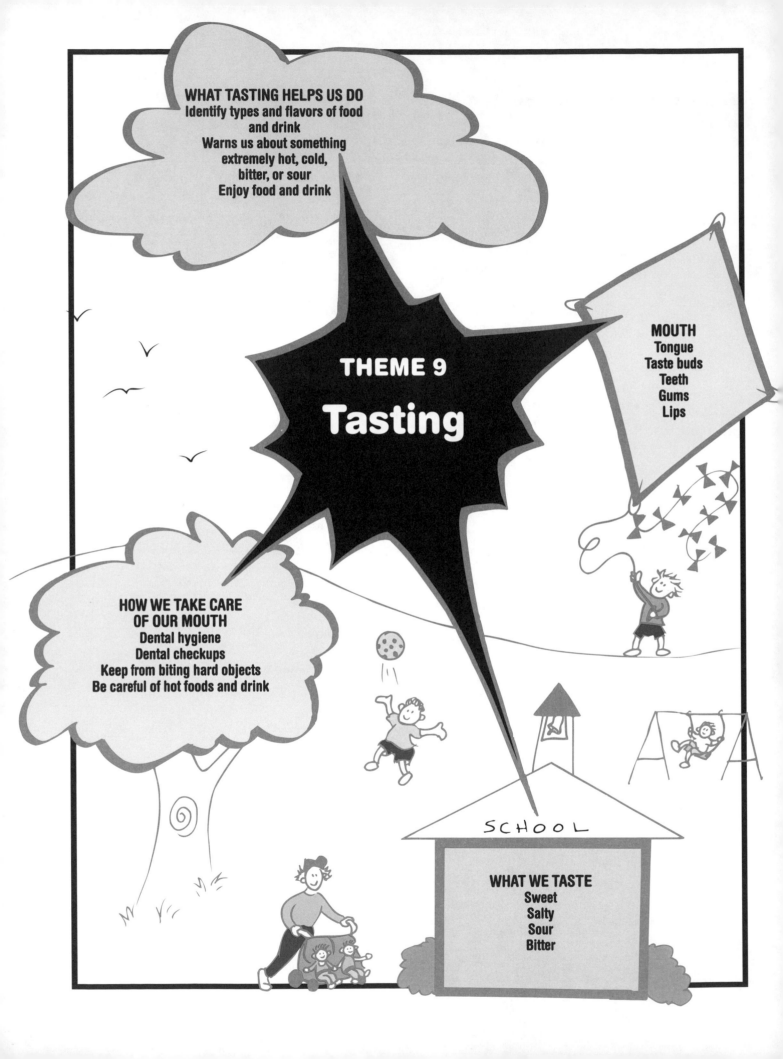

WHAT TASTING HELPS US DO
Identify types and flavors of food and drink
Warns us about something extremely hot, cold, bitter, or sour
Enjoy food and drink

THEME 9
Tasting

MOUTH
Tongue
Taste buds
Teeth
Gums
Lips

HOW WE TAKE CARE OF OUR MOUTH
Dental hygiene
Dental checkups
Keep from biting hard objects
Be careful of hot foods and drink

SCHOOL

WHAT WE TASTE
Sweet
Salty
Sour
Bitter

THEME GOALS

To provide opportunities for children to learn:

1. How the five senses work together.

2. The tongue is the part of the body used to taste.

3. The parts of the tongue called taste buds are used for tasting sweet, sour, salty, and bitter.

4. The sense of taste and the sense of smell work together.

5. We should take care of our mouth, teeth, and tongue.

Children-Created Bulletin Board

This bulletin board is a continuation of the interactive ones in Theme 7 — Seeing, and Theme 8 — Hearing.

✳ Add an open mouth with tongue and teeth to the bottom center of the bulletin board. Leave the eyes and ears already in place.

✳ Add the words "Let's Taste."

✳ Divide the bulletin board into four areas with the words "sweet," "salty," "sour," and "bitter" above the four spaces.

✳ The children add pictures and words of what they taste in the appropriate parts of the bulletin board.

✳ More things can be added as the children become involved with activities relating to this theme.

Vocabulary Starters

Let the children add additional words.

taste — the ability to tell the flavors of what we eat.

taste buds — the places on the tongue that help us taste things.

tongue — the movable muscle inside the mouth that helps us taste and swallow.

flavor — the special taste that something has.

dental — anything having to do with the teeth.

Language Experiences

EXPLORE FAVORITE FOODS

Older infants and toddlers have limited experience with foods. Select one fruit or vegetable each week and explore it thoroughly.

✳ Let the parents know what foods you will be tasting. Infants with limited food experiences may have a reaction to new foods.

✳ For example, let the children look at a tomato, hold it, smell it, and taste it.

✳ Some of the tomatoes may get "squashed" during this process, so have plenty available to share.

✳ Repeat the name of the fruit or vegetable often, so that the children see the food and hear the correct name at the same time.

✳ Follow up with picture books about fruits and vegetables and pictures placed at their eye level.

POEM: "I Eat My Peas"

I eat my peas with honey
Every day at noon.
It makes the peas taste funny,
But it keeps them on the spoon.

THE VERY HUNGRY CATERPILLAR

✳ Read Carle's *The Very Hungry Caterpillar* to the children, see the books section of this theme.

✳ Ask the children to name what they would have eaten if they were very hungry caterpillars.

✳ Write the foods selected on a chart and place it in the art center for the children to refer to later.

✳ Encourage the children to draw the foods they selected, and write the food names on their illustrations.

✳ These pictures can be added to the bulletin board. Some of the children may be creative and cut holes in their pictures, just as Eric Carle did.

✳ As an extension of this activity, select four or five of the children's favorite foods, and have them available for a snack. If possible, select only fruits and vegetables, such as the ones the hungry caterpillar ate.

✳ Ask the children to describe in words what flavors the foods have.

✳ Refer to Theme 23 — Insects for other activities relating to the caterpillar and its metamorphosis into a butterfly.

Dramatic Play

THE GINGERBREAD MAN

✳ Read the story of *The Gingerbread Man* to the children. Three separate books with different styles of illustration are listed in the books section of this theme.

✳ Next, ask the children to act out the story. They can take turns being the different characters.

✳ As an extension, ask the children to think of other endings for this folk tale.

✳ Doing this type of activity helps children with sequencing, recalling, socialization, and stimulating imagination and creativity.

✳ Later, make gingerbread children. The recipe is in the cooking experiences section of this theme.

PANCAKES

✳ Read Carle's *Pancakes, Pancakes* or De Paola's *Pancakes for Breakfast* to the children (see the books section of this theme.)

✳ With older children, ask them to retell the story without using the book.

✳ Have some of the items mentioned in the story available as props to help with the dramatization.

✳ Some children may want to act out the story with or without words, while others may want to orally retell the story. Whatever they do should be okay.

✳ Make the book available if they cannot remember all of the story.

Puppet Play

GINGERBREAD CHILDREN STICK PUPPETS

This activity relates to the cooking one in this theme.

✳ The children can further develop Egielski's *The Gingerbread Boy* story by making stick puppets. Theme 1 contains suggestions for patterns.

✳ Use construction paper reinforced with cardboard or tagboard to make the puppet.

✳ Make many colors of construction paper available for the children. Some may want to have colorful puppet children.

✳ Fasten the puppet to a craft stick or dowel rod.

✳ For younger children, cut smaller child shapes, and attach a straw or small craft stick.

I LIKE SPAGHETTI!

This activity encourages children to think creatively.

PULL

✳ Put paper plates, markers, crayons, scissors, hole punchers, yarn, glue, and construction paper scraps on a table.

✳ Talk about making paper plate puppets.

✳ Ask the children to make a puppet that likes to eat.

✳ Accept whatever the children make.

✳ If some children have difficulty getting started, ask open-ended questions to guide them. "What could you do with this paper plate to make it into a face?" "What could you do to show that this puppet likes to eat?" "What about spaghetti?" "What could you do to this paper plate puppet to make it eat spaghetti?"

✳ Perhaps one or more children will get the idea to make a hole in the puppet's mouth, and use yarn for spaghetti. Knot the yarn on the ends so the "spaghetti" won't pull out of the mouth.

✳ The children will also come up with many other imaginative ways to show how their puppets can "eat."

✳ For younger children, make a puppet and have them play with making the puppet "eat spaghetti."

Music

WHAT'S IN THE BOWL?

✳ Guide the children to sit in a circle.

✳ Sing the following song to the tune of "Farmer in the Dell."

Jello in the bowl, jello in the bowl,
Jiggle, joggle, wiggle, woggle,
Jello in the bowl.
   Popcorn in the bowl, popcorn in the bowl,
   Pop, pop, pop-pop-pop,
   Popcorn in the bowl.
Mix pancakes in the bowl, mix pancakes in the bowl,
Stir, stir, fast and slow,
Mix pancakes in the bowl.
   Soup in the bowl, soup in the bowl,
   Splish, splash, swish, swash,
   Soup in the bowl.

✳ It is fun for the children to "jiggle like jello," "pop like popcorn," "stir fast and slow," and "splish like soup."

✳ Let the children help you make up more verses.

"COOKIES IN THE OVEN"

This song can be sung and acted out by the children. Older children can be divided into groups, with each group singing a different verse or line in each verse. Sing the song to the tune of "Skip to My Lou."

What do I smell? Sniff–sniff–sniff.
What do I smell? Sniff–sniff–sniff.
What do I smell? Sniff–sniff–sniff.
What do I smell with my nose-y.
   It is cookies in the oven. Yum–yum–yum.
   It is cookies in the oven. Yum–yum–yum.
   It is cookies in the oven. Yum–yum–yum.
   That's what I smell with my nose-y.
Open the oven — put them out to cool.
Open the oven — put them out to cool.
Open the oven — put them out to cool.
Then I can eat my cookies.
   Eat my cookies. Chew–chew–chew.
   Eat my cookies. Chew–chew–chew.
   Eat my cookies. Chew–chew–chew.
   I love to eat my cookies!

                           Philip Jackman

Movement

TOOTH TOSS

✳ Draw a happy tooth on the side of a sturdy box.

✳ Cut a hole in the smiley mouth large enough for a beanbag to go through.

✳ Have beanbags of all shapes, sizes, textures, and colors available. Every beanbag should be different so each child can recognize her own.

✳ Toddlers can get close to the box to throw their beanbags in the smiley mouth.

✳ Older children enjoy helping you make up rules for the Tooth Toss Game. For example, the children who brush their teeth each morning get to toss the beanbag three times for each turn.

DENTAL FLOSS

✳ Have the children divide into two equal groups.

✳ Ask each group to choose a leader and to form a line behind the leader.

✳ Give them a jump rope, a piece of clothesline, or a length of garden hose long enough for one group of children to hold one end while the other group holds the other end.

✳ This is a cooperative game. Have the rope represent dental floss. The children work together to wipe out germs and tartar.

Sensory Art

EGG CARTON FLOSS

This is a fun way to teach young children about dental hygiene.

✳ Cut the bottom of an empty egg carton into three pieces. Discard the top of the carton.

✳ Place the three pieces with white yarn and scissors on a table.

✳ Guide two or three children at a time into cutting a long piece of white yarn to be used as "floss."

✳ Turn the carton pieces over so that the bottom will be face up. These will become pretend teeth.

✳ Help the children wrap the yarn around their fingers as they start to floss.

✳ Leave the egg cartons and yarn in the manipulative center so that the children can floss when they choose to do so.

PEANUT SHELL COLLAGE

This project can connect to several activity areas.

✳ Buy some peanuts in the shell from a grocery or farmers' market.

✳ For a snack, have the children take the peanuts out of the shells, save the shells, and eat the peanuts. This is an interesting small muscle activity, too.

✳ Put the peanut shells in a basket or bucket, and make them available in the art center with construction paper, glue, and scissors.

✳ The children can draw and cut out peanut shapes or make any design they wish.

✳ They glue the peanut shells onto their drawings.

✳ Add the finished peanut creations to the bulletin board.

Creative Food Experiences

PEANUT BUTTER BALLS

You will need:

    1/2 cup peanut butter

    1/2 cup nonfat dry milk

    1/2 cup honey

1. Wash hands.
2. With the children's help, measure and put all ingredients in a big bowl. Stir ingredients together.
3. Give each child a portion.

PEANUT BUTTER BALLS

Wash hands.

Measure 1/2 cup peanut butter,

1/2 cup nonfat dry milk,

and 1/2 cup honey.

Put all ingredients in a big bowl and stir together.

Squeeze and pull until it is shiny and soft.

○ ○ ○

Roll into small balls and place on wax paper.

Put in the refrigerator.

Wait 1 hour or more until they are firm.

Then, EAT AND ENJOY!

---

4. Squeeze and pull until the mixture is shiny and soft. (The children love to do this.)
5. Roll into small balls.
6. Identify each child's peanut butter ball with a name label attached to a toothpick inserted in the ball.
7. Place on wax paper and refrigerate one hour or longer, until firm.
8. Then, eat and enjoy!

PANCAKES

✳ Read De Paola's *Pancakes for Breakfast,* or Numeroff's *If You Give a Pig a Pancake,* or Carle's *Pancakes, Pancakes,* all listed in the books section of this theme.

✳ Make pancakes with the children for a morning snack. This is easier to do if you use an electric skillet. Follow the directions on a box of prepared pancake mix.

GINGERBREAD CHILDREN

You will need:

    5 cups flour

    1 1/2 teaspoons baking soda

    1/2 teaspoon salt

    2 teaspoons ginger

    1 teaspoon cinnamon

    1 teaspoon ground cloves

    1 cup shortening

    1 cup sugar

    1 egg

    1 cup molasses

    2 teaspoons vinegar

1. Wash hands.
2. With the children's help, sift dry ingredients together.
3. Cream shortening and sugar.
4. Stir in egg, molasses, and vinegar. Beat well.
5. Stir in sifted dry ingredients, mixing well.
6. Chill.
7. Roll in pecan-size balls.

8. On an individual piece of wax paper, have each child put three balls of dough to use for making the gingerbread child. Each child can make an original design.

9. For younger children, use a cookie cutter or help them flatten one ball with a thumb to make the head, roll one into a rope for arms, and roll and curve the other to form legs.

10. Use raisins or red hots for eyes and buttons.

11. Bake in a 350-degree oven for 10 to 12 minutes.

12. For an extra touch, when cookies are cooled, paint a smile on each face. Use a mixture of powdered sugar and milk for icing, and apply with a toothpick.

13. Mark each child's name on a chart to match the placement on the cookie sheet(s). This way each child will be sure to get his own.

14. If you are limited in time, use a box of gingerbread mix. The children can still make gingerbread children or shapes with the prepared mix.

Math

SHARE A PIZZA

This activity can help children learn about the concepts of how a whole can be divided into halves, fourths, and eighths.

✳ Prior to the activity, create two or more sets of nine-inch plates and plate segments. Each set consists of four plates: one is left whole, one is cut into two halves, one is cut into four quarters, and one is cut into eight eighths.

✳ Put each set in a plastic zip-lock bag.

✳ Encourage two children to assemble each set of parts so that they make three whole plates. The uncut plate is used as a model, making the activity self-correcting.

✳ Have them count the number of parts in each assembled plate.

✳ Younger children like working the puzzle. Older children can comprehend the concept of halves, quarters, and eighths.

✳ Soon after they finish the activity, provide them with one or more nine-inch pizzas, enough to divide up and feed the entire group.

✳ Ask their help to problem-solve: how should the pizzas be divided to provide enough equal-sized pieces to feed the whole class? Then, enjoy the pizza!

Science

TASTING TRAYS

✳ Prepare several trays with various things for the children to taste.

✳ Be sure *not* to include any foods to which children in your class are allergic.

✳ For younger children, include a few of the foods they have had before, and add one or two new ones.

✳ Introduce preschoolers to foods that are divided into the four taste groups: sweet, salty, bitter, and sour. They may need help in naming the tastes, but they can tell you when the food tastes "yuk!"

✳ School-age children can verbalize how something tastes. Ask them to predict the basic taste of each food item. Have them tell you where on the tongue they detect the different flavors.

✳ Place fresh fruits and vegetables (include radishes, turnips, and potatoes), pretzels, popcorn, potato chips, salted nuts, gumdrops, cookies, pickles, parsley, and unsweetened chocolate on the trays.

✳ Cut these tasting foods into cubes for the children to pick up with toothpicks.

✳ Have the children drink water between each taste to reduce the mixing of flavors.

✳ Prepare another tray with items that look alike, such as sugar, baking soda, baking powder, and cornstarch.

✳ Talk about how these substances look the same but are very different. Explain that they should never eat anything if they do not know what it is.

✳ Add a label to each one and ask the children to taste the differences. It is fine if they do not want to taste.

✳ Extend the tasting activity to another day, and introduce the children to spices, such as cloves, cinnamon, nutmeg, ginger, paprika, and pepper. See Theme 10 — "Smell the Spices" for a follow-up activity.

✳ Note: Being able to smell what we are eating is an important part of tasting it. Have the children try closing their eyes and holding their nose while they taste an apple, banana, or orange. Can they tell the difference in how the food tastes?

TASTE BUDS

* Before introducing this concept to older children, draw a large tongue on white posterboard.

* Draw around the **front** of the tongue with a colored marker to indicate that the taste buds here taste **sweet** tastes, such as sugar and honey.

* Draw around the **sides** of the tongue with a different colored marker to show that the taste buds here taste **sour** tastes, such as lemon and vinegar.

* Draw around the **back** of the tongue with another color to point out that the taste buds here taste **bitter** tastes, such as grapefruit and unsweetened baking chocolate.

* Select still another colored marker and make small dots **all over** the tongue to illustrate that the whole surface of the tongue can taste **salty** tastes, such as pretzels and salted nuts.

* Have some sweet, sour, bitter, and salty foods for the children to taste.

* As a follow-up activity, have the children draw a tongue on a piece of paper. Then, cut out pictures of foods from magazines, and glue them on the appropriate taste bud areas of the tongue. Make the drawing of the tongue used in the Taste Bud activity available as a reference for the children.

Social Studies

BREAD, BREAD, BREAD

This activity introduces children to the concept that people all over the world eat bread and that bread comes in all textures, shapes, sizes, and colors. For younger children, just have a bread tasting party.

* Morris's book, *Bread, Bread, Bread,* offers photographs from around the world that show a variety of cultures, as well as the types of bread eaten everywhere. This book is listed in the books section of this theme.

* Ask the children open-ended questions about the families shown in the photographs, the children's own families, what kind of bread they eat at home, and which is their favorite.

* Next, invite the children to the snack table to have a "tasting party" of different kinds of bread. Have several uncut loaves so that the children can cut slices with your supervision.

* Also provide blunt table knives, soft margarine, jellies, and jams.

* Talk about which breads taste the same and which taste differently. Which ones are new to the children?

* Follow up with cooking activities, such as baking corn bread or tortillas.

* Take a field trip to a bakery or bagel shop.

Children's Books

Aylesworth, Jim. (1998). *The Gingerbread Man.* Illustrated by Barbara McClintock. New York: Scholastic.

Barrett, Judith. (1982). *Cloudy with a Chance of Meatballs.* New York: Aladdin Paperbacks.

Carle, Eric. (1994). *The Very Hungry Caterpillar.* (Board book). New York: Philomel Books.

Carle, Eric. (1992). *Pancakes, Pancakes.* New York: Scholastic.

Degan, Bruce. (1985). *Jamberry.* New York: HarperTrophy.

De Paola, Tomie. (1990). *Pancakes for Breakfast.* San Diego, CA: Harcourt Brace.

Egielski, Richard. (1997). *The Gingerbread Boy.* New York: HarperCollins Juvenile.

Ehlert, Lois. (1994). *Eating the Alphabet: Fruits and Vegetables from A to Z.* San Diego, CA: Harcourt Brace.

Gershator, David. (1998). *Bread Is for Eating.* New York: Henry Holt.

McCloskey, Robert. (1987). *Blueberries for Sal.* New York: Viking Press.

McMillan, Bruce. (1991). *Eating Fractions.* New York: Scholastic.

Morris, Ann. (1993). *Bread, Bread, Bread.* Photographs by Ken Heyman. New York: Mulberry.

Numeroff, Laura J. (1998). *If You Give a Pig a Pancake.* Illustrated by Felicia Bond. New York: HarperCollins.

Numeroff, Laura J. (1997). *If You Give a Mouse a Cookie.* Illustrated by Felicia Bond. New York: HarperTrophy.

Numeroff, Laura J. (1991). *If You Give a Moose a Muffin.* Illustrated by Felicia Bond. New York: HarperCollins.

Pallotta, Jerry. (1995). *The Spice Alphabet Book: Herbs, Spices, and Other Natural Flavors.* Watertown, MA: Charlesbridge Publishing.

Ruis, Maria, Jose M. Parramon, and J. J. Puig. (1985). *Taste.* New York: Barrons Juveniles.

Schmidt, Karen. (1986). *The Gingerbread Man.* New York: Scholastic.

Slepian, Jan, and Ann Seidler. (1988). *The Hungry Thing.* New York: Scholastic.

Suhr, Mandy. (1994). *Taste.* Illustrated by Mike Gordon. Minneapolis, MN: Carolrhoda Books.

Westcott, Nadine B. (1992). *Peanut Butter and Jelly: A Play Rhyme.* New York: E.P. Dutton.

Parent Letter (School-age)

Dear Parents,

As we continue to focus on the Five Senses, we are beginning the theme on Tasting. We will provide opportunities for the children to learn:

- How the five senses work together.
- The tongue is the part of the body used to taste.
- Parts of the tongue, called taste buds, are used for tasting sweet, sour, salty, and bitter.
- The sense of taste and the sense of smell work together.
- We should take care of our mouth, teeth, and tongue.

We will be talking about:

- our mouth, taste buds, teeth, gums, and lips
- what tasting helps us do
- how we take care of our mouth
- what we taste

Things to do at home with your child are:

- Conduct taste tests with your child using different healthy snacks. Ask them to tell you where on the tongue they taste each item.
- Bake gingerbread, and make pancakes with your child.
- Let your child buy the next loaf of bread when you go grocery shopping.

Parent participation opportunities at school:

- Help us make beanbags. Stop by any time and you can pick up the materials.
- Come to our tasting party. Bring any favorite family food (enough for all the children to taste).
  Date _____   Time _____

Wish list for this theme:
  peanut shells
  pieces of cardboard and tagboard
  paper plates
  yarn

Thank you for your interest and participation.

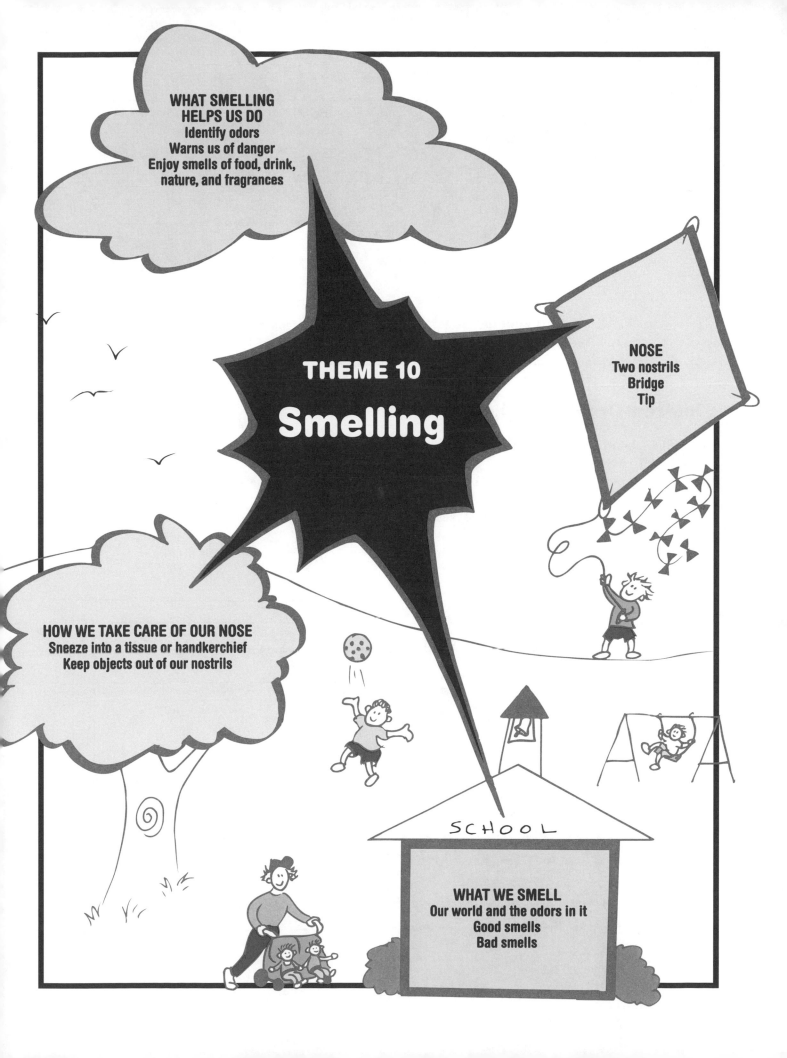

WHAT SMELLING HELPS US DO
Identify odors
Warns us of danger
Enjoy smells of food, drink, nature, and fragrances

THEME 10
Smelling

NOSE
Two nostrils
Bridge
Tip

HOW WE TAKE CARE OF OUR NOSE
Sneeze into a tissue or handkerchief
Keep objects out of our nostrils

SCHOOL

WHAT WE SMELL
Our world and the odors in it
Good smells
Bad smells

THEME GOALS

To provide opportunities for children to learn:

1. How the five senses bring us information about our world.
2. The nose is the part of the body used to smell.
3. The sense of smell helps us find out about odors, enjoy food and drink, and warns us of danger.
4. We should take care of our nose.
5. Some people do not have a strong sense of smell or sense of taste.

Children-Created Bulletin Board

This bulletin board builds on the interactive discovery board introduced in Theme 7 — Seeing, Theme 8 — Hearing, and Theme 9 — Tasting.

✳ Add a nose to the middle of the bulletin board with the words "What's That Smell?" Leave the eyes, ears, and mouth already in place.

✳ Add pieces of fabric or cotton balls scented with various fragrances and spices. This adds an interesting smell to the classroom.

✳ Add more items as the children become involved with activities related to this theme.

Vocabulary Starters

Let the children add additional words.

nose — a part of the body we use to breathe and smell.

nostrils — two holes that let air in and out of the nose.

smell — to be able to notice odors with the nose.

odor — what makes one thing smell different from any other.

sniff — to take air up into your nose so that you can smell something.

Language Experiences

FOOD SMELLS GOOD

For younger children, provide words that go with the smells.

✳ Introduce one food a day.

✳ Have the children smell the food before they taste it. This helps them connect smell and taste in a concrete way.

✳ Talk about what they smell.

✳ Start first with foods that are familiar to the children, such as bananas, peanut butter, and chocolate pudding.

✳ Later in the day, read a book or show the children pictures representing the food they ate earlier.

POEM: "My Favorite Smells"

Chocolate chip cookies baking,
Mommy's perfume,
Pizza!
Daddy's shaving cream,
Fried chicken!
Pine trees,
Fresh popped corn!
If you ask me, then I will tell
The favorite things my nose likes to smell.

✳ Continue with the children saying what their favorite things to smell are.

POPCORN, WE LOVE POPCORN

This activity furthers the children's awareness of the five senses and how they are related to each other. It also introduces new vocabulary words.

✳ Have the children wash their hands.

✳ Place unpopped corn in a bowl and pass it around so that the children can select two or three kernels each.

✳ Ask open-ended questions, such as, "How does the unpopped corn look?" "How does the unpopped corn feel?" "Do the kernels have any smell?"

✳ Throw away the unpopped corn the children have handled.

✳ With a popcorn popper (placed away from the children), begin popping the untouched kernels.

✳ Talk about what sounds the children hear. Ask them to make the sounds. Start with one child, then continue to add the sounds until you have a "popcorn chorus."

✳ Serve each child an individual portion of popped corn.

✳ While they are eating, have them describe how the popcorn tastes.

✳ Continue asking questions while the children are finishing. "What did you learn about popcorn?" "What part of our body helped us know what it looked like before it was popped?" "What part of our body helped us know how the popcorn smells?" "What part of our body helped us know how the popcorn tastes?"

✳ This type of questioning helps children develop skills such as sequencing, recalling, processing, and language acquisition.

Dramatic Play

IT'S A BAKERY!

✳ Turn the dramatic play/home living area into a bakery.

✳ Divide the space into two parts.

✳ The front part should be the counter where "baked goods" are displayed and sold.

✳ The children can make scented play dough or clay cookies, cakes, and breads. See Theme 6 and the sensory art section of this theme for play dough recipes.

✳ Add a cash register, telephone, order pads, pencils, play money, bags, and boxes.

✳ Have the children make signs showing how much the bakery items cost.

✳ Next, make the other part of the area into the "kitchen" of the bakery.

✳ Put bowls, cutting boards, rolling pins, cookie cutters, cookie sheets, candy molds, cookbooks, aprons, hairnets, a broom, and a dust pan in the back part of the bakery.

✳ Make several plastic tubs with warm water and paper towels available for the children.

✳ This is usually a favorite dramatic play area.

Puppet Play

PAPER SACK PUPPET FACE

✳ Put lunch-sized paper sacks, old magazines, catalogs, glue, markers, crayons, yarn, construction paper, and fabric scraps out for the children to use.

✳ Encourage the children to cut out noses, eyes, ears, and mouths from pictures in the magazines.

✳ Guide them into gluing the parts of a face on the sack to make their puppets.

✳ Once the children see how they can make funny faces on their paper sack puppets, they may spend a lot of time making more than one.

✳ As long as the children are interested, give them plenty of time to create.

✳ Older children may add yarn hair, fabric clothes, and construction paper arms, hands, and legs to complete their puppets.

Music

POP GOES THE POPCORN

✳ The children form a circle. They are "unpopped corn."

✳ One child stands in the middle with arms outstretched. She is the "popcorn machine."

✳ As they start singing the song, the children start walking in one direction, the center child rotating with them.

✳ At the word "pop," all the children jump and pretend to be "popcorn popping."

✳ Start singing again, but reverse the direction.

✳ Then, change direction again for the third verse of the song.

✳ Sing to the tune of "Pop Goes The Weasel."

Round and round the popcorn machine
The popcorn tumbles and tumbles,
But when it gets hot in the popcorn machine
POP! Goes the popcorn.
   Turn and turn the popcorn machine.
   We like to hear it popping.
   So let's make more in the popcorn machine,
   Pop! Goes the popcorn.
Circle and circle the popcorn machine,
It is fun to pop the kernels.
Let's try once more with the popcorn machine,
POP! Goes the popcorn!

Movement

LET'S PLAY!

Take this activity outdoors. Smelling the fresh air while actively playing is important for young children.

✳ You will need a medium-sized, lightweight blanket with a hole cut in the middle, and lightweight bouncing balls.

✳ Be sure to have enough balls for each child to have one.

✳ Every player places his ball on the blanket and everyone grabs and lifts the blanket with two hands.

✳ Then, everyone starts pumping the blanket up and down to remove the balls through the hole in the middle.

✳ Once you get the children started, step back and watch the fun.

Sensory Art

SMELL THE WATER

✳ Toddlers love water play. For a change, add different scented extracts to the water table. Try peppermint, lemon, or almond.

✳ For younger toddlers, use tearless baby shampoo to bubble the water.

UNCOOKED PLAY DOUGH

You will need:

    1 cup flour

    1 cup salt

    1 tablespoon cooking oil

    1 cup water

    food coloring (optional)

    scented extracts

1. Wash hands.
2. Mix dry ingredients.
3. Add oil.
4. Slowly add water until the mixture sticks together but does not feel sticky. Knead the play dough well.
5. Add scented extracts, such as vanilla or peppermint.
6. Store in an airtight container.

When the children play with this play dough, it smells so good! Theme 6 has the recipe for cooked play dough.

    Make your favorite play dough recipe, and add one of the following to make it a new kind of sensory experience:

tissue paper	coffee grounds
cornmeal	rose petals
different colors of grated crayons	colored sand

grated lemon or orange rinds (smells great!)

cinnamon, vanilla, mint oils (smells great!)

cake decorating food colors (vivid colors)

Creative Food Experiences

BANANA CHOCOLATE SHAKE

You will need:

    1 cup milk

    1/2 ripe banana

    3 ice cubes

    2 tablespoons sweetened cocoa powder

1. Wash hands.
2. Place all ingredients into a blender.
3. Mix until smooth.
4. Pour into cups and eat with a spoon.
5. Serves 2. It is easier to make small amounts at one time in the blender.

BANANA CHOCOLATE SHAKE

Wash hands.

Place 1 cup milk, 1/2 ripe banana, 3 ice cubes, and

2 tablespoons sweetened cocoa powder into

a blender and mix until smooth.

Pour into cups and eat with a spoon!

GREEN EGGS AND HAM

✳ Read Dr. Seuss's *Green Eggs and Ham.*

✳ Invite the children to imagine and describe how green eggs would smell and taste.

✳ Then, you and the children can make green eggs for morning snack.

✳ In an electric skillet, scramble eggs with green food color added.

✳ Ask the children to talk about how green eggs actually smell and taste. Do they taste any different than regular scrambled eggs?

✳ Encourage the children to tell their parents about this special treat. They can cook some at home too.

Math

GRAPHING FAVORITE SMELLS

This is a good activity to do after the children have been vigorously involved in the discovery of various odors.

✳ Ask the children to tell you what their two favorite smells are.

✳ Write them down exactly as they were dictated.

✳ Then, you and the children make a graph to show which aromas were the most popular. When sharing the graph, use math vocabulary, such as most, more, fewer, and least.

SENSORY BLOCKS

✳ Collect many different types of textures, such as lace, carpet, vinyl, terrycloth, corduroy, sandpaper, and fake fur. Many community businesses will give you odds and ends or remnants of materials.

✳ For samples that do not have a natural odor, spray with pleasant fragrances.

✳ Next, cover small boxes with these different materials. Some of the children may want to help you with this task.

✳ Put the boxes in the block center so the children can explore the smells and textures as they build with boxes and blocks.

Science

WHAT'S THAT SMELL?

Pleasant experiences are often remembered through the sense of smell. There are several ways to get the children involved in identifying odors. One is to make smell bottles.

✳ Accumulate small, clear jars, such as baby food jars. Remove the labels and wash thoroughly.

✳ Put a cotton ball scented with a few drops of extract in each jar.

✳ For a young toddler, hold the cotton balls, one fragrance at a time, under the child's nose. Talk about the odors and show the picture.

✳ Try punching a few holes in the tops of the jars.

✳ You may also leave the lids alone and let the children open and close them, which promotes small muscle development. Remind the children to put the lids back on the jars when they finish their turns.

✳ Suggestions for the smells are: vanilla, lemon, peppermint, almond, and butterscotch extracts; onion juice; pickle juice; vinegar; and colognes.

✳ Fruit peels, such as orange, grapefruit, and lemon, dropped in the jar also are aromatic.

✳ Have pictures, such as an orange, lemon, or onion, for younger children to match with the scents.

✳ Providing words to go with the smells is very important for toddlers.

SMELL THE SPICES

Another way to involve children in the discovery of new smells is to make spice cards. This activity works best when it is done in small groups.

✳ In the art center, put index cards, containers of diluted white glue, small paintbrushes, and a variety of spices.

✳ The children brush glue onto the cards.

✳ Then, sprinkle one spice on each card.

✳ Shake the excess off into a wastebasket or newspaper for easy cleanup.

✳ Include spices that are somewhat familiar to the children: ginger, cinnamon, and nutmeg.

✳ Even though garlic and salt are not spices, it is interesting for the children to discover that garlic salt has a distinctive odor, while salt has none.

OTHER SMELLS IN THE ROOM

✳ Leave scratch-and-sniff stickers and index cards out in the manipulative center for the children to explore.

✳ Additional aromas in the classroom can be provided by placing potpourri, cinnamon sticks, or cloves in baskets.

✳ Put these baskets around the room, preferably using one odor at a time.

✳ To further develop the concept of smells in our environment, bring in a vase of flowers or a potted flowering plant. Place these in the science center.

✳ Let the children discover the flowers without you pointing them out.

Social Studies

LET'S GRIND CORN

Introducing children to the process of grinding corn will help connect them to other cultures. Corn is the staple of many cultures, most of which grind the kernels to produce cornmeal. The children can do the same thing in the classroom. This project can be integrated into many curriculum areas.

✳ Collect an assortment of pictures showing corn growing, being ground, and being used in cooking.

✳ Have actual ears of corn in their husks, as well as dried corn, a box of cornmeal, sifters, spoons, funnels, cups, and a *matate*, or Mexican mortar and pestle.

✳ Place the items in the discovery center, along with the pictures.

✳ Cover a table and floor with newspaper. Place cornmeal with funnels and other utensils on the paper.

✳ Encourage a group of three or four children to practice pouring and measuring.

✳ Put the matate and dried corn on another table. Invite another three or four children to grind the corn. You may have to demonstrate the process for younger children.

✳ Let the children taste the difference between commercial cornmeal and the fresh meal. Use one box of cornmeal just for tasting.

✳ Note: A large, hard, flat rock, washed thoroughly, can be used as the mortar, and a smaller hard rock can be the grinding tool.

✳ Read Politi's *Three Stalks of Corn,* listed in the books section of this theme. Younger children enjoy the pictures, and older children enjoy the story as well.

✳ To further develop this idea, invite a parent or grandparent to cook with the children and share how they use cornmeal in their recipes. Some family members may grind their corn with a metate and offer to bring their own to share with the children.

Children's Books

Cole, Joanna. (1994). *You Can't Smell a Flower with Your Ear!: All About Your Five Senses.* Illustrated by Mavis Smith. Los Angeles, CA: Price Stern Sloan.

De Paola, Tomie. (1989). *The Popcorn Book.* New York: Holiday House.

De Regniers, Beatrice S., Marcia Brown, Jan Carr, and Mary M. White. (1988). *Sing a Song of Popcorn: Every Child's Book of Poems.* New York: Scholastic.

Dr. Seuss. (1960). *Green Eggs and Ham.* New York: Random House.

Fowler, Allan. (1991). *Smelling Things.* San Francisco, CA: Children's Press.

Low, Alice. (1994). *The Popcorn Shop.* Illustrated by Patti Hammel. New York: Cartwheel Books.

Machotka, Hana. (1992). *Breathtaking Noses.* New York: Morrow Junior Books.

Murphy, Mary. (1997). *You Smell: And Taste and Feel and See and Hear.* New York: DK Publishing.

Pinderhughes, John. (1997). *My Five Senses: A Shape Little Nugget Book.* New York: Golden Press.

Pinkney, Andrea. (1997). *I Smell Honey.* New York: Red Wagon.

Royston, Angela. (1993). *The Senses.* (A Lift-the-flap body book.) Illustrated by Edwina Riddell. New York: Barron's Juveniles.

Ruis, Maria, Jose M. Parramon, and J. J. Puig. (1985). *Smell.* New York: Barrons Juvenile.

Shappie, Trisha Lee. (1997). *Where Is Your Nose?: A Peekaboo Book with Flaps and a Mirror!* Illustrated by Judith Moffatt. New York: Cartwheel Books.

Suhr, Mandy. (1994). *Smell.* Illustrated by Mike Gordon. Mineapolis, MN: Carolrhoda Books.

Parent Letter (Preschool)

Dear Parents,

We are beginning our new theme Smelling, as we continue studying the Five Senses. The children will learn:
- How the five senses bring us information about our world.
- The nose is the part of the body used to smell.
- The sense of smell helps us find out about odors and warns us of danger.
- We should take care of our noses.
- Some people do not have a strong sense of smell or sense of taste.

We will be talking about:
- the nose and parts of the nose: nostrils, bridge, and tip
- what smelling helps us do
- how we take care of our nose
- what we smell

Things to do at home to reinforce your child's school activities include:
- Make popcorn.
- Let your child smell the cologne, perfume, or shaving lotion used at your house.
- Talk about the different smells while you cook.

Parent participation opportunities at school will be:
- Come make green eggs with us.
  Date _____ Time _____
- Come grind corn with us.
  Date _____ Time _____

The wish list for this theme is:
paper sacks
tissue paper
index cards
newspapers
empty, clean baby food jars

Thank you for your special friendship.

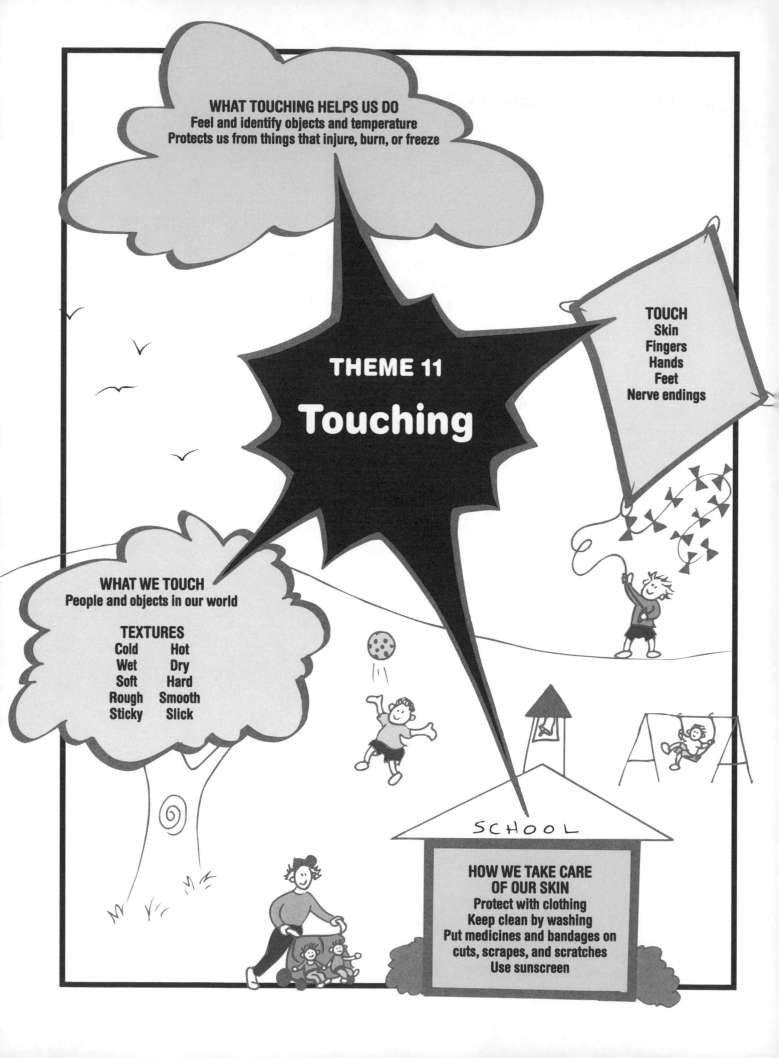

WHAT TOUCHING HELPS US DO
Feel and identify objects and temperature
Protects us from things that injure, burn, or freeze

THEME 11
Touching

TOUCH
Skin
Fingers
Hands
Feet
Nerve endings

WHAT WE TOUCH
People and objects in our world

TEXTURES
Cold   Hot
Wet   Dry
Soft   Hard
Rough   Smooth
Sticky Slick

SCHOOL

HOW WE TAKE CARE
OF OUR SKIN
Protect with clothing
Keep clean by washing
Put medicines and bandages on
cuts, scrapes, and scratches
Use sunscreen

THEME GOALS

To provide opportunities for children to learn:

1. How the five senses help us every day.

2. The skin is the part of the body that gives us our sense of touch.

3. We usually use our fingers to touch and identify things.

4. Our skin protects us and keeps us safe by telling us when things are too hot, if we are too cold, or if we are hurt.

5. We should take care of our skin.

Children-Created Bulletin Board

This bulletin board builds on the ones developed for the four senses presented in Themes 7, 8, 9, and 10.

✳ Add two large hands to the bulletin board. Place one on the bottom left and the other on the bottom right.

✳ Put the words "Please Touch!" on the board.

✳ Attach various textures to the burlap already in place, such as rough sandpaper, smooth plastic, sticky tape, contact paper, soft fabric and cotton balls, and small pieces of wood.

✳ Add more things as the children become involved with activities related to this theme.

Vocabulary Starters

Let the children add additional words.

touch — to feel things through your skin.

skin — the outer covering of our body.

feel — to be able to notice things with our skin.

temperature — how hot or cold something is.

texture — what the outside of something feels like.

Language Experiences

WORD DESCRIPTIONS

✳ Start the children thinking about the sense of touch and how to use words to describe how things feel. For example: soft like a pillow, hard like a rock, smooth like a mirror, rough like sandpaper, wet like water, dry like sand, cold like an ice cube, and hot like a bright light bulb.

✳ Accept whatever words the children use. The objective is to get them associating words with the sense of touch.

✳ Add to this activity. Fill several large plastic tubs with cotton balls, gravel, sand, birdseed, carpet pieces, and rice.

✳ Place these tubs next to each other in a line.

✳ Have the children walk from one tub to another with their *bare feet*.

✳ If some children do not want to take off their shoes, ask if they would like to use their hands to touch instead of their feet.

✳ As they walk, ask them to describe how each texture feels.

✳ Later, they can create pictures to further express their feelings about the experience.

BIG BOOK

This culminating activity helps the children assimilate what they have learned about their five senses. The project provides opportunities for the children to plan, reflect on, and review their learning experiences.

✳ Create a class Big Book on the senses.

✳ The children should be the decision makers on what goes into the book.

✳ With their input, design a cover and a table of contents. How many pages should there be for each one of the senses? How should the children's drawings and dictated words be incorporated into the book? Should they create new content?

Dramatic Play

HOT POTATO

This game can be played inside or outdoors, with the children sitting or standing in a circle.

✳ Give them a lightweight beanbag. This can be stuffed with newspaper, small Styrofoam packing pieces, wadded balls of newspaper, or tissue paper instead of beans.

✳ Pretend the beanbag is a "hot potato."

✳ As it is passed to the children, they quickly toss it to someone else.

"PLEASE TOUCH" STORE

✳ With the children's help, make the dramatic play area a special place by putting up a sign that says "Welcome to the Touch Store! Please touch everything!"

✳ Label the areas with signs that say "Soft," "Hard," "Rough," "Smooth," "Sticky," "Prickly," and other texture words.

✳ Let the children explore the classroom. When they find something that belongs in an area of the "store," they bring it there.

✳ Be sure to have unique items placed around the room so that the children have fresh things to examine.

✳ The children may find that they need more space to expand the store. Be prepared to open the classroom even more.

Puppet Play

HUMPTY DUMPTY

This puppet can be made by you and your preschoolers. Primary-grade children can make the puppets to give to the younger children to enjoy.

✳ Place cardboard or tagboard sheets, sandpaper, construction paper, yarn, ribbon, markers, and crayons on a table.

✳ Have the children draw an egg-shaped Humpty Dumpty sitting on a sandpaper wall.

✳ Cut two holes for the children to place two fingers in the puppet. The fingers become Humpty's legs.

✳ It is fun for the children to sing or say the nursery rhyme while playing with their puppet.

✳ They like to place Humpty in other situations besides falling off the wall.

✳ They may suggest making more nursery rhyme puppets. Have plenty of materials available so that they can continue to create puppets.

Music

A MUSICAL GAME

The object of this activity is to encourage the children to imagine objects of different sizes, shapes, and textures, and sing a song at the same time.

✳ Each verse of the song presented in this activity suggests picking up a different type of object.

✳ As the song is sung, the children can walk around the play area, indoors or outdoors, while picking up imaginary objects and putting them in imaginary baskets.

✳ Give toddlers actual little baskets and ask them to walk around and put things in their baskets while you sing. Put out small blocks and toys for them to pick up.

✳ The song is sung to the tune of "Paw-Paw Patch." This is a traditional song with some new words added. You may want to explain to the children that paw-paws are a small, brown podlike fruit named by Native Americans. They do not taste very good, but early settlers in the eastern part of the United States ate them as food.

Let's take a walk and look around.
Let's take a walk and look around.
Let's take a walk and look around
Way down yonder in the paw-paw patch.
  Picking up paw-paws, put 'em in a basket.
  Picking up paw-paws, put 'em in a basket.
  Picking up paw-paws, put 'em in a basket
  Way down yonder in the paw-paw patch.
Find a little feather and put it in my basket.
Find a little feather and put it in my basket.
Find a little feather and put it in my basket.
Way down yonder in the paw-paw patch.
  Find a wiggly worm and put it in my basket, etc.
Find a big rock and put it in my basket, etc.
  Find a cute bunny and put it in my basket, etc.
Find an ice cube and put it in my basket, etc.
  Find a little bug and put it in my basket, etc.

Movement

WATER PLAY RELAY

✳ Divide the children into two equal groups for this outdoor activity.

✳ Have each group form a line and stand at least six feet from the other group.

✳ Give the first child in each line a small plastic bucket full of water.

✳ At the other side of the play area, draw a line on the ground that each child must run to and cross before returning with the bucket and handing it to the next child in line.

✳ At a signal to start, the first child in line runs to the line and back, taking care not to spill the water. If the bucket is prematurely emptied, the game is over. Time to start a new one.

✳ Each returning child hands the bucket off to the next child until all children have run with the bucket to the line and back.

✳ The object of the game, in addition to being the first to finish, is to try and complete the game without spilling the water.

✳ After playing this once, the children can make up their own rules.

TEXTURE WALK

This is an extension of the Word Descriptions activity in the language experiences section of this theme.

✳ Collect all kinds of texture squares, such as carpet samples, doormats, packing materials, linoleum and wooden floor tiles, foam rubber cushions or pillows, and artificial grass.

✳ Take the squares and line them up to make a textured walk.

✳ Have the children take off their shoes and socks, and put them in their cubbies.

✳ The children take turns walking along the textured squares and describing what they feel with their bare feet.

✳ They can walk forward, sideways, backward, and on tiptoe. Older children can experiment with other ways of getting across the textured walk.

✳ To vary the activity, put on a record, cassette, or CD, and ask the children to take a texture walk while "moving to the music."

✳ Put the texture walk in an out-of-the-way space in the room or on the playground, and leave it there for the duration of the theme so that the children can return to it often.

✳ Primary-grade children can work with a partner and think up additional uses for the texture walk.

Sensory Art

LET'S TOUCH

Infants and toddlers learn by touching things and exploring them with their mouths as well.

✳ Give an infant a small paper bag or a piece of brown wrapping paper, and watch all the sensory exploration that occurs.

✳ For toddlers, make a touch bag for each child by placing five or six items in a large paper bag, such as a soft stuffed animal, a feather, a washcloth, a piece of wood, and a rubber ball.

✳ Ask the children to reach inside their bags and, without looking, guess what the objects are. Ask them to name them. You supply the words if they cannot.

✳ Continue this activity, also asking them such questions as, "Does it feel soft?" "Does it feel rough?"

"Does it feel round?" Helping the children discover appropriate words encourages language development.

✳ Leave the bags on a table so that the children can return to them whenever they wish.

MAKE TEXTURE BOXES

There are several ways to create a sensory touch box for toddlers.

Individual Texture Boxes

✳ Make several individual boxes using shoe boxes.

✳ Let the children help you make these by gluing different things inside each box. For example, use sandpaper, scraps of fabric, yarn, feathers, pieces of fur, and leather.

✳ Leave enough room so that other items the children find can be added. Some of these are leaves, flowers, and sticks.

Group Texture Box

✳ Using an appliance box, at least three to four feet square, is another way to create a texture box.

✳ Put several pounds of sand or gravel in the bottom of the box to stabilize it.

✳ Close the box and tape down the flaps securely.

✳ Ask the children to join you in painting the box.

✳ Glue or tape (with double-sided tape) various materials onto the box. Use items that have tactile and three-dimensional qualities; i.e., egg cartons, cotton balls, thread spools, several small nonbreakable mirrors, bells, foil, string, yarn, and other items suggested by the children.

LET'S TOUCH AND MATCH

✳ Precut two pieces of each of the following articles: sandpaper, foil, corrugated cardboard, sponges, silk, corduroy, leather, lace, wallpaper, washcloths, butcher paper, and construction paper.

* Gather two of the following: craft sticks, feathers, plastic tops from food containers, hair curlers, golf balls, and bells.

* Separate the textured pairs by putting one mate in a paper bag numbered 1 and the other in a paper bag marked 2, or A and B.

* For younger children, use fewer pairs.

* Ask one child to reach into bag 1 without looking and pull out an item.

* Have the same child reach into bag 2, again without looking, and try to find the matching piece using her sense of touch.

* If a child misses the match, reassure him or her that it's all right. There will be another turn later.

* Continue going around the circle until each child has had a turn to guess correctly.

Creative Food Experiences

MARSHMALLOWS AND COCONUT TREAT

You will need:

    large marshmallows

    shredded coconut

1. Wash hands.

2. Sprinkle coconut on a long sheet of wax paper.

3. You place marshmallows in a slotted spoon, and dip them quickly into a pot of hot water that is well out of reach of the children.

4. Place the slightly cooled marshmallows on the long strip of wax paper covered with coconut.

5. Let the children roll the marshmallows in the coconut, and then place the coated marshmallows on another piece of wax paper to dry.

6. Enjoy!

NO COOK ORANGE COOKIES

You will need:

    30 to 40 vanilla wafers

    1/4 cup orange juice

    2 tablespoons granulated sugar

    powdered sugar

1. Wash hands.

2. Divide the children into small groups. Each group has a specific task to complete.

3. Place vanilla wafers in a plastic zip-top bag, and crush with a rolling pin until finely crumbled. The children can take turns with the rolling pin.

4. Put the crumbs in a large bowl, and add the sugar and orange juice.

5. Mix well.

6. Roll into balls with moistened hands.

7. In a separate bowl, roll balls in powdered sugar. Place on wax paper.

8. If mixture is too sticky, add more vanilla wafers.

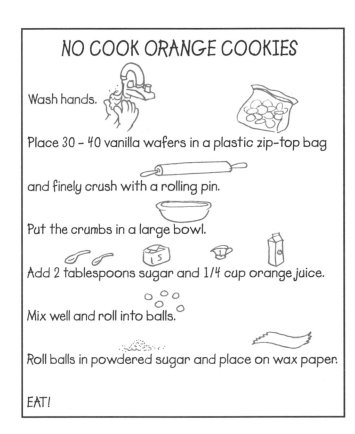

NO COOK ORANGE COOKIES

Wash hands.

Place 30 – 40 vanilla wafers in a plastic zip-top bag and finely crush with a rolling pin.

Put the crumbs in a large bowl.

Add 2 tablespoons sugar and 1/4 cup orange juice.

Mix well and roll into balls.

Roll balls in powdered sugar and place on wax paper.

EAT!

Math

FINE MOTOR TOUCH

When children play this math game of putting the correct number of objects into numbered compartments, they develop one-to-one correspondence recognition and fine motor skills.

* Save egg cartons.

* In the bottom of each egg compartment, write a numeral with a permanent marker.

* Place several of these numeral recognition egg cartons in the math center with small plastic

tongs and dried beans, small buttons, or pennies. The tongs usually are available in the science section of educational products stores.

✳ Encourage the children to use the tongs to place the correct number of beans, buttons, or pennies in the numbered spaces, and to return them to their original containers.

BUTTON, BUTTON, WHO'S GOT THE BUTTON?

Keep a large plastic jar or other container with a lid filled with buttons of many sizes, colors, and shapes. Many parents and family members usually have loose, mismatched buttons around the house. Ask them to contribute some.

✳ Place the button jar in the math or manipulative center.

✳ The children can count, sort, classify, make collages, and match the buttons.

✳ For younger children, use only large-size buttons.

✳ Older children enjoy tossing the buttons into plastic containers and paper cups and counting how many they get into the container.

✳ The buttons can provide the children with a meaningful activity to occupy them when bad weather cancels their outdoor time.

Science

IMAGINOLOGY

The focus of this concept is that children like to do new things with familiar materials. This helps to encourage problem-solving, imaginative thinking, and creativity. Many items around the classroom can be used for this activity.

✳ The children may work individually or with partners. Ask the children to think about and then describe all the things they can do with the following, one item at a time:

a piece of string or a ball of string

a box	egg cartons
paper sacks	wrapping paper
sandpaper	envelopes
straws	craft sticks

✳ The children will think of more items. Support their ideas by giving them unlimited time, materials, supplies, and plenty of space in which to develop unique creations.

Social Studies

THE BRAILLE ALPHABET

✳ Discuss with the class different ways we communicate with others, such as written words, spoken words, nonverbal reactions, body language, and sign language.

✳ Introduce them to Braille, which is a system of letters and numbers communicated through touch.

✳ Explain that instead of words and letters printed on a page or in a book, Braille letters and numbers are "bumps" on a page.

✳ Ask someone from one of the local associations or services for visually impaired children and adults to visit your class. This person usually can bring copies of the Braille alphabet to show the children.

✳ You may obtain a card with the alphabet and numbers in Braille at no cost by sending a postcard to the American Foundation for the Blind, 15 West 16th Street, New York, NY 10011.

GO ON A FIELD TRIP

✳ Visit a fabric or carpet store by yourself first to arrange a special time for the field trip and to be sure the store is appropriate for young children to visit. Ask the store manager if the children may take a collection of carpet samples back to school.

✳ It is important the people be available at the store to show the children many textures they can touch.

✳ Suggest that the individuals set up a special area in the store with preselected materials to share with the group.

✳ Allow enough time for the children to ask questions and talk to the salespersons.

✳ Follow up by sending thank-you notes from the class.

✳ Encourage the children to talk about the experience, draw pictures, and dictate stories about it.

Children's Books

Harlow, Rockwell. (1987). *The Touch Me Book.* New York: Golden Books.

Hill, Eric. (1997). *Spot's Touch and Feel Day.* New York: Putnam Publishers.

Isadora, Rachel. (1991). *I Touch.* New York: Greenwillow.

Johnson, Audean. (1982). *Soft as a Kitten.* (Board book). New York: Random House.

Kunhardt, Dorothy, and Edith Kunhardt. (1993). *Pat the Puppy.* New York: Golden Press.

Kunhardt, Dorothy, and Edith Kunhardt. (1990). *Pat the Bunny.* (Board book). New York: Golden Press.

Muntean, Michaela. (1996). *Elmo Can . . . Taste! Touch! Smell! See! Hear!* Illustrated by Maggie Swanson. New York: Golden Books and Children's Television Workshop.

Otto, Carolyn B. (1994). *I Can Tell by Touching.* Illustrated by Nadine Bernard Westcott. New York: HarperTrophy.

Oxenbury, Helen. (1995). *I Touch.* (Board book). Cambridge, MA: Candlewick Press.

Rose, Julian, and Molly Perham. (1993). *Feel and Touch!* San Francisco, CA: Children's Press.

Wood, Nicholas. (1991). *Touch . . . What Do You Feel?* Mahwah, NJ: Troll Associates.

Parent Letter (School-age)

Dear Parents,

We are studying the last of the Five Senses. Our theme is Touching. The children will learn:
- How the five senses help us every day.
- The skin is the part of the body that gives us our sense of touch.
- We usually use our fingers to touch and identify things.
- Our skin protects us and keeps us safe by letting us know when things are too hot or cold or if we are hurt.
- We should take care of our skin.

We will be talking about:
- our skin and nerve endings
- what touching helps us do
- how we take care of our skin
- what we touch

Things to do at home with your child are:
- Talk about what is going on in the classroom.
- Encourage your child to investigate the textures around the house and yard.
- Use word descriptions of how things feel when you and your child touch various surfaces.
- Let your child share cooking experiences with you. It is important for the child to make something and contribute to family meals.

Join us for parent participation opportunities at school:
- Visit our classroom any time to see what we have been creating and discovering.
- Join us for our field trip to the fabric or carpet store.
    Date _____ Time _____

Our wish list for this theme is:

egg cartons

straws

wrapping paper

buttons of all shapes, sizes, and colors

sandpaper

thread spools

rolling pins

Thank you for being part of our class family.

SECTION III

Seasons

Young children are active learners. They enter into what-ever they do with spontaneity and energy. The seasons of the year and young children are easily connected. Both are filled with the rhythms and energy of life. The thematic activities in this section offer children opportunities to grow and learn while actively enjoying the rhythms of the changing seasons.

The activities are easily adaptable to large group, small group, or individual instruction. This allows the children to learn at their own pace and style.

The following themes are included in Section III — Seasons:

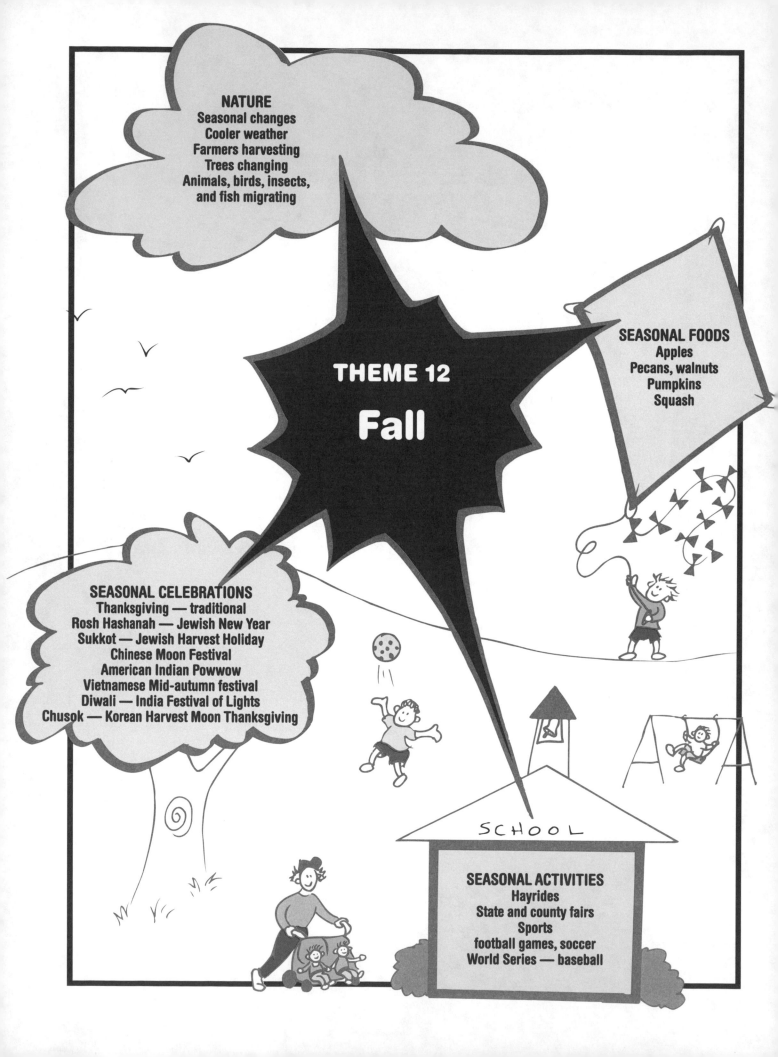

NATURE
Seasonal changes
Cooler weather
Farmers harvesting
Trees changing
Animals, birds, insects,
and fish migrating

THEME 12

Fall

SEASONAL FOODS
Apples
Pecans, walnuts
Pumpkins
Squash

SEASONAL CELEBRATIONS
Thanksgiving — traditional
Rosh Hashanah — Jewish New Year
Sukkot — Jewish Harvest Holiday
Chinese Moon Festival
American Indian Powwow
Vietnamese Mid-autumn festival
Diwali — India Festival of Lights
Chusok — Korean Harvest Moon Thanksgiving

SCHOOL

SEASONAL ACTIVITIES
Hayrides
State and county fairs
Sports
football games, soccer
World Series — baseball

THEME GOALS

To provide opportunities for children to learn:

1. Fall is a season of the year that comes after summer and before winter.
2. Fall is the time of year that has many changes in nature, such as shorter days and longer nights.
3. In the fall, many birds and some animals, fish, and insects migrate to warmer climates.
4. The leaves of trees may change color, and many trees lose all their leaves.
5. Fall weather becomes cooler, and we start wearing warmer clothing.

Children-Created Bulletin Board

The children will be active participants in making this bulletin board for the fall theme. The board will change to reflect what happens during each season.

✳ Cover the entire board with pale blue, pink, or green paper. This becomes the background for all four season themes.

✳ With the children's help, cut out a tree trunk from corrugated paper, or crumple paper bags to form a tree trunk.

✳ Staple the trunk to the bulletin board. Add tree branches with black or brown crayons or markers.

✳ Trace each child's hand on medium green construction paper.

✳ Have each child cut out the hand shape and place it where a leaf would be on the tree.

✳ As the leaves on real trees start changing color, place individual water color tablets of yellow, orange, red, or brown on a tray. You can usually push out the tablets from watercolor paint sets available at most stores.

✳ The children, a few at a time, dip their index fingers into a small glass of water. Each child then selects a color and rubs the finger on a paint tablet. The more they rub, the more colorful their prints will be.

✳ Their paint-loaded fingers are then used to make "fingerprint leaves" all over the tree branches, on the ground, or blowing in the wind.

✳ Collect fallen leaves from a walk around the neighborhood, and glue these onto the bulletin board.

✳ At Thanksgiving time, write what each child is thankful for on colored leaf shapes, and add these to the fall scene.

✳ When the class focuses on planting, growing, and harvesting apples, have the children turn the tree into an apple tree. October is Apple Month.

Vocabulary Starters

Let the children add additional words.

fall — one of the four parts of the year.

autumn — another name for fall, the season that comes after summer and before winter.

temperature — hotness or coldness of anything.

migration — the movement of birds, fish, and butterflies from one place to another.

harvest — the gathering of ripe grains, fruits, and vegetables from farms, gardens, and orchards.

orchard — a large piece of land where fruit trees are grown.

Language Experiences

SOUNDS ALL AROUND

✳ Have interesting sounds in the environment for infants.

✳ Hum, sing, and talk to them when you are changing their diapers, feeding them, and holding them.

✳ Respond to their "talking" sounds.

✳ Musical toys, musical mobiles, and the voices of adults and other children are important to infants.

✳ Have picture books to share with an individual child.

✳ Each child should be able to interact with the book as well. This means holding, touching, and chewing the book.

✳ Select board books that encourage this interaction, as well as presenting rhythmic language, rhymes, chants, and songs. Here are some suggestions:

Ahlberg, Allan, and Janet Ahlberg. (1981). *Peek-a-Boo*. New York: Viking.

Brown, Margaret Wise. (First board book edition, 1991). *Goodnight Moon*. Illustrated by Clement Hurd. New York: HarperCollins.

Hathon, Elizabeth. (1993). *Soft as a Kitten*. New York: Grossett & Dunlap.

Kemp, Moira. (1987). *Pat-a-Cake*. Los Angeles, CA: Price Stern Sloan.

Titherington, Jeanne. (1990). *Pumpkin, Pumpkin*. New York: Mulberry.

THE LITTLE RED HEN

Retelling stories using a flannelboard helps the children sequence a story, repeat the language of the story, and dramatize concepts.

* Read the story of *The Little Red Hen.* Four versions are listed in the books section of this theme.

* Ask the children to help you retell the story with the flannelboard characters you have made. Use felt or nonwoven interfacing, found at a fabric store, to make the characters.

* After repeating the story, place the flannelboard and character pieces in any activity center or curriculum area.

* Flannelboard figures can be touched, held, and moved, thus helping the children move between real and abstract.

POEM: "Fall"

Where did the summer go?
First it was hot, but now it's so cool.
We were on vacation, but now we're in school.
Where did the green go?
First plants looked green as green plants could be.
Now they look brown, red, and yellow to me.
Where did the leaves go?
The trees and their branches had leaves all around.
Oh my, now they're falling all over the ground.
What's going on here?
I think that I've figured out what's happening here.
It's what they call "Fall." It's that time of the year.

Philip Jackman

Dramatic Play

"A" IS FOR APPLE AND "P" IS FOR PUMPKIN

If possible, visit a farmer's market or the produce section of a grocery store with the children. Turn the homeliving/dramatic play area into a produce stand. This can be accomplished indoors and continued outdoors as a "drive-up" market stand.

* Collect recycled paper grocery bags and fruit baskets.

* Add aprons, a toy cash register, a scale, and real or plastic apples, pumpkins, onions, corn, squash, and nuts.

* Make one side of the produce stand into a "pumpkin patch."

* Add corn stalks, hay bales, straw hats, a scarecrow, and plenty of real pumpkins and gourds. Let the children make the scarecrow.

* Give the children an opportunity to investigate all of these items firsthand.

Puppet Play

IT'S A TURKEY!

Introduce the children to this activity by showing pictures of turkeys and reading books, such as Arnosky's *All About Turkeys,* listed in the books section of this theme.

* For children who are interested in making puppets, use the same approach used in making some of the leaves for the bulletin board.

* Invite the children to trace around their hands on brown wrapping paper or construction paper.

* If needed, help the toddlers and young preschoolers who want to do this activity.

* Have the children cut out the hands.

* The thumb becomes the turkey's face, and the four fingers become the turkey's back.

✳ Add paper, real feathers, or anything else the children decide that will personalize their puppets.

✳ Attach a craft stick to make a puppet.

✳ Give the children time to explore the materials and their puppets.

SCARECROW PUPPET

✳ Make materials available so the children can make scarecrow hand puppets from two pieces of felt or other fabric cut to fit the child's hand.

✳ Glue or sew the two pieces together.

✳ Eyes, nose, mouth, ears, hair, and hat can be attached with Velcro or glue.

✳ Use straw for hair and extra decoration. Straw can usually be found at craft stores.

✳ The children can use their puppets in the dramatic play areas as well.

Music

"PICKING APPLES"

This is a rhythm activity appropriate for all ages of children. It encourages them to play with the *rhythm of language*.

Let's go find an apple tree,
Fiddle-dee-dum and fiddle-dee-dee.
There's a nice one. Let me see —
Fiddle-dee-dum and fiddle-dee-dee.
Lots of apples, let's pick some,
Fiddle-dee-dee and fiddle-dee-dum.
I'll pick an apple, and you pick one,
Fiddle-dee-dee and fiddle-dee-dum.
Let's pick more, how about two?
Fiddle-dee-dum and fiddle-dee-doo.
That's not enough. How about three?
Fiddle-dee-doo and fiddle-dee-dee.
Now we've enough for you and me,
Fiddle-dee-dum and fiddle-dee-dee.

Philip Jackman

"OATS, PEAS, BEANS, AND BARLEY GROW"

This traditional song has been passed down from one group of children to the next. Perhaps some of the verses will be new to you and your children. It is fun for the children to act out the words as they are singing.

Chorus:

Oats, peas, beans, and barley grow,
Oats, peas, beans, and barley grow,
Can you or I or anyone know
How oats, peas, beans, and barley grow?

Verse:

First the farmer sows the seed,
Stands erect and rests with ease,
He stamps his foot and claps his hands,
And turns around to view his lands.

Chorus:

Oats, peas, beans, and barley grow,
Oats, peas, beans, and barley grow,
Can you or I or anyone know
How oats, peas, beans, and barley grow?

Verse:

Next the farmer waters the seed,
Stands erect and rests with ease,
He stamps his foot and claps his hands,
And turns around to view his lands.

Repeat chorus.

Verse:

Next the farmer hoes the weeds,

Repeat the rest of the verse.

Repeat chorus.

Verse:

Last the farmer harvests the seed,

Repeat the rest of the verse.

Repeat chorus.

Movement

LEAF DANCING

Play recorded instrumental music in the background as the children move around, acting out the words to the poem. Ask them to help you make up other verses and actions.

Like a leaf or feather,
in the windy, windy weather,
we'll whirl around and twirl around,
and all fall down together.
Like the birds covered in feathers,
in the windy, windy weather,
we'll fly around and twirl around,
and feel the wind together.

Sensory Art

LET'S TEAR

This activity helps the children with small muscle development and hand-eye coordination. This also gives them a sense of autonomy within appropriate boundaries.

✳ Have children who are interested tear small pieces of tissue and construction paper and glue them onto pumpkin shapes.

✳ Let them make as many pumpkins as they want.

✳ Leave the materials out and let them come back to the table whenever they want to do so.

COLLECT FALL LEAVES

✳ With the children, collect fall leaves.

✳ Dry them. Pressing leaves in an old telephone book for several days works well.

✳ Toddlers and preschoolers enjoy crumbling up the dried leaves. Place these on a tray.

✳ Put glue out in small containers along with small brushes or cotton swabs for the children to use to spread glue on construction paper.

✳ The children can create pictures with the dried leaves by experimenting with the materials and random placement of the leaves.

✳ Let the pictures dry flat.

PARTNER COLLAGE

✳ Guide the children, each with a partner or in a small group, into making a tree, pumpkin, apple, or fall sports collage.

✳ Place magazines, calendars, colored tissue paper, posterboard, construction paper, glue, scissors, yarn, and fabric scraps out for the children to use.

✳ Working cooperatively, let them decide what they want their collage to be and how it should look.

✳ Ask the children to title their collages and write the names at the top.

Creative Food Experiences

IT LOOKS LIKE A PUMPKIN FACE

You will need:

English muffins (enough for each child to have one-half)

spreadable orange colored cheese spread

vegetables cut into slices and pieces (celery, carrots, black olives, green peppers)

1. Wash hands.

2. Spread orange colored cheese spread over an English muffin half.

3. Add various vegetables to make silly faces.

LET'S MAKE APPLESAUCE

You will need:

    6 apples
    1/2 cup water
    1/8 teaspoon cinnamon
    1 teaspoon lemon juice
    sugar to taste

1. Wash hands.
2. Peel apples. Remove core from each apple.
3. Cut up the apples and add water, sugar, and lemon juice.
4. Put apple mixture in a pan, cover, and cook until tender on medium heat, approximately 15 to 20 minutes.
5. Add cinnamon.
6. Mash apples with a fork or potato masher, or press through a colander.
7. Serve and eat!

LET'S MAKE APPLE SAUCE!

Wash hands.

Peel 6 apples. Remove core from each apple.

Cut up the apples and add 1/2 cup water,

sugar to taste, and 1 teaspoon lemon juice.

Put in a pan, cover, and cook until tender on a

medium heat. Add 1/8 teaspoon cinnamon.

Mash apples with a fork or potato masher or

press through a colander.

Serve and eat!

JOHNNY APPLESEED DAY (SEPTEMBER)

Here is another "apple" idea for the children on a fall day.

✳ Warm some apple cider in a crock pot and serve for snack.

✳ Talk about how it tastes and smells.

Math

SHOE BOX FOREST

✳ Cover a shoe box with wood-patterned contact paper. Cover the lid *and* the bottom of the box.

✳ Place slits in the box. The number of slits depends on the developmental stage of the children.

✳ For toddlers, use large tongue depressors with leaves drawn or pasted on them.

✳ Let each child insert the "tree sticks" and take them out. Use words to go with the actions, such as, "You're putting the sticks *in* the box." "Now you're taking the sticks *out* of the box."

✳ Step back and let the children play with this math game.

✳ With preschoolers, make slits in the top of the box and write numerals from 1 to 10 under each slit.

✳ Make craft sticks into trees by adding green tree-top shapes glued to each stick.

✳ Put dots on the trees that correspond to each slit in the box.

✳ The children match the tree with the number of dots on it to the slit on the box with that numeral.

✳ Put the tree sticks into a resealable plastic bag, and store them in the bottom of the shoe box. When the children are through playing with this math game, they just place the pieces into the bag, put them into the box, and put the lid on.

MATCH THE APPLE SEEDS

✳ Take an ordinary file folder, open it, and draw an apple on the right side.

✳ The apple can be bright red, yellow, or green. See the science section of this theme for information about different types of apples. You many decide to make several folder games.

* Divide the apple into puzzle parts, and number them from 1 to 9.

* On the cover of the file folder, write "Apple Seeds."

* Laminate the file folder.

* Draw another apple exactly the same, except place this apple on a piece of tagboard. Divide this apple into puzzle parts, and place apple seeds on each piece, numbering from 1 to 9. Outline each puzzle piece in black (see illustration).

* Laminate the apple.

* Cut the apple into the puzzle slices you have previously marked.

* Place pieces into a resealable plastic bag and staple or glue to the back of the folder.

* Place the folder game in the math or manipulative center for the children to discover.

Science

APPLE VARIETIES

Introduce the children to the many kinds of apples and how they are grown. Introduce toddlers to the different kinds of apples by preparing a tasting tray. Show them the actual whole apples before cutting them. It is important for the children to see, touch, smell, and taste real apples. Show them pictures of an apple tree.

* An individual apple tree may grow to be forty feet high and live more than a hundred years.

* Each tree begins with one small seed.

* Read Micucci's *The Life and Times of the Apple,* Gibbons' *The Seasons of Arnolds's Apple Tree,* and Aliki's *The Story of Johnny Appleseed* to the children. These are listed in the books section of this theme.

* Bring several kinds of apples to class for the children to *see, smell, feel,* and *taste.* They can even *hear* an apple when they take a bite.

* Some varieties of apples are:

  Red Delicious — sweet and juicy, eat fresh

  Golden Delicious — good in pies or eat fresh

  McIntosh — make applesauce or eat fresh

  Winesap — good for cider or eat fresh

  Granny Smith — tart taste, use in pies, or eat fresh

  Jonathan   use in pies or eat fresh

  Rome — nice size for baking or eat fresh

* Have the children help you make a list of the many uses of the apple, including apple vinegar, apple bread, and apple butter. Add this list to the bulletin board.

THE SEASONS OF THE APPLE TREE

* Introduce the children to the life cycle of the apple tree.

* Give each child a large piece of paper and crayons or markers.

✳ Guide them into dividing their paper into fourths, one section for each season of the year.

✳ Write the name of a season in each section.

✳ Have them draw an apple tree as it looks in each season. They can use the books about apples for reference. In winter, the tree has bare branches and tiny buds at the end of each branch; in spring, the tree has small green leaves and apple blossoms; in summer, the tree has leaves and small green apples; and in fall, the tree has big apples on the branches and on the ground.

✳ The children can create other things that are happening, such as honeybees flying around the blossoms in the spring and people picking the apples in the fall.

Social Studies

CHINESE MOON FESTIVAL

✳ The Chinese hold a festival in September to celebrate the harvest of crops. Since there is a full moon around harvest time, they call the celebration the **Moon Festival.** This is similar to the American tradition of Thanksgiving.

✳ Moon Cakes (round, yellow cakes filled with red bean paste and sesame seeds, or fruits, nuts, and spices) are enjoyed by everyone during this time of year.

✳ The Moon Cake symbolizes the moon and family unity.

✳ Perhaps one of the children in your classroom has a family member who would visit and share how the Chinese Moon Festival is celebrated in her family.

✳ Serve Moon Cakes to the children. These are available at bakeries or grocery stores that sell Asian food.

SUKKOT

✳ **Sukkot** (sŏŏ-koat) is the Jewish harvest festival celebrated in the fall.

✳ During the holiday a sukkah (sŏŏ-kah), a small hut or booth, is built in the courtyard of a Jewish temple or synagogue by the members of the congregation, or in individual family backyards. These

structures remind Jewish people of the booths lived in by their ancestors in the desert.

✳ The sukkah is covered with evergreen boughs, palm fronds, or tree branches. The children decorate it with flowers, fruits, and vegetables.

✳ This is a happy festival. Families visit the sukkah and share the fruits of the harvest.

✳ Plan a field trip to visit a Jewish temple or synagogue during the holiday of Sukkot. This gives the children an opportunity to learn about another festival of Thanksgiving.

POWWOW

✳ A **Powwow** is another tradition that takes place in the fall. This is an important experience for many American Indian tribes.

✳ Some Powwows and other ceremonies are also held during the year by tribes throughout the United States.

✳ This occasion brings tribes and families together.

✳ Food, singing, drums, and dancing are all part of the Powwow.

✳ The dancers wear colorful feathers just as their ancestors did. This is a time when ancient traditions are passed from one generation to another.

✳ Invite a family or community individual to visit the class and share the music, drums, or costumes that are part of the Powwow.

✳ Visit your local library or bookstore for further information.

Children's Books

Aliki. (1963). *The Story of Johnny Appleseed.* New York: Aladdin.

Aronosky, Jim. (1998). *All About Turkeys.* New York: Scholastic.

Behn, Harry. (1992). *Trees: A Poem.* Illustrated by James Endicott. New York: Henry Holt.

Berg, Jean H. (1962). *The Little Red Hen.* Illustrated by Mel Pekarsky. Chicago, IL: Follett Publishing.

Birdwell, Norman. (1997). *Clifford's Thanksgiving Visit.* New York: Scholastic.

Bunting, Eve. (1988). *How Many Days to America? A Thanksgiving Story.* Illustrated by Beth Peck. New York: Clarion Books.

Carle, Eric. (1987). *The Tiny Seed.* Saxonville, MA: Picture Book.

Chanin, Michael, and Sally Smith. (1994). *Grandfather Four Winds and Rising Moon.* New York: Starseed Press.

Ehlert, Lois. (1991). *Red Leaf, Yellow Leaf.* San Diego, CA: Harcourt Brace.

Galdone, Paul. (1973). *The Little Red Hen.* Boston, MA: Houghton Mifflin.

George, Lindsay B. (1995). *In the Woods: Who's Been Here?* New York: Greenwillow.

Gibbons, Gail. (1984). *The Seasons of Arnold's Apple Tree.* San Diego, CA: Harcourt Brace.

Golden, Barbara Diamond. (1995). *Night Lights: A Sukkot Story.* San Diego, CA: Harcourt Brace.

Golden, Barbara Diamond. (1995). *The World's Birthday: A Rosh Hashanah Story.* San Diego, CA: Harcourt Brace.

Hall, Zoe. (1994). *It's Pumpkin Time.* Illustrated by Shari Halpern. New York: Scholastic.

Howe, James, and E. Young. (1994). *I Wish I Were a Butterfly.* San Diego, CA: Harcourt Brace.

Kalman, Bobbie. (1997). *Celebrating the Powwow.* New York: Crabtree Publishing.

Maass, Robert. (1992). *When Autumn Comes.* New York: Henry Holt.

Marzollo, Jean. (1997). *I Am an Apple.* Illustrated by Judith Moffatt. New York: Scholastic.

McQueen, Lucinda. (1995). *The Little Red Hen/La Gallinita Roja.* New York: Scholastic.

Micucci, Charles. (1992). *The Life and Times of the Apple.* New York: Orchard Books.

Muller, Gerda. (1995). *Circle of Seasons.* New York: Dutton.

Rendon, Marcie R. (1996). *Powwow Summer: A Family Celebrates the Circle of Life.* Minneapolis, MN: Carolrhoda Books.

Rius, Maria, U. Wensel, and Jose M. Parramon. (1998). *Fall (The Four Seasons).* New York: Barrons Juveniles.

Rockwell, Anne. (1989). *Apples and Pumpkins.* Illustrated by Lizzy Rockwell. New York: Simon and Schuster.

Schweninger, Ann. (1993). *Autumn Days.* New York: Puffin Books.

Sundgaard, Arnold. (1996). *The Lamb and the Butterfly.* Illustrated by Eric Carle. New York: Scholastic.

Titherington, Jeanne. (1990). *Pumpkin, Pumpkin.* New York: Mullberry.

Zemach, Margot. (1983). *The Little Red Hen.* New York: Farrar, Straus, and Giroux.

Parent Letter (Toddler)

Dear Parents,

We are starting to learn about the seasons. Our first theme is Fall.

The children will learn:
- Fall is the season of the year that comes after summer and before winter.
- Fall is a time of the year that has many changes in nature.
- In the fall, many birds and some animals, fish, and insects go where the weather is warm.
- The leaves of trees may change color, and many trees lose their leaves.
- Fall weather becomes cooler, and we start wearing warmer clothing.

We will be talking about:
- fall changes in trees and weather
- farmers harvesting fruits, vegetables, and grain — especially apples, pumpkins, and nuts
- fall holidays and celebrations
- fall family activities

Things to do at home with your child to support our classroom activities are:
- Go for a walk and look at trees, collect fallen leaves, watch the birds fly south, and notice other changes.
- Talk about what you see.
- Point out fall colors.
- Carve a pumpkin, and eat pumpkin pies.
- Take your child to the grocery store to buy apples. Taste the different kinds.
- Read books about fall and the other seasons.

Parent participation opportunities at school will be to:
- Come help us make applesauce.
  Date _____   Time _____
- Go with us on a field trip.
  Date _____   Time _____

Our wish list for this theme:

shoe boxes

paper grocery bags

magazines and calendars

feathers

fall leaves

Thank you for all you do for the children.

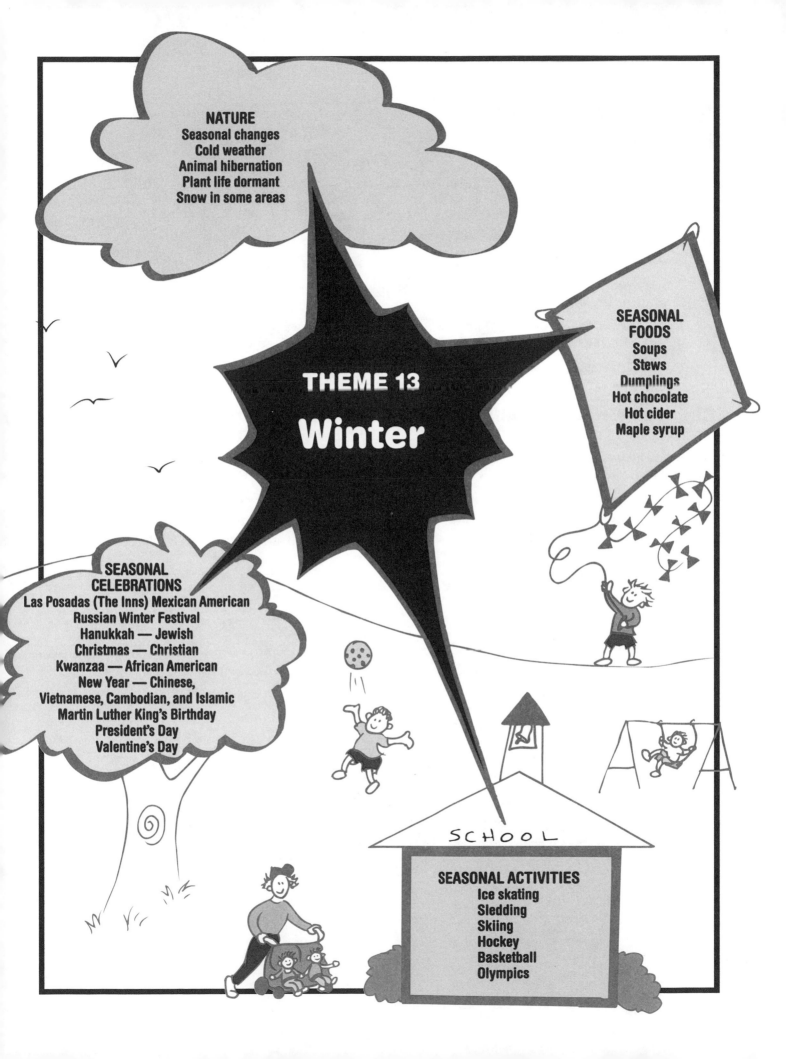

NATURE
Seasonal changes
Cold weather
Animal hibernation
Plant life dormant
Snow in some areas

THEME 13
Winter

SEASONAL FOODS
Soups
Stews
Dumplings
Hot chocolate
Hot cider
Maple syrup

SEASONAL CELEBRATIONS
Las Posadas (The Inns) Mexican American
Russian Winter Festival
Hanukkah — Jewish
Christmas — Christian
Kwanzaa — African American
New Year — Chinese,
Vietnamese, Cambodian, and Islamic
Martin Luther King's Birthday
President's Day
Valentine's Day

SCHOOL

SEASONAL ACTIVITIES
Ice skating
Sledding
Skiing
Hockey
Basketball
Olympics

THEME GOALS

To provide opportunities for children to learn:

1. Winter is a season of the year that comes after fall and before spring.
2. Winter is the time of year with the shortest days and longest nights.
3. In the winter, many animals and insects hibernate.
4. Many plants stop growing and their seeds, roots, or bulbs live underground waiting for warmer weather.
5. Winter weather usually becomes very cold, often with snow, sleet, and ice. Heavy clothing helps protect us, and keeps us comfortable and warm.

Children-Created Bulletin Board

As the weather changes into winter, so does the interactive bulletin board. Encourage the children to think of what can be added or deleted from the board to show that winter has arrived.

* There can be pictures of bears hibernating, children sledding, and sleet or snow falling.
* Cotton balls or Styrofoam "squiggles" can be glued on to create "snow people" or snow on the tree.
* This is an opportunity for the children to work cooperatively in adding winter scenes to the board.

Vocabulary Starters

Let the children add additional words.

hibernation — a time when many animals are resting or sleeping during the winter months.

frost — ice crystals that form on a surface, such as the ground.

sleet — frozen raindrops.

ice — frozen water.

snow — frozen water crystals, or flakes, that fall from the sky.

blizzard — a very big and strong snowstorm.

Language Experiences

POEM: "Winter Time"

Woo! Woo! Woo-woo-woo!
When winter comes, hear the cold wind blow.
Look! Look! Look-look-look!
Out of the clouds, here comes the snow!
Hop. Hop. Hop-hop-hop.
The rabbit hurries to his hole so deep.
Shhh. Shhh. Shhh-shhh-shhh.
Don't make a sound — now he's fast asleep.

GETTING DRESSED FOR WINTER

✳ Read Neitzel's *The Jacket I Wear in the Snow* or London's *Froggy Gets Dressed,* listed in the books section of this theme.

✳ These books are a lot of fun for the children. Neitzel's cumulative rhyme (a takeoff of *The House That Jack Built*) and the lively illustrations describe every stitch of clothing the little girl wears in the snow. London's Froggy keeps forgetting key articles of clothing needed for going out into the snow.

✳ Have the children go through the books' sequence of identifying the appropriate clothes to wear, building on vocabulary.

✳ Have all the pieces of clothing mentioned in the books available for one or two of the children to dress as the characters in the book. The children love to do this, and it offers a hands-on experience.

Dramatic Play

THE THREE BEARS

✳ Turn your dramatic play area into the house of "The Three Bears."

✳ Make three sets of ears from fake fur, construction paper, or tagboard, and attach them to headbands.

✳ Get a girl's headband with a bow on it for Goldilocks.

✳ You will need three sets of dishes, eating utensils, and chairs in three different sizes.

✳ Use colored masking tape to make a "path" for the bears to follow when they leave their house for a walk in the woods.

✳ Extend this activity by setting up an adjacent area where the bears will hibernate for the winter.

✳ Ask the children to decide what the bears will need for their long sleep. Add these items gradually.

GIFT WRAPPING CENTER

As the children experiment with wrapping beautiful packages, they are developing small muscles, problem-solving, and working cooperatively with other children.

✳ Collect empty boxes of all sizes, wrapping paper of many colors and textures, yarn, ribbon, bows, tape, and scissors.

✳ Set up the dramatic play area as a gift wrapping center, and invite the children to wrap and decorate packages.

Puppet Play

PUSH-UP CANDLE PUPPETS

Festivals of light are held worldwide during the winter months. The candle is an important symbol of these celebrations. The books section of this theme offers related stories.

✳ To introduce this puppet project, bring different sizes of candles to show the children. Show pictures and read books.

✳ Talk about the candles that are carried door to door during Las Posadas in Mexico.

✳ Have a Hanukkah menorah with candles to demonstrate how candles are lit during this Jewish holiday.

✳ Show how candles are used during the African American celebration of Kwanzaa.

✳ Talk about how at Christmas candles are used to make homes look warm and cheerful.

✳ The children can go to the art table to make their "candles" and "candle puppets" whenever they choose.

✳ Put paper towel rolls that have been cut in half, colored tissue and construction paper, foil, tape, glue, scissors, crayons, and craft sticks on a table.

✳ Let the older children experiment with ways to make "flames" push up through the "candle."

✳ Let those toddlers who want to explore the materials do so.

✳ Precut candle "flames" and help the toddlers glue the "flames" onto craft sticks to push up through the paper towel rolls.

✳ Leave the materials in the art center for several days. Some children like to make more than one puppet.

Music

SONG: "Jingle Bells"

✳ Sing the song "Jingle Bells." Play a record or tape of this as well, and fill the environment with music and bells.

✳ With one or two infants at a time, introduce a variety of bells to them.

✳ As you play the bells, talk about their shapes and the sounds they make.

✳ Guide each child into holding a bell and making it ring.

✳ Repeat this activity throughout the holiday season.

DANCE WITH TEDDY

✳ Encourage the children to bring their favorite stuffed animal to play with in the classroom. Many of these will be teddy bears. Add any teddy bears already in the room to these.

✳ Invite the children to dance and sing with their teddy bears.

✳ The older children can help you sing and act out this traditional song: "Teddy Bear, Teddy Bear"

Teddy bear, teddy bear,
Turn around.
Teddy bear, teddy bear,
Touch the ground.
Teddy bear, teddy bear,
Skidoo.
Teddy bear, teddy bear,
Go upstairs.
Teddy bear, teddy bear,
Say your prayers.
Teddy bear, teddy bear,
Turn out the light.
Teddy bear, teddy bear.
Say good night.

SONG: "Brr, It's Cold Today!" by Jo Eklof

(See page 300 for enlargement.)

Movement

IN AND OUT

This activity promotes gross motor development.

* Wrap several very large boxes with wrapping paper and bows. Leave the ends open.
* Place these in the classroom.
* Encourage the children to climb in and out of the decorated boxes.
* After a while, add a pillow at one end of the box. The children will then have to crawl over the pillow to get out.

ICE SKATING

* Give each child two pieces of wax paper (for use on a carpeted floor), or two pieces of cardboard or tagboard (to use on uncarpeted areas).
* Play "The Skater's Waltz" or other appropriate music.
* Suggest to the children that they "ice skate" using the wax paper or cardboard as skates.

* Encourage them to try different arm movements as well as leg and body movements.
* Ask them to act out other winter sports, such as skiing or sledding. This is a good activity to relate to the Winter Olympic Games.

JACK FROST

* Play some music in the background that suggests winter time, such as Tchaikovsky's *The Nutcracker Suite.*
* Have the children sit in a circle. One child is Jack Frost, who sits inside the circle.
* Jack closes his eyes.
* While the music is playing, have the other children pass an ice cube, enclosed in a plastic bag, from child to child around the circle.
* Then, stop the music! The child with the ice hides it by placing it behind his back.
* Jack Frost opens his eyes and tries to guess who has the ice cube.
* After the guess, the children trade places. The game begins again when the music starts.

LION DANCER

* Read Waters and Slovenz-Low's *Lion Dancer, Ernie Wan's Chinese New Year.*
* Give one or two of the children drums.
* Ask them to play the drums as though they were playing for the Lion Dance.
* Next, give the other children various kinds of percussion instruments to play along with the drums. Here are some with suggestions for creating different sounds:
  — cymbals (crashing)
  — wood blocks (clapping)
  — triangle (ting-a-linging)
  — Chinese gong (smashing)
  — tambourines (slapping)
  — many sizes of drums (pounding)
  — chimes (striking)
  — bells (jingling)
  — castanets (shaking)
  — maracas (shaking)
* The children can make some of their own instruments. See Theme 6 for suggestions.

Sensory Art

IT'S COLD!

✳ To introduce the concept of cold to very young children, put a small amount of cold water in a plastic tub or the sand and water table.

✳ Talk about how cold the water is.

✳ Start with helping them put just one finger in the water and taking it out quickly.

✳ You can model putting your hand in and letting the water run through you fingers. After that, let the children decide if they want to play in the water or not.

✳ Once the children are playing in the water, add a few ice cubes.

✳ Continue talking about how cold the ice cubes make the water.

✳ This activity can be repeated easily.

MITTENS

✳ Trace each child's handprint on a colorful piece of felt.

✳ Let interested children decorate their mitten using markers, crayons, and stickers.

✳ Punch a hole at the top of the felt and string yarn through it.

✳ Hang the mittens around the room for decoration.

✳ Some parents like to use these as holiday ornaments.

SNOWFLAKES

✳ Each snowflake is one-of-a-kind. Let the children make their unique snowflakes with marshmallows and toothpicks.

✳ Put mini marshmallows, regular-size marshmallows, and toothpicks out for the children to make as many snowflakes as they wish.

✳ They stick toothpicks into the marshmallows and then connect the marshmallows to other toothpicks.

✳ They will soon have unusual snowflakes to show each other.

✳ Ask them questions about their creations. "Did you use different size marshmallows?" "What different patterns did you make?" "How is this snowflake different from this other one?" "Now that you've made this snowflake, what else can you add to it?"

LIGHT-UP PICTURES AND LANTERNS

✳ Provide cotton swabs, tempera paint, manila paper, and salad oil for the children to use.

✳ Place the cotton swabs and tempera paint on separate trays for each child.

✳ Guide the children who are interested to paint designs on the nine-by-twelve-inch manila paper.

✳ After the paint is dry, have the children use a paintbrush or basting brush to quickly spread a layer of salad oil over the entire picture.

✳ If they spread too much oil on their picture, this is part of the process. They are learning by doing.

✳ Light should shine through and brighten up the picture when it is hung in a window.

✳ For older children, extend this project by making their light picture into a Chinese festival lantern. To do this:

— Fold the picture.

— Cut lines across the fold of the paper, almost to the other edge, but not quite (see illustration).

— Unfold the picture. Hold it so the cut lines go up and down.

— Bring the two sides around together.

— Tape the sides together. The lantern will bend on the fold.

— Tape a piece of ribbon or yarn to the top of each lantern, and hang the lanterns around the room as decorations.

Creative Food Experiences

MEXICAN HOT CHOCOLATE — CHOCOLATE CALIENTE

You will need:

4 cups milk

5 tablespoons Mexican chocolate or unsweetened chocolate

4 tablespoons brown sugar

2 cinnamon sticks, broken in half

l teaspoon vanilla

1. Wash hands.
2. Combine milk, chocolate, sugar, and cinnamon in a saucepan.
3. Cook over low heat until the chocolate melts and the sugar dissolves.
4. Remove from heat and add vanilla to milk mixture, beating with an egg beater.
5. Place a piece of cinnamon stick in a cup for each child, and pour the warm chocolate into the cups.

Safety reminder: Show the children all the steps in this recipe, but only the teacher should work with the heating of this mixture.

STONE SOUP

Read Brown's *Stone Soup,* listed in the books section of this theme. Next, you and the children make your own Stone Soup.

You will need:

3 small clean rocks, found and washed by you and the children, if possible.

3 stalks of celery

2 large carrots

2 medium onions

2 medium potatoes

3 medium tomatoes

1/2 cup rice

1/2 teaspoon basil

1/2 cup fresh parsley

1 1/2 tablespoon salt

1/2 teaspoon pepper

1/2 cup rice

1. Wash hands.
2. Everyone helps to chop or measure an ingredient.
3. Put the ingredients into a big pot, and place on the stove.
4. Add water to cover the vegetables, and cook on low heat for two to three hours. The soup smells so good as it cooks!
5. Add the rice to thicken the soup, and cook longer until rice is tender.
6. Enjoy!

STONE SOUP

Wash hands. Wash 3 clean rocks.

Chop and measure 3 stalks of celery, 2 large carrots,

2 medium onions, 2 medium potatoes, 3 medium tomatoes,

1/2 teaspoon basil, 1/2 cup fresh parsley,

1 1/2 tablespoon salt, and 1/2 teaspoon pepper.

Put all ingredients in a big pot and place on the stove.

Add water to cover the vegetables. Cook for 2 - 3 hours.

Add 1/2 cup rice to thicken the soup. ENJOY!

Math

HIBERNATION HELPER GAME

This game is for two to four children at a time. Its object is for each child to help her "bear" move from Start to safe winter hibernation in the "cave."

✳ On posterboard, draw an enlarged version of the sample gameboard shown in the illustration. School-age children can make the gameboard and pieces, with your assistance, if needed.

✳ Using posterboard or tagboard, cut out four bears. Color one black, one brown, one tan, and one red.

✳ Laminate the bear pieces.

✳ From the same material, cut out thirty 2-inch by 2-inch squares. In the center of twenty of these, draw a triangle. In the remaining ten, draw a circle.

✳ A triangle shows the number of squares a player can move *forward,* and circles show the number a player must move *backward.*

— Inside *five triangles,* write the numeral 1.

— Inside *five more triangles,* write the numeral 2.

— Inside an additional *five triangles,* write the numeral 3.

— Inside the last *five triangles,* write the numeral 4.

— Inside *three circles,* write the numeral 1.

— Inside *three circles,* write the numeral 2.

— Inside *three circles,* write the numeral 3.

— Inside *three circles,* write the numeral 4.

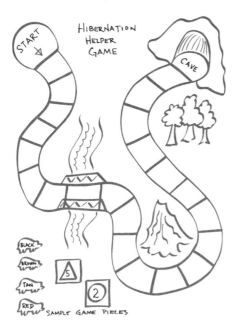

HIBERNATION HELPER GAME

SAMPLE GAME PIECES

✳ Laminate the square pieces.

✳ Before starting, have each player select a bear to move. Also, put the thirty numbered pieces in a bag or box, and shake them up.

✳ Each child, in turn, draws a numbered piece and moves her bear forward or backward the number of spaces indicated. Players cannot move back further than Start.

✳ Play continues until each bear is safely hibernating in the cave. If all the numbers are drawn before the bears reach the cave, put the numbers back in the bag, shake them up, and keep drawing.

Science

WHAT'S THE TEMPERATURE?

✳ Show the children several different kinds of thermometers. Talk about them. Discuss how thermometers are used. "What do you think this big thermometer does?" Point out the vertical number line.

✳ Measure and record the morning outside temperature for one week. Use the large thermometer.

✳ Draw a large thermometer on posterboard and put it in the classroom. Also create a chart with the days of the week along the top, and temperatures up the side.

✳ Use strips of red paper to graph the temperature measured by the mercury on the real thermometer outside.

✳ At the end of the week, the children can see which day was coldest or warmest.

Social Studies

INTERVIEW THE ANIMALS

To help children understand seasonal changes and how animals adapt to these changes, have them "interview the animals."

✳ Decide which children will be the television news or newspaper reporters, and which children will be the animals being interviewed.

✳ Provide microphones (play ones or ones the children have made out of paper towel rolls), bear ears, bunny ears, bird feathers, and other objects the children help think of.

* Make up a list of questions to be asked, such as, "Do you sleep all through the winter?" "How do you know when it is time to wake up?" "Do you sleep for part of the winter?" "What do you eat?" "Why do you migrate?" "How do you know where you are going?" "Why don't you go to sleep during the winter?" "Why do you stay active and search for food all winter?"

* Discuss how some of these questions can be answered. Provide correct information for the children. For example, deep hibernators that sleep most of the winter are groundhogs, frogs, box turtles, and snakes. Bears, raccoons, and skunks are light hibernators, sleeping for weeks and snacking on food they have stored in their dens. Cardinals, deer, and snowshoe hares stay active during the winter.

* Everyone has a lot of fun with this activity. You will also find out what misconceptions the children have.

Children's Books

Adoff, Arnold. (1991). *In for Winter, Out for Spring.* Illustrated by Jerry Pickney. San Diego, CA: Harcourt Brace.

Berenstain, Stan, and Jan Berenstain. (1996). *The Berenstain Bears Four Seasons.* New York: Random House.

Borden, Louise, (1992). *Caps, Hats, Socks, and Mittens: A Book About the Four Seasons.* Illustrated by Lillian Hoban. New York: Scholastic.

Brown, Marcia. (1975). *Stone Soup.* New York: Aladdin Books.

Bunting, Eve. (1994). *Night Tree.* Illustrated by Ted Rand. San Diego, CA: Harcourt Brace.

Burden-Patmon, Denise. (1992). *Imani's Gift at Kwanzaa.* Illustrated by Floyd Cooper. New York: Simon & Schuster.

Chiemruom, Sothea. (1994). *Dara's Cambodian New Year.* Illustrated by Dam Nang Pin. New York: Simon & Schuster.

De Paola, Tomie. (1997). *The Legend of the Poinsettia.* New York: Paper Star.

Ehlert, Lois. (1995). *Snowballs.* San Diego, CA: Harcourt Brace.

Ets, Mary Hall, and Aurora Labastida. (1991). *Nine Days to Christmas (Los Posadas).* New York: Puffin.

Fuchs, Diane M. (1995). *A Bear for All Seasons.* New York: Henry Holt.

George, Jean C. (1995). *Dear Rebecca, Winter Is Here.* Illustrated by Loretta Krupinski. New York: HarperCollins.

George, Linda B. (1995). *In the Snow: Who's Been Here?* New York: Greenwillow.

Greene, Carol. (1982). *Read Holidays Around the World.* Chicago, IL: Children's Press.

Guiberson, Megan L. (1995). *Winter Wheat.* New York: Henry Holt.

Hirschi, Ron. (1990). *Winter — Invierno.* New York: Dutton.

Keats, Ezra Jack. (1996). *The Snowy Day.* (Board book). New York: Viking.

Lemelman, Martin. (1998). *Chanukah Is . . .* (Board book). New York: UAHC Press.

London, Jonathan. (1995). *Froggy Gets Dressed.* Illustrated by Frank Remkiewicz. New York: Puffin Books.

Lotz, Karen E. (1993). *Snowsong Whistling.* Illustrated by Elisa Kleven. New York: Dutton.

Neitzel, Shirley. (1994). *The Jacket I Wear in the Snow.* Illustrated by Nancy W. Parker. New York: Mulberry.

Pinkney, Andrea Davis. (1998). *Seven Candles for Kwanzaa.* Illustrated by Brian Pinkney. New York: Puffin.

Preller, James. (1994). *Wake Me In Spring.* New York: Scholastic.

Prelutsky, Jack, and Jeanne Titherington. (1984). *It's Snowing, It's Snowing: Poems.* New York: William Morrow.

Scharfstein, Sol. (1985). *Hanukah Pop-Up Book.* Hoboken, NJ: KTAV Publishing.

Schweninger, Ann. (1993). *Wintertime.* New York: Puffin Books.

Shostak, Myra. (1997). *Rainbow Candles: A Chanukah Counting Book.* (Board book). New York: KarBen Press.

Tran, Kim-Lan. (1992). *Tet: The New Year.* Illustrated by Mai Vo-Dinh. New York: Simon & Schuster.

Tresselt, Alvin R., and Roger Duvoisin. (1988). *White Snow, Bright Snow.* New York: William Morrow.

Waters, Kate, and Madeline Slovenz-Low. (1990). *Lion Dancer, Ernie Wan's Chinese New Year.* Photographed by Martha Cooper. New York: Scholastic.

Yerxa, Leo. (1994). *Last Leaf, First Snowflake to Fall.* New York: Orchard Books.

Parent Letter (Preschool)

Dear Parents,

Our new theme is Winter. We will provide opportunities for the children to learn:

- Winter is a season of the year that comes after fall and before spring.
- Winter is the time of year with the shortest days and longest nights.
- In the winter, many animals and insects hibernate.
- Many plants stop growing and their seeds, roots, or bulbs live underground, waiting for warmer weather.
- Winter weather usually becomes very cold, often with snow, sleet, and ice. Heavy clothing helps protect us and keeps us comfortable and warm.

We will be talking about:

- seasonal changes of nature
- animal hibernation
- season activities
- cold weather
- seasonal celebrations
- seasonal foods

Try some of these things to do at home with your child:

- Talk about the changes in the weather.
- Let your child help you bring out winter clothes and put away summer ones.
- Let your child help you prepare for your family's holiday celebration.
- Enjoy the sights and sounds of the season with your child.

You are welcome to join us for these parent participation opportunities at school:

- Help us make "Stone Soup."
  Date _____ Time _____
- Come visit us during our "animal interviews."
  Date _____ Time _____

Our wish list for this theme is:

cotton balls and cotton swabs

Styrofoam "squiggles" or packing shapes

paper towel rolls

wrapping paper

small boxes

Thank you for sharing your child with us.

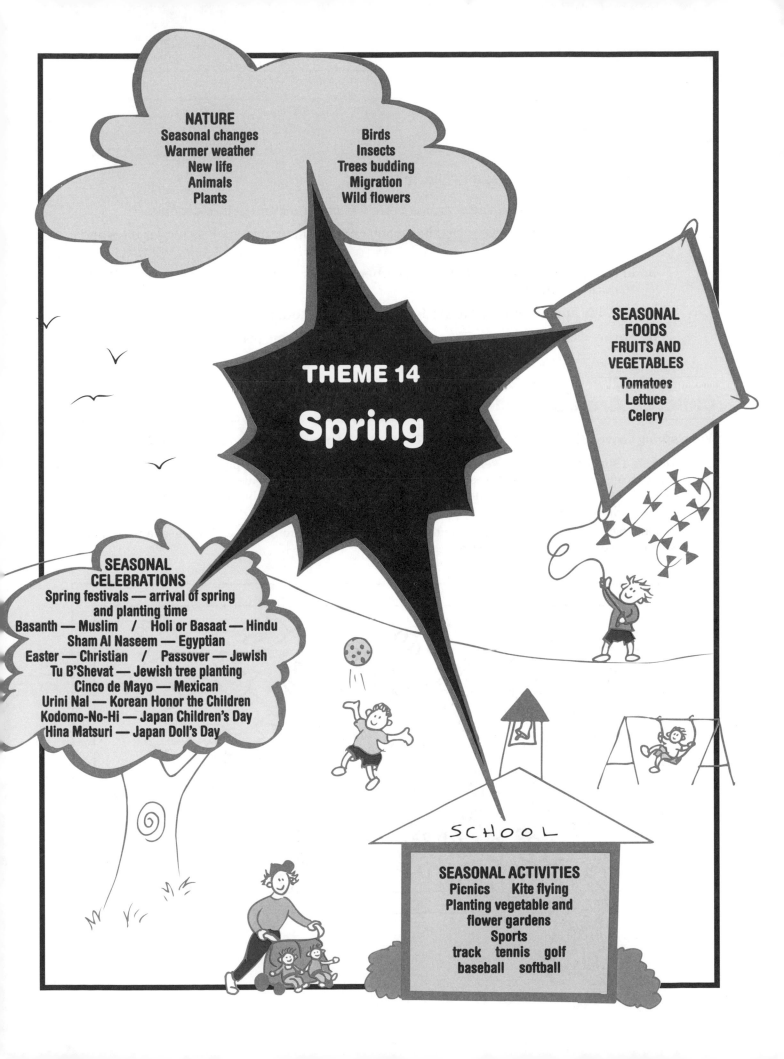

NATURE
Seasonal changes
Warmer weather
New life
Animals
Plants

Birds
Insects
Trees budding
Migration
Wild flowers

THEME 14
Spring

SEASONAL FOODS
FRUITS AND VEGETABLES

Tomatoes
Lettuce
Celery

SEASONAL CELEBRATIONS
Spring festivals — arrival of spring
and planting time
Basanth — Muslim / Holi or Basaat — Hindu
Sham Al Naseem — Egyptian
Easter — Christian / Passover — Jewish
Tu B'Shevat — Jewish tree planting
Cinco de Mayo — Mexican
Urini Nal — Korean Honor the Children
Kodomo-No-Hi — Japan Children's Day
Hina Matsuri — Japan Doll's Day

SCHOOL

SEASONAL ACTIVITIES
Picnics   Kite flying
Planting vegetable and
flower gardens
Sports
track   tennis   golf
baseball   softball

THEME GOALS

To provide opportunities for children to learn:

1. Spring is a season of the year that comes after winter and before summer.

2. Spring is the time of year that has many changes in nature, such as longer days and shorter nights.

3. In the spring, many birds and some other animals, such as fish and insects, migrate to cooler climates.

4. New life and growth begin: seeds sprout, leaves grow, and flowers bloom.

5. Spring weather becomes warmer and we begin wearing less clothing.

Children-Created Bulletin Board

When spring arrives, the bulletin board starts blooming with flowers, fruits, and vegetables.

✳ Here is a suggestion for a flower garden. Provide assorted tissue paper, pipe cleaners, yarn, Styrofoam egg cartons, small paper plates, art foam, construction paper, tape, glue, and scissors. Each child can create many flowers for the garden. See the sensory art activities in this theme for other additions to the spring bulletin board.

✳ Again, trace around the children's hands on light green construction paper. Cut the shapes to make spring leaves for the bulletin board tree.

Vocabulary Starters

Let the children add additional words.

garden — a place where vegetables and flowers grow.

rain — water that drops from the clouds.

seed — the tiny pod that has inside it the beginning of a new plant or tree.

bud — a bump on a plant where a branch, leaf, or flower grows.

root — the part of the plant that grows underground.

blossom — a flower on a plant.

Language Experiences

FINGERPLAY:
The Little Acorn

I took a little acorn
And put it in the ground.
   (pick up imaginary acorn with fingers of one hand,
   put it into the other cupped hand)
I filled up the hole
And smoothed it all around.
   (pour in "dirt," rub hand over "hole")
Took my watering can
And made the ground all wet.
   (pick up "can," pour over "ground")
Then the seed began to sprout
And poked up its head.
   (point index finger up from "ground" hand)
It grew and it grew
And made a lot of leaves.
   (slowly raise arm above head and open up hand so
   that fingers become leaves)
It's an oak tree as big
As the tallest trees.
   (extend hand and arm high over head)

Philip Jackman

POEM:
Seeds

SEEDS

The little seeds are sleeping under their blanket made of earth.

They dream until the rainclouds cover the sky;

then all the little seeds begin to sigh,

"We are thirsty! We're thirsty!

We need some rain to drink!"

And now there are raindrops falling, raindrops falling,

and all the little seeds are busy drinking up all the

raindrops falling, raindrops falling, and soon ------

the little seeds begin to grow -------

s l o w l y . . . s l o w l y . . .

and some turn into flowers . . . .

and others turn into trees,

and many turn into good things to eat!

And all of them are beautiful;

they're very beautiful, reaching up so high

as they try to touch the sky!

Reproduced by permission of B. Wolf – 1995
Copyright B. Wolf – 1993

STORY STARTER:
"When the Wind Blows"

With younger children:

✳ Let them tell you a story about what happens when the wind blows.

✳ You can do this as a group activity or one-on-one with each child.

✳ Write down what the children say. Later read it back to them, and let them draw pictures about the wind blowing.

With older children:

✳ Let them dictate or write story sentences about what happens when the wind blows. Put these on sentence strip paper.

✳ Mix the sentences up. Have the children read each line and arrange them in the correct sequence.

✳ This activity can be extended by the children. They can make a book of the story and illustrate each line.

Dramatic Play

FLOWER SHOP

✳ In the spring, flowers bloom in the dramatic play area's flower shop. The children begin by choosing a name for their shop.

✳ If possible, visit a flower shop and have the florist talk to the children and show them different areas of the shop. Sometimes the florist gives the children flowers to take back to the classroom.

✳ Stock the shop in the dramatic play area with silk flowers, flower pots, watering cans, gardening gloves, aprons, spray bottles, plastic vases, packets of seeds, and Styrofoam balls.

✳ Let the children discover how to stick the flowers into the Styrofoam, and put these into the flower pots. This eliminates the need for dirt or potting soil.

✳ If dirt or potting soil is added, place several layers of newspaper on the floor to catch spills for easy clean-up.

✳ The children can pretend to grow seeds, care for the flowers, and make flower arrangements in one part of the shop.

✳ In another area of the shop, place a cash register, telephone, order pad, pencils, and pictures of flowers, and flower displays. These can be drawn by the children or cut from magazines. The children may also draw their own flower posters and brochures to place around the area.

✳ Allow plenty of time for this creative play. Sometimes the flower shop lasts for weeks. Observation of the children's play will tell you when it is time to change.

FROM CATERPILLAR TO BUTTERFLY — FROM SEED TO GROWING PLANT

✳ To help the children assimilate all the information about what happens in the spring, have them act out the story of Carle's *The Very Hungry Caterpillar* or Ehlert's *Planting a Rainbow.*

✳ This process encourages children to apply new vocabulary, sequence events, and use their imagination and creativity.

✳ Repeat this activity. Change it by reading different books to the children, adding props, and taking the dramatic play area outdoors on the playground.

✳ The action and reenactment changes with each telling.

Puppet Play

BUTTERFLY PUPPET

✳ To make the butterfly puppet, you need to supply nine-inch paper plates, tagboard cut into strips approximately one inch wide and four to five inches long, pieces of colored tissue paper, crayons, markers, glue, and scissors.

✳ Let the children decide when they are interested in making puppets.

✳ They can color the entire bottom of a plate with whatever colors and patterns they choose.

✳ Next, they bend the plate in half, with the colored halves showing. These become the wings of the butterfly puppet.

✳ With your assistance, on each side of the plate next to the crease, have the children position a tagboard strip and staple each end to the plate, allowing a little slack where children can insert their fingers.

✳ Finally, have the children glue pieces of colored tissue paper to the inside of the folded plate, allowing the tissue to overhang the edges so that they "float" when the wings are flapped.

✳ For older toddlers and young preschoolers, simplify the puppet by having interested children color the plate and glue on the tissue paper. You attach the strips for their fingers.

✳ Each child inserts the thumb under one strip and the other four fingers under the other strip. When the wings flap, away flies the butterfly!

Music

SPRING RAIN

The following is a *musical beat* activity. It can also be chanted.

Listen to the rain, pretty rain.*
Listen to the rain, pretty rain.*
Listen to it drip.
Listen to it drop.
Listen to the rain, pretty rain.*
   Listen to it patter on the roof.*
   Listen to it patter on the roof.*
   Listen to it drip.
   Listen to it drop.
   Listen to it patter on the roof.*

Philip Jackman

This method of indicating beat was introduced in Theme 4 and is adapted from Moomaw's *More Than Singing*. Accent syllables with a vertical line (ı) above them, and pause (rest) where an asterisk (*) is shown. Use a drum or other musical instrument to help reinforce the beat.

Movement

MOVE WITH THE WIND

This activity works very well outdoors.

✳ Choose music with varied tempos, some instrumental and some that ask children to sing along.

✳ Let each child select crepe paper streamers or scarves.

✳ The children pretend they are being moved by the wind as they dance and sing with the music.

CATERPILLAR HOPSCOTCH

✳ With the children's help, make a hopscotch game outdoors using sidewalk chalk. Draw circles until you have the length of the caterpillar you want, varying the sizes of the circles.

✳ Make a face and antenna on the first circle, and draw simple legs on the other circles.

✳ On some of the circles, draw a vertical line down the middle; leave some with no lines.

✳ Encourage the children to find different ways of jumping from circle to circle. Jump on one foot, hop into only the unlined circles, place both feet on the lined ones, and jump with both feet.

✳ Emphasize the fun of jumping. This skill improves with each child's developmental growth.

✳ To extend the activity, number the circles. A child calls out a number and tries to throw a bean bag into the circle with the number selected.

✳ Older children make up their own rules and expand the game as well.

Sensory Art

FRUIT AND VEGETABLE COLLAGE

This is a one-on-one activity. Help older infants make a collage.

✳ Precut pictures of fruits and vegetables.

✳ Cut a piece of clear contact paper, about the size of a large piece of construction paper, and place it sticky side up in front of the child.

✳ While sitting with the child in your lap or next to you, guide her to put a picture on the contact paper.

✳ Talk to the child as you do this. Say the name of the fruit or vegetable.

✳ Continue as long as the child wants to.

SPRING COLLAGE

✳ Collect eggshells.

✳ Place the shells, a small amount at a time, in a paper towel, and crush them. The older children can help do this.

✳ Place the crushed shells, different colors of paper, and glue at the art table.

✳ Let the children have fun making a collage with the crushed eggshells and other materials.

FLOWERS EVERYWHERE

✳ Ask your local florist for discarded flowers. Collect as many roses as you can before they turn brown.

✳ Pull the petals off all the flowers.

✳ Make the petals available for the children to glue onto construction paper to make aromatic flower pictures.

✳ You can also create a pleasant sensory experience by adding the flower petals to the sand and water table.

✳ Encourage the children to compare sizes, discuss shapes, identify colors, smell and feel different textures.

SPRING FLOWERS

✳ To create "spring flowers," gather together coffee filters, pipe cleaners, the bottoms of egg cartons, crayons, and markers.

✳ Cover the table with two or three layers of newspapers. The papers will provide padding and absorb colors that soak through as the children work.

✳ Let the children experiment with the materials. They can decorate a filter, poke a finger in the center, and make a small twist at the bottom.

✳ Fasten a pipe cleaner stem by giving one end of the pipe cleaner a few turns around the twist.

✳ Make a small hole in each of the twelve egg-holders in the inverted lower half of an egg carton to create a "garden." The children can "plant" their flowers by inserting the pipe cleaners into the holes.

✳ Children identify their flowers by writing their names on the egg carton at the base of the flowers. They also can place their flowers in the dramatic play flower shop.

Creative Food Experiences

BANANA SNACK

✳ Bananas are a favorite food of infants. Older babies like to squeeze banana slices through their fingers and then taste them.

✳ For a change, let the children try to "cut" the banana into slices themselves by using craft sticks.

✳ Place a section of a banana in front of the child, and demonstrate how this is done with each individual child. At first, hold the child's hand while placing the craft stick in it and gently "cutting down" on the banana.

✳ Talk about what you are doing.

✳ This activity should be repeated several times while the child is gaining control over his muscles.

BUTTERFLY SALAD

You will need the following ingredients for each individual serving:

> 2 pineapple rings
>
> lettuce leaf
>
> cottage cheese
>
> celery stick
>
> green and black olives

1. Wash hands.

2. Place lettuce leaf onto a paper plate.

3. Slice pineapple rings in half to use as an outline of the butterfly's wings.

4. Use the celery stick as the body.

BUTTERFLY SALAD

Wash hands.

Place one lettuce leaf onto a paper plate.

Slice 2 pineapple rings in 1/2 to use as an outline of

the butterfly's wings. Use one celery stick as the body.

Place a small amount of cottage cheese inside of

pineapple rings. Decorate the cottage cheese with

green and black olives.

5. Place a small amount of cottage cheese inside the pineapple.

6. Decorate the cottage cheese with green and black olives.

Math

LET'S GO FISHING

✳ Make several fishing poles using dowel rods that are approximately two to three feet long. Tie a piece of yarn or string to one end, and attach a magnet to the end of the yarn. You might use a hot glue gun to attach the yarn to the magnet.

✳ Let the children help you make, decorate, and cut out the fish for the fishing pond.

✳ Attach paper clips to the ends of the fish.

✳ Place a large piece of blue craft or construction paper on the floor. Cut in the shape of a pond.

✳ Put the "fish" into the pond.

✳ Younger children take turns using the fishing rod to try picking up the fish with the magnet.

✳ To make it more interesting for older children, number the fish from 1 to 10. After they catch the fish, they add up the numbers and see who caught the highest number. Help them add up the numbers as needed.

WHERE'S THE BUTTER?

✳ To create this game, you will need to make and laminate a game folder, "potatoes," and "butter squares."

✳ The object of the game is for the child to match each "butter square" with a numeral on it to the potato showing the same number of "eyes."

✳ Laminate a standard file folder. Create ten potatoes out of brown or tan construction paper showing "one eye," "two eyes," up to "ten eyes."

✳ Write the numeral corresponding to the number of eyes on the back of each potato.

✳ Cut ten "butter squares" out of yellow construction paper, and number them from 1 to 10.

✳ Place the potatoes on the open folder in a random arrangement. Then, cut a strip of clear tape and press it down, lower half on the potato and upper half on the folder, to form a hinge.

✳ This makes the game self-correcting. If the child is unable to match the "butter" numeral to the potato "eyes," he can lift up the potato to see if the numbers match.

✳ Let the children know you have created a new math folder for them.

✳ Place this game in the math center for the children to play whenever they wish.

Science

WHAT HAPPENED TO THE WHITE CARNATION?

✳ After reading books, showing pictures, planting gardens, and visiting a florist shop, continue to talk about the similarities and differences of the plants.

✳ Carefully remove a plant from its container, and place it on newspaper so the roots are visible.

✳ Point to the roots, leaves, stems, and flowers of the plant. Explain that each part of a plant has a certain job to do. The roots help to hold plants in place. Water and food move through the stems. The stems also help the plant stay upright. A tree has a woody, hard stem.

✳ To demonstrate how water moves up through a stem, place a long-stemmed white carnation into a clear container with some water and a few drops of red or blue food coloring. The darker the color, the more dramatic the outcome. For best results, the stem should be freshly cut on a diagonal.

✳ Try this with several flowers. Have the children observe the flower every ten to fifteen minutes and describe any change in the petals. They will notice the petals begin to take on the color of the food coloring.

✳ With toddlers, simplify the activity by showing them the colored water, and watching with them as the tinted liquid moves up the stem, changing the color of the carnation. Talk about the color of the flower. What are their favorite colors?

EARTHWORMS

* Collect a few earthworms.
* Punch holes in the lids of two plastic jars.
* Conduct an experiment to help the children understand that earthworms help keep the soil healthy.
* Give the children the two jars and ask them to put a layer of potting soil in the bottom of each.
* Next, they add a layer of sand. Continue alternating layers until the jar is almost full.
* Spread grated carrots on the top of the soil in each jar.
* Sprinkle just enough water in each jar to moisten the soil.
* Place a few earthworms in *one* of the jars.
* Place the lids on the jars and cover them with a dark cloth. Ask the children not to disturb the jars until the next day.
* Ask the children to predict what changes they might see in the jars the next day. Write down or have them write what they think will occur.
* Do this for several days. Each morning uncover the jars and encourage the children to note the changes that have taken place.
* If the soil has dried out, add enough water to moisten.
* Over time, the children will discover that the earthworms have mixed the layers of potting soil and sand in the jar.
* What happened to the carrots?
* In the jar without worms, nothing will change.
* Explain to the children that the earthworms tunnel through the soil and mix in nutrients, which help plants to grow.

Social Studies

WHERE DOES FOOD COME FROM?

This is an exploration you and the children can enjoy together. Though children eat foods every day, they probably have little idea how it travels from field or garden to plate, starting as seeds or bulbs, growing,

being harvested, then being processed for eating by canning and freezing.

* First, talk about the "families" of fruits, grains, and vegetables and how they are determined by the part of the plant we eat. Some examples are:

  Fruit — apples, oranges, and pears

  Root or bulb — onions, carrots, potatoes, and radishes

  Stems — celery and asparagus

  Seeds — wheat, rice, peas, corn, and beans

  Leaves — cabbage, spinach, and lettuce

  Flowers — broccoli and cauliflower

* Show pictures of these foods from books, magazines, and seed catalogs. Select some pictures that show the trucks and trains that take the food from farm to farmer's markets and grocery stores. The books section of this theme includes some suggestions.
* Older children also enjoy reading about the canning process or visiting a local plant, if possible.
* Talk about their favorite kinds of fruits, vegetables, and grains.
* Pick out one or more examples of plant-grown food, and set up a "laboratory" to examine them. A common food, such as peas, is a good sample.
* On a table, place several seeds or growing plants, and label them. Next to them, place several fresh peapods, then a can of peas, and finally a frozen food container of peas.
* Have a taste test by heating some canned peas, cooking some frozen peas, and having some thoroughly washed raw peas for the children to sample.
* Ask the children to describe how they taste. Do they taste the same? Different?
* If possible, ask a farmer, gardener, or fruit grower to visit the classroom and tell the children all about their farm, garden, or orchard. Ask if this person can bring some of the produce they grow.

Children's Books

Bacon, Ron. (1993). *Wind.* New York: Scholastic.

Brown, Craig. (1994). *In the Spring.* New York: Greenwillow.

Carle, Eric. (1998). *Let's Paint a Rainbow.* New York: Cartwheel Books.

Carle, Eric. (1994). *The Very Hungry Caterpillar.* (Board book). New York: Philomel.

Cassie, Brian, and Jerry Pallotta. (1995). *The Butterfly Alphabet.* Illustrated by Mark Astrella. Watertown, MA: Charlesbridge.

Cooney, Barbara. (1985). *Miss Rumphius.* New York: Puffin.

De Coteau Orie, Sandra. (1996). *Did You Hear Wind Sing Your Name?* Illustrated by Christopher Canyon. New York: Walker and Company.

De Paola, Tomie. (1983). *The Legend of the Bluebonnet.* New York: G.P. Putnam's Sons.

Demi. (1993). *Little Baby Lamb.* (Soft and furry board book). New York: Grossett and Dunlap.

Ehlert, Lois. (1988). *Planting a Rainbow.* San Diego, CA: Harcourt Brace.

Ets, Marie Hall. (1978). *Gilberto and the Wind.* New York: Puffin.

George, Lindsay B. (1996). *Around the Pond: Who's Been Here?* New York: Greenwillow.

Gibbons, Gail. (1991). *From Seed to Plant.* New York: Holiday House.

Hill, Eric. (1991). *Spot in the Garden.* (Board book). New York: Putnam Publishing.

Hirschi, Ron. (1996). *Spring/Primavera.* New York: Puffin.

Johnson, Neil. (1997). *A Field of Sunflowers.* New York: Cartwheel Books.

Kalan, Robert. (1991). *Rain.* Illustrated by Donald Crews. New York: Mulberry Books.

Kroll, Virginia. (1993). *A Carp for Kimiko.* Illustrated by Katherine Roundtree. Watertown, MA: Charlesbridge.

Lionni, Leo. (1995). *Inch by Inch.* New York: Mulberry.

Marzollo, Jean. (1997). *I'm a Caterpillar.* Illustrated by Judith Moffatt. New York: Scholastic.

Marzollo, Jean. (1995). *I'm a Seed.* Illustrated by Judith Moffatt. New York: Scholastic.

Mudd, Maria M. (1991). *The Butterfly.* Illustrated by Wendy Smith-Griswold. New York: Steward, Tabori & Chang.

Pfister, Marcus. (1998). *Hopper Hunts for Spring.* New York: North South.

Polacco, Patricia. (1997). *Thunder Cake.* New York: Putnam Publishing.

Rockwell, Anne F. (1996). *My Spring Robin.* Illustrated by Harlow and Lizzie Rockwell. New York: Demco Media.

Rucki, Ani. (1998). *When the Earth Wakes.* New York: Scholastic.

Scheer, Julian, and Marvin Bileck. (1985). *Rain Makes Applesauce.* New York: Viking.

Schweninger, Ann. (1995). *Springtime.* New York: Puffin.

Serfozo, Mary. (1990). *Rain Talk.* Illustrated by Keiko Narabasbi. Chicago, IL: Children's Press.

Spier, Peter. (1997). *Rain.* New York: Bantam Dell.

Tresselt, Alvin. (1990). *Rain Drop Splash.* Illustrated by Leonard Weisgard. New York: Morrow.

Parent Letter (School-age)

Dear Parents,

We are studying the four seasons. Our theme is Spring, and we will provide opportunities for the children to learn:

- Spring is a season of the year that comes after winter and before summer.
- Spring is the time of the year that has many changes in nature, such as longer days and shorter nights.
- In the spring, many birds and some other animals, such as fish and insects, migrate to cooler climates.
- New life and growth begin: seeds sprout, leaves grow, and flowers bloom.
- Spring weather becomes warmer, and we begin wearing less clothing.

We will be talking about:

- seasonal changes and the new growth of animals, plants, birds, and insects
- seasonal celebrations, and the arrival of spring and planting time
- seasonal activities, such as picnics, kite flying, planting vegetable and flower gardens, and sports
- seasonal fruits and vegetables

Strengthen your child's learning by doing some of these things at home:

- Take walks and look at what is happening to nature in the spring. Talk with your child about what she observes.
- Enjoy kite flying and family walks in the rain.
- Plant a garden with your child. Make it a family event.
- As a family, visit the parks and arboretums in your city.

Parent participation opportunities at school will be to:

- Go with us on our field trip to a local florist.
  Date _____ Time _____
- Spend some time with us in the classroom and see all the activities in which we are involved.
  Date _____ Time _____

Our wish list for this theme includes:

  flower pots of all sizes
  clean, unused coffee filters
  clean baby food jars with lids
  plastic vases
  earthworms
  potting soil

Thank you for your special friendship.

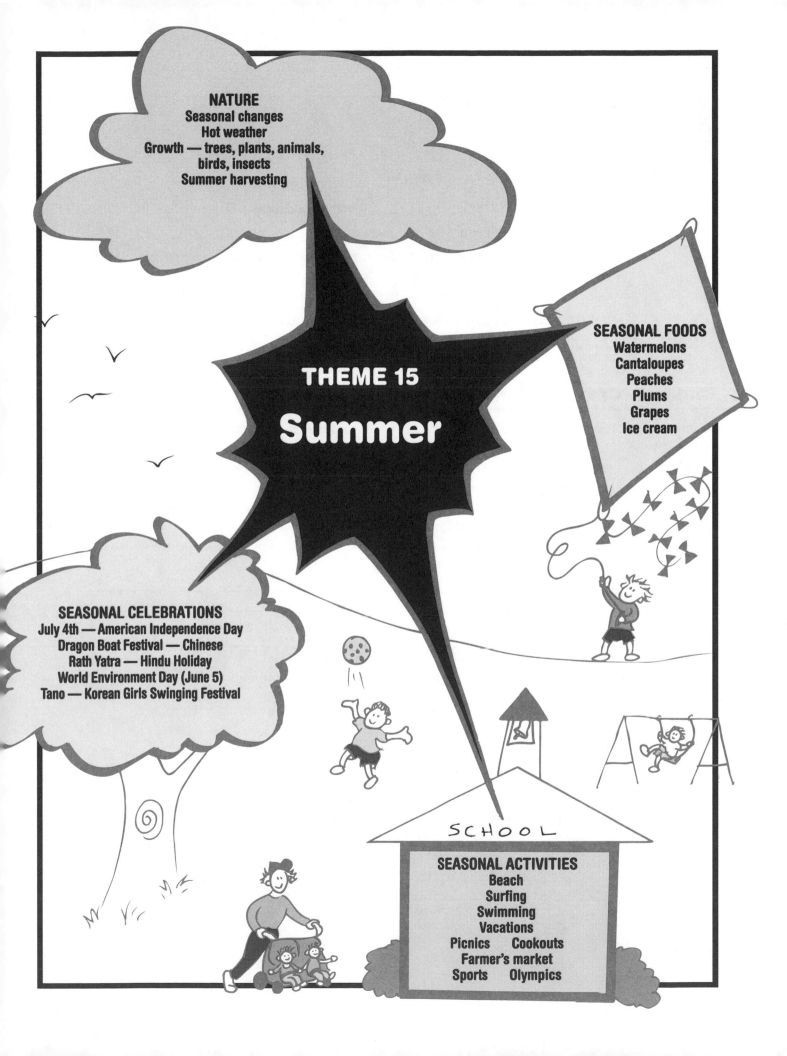

NATURE
Seasonal changes
Hot weather
Growth — trees, plants, animals,
birds, insects
Summer harvesting

THEME 15

Summer

SEASONAL FOODS
Watermelons
Cantaloupes
Peaches
Plums
Grapes
Ice cream

SEASONAL CELEBRATIONS
July 4th — American Independence Day
Dragon Boat Festival — Chinese
Rath Yatra — Hindu Holiday
World Environment Day (June 5)
Tano — Korean Girls Swinging Festival

SCHOOL

SEASONAL ACTIVITIES
Beach
Surfing
Swimming
Vacations
Picnics   Cookouts
Farmer's market
Sports   Olympics

THEME GOALS

To provide opportunities for children to learn:

1. Summer is a season of the year that comes after spring and before fall.
2. Summer is the time of year with the longest days and shortest nights.
3. In the summer, baby birds and other animals grow and learn to take care of themselves.
4. Most fruits and vegetables grow until they become ripe enough to eat.
5. Summer weather becomes very hot, and we need to wear lightweight clothing.

Children-Created Bulletin Board

Summer is a continuation of the Seasons theme. As before, continue to make the bulletin board interactive. The look of the board will change throughout the summer season.

* With the children's help, create a beach scene. Glue sand on the bulletin board's background paper.
* Add seashells, real or drawn by the children.
* Have the children tear pieces of construction paper in assorted shades of blue, or paint paper blue to make an ocean or lake. Add sailboats, clouds, and sun.
* Once you get started, the children can work together to make the bulletin board three-dimensional.

Vocabulary Starters

Let the children add additional words.

temperature — how hot or cold something is.

hot — a very high temperature.

beach — a sandy place near a lake or an ocean for playing and sunbathing.

shade — a place protected from the heat and light of the sun.

ripe — when fruits and vegetables are ready to eat.

Language Experiences

FUN IN THE SUN INDOORS

✳ Use a flannelboard and large flannelboard pieces to tell a story about the summertime.

✳ Make flannelboard pieces that correspond to the experiences of the children, such as the sun, beach ball, sand, small buckets, and shovels. The actual objects should be available in the classroom indoor or outdoor environment.

✳ After you tell a short story, let the older infants and the toddlers place the pieces on the flannelboard, name the articles, and "tell" their story.

LET'S HAVE A READING PARTY OUTDOORS

✳ Take a basket of books, pillows, blankets, and teddy bears outdoors, and have a reading party with the children!

✳ You can pitch a tent for a pretend camp-out, and tell stories.

✳ Have a snack in the tent. Make a "trail mix" with dry cereal pieces, raisins, nuts, and dried fruit.

POEM: "Summertime"

I love to swim in the summertime,
The summertime, the summertime.
I love to swim in the summertime
When the sky is clear and bright.

When we go to the beach in the summertime,
The summertime, the summertime,

When we go to the beach in the summertime,
I like to fly my kite.

I love to sail in the summertime,
The summertime, the summertime.
I love to sail in the summertime,
In a boat that's white and blue.

When we go to the lake in the summertime,
The summertime, the summertime,
When we go to the lake in the summertime,
We'll go fishing. How about you?

Philip Jackman

Dramatic Play

SURPRISE ENVIRONMENTS

✳ Close off the dramatic play area with a large sheet while "creating" is in progress.

✳ Have a few children set up a special dramatic play area with items they make or bring from home and that are unknown to the other children.

✳ They will decide what the area will be, what props are needed, and what they will name the dramatic play area. The process is their responsibility.

✳ Add items only if the children ask you to do so.

✳ After you do this, other children will want to set up surprise environments, too. That's the whole idea — to get the entire class involved in diverse thinking, problem-solving, working together cooperatively, and using their imagination and creativity.

IN THE GOOD OLD SUMMERTIME

✳ Set up a dramatic play ice cream stand outdoors for the children.

✳ Have the children make a sign with the name of the ice cream store, as well as labels for the kinds of ice cream sold and how much the cones cost.

✳ You will need cotton and cotton balls for the ice cream. Color some of the balls with food coloring before setting up. Also gather together containers of sprinkles and toppings, colored pompoms, scoops, cones, napkins, and pretend money.

MORE OUTDOOR FUN

✳ Create an island! It can be Hawaii, Jamaica, or any name the children choose.

✳ Get a few grass skirts, sunglasses, shells, and non-working cameras.

✳ You and the children can make palm trees, create a beach area by putting sand on a large piece of plastic, and add blue food coloring to a large plastic tub filled with water.

✳ How about some cold lemonade to drink too!

✳ The children will tell you what else is needed on their island. They will have a great time, and so will you!

Puppet Play

BEACH PEOPLE PUPPETS

Have fun at the beach! To do that, you will need to create an environment to help children act out what it is like to be at the beach.

✳ Make people puppets! Each one is built around a child's face. For example, one child can be the "sun," a "cloud," or "a wave." (See the illustration.) Help younger children and those who have not been to a beach to create their puppets.

✳ Create each puppet with heavy or corrugated cardboard. Out of a large, rectangular piece, cut a face-sized hole in the center.

✳ The child who wants to be a sun can decorate the puppet with crayons, markers, or tempera paint in sunny colors.

✳ The children will think of other beach puppets they want to make, such as a beach ball, a round life preserver, or a sand castle.

✳ Encourage the children to create "beach stories" using their puppets. Get them started by sharing books, photographs, and other pictures of beach activities.

Music

LET'S CELEBRATE

✳ Celebrate the 4th of July with an outdoor "concert."

✳ Make drums (use oatmeal containers), shakers (use paper plates stapled together with birdseed inside), and flutes (use paper towel rolls with wax paper covering one end and holes punched in one side).

✳ Take these "instruments" outside along with all the rhythm instruments and a tape player.

✳ Spread blankets on the grass.

✳ Serve lemonade.

✳ Decorate the playground equipment with red, white, and blue crepe paper.

✳ Let the concert begin. Play festive march music and have the children play along and march along with their musical instruments.

✳ Hold babies in teachers' laps and help them clap with the music. Some can crawl around on the blankets, while older infants can be pulled around the playground in decorated wagons.

RAINDROPS PITTER-PATTER AND SUNBEAMS GLOW

This is a *rhythmic* poem. Each verse emphasizes a different mood and a different season.

✳ Try saying each verse differently. Rain might have a light staccato quality, summer an expansive tone, fall a back-and-forth lilt, and winter a hushed tone.

✳ The words offer children an opportunity to play with language.

✳ Each verse suggests an appropriate arm-hand activity. For example, descending hands with wiggling fingers for rain, waving hands with spread fingers for sun, dropping hands sliding back and forth for leaves, and softly swaying falling hands for snow.

In the spring the raindrops go pitter-patter-pit,
Pitter-patter, pitter-patter, pitter-patter-pit.

In the summer the sunbeams glow shiny-shony-shine,
Shiny-shony, shiny-shony, shiny-shony-shine.

In the fall the red leaves dip flitter-flutter-flit,
Flitter-flutter, flitter-flutter, flitter-flutter-flit.

In the winter the snowflakes slip softly-siftly-soft,
Softly-siftly, softly-siftly, softly-siftly-soft.

Philip Jackman

Movement

SUMMER OLYMPICS

✳ Turn your playground into an Olympic Games site.

✳ Put some napping mats out for the gymnastics event, use the balance beam, set up a track for the runners, and add a sprinkler for the water event.

✳ Be sure to design the activities for the different developmental stages of the children in your class.

✳ The children will suggest additional events — be flexible.

✳ At the end of the day, each child receives a ribbon that says "First Place."

Sensory Art

WATER EVERYWHERE

✳ Older infants and toddlers enjoy outdoor water play. Sprinkler play, with children walking or running through the water, trying to catch the water in a plastic bucket, or just sitting where the sprinkler "rains" on them, can continue for long periods of time.

✳ Turn the sprinkler on and off while the children play.

✳ Tell the children what you are doing. "I'm turning the water off." "See, it is all gone." They'll look closely at the sprinkler to see where the water goes.

✳ "Look! Here it comes."

✳ Let the children help you turn the water on and off.

SUMMER SPRAY

✳ Painting outdoors with spray bottles is fun for preschoolers.

✳ Take a large piece of butcher paper and tape or tie it with yarn to the playground fence.

✳ Cover the grass or ground with a dropcloth.

✳ Fill three small spray bottles with watered-down paint in primary colors, one each of red, yellow, and blue.

✳ The more water you add to the paint, the more the children's creations will look like watercolor paintings.

✳ Ask the children to put on smocks, just as they do when painting indoors.

✳ Let the children, one at a time or in pairs with one at each end of the paper, spray paint the paper. They choose which of the three colors to use, or they may even choose all three.

✳ After the painting dries, create a banner and hang it from the classroom ceiling, or hang it as a mural on a wall in the classroom for all to see.

WATERCOLOR BUTTERFLIES AND IMAGINATIVE DESIGNS

For this project, supply white paper, watercolors, paintbrushes, water, scissors, and a butterfly design, if desired. This activity is designed to introduce the children to a new sensory art technique. Ask the children who are interested to create several designs on the sheets of paper using the following techniques.

Wet on Wet

On one of the pictures they use the "wet on wet" technique by painting with plain water first. Then, they paint over the water design with watercolors. The children see how the colors run together, creating new colors and interesting patterns.

Wet on Dry

Next, the children paint a picture using the "wet on dry" technique. They paint with watercolors on a dry piece of paper.

✳ Ask open-ended questions, such as, "Do you see a difference in your two paintings?" "Which do you think is your favorite?" "When the pictures dry, would you like to cut the designs out and display them?" "Would you like to put a frame around either of your pictures?" "Would you like to draw some flowers or butterflies and paint them?" "Will you paint your next picture with the *wet on wet* or *wet on dry* technique?"

Creative Food Experiences

SHAKE IT UP

You will need:

> 2 scoops of ice cream, preferably vanilla
> 1 scoop of orange sherbet
> 1/3 cup milk
> 2 or 3 tablespoons of orange juice

1. Wash hands.
2. Place all ingredients in a blender.
3. Mix until all the ingredients are well combined.
4. Enjoy!

EASY SANDWICH SURPRISE

You will need:

> a loaf of bread
> fillings such as peanut butter and jelly, or tuna spread

1. Wash hands.
2. Roll out a slice of bread with a rolling pin until it becomes very thin.
3. Spread the filling over the bread.
4. Carefully roll bread lengthwise and hold together with toothpicks if needed.
5. Slice into bite-size pieces.

The children love making this kind of sandwich, and it is self-correcting — if a piece of bread with filling doesn't roll, they can eat it anyway!

HAY STACKS

You will need:

> 1 small package butterscotch chips
> 1 small package chocolate chips
> 1 6-ounce package of Chinese noodles

1. Wash hands.
2. Melt the butterscotch and chocolate chips over low heat.
3. Add the package of Chinese noodles.
4. Place on wax paper in large spoonfuls, and shape into balls.
5. Let set. Eat!

HAY STACKS

Wash hands.

Melt 1 small package butterscotch chips and 1 small package chocolate chips over low heat.

Add 1 6-ounce package of Chinese noodles.

Place on wax paper in large spoonfuls.

Shape into balls. Let set.

EAT!

Math

MATCHING GAME

* Children love to find fun things to do in baskets placed around the room.
* Fill one basket with a variety of plastic containers and their lids.
* The containers should be small enough for the children to handle on their own. Provide plastic ones with tops and some with screw-on lids.
* A child can match the containers to their corresponding lids independently or by playing cooperatively with others.
* Make this activity available for the children to return to anytime they wish.

BLOCKS AND MATH ARE PARTNERS

* Block play is ongoing in every early childhood classroom, no matter what the season of the year.
* Stimulate block play by placing some colorful cards nearby with simple pictures of long, short, high, wide, narrow, straight, curvy, and zig-zag block designs, along with appropriate word labels.
* This is a nonintrusive way to increase mathematical concepts and vocabulary.
* Remember to take photographs of the block center creations, or make a simple sketch of the original designs. Be sure to label each picture with the "architect's" name.

Science

SUN PRINTS

* Place objects from the classroom, such as blocks, Styrofoam pieces, lids from containers, flannelboard pieces, buttons, shells, and a plastic knife or fork, on dark construction paper, and expose them to sunlight for several hours.
* At the end of the day, let the children remove the items and discuss what has happened.

EVAPORATION

* Discuss the process of evaporation with the children.
* Take two identical small jars, and fill them one-half full with colored water. Do not cover the jars.
* Put one jar in the sun and the other in the shade.
* Have the children predict which will evaporate first.
* Discuss and record their observations each day.
* How many days does it take for the water in each to evaporate?

Social Studies

LET'S GO TO THE BEACH!

Summer is the time when people all over the country love to swim, sunbathe, and play at lakes and beaches in our coastal areas.

* Read Hayles' *Beach Play* to the children to set the scene; see the books section in this theme.
* Help the children learn more about beaches through the aid of pictures, a map, and a miniature beach in your outdoor play area.
* Using pictures of beaches you have collected from travel brochures and magazines, talk with the children about what beaches are (sandy areas where the land meets the oceans).
* Ask them if they have ever been to a beach. What do people do there? What do they wear? What do they take with them?
* Using a map of the United States that includes an inset map of the Hawaiian Islands, explain that the blue area next to the coastline on our east is the Atlantic Ocean; on the west shore is the Pacific Ocean; and on the south shore is the Gulf of Mexico.
* Beaches are located where these blue areas touch the darker-colored land areas.
* Have the children show you where beaches are located on your map.
* If they ever want to go to a beach, the children should know directions: north, south, east, and west.
* Guide them into showing you where the directions are on the map. Show them the arrow pointing north, usually found in one corner of a map.

✳ It is helpful to write "north," "south," "east," and "west" on the map's four sides.

✳ Invite the children to locate where they live on the map. Ask them in what directions they would have to travel to visit beaches on the west, east, or south. Have them point to the directions on the map.

✳ To extend this activity, have the children make a beach on the playground, and plan a trip to their beach. The existing sandbox or a large piece of plastic on the grass covered with sand becomes the beach. Provide sunscreen, beach balls, a beach umbrella, towels, shells, pails, and shovels.

✳ The children may wear swimsuits and play in the waves (the sprinkler) to complete the environment.

Children's Books

Archambault, John, and David Plummer. (1996). *Grandmother's Garden.* Illustrated by Raul Colon. New York: Silver Burdett.

Boelts, Maribeth. (1995). *Summer's End.* Illustrated by Ellen Kandoian. New York: Houghton Mifflin.

Bunting, Eve. (1996). *Sunflower House.* Illustrated by Kathryn Hewitt. San Diego, CA: Harcourt Brace.

Bunting, Eve. (1994). *Flower Garden.* Illustrated by Kathryn Hewitt. San Diego, CA: Harcourt Brace.

Crews, Nina. (1995). *One Hot Summer Day.* New York: Greenwillow.

De Paola, Tomie. (1994). *Four Stories for Four Seasons.* New York: Aladdin.

Ehlert, Lois. (1996). *Eating the Alphabet: Fruits and Vegetables from A to Z.* (Board book) New York: Red Wagon.

Euvremer, Teryl. (1987). *Sun's Up.* New York: Crown Publishers.

Fleming, Denise, (1995). *In the Small, Small Pond.* New York: Henry Holt.

Florian, Douglas. (1998). *A Summer Day.* New York: William Morrow.

Garland, Sherry. (1995). *Summer Sands.* Illustrated by Robert J. Lee. San Diego, CA: Harcourt Brace.

Gershator, Phillis, and David Gershator. (1998). *Greetings, Sun.* New York: Dk Ink.

Haas, Irene. (1997). *A Summertime Song.* New York: Margaret K. McElderry Books.

Hall, Donald. (1995). *Lucy's Summer.* Illustrated by Michael McCurdy. San Diego, CA: Harcourt Brace.

Hayles, Marsha. (1998). *Beach Play.* Illustrated by Hideko Takahashi. New York: Henry Holt.

Hirschi, Ron. (1991). *Summer.* Photographed by Thomas D. Mangelsen. New York: Cobblehill Books.

Kesselman, Windy. (1995). *Sand in My Shoes.* Illustrated by Ronald Himler. New York: Hyperion Books.

Lee, Huy Voien. (1997). *At the Beach.* New York: Henry Holt.

Lerner, Carol. (1996). *Backyard Birds of Summer.* New York: William Morrow.

MacKinnon, Debbie. (1995). *The Seasons: Spring, Summer, Autumn, Winter.* Photographed by Anthea Sieveking. New York: Barrons Juveniles.

Peters, Lisa W. (1995). *The Hayloft.* Illustrated by K. D. Plum. New York: Dial Books.

Peters, Lisa W. (1995). *The Sun, the Wind, and the Rain.* Illustrated by Ted Rand. New York: Henry Holt.

Rius, Maria, and Jose M. Parramon. (1998). *Summer: The Four Seasons.* New York: Barrons Juveniles.

Sanchez, Isidro, and Carmen Peris. (1992). *Summer Sports.* New York: Barrons Juveniles.

Van Leeuwen, Jean. (1997). *Touch the Summer Sky.* Illustrated by Dan Andreasen. New York: Dial Books.

Yolen, Jane. (1995). *Before the Storm.* Illustrated by Georgia Pugh. New York: Boyds Mills Press.

Parent Letter (Toddler)

Dear Parents,

As we continue to study the seasons, we are now starting our theme of Summer. We will offer opportunities for the children to learn:

- Summer is a season of the year that comes after spring and before fall.
- Summer is the time of year with the longest days and shortest nights.
- In the summer, baby birds and other animals grow and learn to take care of themselves.
- Fruits and vegetables grow until they become ripe enough to eat.
- Summer weather becomes very hot, and we need to wear lightweight clothing.

We will be talking about:

- nature and seasonal changes
- the growth of trees, plants, animals, birds, and insects
- seasonal celebrations, such as the Fourth of July
- seasonal activities, such as going to the beach, swimming, picnics, and the Olympic games
- seasonal foods, such as watermelons, cantaloupes, and ice cream

To reinforce what your child is learning in school, try some of these things to do at home:

- Go on a family picnic.
- Enjoy July 4th with your child.
- Decorate your child's tricycle with red, white, and blue crepe paper streamers.
- Enjoy water play with your child.

Parent participation opportunities at school will be to:

- Come to our Fourth of July outdoor "concert" on the playground.
  Date _____ Time _____
- Come and help us with our summer recipes.
  Date _____ Time _____

Our wish list for this theme includes:

    small baskets
    clean plastic containers with lids
    plain and corrugated cardboard
    seashells
    plastic buckets with shovels

                        Thank you for your continued support and interest in your child's learning program.

Environment

*C*hildren learn by doing. Young children must explore, dis-cover, and create the environment around them. Encour-age children to do what they can for themselves, but provide guidance with some tasks before they become too difficult and frustration begins.

The thematic activities in this section have been developed to assist young children in growing up with a joy of explora-tion and an appreciation of the environment. A wide variety of experiences, materials, and equipment are included to accommodate the children's developmental ages and stages.

The following themes are included in Section IV — Environment:

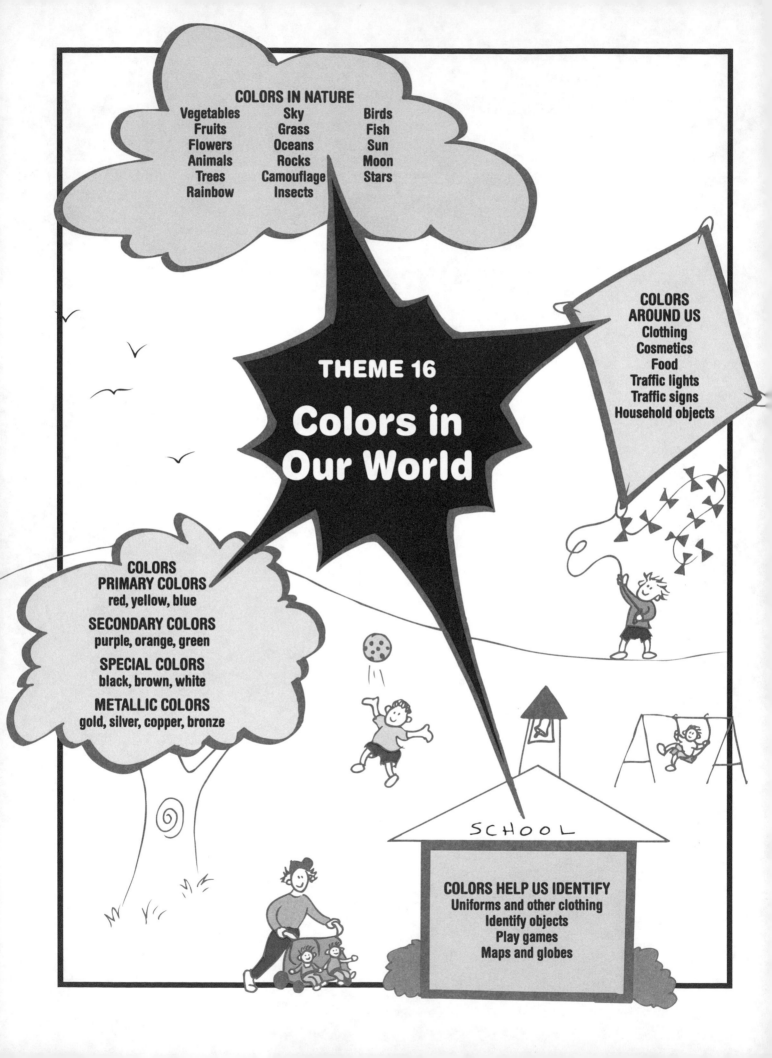

COLORS IN NATURE

Vegetables	Sky	Birds
Fruits	Grass	Fish
Flowers	Oceans	Sun
Animals	Rocks	Moon
Trees	Camouflage	Stars
Rainbow	Insects	

THEME 16

Colors in Our World

COLORS AROUND US
Clothing
Cosmetics
Food
Traffic lights
Traffic signs
Household objects

COLORS
PRIMARY COLORS
red, yellow, blue

SECONDARY COLORS
purple, orange, green

SPECIAL COLORS
black, brown, white

METALLIC COLORS
gold, silver, copper, bronze

SCHOOL

COLORS HELP US IDENTIFY
Uniforms and other clothing
Identify objects
Play games
Maps and globes

THEME GOALS

To provide opportunities for children to learn:

1. Our world is full of color.

2. Color is important for identifying most things in our world.

3. Color makes our world more interesting and enjoyable.

4. Colors have names.

5. The primary colors are red, yellow, and blue, and when mixed they produce new colors.

6. The secondary colors are orange, green, and purple, and are created by mixing two primary colors.

7. There are many ways of experimenting with and exploring colors.

Children-Created Bulletin Board

Use this bulletin board to provide the children with concrete examples of how their world is filled with color. As always, include the children in your planning. They will give you a lot of colorful ideas and help you to make the board an ongoing project.

✳ Cover the bulletin board with a pastel shade of paper for background.

✳ In the upper left side of the board, place a rainbow made of colored crepe paper or ribbons that the children cut.

✳ Have them crumple up white tissue paper to make a cloud. Place this in the upper right side.

✳ Have a bright yellow sun peek out from behind the cloud.

✳ In the lower left corner of the bulletin board, have a flower garden made by the children. See the science activity, A Garden of Color, in this theme for ways to create the garden.

✳ In the lower right corner of the board make a blue ocean with waves using cellophane or tissue paper.

✳ Ask the children to draw pictures of themselves or other children, cut these out, and place them anywhere they want on the bulletin board. See the social studies part of this theme.

✳ Title the board "Colors in Our World."

✳ Continue to add to the bulletin board throughout the theme.

Vocabulary Starters

Let the children add additional words.

primary colors — three colors, red, yellow, and blue, from which all the colors in the rainbow are created.

secondary colors — orange, green, and purple, which are created by mixing any two primary colors.

black — created by mixing all three primary colors.

brown — created by mixing red, yellow, and black.

white — the absence of color.

shade — the darkness of or amount of black in a particular color.

tint — the lightness of or amount of white in a particular color.

Language Experiences

COLORFUL PEEKABOO

✳ Play Peekaboo with the babies.

✳ To make this activity colorful, collect solid-colored scarves that can be seen through.

✳ Hold up a scarf between you and the little one. Play peekaboo.

✳ Talk about the color of the scarf.

✳ Repeat this activity often. It is a fun way to share colors with babies.

A COLOR A DAY

✳ To begin this theme, totally surround the children in a color each day. It is important for children to *experience* color.

✳ For example, children paint with red, wear red, sing about red, eat a red snack, read books about red, and build with red blocks or Legos.

✳ In small groups, talk about the color of the day. To get them started, ask open-ended questions such as, "What do you see that is red?" "How does red taste?"

✳ Write what the children say about each color on a chart. It can be made into a book with their drawings and placed in the book center.

POEM:
"Primary Colors"

The primary colors look bright to me.
The first is red, as we all can see,
The second is yellow, plain as can be,
And the third looks blue to me.
  Mix red and yellow — it's orange you'll see,
  Mix red and blue — it's purple you'll see,
  Mix blue and yellow — it's green you'll see,
  And they all look good to me.

Philip Jackman

COLORFUL LANGUAGES

Young children enjoy learning languages. The following names for colors are another way to introduce the colors of the world.

English	Spanish	French	German
red	rojo	rouge	rot
	ró-ho	roozh	rote
yellow	amarillo	jaune	gelb
	ah-ma-reé-yo	zhōne	gelb
blue	azul	bleu	blau
	ah-zoóĺ	bloō	bla-oh
green	verde	vert	grun
	vaiŕ-day	vair	green
purple	morado	violet	purpur
	mo-rah́-do	vee-o-lay	poōŕ-poōr
orange	naranja	orange	orangefarben
	na-rah́n-ha	o-ranzh	o-rah́nj-fár-ben
brown	marron	brun	braun
	mah-roñe	broōn	brown
black	negro	noir	schwarz
	néh-gro	nwahr	shvarts
white	blanco	blanc	weiss
	blah́n-co	blahnc	vice

English	Italian	Japanese
red	rosso	akai
	róh-so	ah-káh-ee
yellow	giallo	kiiro
	jee-ah́-lo	kée-ro
blue	blu	aoi
	blue	ah-oh́-ee
green	verde	midori
	vaiŕ-day	mee-dóh-ree
purple	porpora	murasaki-iro
	por-pór-a	moō-ruh-sáh-kee-eé-ro
orange	arancio	mikan
	ah-rah́n-chee-o	mée-kahn

brown	bruno	kasshoku
	broō´-no	kah-shó-koō
black	nero	kuroi
	náy-ro	koo-róh-ee
white	bianco	shiroi
	bee-ah́n-co	she-róh-ee

Dramatic Play

CRAYON MELT

✳ Ask the children to tell you their favorite color of crayon.

✳ They are going to pretend to be that crayon dancing on a sunny day. This activity works well outdoors.

✳ Children raise their hands above their heads, palms together and fingers pointing up, to make the point of the crayon. Toddlers can just put their hands on their heads.

✳ Play some music for the "dancing crayons."

✳ Remind them that the sun is shining brightly. What will happen to the colorful crayons?

✳ Comment on the children's actions as they begin to melt. "I think Jared is all melted." "Tamera is melting into a yellow puddle." "Now we have a beautiful lake of many colors."

✳ Continue playing as long as the children want to do so. They can suggest other things that will melt in the sun, such as ice cream cones.

Puppet Play

PURPLE POLKA-DOT PUPPET

✳ Collect clean white socks, child-sized if possible.

✳ Give each child a sock, and ask him to put the sock on his hand.

✳ Ask open-ended questions, such as, "What does the sock look like?" "What kind of puppet can it become?" "What color should it be?"

✳ At the art table, guide the children into making their sock puppets. Provide markers, crayons, and colored plastic tape.

✳ If some children do not want to do anything to the white sock, then that can be the color they choose.

I see two red blocks,
Red blocks, red blocks,
I see two red blocks
In the yellow box.

SONG: "When I Wear Red" by Jo Eklof

Additional verses:

Have children make up what to action to do with other colors, for instance, "When I wear green, I always lean."

© 1982 by Jo Eklof. All rights reserved. Used with permission.

(See page 301 for enlargements.)

✳ Older children may decide to be more creative with their puppets. Ask them if they know what striped, polka-dot, or plaid looks like? Show them with a piece of paper and a marker. The colored plastic tape makes this easy to do.

✳ The main objective is to get the children playing with puppets.

Music

TRADITIONAL SONG: "Mary Wore Her Red Dress"

This activity is to encourage young children to look at the colors they and their friends are wearing. It also makes them become more aware of the colors in their environment.

✳ After introducing the children to this traditional song, ask them to make up additional words. Examples might be blue jeans, sneakers, shoes, shirt, blouse, hat, ribbon, and head band.

Mary wore her red dress,
Red dress, red dress,
Mary wore her red dress
All day long.

✳ The children can change the focus away from clothing to objects in the room or outdoors

I see a blue ball,
Blue ball, blue ball,
I see a blue ball
On the playground.

LET'S PAINT TO MUSIC

✳ Children love to move to music. Select appropriate music from cassettes and CDs of Ella Jenkins, Raffi, Jack Grunsky, Thomas Moore, Steve and Greg, Hap Palmer, Sesame Street, and Red Grammar.

✳ Tape butcher paper to a long table or several round tables.

✳ Set up small containers of different colors of tempera paint, with a brush for each container, at various points around the table.

✳ Each child starts this activity standing at a paint container.

✳ When the music starts, each child begins painting.

✳ The children will play a kind of musical chairs. They stop painting when the music stops. Then, they move to another point and paint as the music starts again. Everyone stays in and keeps painting. No one gets left out.

✳ The first time you do this, it might be helpful to have the children practice moving around the table, making pretend marks with the brushes as they go.

✳ Hang the "music mural" up in the classroom as a wall mural, a banner, or a hanging center divider.

Movement

COLORS FALL DOWN

This movement activity works best either indoors in a carpeted area, or outdoors in a grassy area, where the children can most safely "fall down."

✳ With young toddlers, simply say or chant the song. They can do the actions together.

✳ Have color samples on hand to use as visual clues.

✳ Sing the following song, based on the traditional rhyme:

Ring around a rosey
A pocket full of posies,
Red, yellow, blue,
Red (or yellow or blue) fall down.

✳ For older children, have them divide into three groups. Designate one as the "red" group, one as "yellow," and the third as "blue."

✳ You name one or more colors to fall down.

✳ The children join hands in a circle and all move in one direction as they sing.

✳ After you lead the activity, the children can take turns saying which color(s) should fall down.

✳ You can vary the activity by announcing which colors are to fall down before they sing, or waiting until the last line to surprise them with which group(s) will fall down.

COLOR RUN

Younger children need help with this activity, but older children can do it by themselves.

✳ Cut large paper plates in half.

✳ Attach various colors of ribbon or crepe paper streamers along the straight edge by stapling them or tying them through holes punched along the edge.

✳ The children take their rainbow streamers outside and run with them overhead. The faster they run, the more the colors will fly.

Sensory Art

COLORFUL PLACEMATS

With the children's help, make colorful construction paper placemats.

✳ Trace around a plate, spoon, fork, and glass with a black marker.

✳ Laminate each placemat for easy cleaning and durability.

✳ When first introducing colors, use placemats of only one color so all the children have the same color.

✳ Later, the children can choose which colors they want. They can change placemats daily or keep the same color all the time. Children make the decision.

PASTELS GALORE

✳ Give the children red, yellow, and blue paints.

✳ Encourage them to create as many colors as they can using these primary colors.

✳ Introduce pastels by adding white to all the other colors they created using red, yellow, and blue.

✳ Add watercolors and colored chalk for the children to experiment with.

✳ Later, talk about what the children experienced. Write the names of all the different colors they discovered. Place this information on the bulletin board.

SHADES OF COLOR

Introduce children to the concept of how a color can have many different shades. Show them a red, yellow, blue, or green ball, the same color construction paper, and a picture with that color in a book. They are different shades of the same color.

✳ What else do they see in the classroom that is a different tint or shade of the same color?

✳ Collect magazines, catalogs, and travel brochures. Put these along with glue, scissors, and various colors of construction paper on a table.

✳ Ask the children to choose one color and one piece of construction paper.

✳ Explain that they are going to make a "one-color collage" of pictures from the magazines. They then search for all the shades of the color they chose.

✳ Next, glue the pictures on the construction paper.

✳ Younger children may want to work with a partner.

✳ Older children can extend the activity by designing their collages to range from the darkest shade of a color to the lightest.

✳ Follow up with a discussion of the many shades of colors they have discovered. Write down the new words they use to *describe* the colors, such as dark, light, bright, pale, dull, and shiny.

✳ Make the materials available to the children so that they can make additional collages if they wish.

SURPRISE PLAY DOUGH

✳ Put the following items on the art table:

aprons

large mixing bowl

pitcher of water

measuring cup

tablespoon

red, blue, and yellow food coloring

container of salt

container of flour

bottle of vegetable oil

large spoon

sandwich-size bags

✳ Have a small group of children wash their hands and put on aprons. You can repeat this activity as many times as needed to give all the children a chance to participate.

✳ Have several children measure one-half cup of flour each into the bowl until it totals three cups of flour.

✳ Ask another child to measure one cup salt, and mix it together with the flour.

✳ Ask another child to make a well in the dry ingredients, and measure a tablespoon of oil into the well.

✳ Add water slowly until the dough is like pie dough.

✳ Divide the dough into sections, and have the children shape the dough into balls.

✳ Place each ball into a plastic sandwich bag labeled with the child's name on masking tape, and close each bag with a rubber band.

✳ Place these on a teacher's shelf.

✳ Before the children arrive the next day, punch an indentation in each ball, and carefully put in a drop of food coloring and reseal the ball.

✳ Reclose each bag.

✳ When the children ask about their balls of dough, give out the dough and ask them to knead it in the bag.

✳ The children will really be surprised when they see what happens! They can then take the dough out and play with it.

Creative Food Experiences

LET'S DRINK PURPLE

You will need:

1 cup milk

1/4 cup grape juice

1 sliced banana

1. Wash hands.
2. Place all ingredients into a blender and mix together.
3. Yum!

Serves approximately 3.

LET'S DRINK PURPLE

Wash hands.

Place 1 cup milk,

1/4 cup grape juice, and

1 sliced banana

into a blender and mix together.

YUM!

COLORFUL SALAD

You will need:

    strawberries

    blueberries

    bananas

    green or yellow apples

    red or green grapes

1. Wash hands.
2. Wash fruit.
3. Cut up bananas and apples into bite sizes.
4. Let children taste each kind of fruit separately before mixing together.
5. Place fruit pieces in a big bowl, and mix gently to combine all the fruits.
6. Let's eat!

Math

COLORED STACKING RINGS AND BLOCKS

This exercise is an opportunity to remember that developmentally appropriate basic toys and equipment are the foundation of themes and concepts for young children.

✳ With older infants and younger toddlers, have colored stacking rings and blocks available for them every day.

✳ This individual activity keeps colors and shapes in young children's environment and provides new vocabulary as language skills develop.

COLOR CHALLENGE

✳ Place additional items of one color around the room without the children knowing.

✳ Count and list the number of items of a specific color in the room. For example, count and list all the blue items.

✳ Place this information on a chart for the children to refer to *later*.

✳ Ask each child to find blue items in the room, pick up those that can be picked up, and put them in a separate pile next to him.

✳ They will need to notice items such as the blue on the bulletin board or someone's shirt.

✳ Each child counts the number of items she found and writes the number.

✳ With your help, they add all the numbers together to find the total.

✳ Check the total with your list. Were any items missed? If so, have the children look again to find the missing items.

✳ Have the children count all the items again and compare with your list.

✳ Change this activity on another day. Place items of several colors around the room. This time, tell the children the number of items of each color you have counted.

✳ You will find the children adding up what others find to see if all items have been found.

Science

WATERCOLORS

✳ A simple way to bring color to the toddler environment is to add a few drops of food coloring to the water table. This can be changed easily and often.

✳ For toddlers and young preschoolers, demonstrate how one color can change into another color by having them add a few drops of yellow food coloring to a glass of water. They watch the color sink and spread.

✳ Then add blue drops. What happens when the colors mix? Continue this activity using different combinations of colored drops to create more colors.

A GARDEN OF COLOR

This activity promotes creativity, problem-solving, working together cooperatively, and thinking about how many beautiful colors appear in nature.

✳ Collect books, magazines, and catalogs that have many colorful pictures of all kinds of flowers.

✳ Make these available for the children to look at, not cut up.

✳ Have the children point out and name the different flowers they know. Talk about the different colors of the flowers. For example, a rose can be red, white, pink, or a combination of colors. Can daisies be any other color than white?

✳ Suggest to the children that they can create a garden of colors to put in the flower garden on the bulletin board.

✳ Guide them to make as many different kinds of flowers as they can out of construction paper. The children will tell you what other materials they need to create their garden.

✳ Another decision they will make is how to group the flowers in the garden. Perhaps they will want to draw them on paper first, plotting out how the flowers will look.

Social Studies

HAROLD AND THE PURPLE CRAYON:

Introduce the children to the wonderful world of *Harold and the Purple Crayon* by Crockett Johnson, listed in the books section of this theme. This book can be the beginning of many fun activities.

✳ After reading *Harold and the Purple Crayon,* give the children paper and purple crayons. Let them tell you where their purple crayons are taking them and what it is like there.

✳ If some children want a color other than purple, that is fine. Different colors can take them different places in our world of colors.

✳ With preschoolers and kindergartners, you can expand this activity. Attach white butcher paper to the lower part of the walls all around the classroom.

✳ Give each child a portion of the paper and a purple crayon. She can draw pictures and go for a walk, just like Harold.

✳ What a wonderful world the children will create from their imaginations!

THE LAND OF MANY COLORS

The Klamath County YMCA Family Preschool's *The Land of Many Colors,* listed in the books section of this theme, is another special book you will want to share with the children. It is written by children for children.

✳ Talk about the story with the children. Discuss the messages of peace and respect for differences.

✳ Make purple, blue, and green people, and put them on the bulletin board to add to the Colors in Our World.

✳ After reading this, the children may want to write and illustrate a story of their own.

✳ They may want to act out the story with props and simple costumes.

✳ They can draw and cut out felt characters, then retell the story on the flannelboard.

✳ Together, you and the children can find many ways to expand this activity.

Children's Books

Burton, Katherine. (1997). *One Gray Mouse.* New York: Kids Can Press.

Cabrera, Jane. (1997). *Cat's Colors.* New York: Dial Books.

Carle, Eric. (1998). *Hello, Red Fox.* New York: Simon & Schuster.

Carle, Eric. (1998). *Let's Paint a Rainbow: A Play-and-Read Book.* New York: Cartwheel Books.

Crews, Donald. (1995). *Ten Black Dots.* New York: Mulberry.

Demi. (1980). *Liang and the Magic Paint Brush.* New York: Henry Holt.

Dr. Seuss. (1996). *My Many Colored Days.* New York: Knopf.

Dundon, Caitlin. (1994). *The Yellow Umbrella.* Illustrated by Sandra Speidel. New York: Simon & Schuster.

Ehlert, Lois. (1997). *Color Farm.* New York: HarperCollins.

Ehlert, Lois. (1997). *Color Zoo.* New York: HarperCollins.

Ehlert, Lois. (1991). *Red Leaf, Yellow Leaf.* San Diego, CA: Harcourt Brace.

Fleming, Denise. (1998). *Lunch.* New York: Henry Holt.

Heller, Ruth. (1995). *Color.* New York: Scholastic.

Hill, Eric. (1997). *Spot's Big Book of Colors, Shapes, and Numbers.* New York: Puffin.

Hoban, Tana. (1995). *Colors Everywhere.* New York: Greenwillow.

Hoban, Tana. (1993). *Black on White* and *White on Black.* (Board books). New York: Greenwillow.

Hoban, Tana. (1989). *Of Colors and Things.* New York: Greenwillow.

Hoban, Tana. (1986). *Red Blue Yellow Shoe.* (Board book). New York: William Morrow.

Johnson, Crockett. (1983). *Harold and the Purple Crayon.* New York: HarperTrophy.

Jonas, Ann. (1989). *Color Dance.* New York: Greenwillow.

Kissinger, Katie. (1994). *All the Colors We Are — Todos los Colores de Nuestra Peil.* Photographed by Wernher Krutein. St. Paul, MN: Redleaf Press.

Klamath County YMCA Family Preschool. (1993). *The Land of Many Colors.* Illustrated by Rita Pocock. New York: Scholastic.

Littlefield, Holly. (1997). *Colors of Japan (Colors of the World).* Illustrated by Helen Byers. New York: Lerner Publications.

Martin, Bill Jr. (1983). *Brown Bear, Brown Bear.* Illustrated by Eric Carle. New York: Henry Holt.

McCloskey, Robert. (1987). *Blueberries for Sal.* New York: Viking.

Olawsky, Lynn A. (1997). *Colors of Mexico (Colors of the World).* Minneapolis, MN: Carolrhoda Books.

Onyefulu, Ifeoma. (1997). *Chidi Only Likes Blue: An African Book of Colors.* New York: Cobblehill Books.

Peek, Merle. (1988). *Mary Wore Her Red Dress, and Henry Wore His Green Sneakers.* (Reprint edition). Boston, MA: Houghton Mifflin.

Van Der Leeden, Ingrid. (1997) *Colors, Colors, Everywhere! (Teething Time Books).* New York: Little Simon Books.

Walsh, Ellen Stoll. (1995). *Mouse Paint.* New York: Voyager.

Wylie, Joanne, and David Wylie. (1983). *A Fishy Color Story.* Chicago, IL: Children's Press.

Yenawine, Philip. (1991). *Colors.* New York: Delecorte.

Parent Letter (Toddler)

Dear Parents,

We are beginning our new theme, Colors. The children will learn:

- Our world is full of color.
- Color is important for identifying most things in our world.
- Color makes our world more interesting and enjoyable.
- Colors have names.
- The primary colors are red, yellow, and blue. When mixed, primary colors produce new colors.
- The secondary colors are orange, green, and purple. Secondary colors are created by mixing two primary colors.
- There are many ways of experimenting with and exploring colors.

We will be talking about:

- primary colors
- special colors
- how colors help us
- colors of skin, hair, and eyes
- colors in nature
- colors around us

Try these fun things to do at home with your child:

- Help your child identify objects of different colors in the environment.
- Walk around the house and talk about all the colors, both inside and outside.
- Talk about the colors of the food you eat.

Parent participation opportunities at school will be to:

- Come visit our class and share our colorful experiences with us.
  Date _____ Time _____
- Come help us make flowers for our garden of color.
  Date _____ Time _____

Our wish list for this theme includes:

children's socks
pictures of flowers
colored tissue paper
colored ribbon
old magazines
paper plates

Thank you for sharing your child with us.

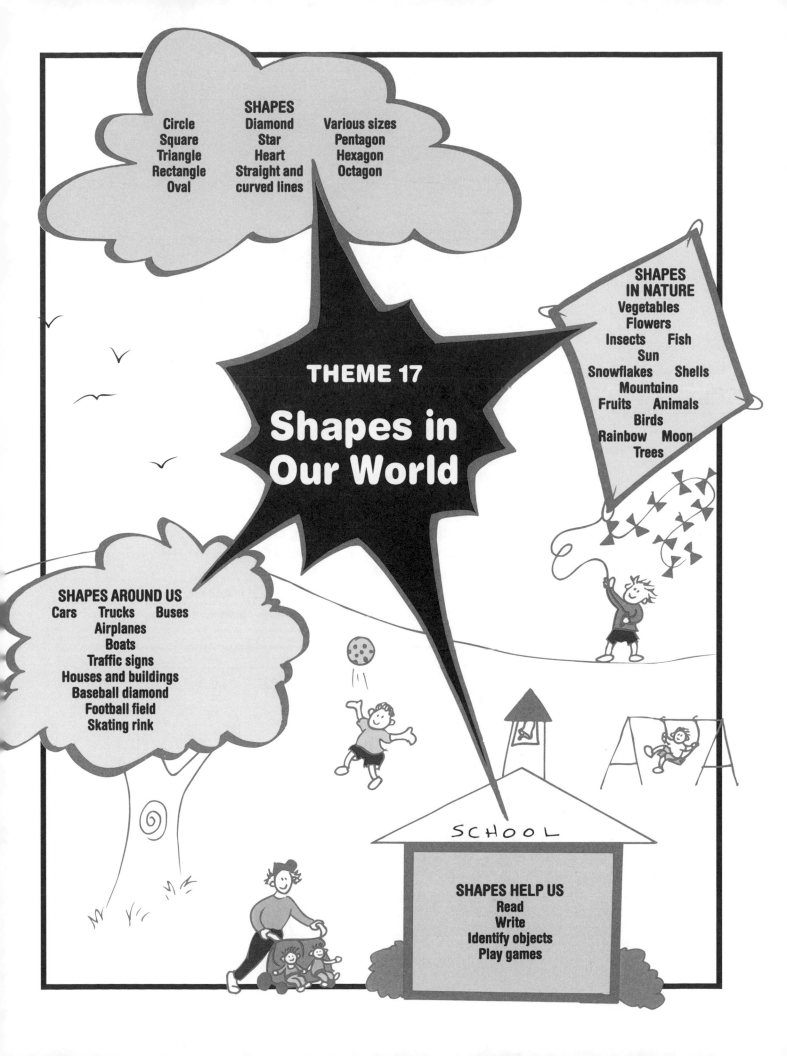

SHAPES
Circle
Square
Triangle
Rectangle
Oval

Diamond
Star
Heart
Straight and
curved lines

Various sizes
Pentagon
Hexagon
Octagon

SHAPES IN NATURE
Vegetables
Flowers
Insects   Fish
Sun
Snowflakes   Shells
Mountains
Fruits   Animals
Birds
Rainbow   Moon
Trees

THEME 17

Shapes in Our World

SHAPES AROUND US
Cars   Trucks   Buses
Airplanes
Boats
Traffic signs
Houses and buildings
Baseball diamond
Football field
Skating rink

SCHOOL

SHAPES HELP US
Read
Write
Identify objects
Play games

THEME GOALS

To provide opportunities for children to learn:

1. Our world is full of shapes.
2. Shape is important for identifying everything in our world.
3. We can see shapes with our eyes and feel them with our hands.
4. Shapes have names.
5. The basic shapes are circle, square, rectangle, and triangle.
6. A shape comes in many sizes, but it still is the same shape.

Children-Created Bulletin Board

The bulletin board that was created by you and the children for Theme 16 — Colors in Our World can be used for this theme, Shapes in Our World, by adding and changing some elements.

✳ Change the title of the board to read "Colors and Shapes in Our World."
✳ Let the children create a border around the bulletin board. There are several ways to do this.
✳ Begin with pre-cut strips of paper in lengths equal to the sides of the bulletin board.
✳ The children can do stamp printing with assorted shapes on the strips of paper.
✳ They can cut out shapes from construction paper scraps and make a collage of shapes on the strips.
✳ They can draw favorite shapes on the border strips.
✳ Remove the cloud covering part of the sun to leave a bright sun, a large round circle.
✳ Let the children help you add more Shapes to the board as the Shapes theme continues.

Vocabulary Starters

Let the children add additional words.

circle — a perfectly round shape.

square — a shape with four equal sides.

rectangle — a shape with four sides that are not all equal.

triangle — a shape with three sides.

oval — a shape like an egg.

line — a long mark or the edge of something, either straight or curved.

Language Experiences

INFANT TALK

✳ Talk about shapes to the babies.

✳ When you roll a ball, talk about circles. "This is a big ball, and it is a round circle." "This is a little ball, and it is a round circle."

✳ When the infants play with empty boxes, such as tissue boxes, small gift boxes, or shoe boxes, talk about the shapes of the boxes.

✳ Cut textured fabric shapes, and glue them to thick pieces of cardboard. Give the shapes to the babies to play with.

✳ Talk about triangles, squares, rectangles, and circles.

✳ Share shapes with the infants as part of their environment.

POEM: "I Am a Shape"

I am a square, a square am I,
I have four sides that you can spy.
I have four corners, all the same,
I am a square, that is my name.
   I am a circle, a circle you see,
   I'm round and round as a ball can be.
   My circling side looks all the same,
   I am a circle, that is my name.
I am a triangle, just look at me,
I have three sides, as you can see.
I have three corners, all the same,
I am a triangle, that's my name.

I am a rectangle, four sides are there,
I have four corners just like a square.
But my sides are different, not all the same,
I am a rectangle, that's my name.

Philip Jackman

A SHAPE STORY

✳ Tell a story to the children.

✳ You can tell the story using the flannelboard and flannelboard characters, or you can draw the story on a flip chart, changing the pages as you progress through the story.

A Shape Story

Once upon a time, there lived a group of circles. They lived and played all by themselves.

(Put the circles, all sizes and colors, on the upper left side of the flannelboard or flip chart.)

In the same town lived a group of squares. They lived and played all by themselves.

(Put the squares, all sizes and colors, on the upper right side of the flannelboard or flip chart.)

There also lived in the town a group of triangles. They lived and played all by themselves.

(Put the triangles, all sizes and colors, on the lower left side of the flannelboard or flip chart.)

And down the street in the same town there lived a group of rectangles. They lived and played by themselves.

(Put the rectangles, all sizes and colors, on the lower right side of the flannelboard or flip chart.)

One day one of the small circles rolled into the center of town and began playing all alone.

(Place a small circle in the center of the flannelboard or flip chart.)

A small square saw the little circle playing all alone and decided to join in the fun.

(Move a small square to the center to join the small circle.)

The circle and the square enjoyed playing together. Just then, the small triangle saw the two shapes playing and wanted to play too. So, the triangle joined in the fun.

(Move a small square to join the circle and square in the center of the flannelboard or flip chart.)

What do you think happened next?

(The children should answer "a small rectangle joined in the fun." Add a small rectangle to the other squares in the center of the flannelboard or flip chart.)

What do you think will happen now?

(As the children start telling you what they think will happen, start moving all the shapes together and jumble them up all over the flannelboard or flip chart.)

Everyone is having so much fun. Look! Look at what the shapes have done. They've made themselves into a house, and a wagon.

(Make a house and a wagon on the flannelboard or flip chart.)

What else can we make?

(Put all the shape pieces out for the children to pick up. Let a child come up to the flannelboard and make a picture with the shapes. If you are using a flip chart, give the marker to a child and let her make a shape picture. Children can work with a partner to make the picture.)

And now my story is over. The End!

Dramatic Play

THE SHAPE OF THINGS

Start this activity by clearing a large space in the classroom, or go outdoors on the playground where there is open space.

✳ Help the children define the personal space each will need within the area.

✳ Explain that you are going to ask the children to form shapes with their bodies. There is no right or wrong way to do this.

✳ Ask all the children to form a straight line with their bodies, either vertical or horizontal.

✳ Ask them to make their bodies into circles. Then become triangles.

✳ What other shapes can they make?

✳ Talk about how everything has a shape, and many things combine shapes.

✳ Ask the children to show the shape of a tall candle as it burns down.

✳ Ask them to demonstrate the shape of a pretzel. Accept any shape they form. (There is a recipe for making pretzels in the creative food experiences of this theme.)

✳ How does a growing plant change its shape?

✳ Make an oval shape of an egg and show a bird hatching from the egg.

✳ Let the children come up with other shapes to make.

Puppet Play

SACKS AND SHAPES PUPPETS

✳ Put lunch-size paper sacks, glue, markers, crayons, yarn, construction paper, and fabric scraps out for the children to use.

✳ Encourage the children to make a puppet by creating a large shape (circle, triangle, square, rectangle, or oval) for the face, adding facial features to the shape, and then gluing this face onto the paper sack.

✳ Allow enough time for them to create as many shape puppets as they wish.

✳ Older children may add yarn hair, fabric clothes, and construction paper arms, hands, and legs to complete their puppets.

Music

CIRCLE SONG

This can be sung to the melody of the traditional tune "Have You Ever Seen a Lassie?," or said as a poem.

Have you ever seen a circle, a circle, a circle?
Have you ever seen a circle, which goes 'round and
*   'round?*
It rolls this way and that way, and that way and this way.
Have you ever seen a circle, which goes 'round and round?

MUSICAL SHAPES

✳ Ask all the children to sit on the floor in a circle with you.

✳ Place the following rhythm instruments in the middle of the circle:

triangles

rhythm sticks

sandpaper blocks

drums

bells

castanets

finger cymbals

cymbals

egg-shaped shakers

round maracas

✳ Include enough instruments so that each child will have one.

✳ After each child has selected his instrument, ask the child to talk about what shape it is.

✳ Have each child play the instrument so that everyone can hear the sound each makes.

✳ Next, have everyone play together.

✳ Choose an appropriate cassette or CD, and let the "shape orchestra" play along with the music.

Movement

LET'S MOVE!

✳ Continue emphasizing the shape concept by asking the children to move in the way you ask.

— Walk in a line.

— Walk in a circle.

— Walk in a square.

— Walk in a triangle.

— Run in a circle.

— Run in a zigzag pattern.

— Jump in place.

— Jump around a square.

— Hop in place.

— Hop around a triangle.

— Skip in a circle.

— Skip in a rectangle.

Developmentally, some of these instructions may be difficult for the younger preschoolers. Accept any way the children move.

CIRCLE GAME

✳ Have the children form a circle, feet apart and touching their neighbor's feet.

✳ One child stands inside the circle with a volley ball or similar type of ball, and tries to throw the ball out of the circle between the players' legs.

✳ The players stop the ball by using their hands.

✳ If the ball goes through, then that child goes in the center and continues the game.

RED LIGHT/GREEN LIGHT

✳ In this game, one child plays the "traffic light," and the rest of the children try to touch "it."

✳ At the start, all the children form a line about fifteen feet away from the "traffic light."

✳ The light faces away from the line of children and says "green light!" At this point, everyone moves slowly toward the traffic light.

✳ At any point, the light may say "red light!" and turn around.

✳ If the children are caught moving after this has occurred, they are out.

✳ Play resumes when the traffic light turns back around and says "green light!"

✳ The traffic light wins if all the children are out before anyone is able to touch her. Otherwise, the first player to touch the "light" wins the game and becomes the traffic light for the next game.

Sensory Art

PAPER SHAPES

✳ Use various shapes of paper for art activities instead of the standard rectangle sheets.

✳ Place easel paper cut in the shape you are studying on each painting easel in the classroom.

SURPRISE SHAPES

✳ Without the children knowing, make glue shapes on tagboard, and let them dry.

✳ Let the children discover and name the shapes by rubbing a crayon over a piece of thin drawing paper on top of the tagboard. Have them use the side of crayon for best results.

SKYLINES

The main objective of this activity is to have the children identify shapes.

✳ Collect old magazines with a lot of colorful pictures and advertising.

✳ Encourage the children to look for rectangles, squares, and triangles in the magazines. After they find the shapes, ask them to cut the shapes out.

✳ The rectangles, squares, and triangles can be pictures, words, or a combination of both.

✳ Glue the shapes onto a half sheet of light blue construction paper to form a skyline. The illustration is one example of using word shapes to form a skyline.

✳ Both you and the children can have a lot of fun with this project.

Creative Food Experiences

SHAPE SNACK MIX

You will need:

    raisins

    dry cereal (round and square)

    sunflower seeds

    butterscotch chips

    sesame seeds

    peanuts

    chocolate chips

1. Wash hands.
2. Mix ingredients together.
3. Enjoy!

PRETZELS AND CHEESE SHAPES

You will need:

    14-ounce block of cheddar cheese or cubed cheese

    package of stick pretzels

1. Wash hands.
2. Cut cheese into various shapes.

3. Put the ends of pretzels into the cheese cubes. The children really have fun with this.

4. Eat and talk about the shapes the children are eating.

LET'S MAKE PRETZEL SHAPES

You will need:

    1 package yeast

    1 tablespoon sugar

    1 teaspoon salt (optional)

    1 1/2 cups warm water

    4 cups flour

    1 egg

1. Wash hands.

2. Children help you mix yeast, warm water, and sugar.

3. Stir in flour.

4. Knead until smooth.

5. Give each child a small ball of dough.

6. Roll between hands until approximately $\frac{1}{4}$ inch across.

7. Form into desired shape.

8. Brush top with egg to make the shape shiny during baking.

9. Sprinkle with salt if desired. Bake at 425 degrees for 15 minutes.

10. Let's eat!

Math

SHOE BOX SORTER

Many shape sorters are available for infants commercially. Here is a suggestion for making an inexpensive one for the infants in your care.

✳ Cut holes in the top of a large shoe box. The holes need to be large enough for shapes to fit through easily, and of the same shapes as the objects.

✳ Use small square and rectangular blocks, and large peglike objects, such as the bottoms of plastic film containers, to fit into the sorter.

✳ For infants who have mastered this task, line the hole openings with foam rubber. This provides resistance for the baby to push the shapes through.

SHAPES GALORE

✳ Take a walk with the children around the school, playground, and neighborhood.

✳ Talk about basic shapes. Have the children find examples of those shapes around the room, building, playground, and neighborhood.

✳ Cut fabric scraps into squares, circles, triangles, rectangles, and ovals.

✳ Make sets of the same color, size, shape, and pattern.

✳ Put these in the manipulative center for children to match fabric pieces.

✳ They can also sort the shapes according to texture, size, color, or pattern.

✳ To expand this activity, put a variety of paper and fabric pieces on a table.

✳ Let the children cut the shapes themselves.

✳ Ask them to name the shapes as they cut. Talk about the sizes and colors, too.

LET'S MAKE PRETZEL SHAPES

Wash hands.

Mix 1 package yeast, 1 1/2 cups warm water, and

1 tablespoon sugar. Stir in 4 cups flour and knead until smooth.

Roll a small ball of dough between hands. Make into shape.

Brush 1 egg across top of shape to make shiny.

Sprinkle with salt if desired. Bake at 425 degrees for 15 min.

Let's Eat!

SHAPE PATTERNS

This is a small group activity.

✳ Put a large flannelboard and shapes of many sizes and colors in the math center. You can also have small individual flannelboards, chalkboards, and chalk there as well.

✳ Ask the children to choose partners. The pairs of children will take turns with other pairs at the large flannelboard.

✳ On a large card set up a simple pattern. Ask the children to arrange the same pattern on the flannelboard. For example, place a circle, square, another circle, and a triangle.

✳ Continue holding up patterns for the children to duplicate. Increase the difficulty of each pattern. (A square, two circles, a star, two triangles, a rectangle, an oval, and two more rectangles.)

✳ For older children, add colors and sizes to the shape patterns. Add new shapes, such as the pentagon, hexagon, and octagon.

✳ Leave the flannelboard(s) and shapes in the math center for the children to create patterns by themselves.

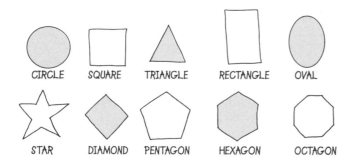

Science

NATURAL SHAPES

This activity encourages children to look for the beauty of nature while developing an awareness of color and shape.

✳ Go on a neighborhood walk and look for shapes in the environment.

✳ Visit an arboretum, flower shop, or grocery store.

✳ Look for all the different shapes in nature.

✳ Talk about the colors and shapes the children see.

Social Studies

FLAGS OF THE WORLD

This activity is designed to help the children become more aware of the many ways shapes are used in our world. Introduce the children to the symbol of a flag by first talking about the flag of the United States. Have an actual flag available, along with pictures of other flags of the world's countries.

✳ Ask the children to look for shapes in the American flag. Then, ask them to point out shapes in the other flags.

✳ Have the children make a flag. They can make the United States flag, a flag from another country, or one that they create themselves.

HOUSE SHAPES DRAWING GAME

✳ Before beginning this activity, talk about how many doors and windows are in the children's homes. Have they noticed the shapes around where they live? What shapes can they find in the houses and buildings around their neighborhoods?

✳ Have construction paper, crayons, markers, and chalk available for the children.

✳ Create cards and pictures for the children to use in drawing houses and parts of houses. For example, draw a rectangular door on the cards, windows with squares of glass, and show pictures of a triangular roof, a chimney, steps, and other parts of the house.

✳ You also can number cards to indicate how many doors or windows should be in the house.

✳ Sort the cards by category. Label the piles with a picture indicating each category.

✳ Turn each category of cards face down.

✳ The children select a card from each category and draw their houses using the information on the cards.

✳ The children decide what color to make their houses.

✳ Place the pictures in a special display or on the bulletin board.

Children's Books

Albee, Sarah. (1996). *Allegra's Shapes.* (Board edition). Illustrated by Peter Panas. New York: Simon & Schuster.

Bolton, Janet. (1994). *My Grandmother's Patchwork Quilt.* New York: Mulberry.

Callin, Karen. (1992). *Rectangles.* Mankato, MN: Capstone Press.

Dillon, Leo, Diane Dillon, and N. N. Charles. (1994). *What Am I?: Looking through Shapes at Apples and Grapes.* New York: Scholastic.

Fatus, Sophie. (1997). *Holes. (Sally shape series).* New York: Abbeville Press.

Hill, Eric. (1986). *Spot Looks at Shapes.* (Board book). New York: Putnam.

Hoban, Tana. (1998). *So Many Circles, So Many Squares.* New York: Greenwillow.

Hoban, Tana. (1996). *Shapes, Shapes, Shapes.* New York: Mulberry.

Hoban, Tana. (1988). *I Read Symbols.* New York: William Morrow.

Hoban, Tana (1987). *I Read Signs.* New York: William Morrow.

Lamut, Sonja. (1998). *Turn and Learn Shapes.* New York: Grossett & Dunlap.

Mahan, Ben. (1992). *See a Circle.* New York: McClanahan Books.

Mahan, Ben. (1992). *See a Square.* New York: McClanahan Books.

Mahan, Ben. (1992). *See a Triangle.* New York: McClanahan Books.

Morgan, Sally. (1995). *Triangles and Pyramids (The World of Shapes).* New York: Thomson Learning.

Murphy, Stuart J. (1998). *Circus Shapes.* New York: HarperCollins.

Serfozo, Mary. (1996). *There's a Square: A Book about Shapes (Story Corner).* Illustrated by David A. Carter. New York: Scholastic.

Shannon, David. (1998). *A Bad Case of Stripes.* New York: Scholastic.

Van Fleet, Matthew. (1995). *Fuzzy Yellow Ducklings: Fold-Out Fun with Textures, Colors, Shapes, Animals.* New York: Dial.

Parent Letter (Preschool)

Dear Parents,

We will be talking about Shapes, our new theme. We will provide opportunities for the children to learn:

- Our world is full of shapes.
- Shape is important for identifying in our world.
- We can see shapes with our eyes and feel them with our hands.
- Shapes have names.
- The basic shapes are circle, square, rectangle, and triangle.
- A shape comes in many sizes, but it still is the same shape.

We will be talking about:

- shapes: circle, square, triangle, rectangle, oval, diamond, star, heart, pentagon, hexagon, octagon, and straight and curved lines
- shapes in nature
- how shapes help us
- shapes around us

Some things to do at home with your child are:

- Talk about all the shapes you and your child can find at home, in the yard, and around the neighborhood and community.
- When you are in the car, look for shapes in traffic lights and signs.
- Play board games with your child. These offer different shapes and colors to talk about.
- Let your child help you fold the laundry. Talk about the different shapes you see.

Join us at school for some parent participation opportunities:

- Visit our classroom, and join in on activities.
  Date ——————   Time ——————
- Go with us to the arboretum or grocery store.
  Date ——————   Time ——————

Our wish list for this theme includes:

paper sacks

old magazines

shoe boxes

fabric scraps

wallpaper scraps

pictures of flags

Thank you for your continued support and interest in our experiences.

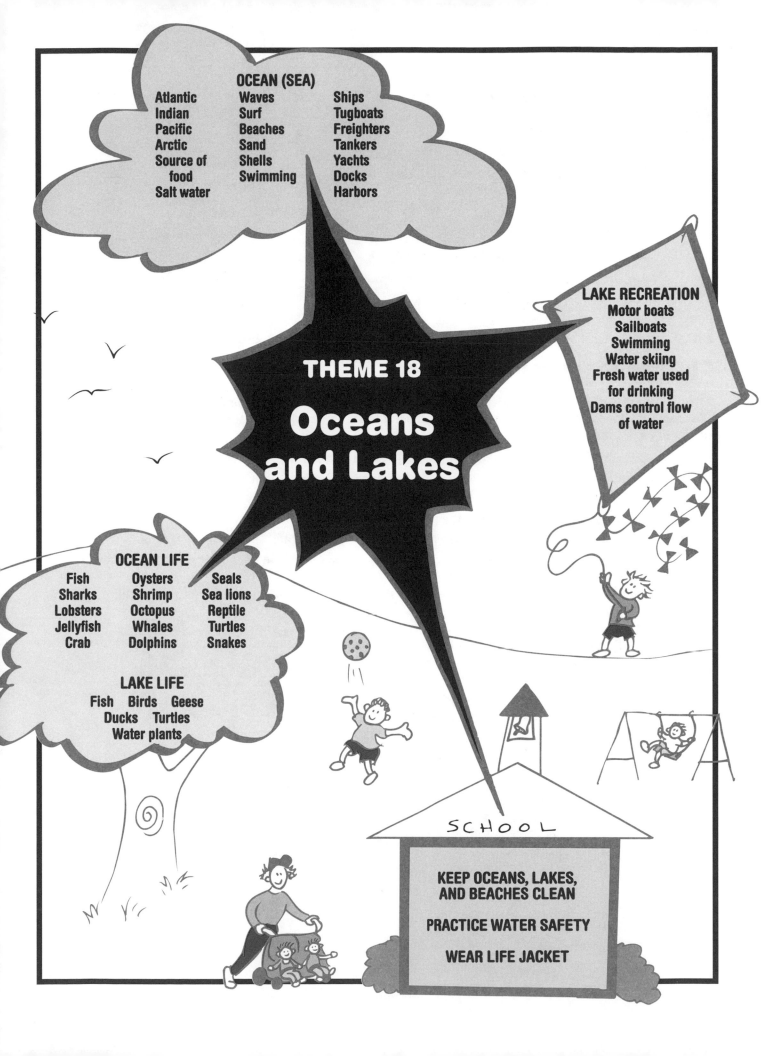

OCEAN (SEA)

Atlantic	Waves	Ships
Indian	Surf	Tugboats
Pacific	Beaches	Freighters
Arctic	Sand	Tankers
Source of	Shells	Yachts
food	Swimming	Docks
Salt water		Harbors

THEME 18

Oceans and Lakes

LAKE RECREATION
Motor boats
Sailboats
Swimming
Water skiing
Fresh water used
for drinking
Dams control flow
of water

OCEAN LIFE

Fish	Oysters	Seals
Sharks	Shrimp	Sea lions
Lobsters	Octopus	Reptile
Jellyfish	Whales	Turtles
Crab	Dolphins	Snakes

LAKE LIFE
Fish   Birds   Geese
Ducks   Turtles
Water plants

SCHOOL

KEEP OCEANS, LAKES, AND BEACHES CLEAN

PRACTICE WATER SAFETY

WEAR LIFE JACKET

THEME GOALS

To provide opportunities for children to learn:

1. Water is necessary to all living things.
2. *Ocean* water is salty.
3. Most *lakes* have fresh water in them.
4. Many plants and animals, especially fish, live in oceans and lakes.
5. The four biggest oceans in the world are the Atlantic, Pacific, Indian, and Arctic.

Children-Created Bulletin Board

Throughout this theme of Oceans and Lakes, the children can change the bulletin board frequently. The study of water and waves, and the fish, mammals, and plant life that inhabit the water offers many opportunities for discovery and exploration.

✳ Title this bulletin board "Oceans and Lakes — Don't Pollute!"

✳ The water background for the board can be done with watercolor paints on butcher paper.

✳ Colored rickrack looks great as the waves.

✳ Form a beach with sand glued on the paper.

✳ Have the children cut out sandpaper starfish to glue on the beach, along with seashells.

✳ Place a frog with a long, sticky tongue made from contact paper on the board. Ask the children to put "objects" the frog has caught on his tongue.

✳ You will find activities to add to the bulletin board as you explore this theme with the children.

Vocabulary Starters

Let the children add additional words.

ocean — a great body of salt water.

lake — a body of fresh water surrounded by land.

pond — a small lake.

sea — another name for ocean.

shore — where the land meets the ocean.

wave — a movement of the surface of the water caused by wind.

surf — waves hitting the shore.

Languages Experiences

POEM:
"Ocean Friends"

Children enjoy adding hand and body movements to this poem.

When our friends who swim in the ocean blue
Want to say hello, what do they do?
The silvery fish gives its tail a flick,
The lobster's claws go click-click-click,
The great big whale makes a great big splash,
The shark opens wide, then he's gone in a flash,
The octopus waves all his arms at you,
And that's how they say "How do you do?"

Philip Jackman

POEM:
"What a Splash!"

If all the lakes were one lake,
What a great lake that would be!
And if all the oceans were one ocean,
What a great sea that would be!
And if all the people were one person,
What a great person that would be!
And if the great person took a great jump
And jumped as high as could be,
And jumped into the great ocean
What a great splash that would be!

Philip Jackman

A HOUSE FOR HERMIT CRAB

* Read Carle's *A House for Hermit Crab,* listed in the books section of this theme.

* This delightful book offers an imaginative look at the underwater neighborhood of Hermit Crab. It also offers many ways to stimulate creativity and language development.

* Let the children help you make a list of the things Hermit uses to decorate his houses. Older children can write the list themselves.

* Some children may want to draw a picture of the new shell.

* Look through other books to find additional sea creatures whose shells could have been used.

* Talk about the items the children have outgrown.

* Act out the story of *A House for Hermit Crab.*

Dramatic Play

CAN YOU?

* Introduce children to ocean animals they may not have seen before.

* Invite someone from a local aquarium or pet store to visit the children and show them a crab, lobster, eel, or other animal whose usual home is the ocean.

* If possible, plan a field trip to the aquarium or pet store.

* Select a video that shows dolphins, an octopus, and other ocean creatures.

* After the children have become somewhat familiar with inhabitants of the ocean, ask them if they can:

— Swim like a fish?

— Crawl like a crab?

— Slither like an eel?

— Jump like a frog?

— Dance like a dolphin?

— Hug like an octopus?

* Many children will want to show you how they can do all of the movements. Accept whatever they do.

* For the younger group, you might need to model the pantomimes for them.

✻ Have pictures and books about ocean life available to show the children.

✻ Have some appropriate music playing in the background.

✻ Let the children add their own animal ideas to the activity.

UNDERSEA ENVIRONMENT

Let the children change the dramatic play area into an underwater environment. Allow plenty of room and lots of time for this project. This is a cooperative activity. All interested children should be involved.

✻ Have plenty of books, pictures, maps, and research materials available so the children can discover interesting facts about the ocean and the fish, mammal, and plant life that live there.

✻ Have crayons, colored pencils, markers, crepe paper, construction paper, paper plates, yarn, scissors, and glue available.

✻ Children begin to decorate by hanging blue and green crepe paper across the dramatic play area.

✻ Then, they can make and hang fish, whales, dolphins, and seaweed from the ceiling or on mobiles attached to a clothesline. You will have to help with this. The clothesline should be above their heads and out of the way of the adults in the room.

✻ Discuss with the children what might be found on the ocean floor. Suggestions could be an octopus cave, a sunken ship, or a coral reef. Any of these can lead to more exploration and research.

✻ This becomes an ongoing project as you and the children add seashells, boats, ships, music, and the sounds of the ocean and lakes. Be prepared to close some centers as the underwater environment continues to grow.

Puppet Play

SPONGE PUPPETS

✻ Collect all sizes of sponges.

✻ Put these, with scraps of yarn, crepe paper, felt, fabric, toothpicks, craft sticks, and scissors, on a table.

✻ Have the children make ocean creature puppets out of the sponges. Attach yarn or crepe paper "arms" to make an octopus.

✻ Wrap the yarn around toothpicks and stick them into the sponge, or stick toothpicks through the crepe paper and into the sponge.

✻ If the sponge is small enough for the child to hold in her hand, the puppet can be moved around easily.

✻ If the sponge is larger, help the child make some finger holes. Another way to use the puppet is by inserting craft sticks into the sponge to make a stick puppet.

✻ Encourage the children to create voices for their puppets and to act out an underwater adventure in the dramatic play area.

Music

SONG: "The Frog Song" by Jo Eklof

Extend this song by having the children sing additional verses using different animal sounds.

Late last night while you and I were in our beds a-sleep, the frogs came out and sang this song, "rib-bit rib-bit rib-bit rib-bit rib-bit ba-reep!"

(See page 302 for enlargement.)

Movement

SAIL THE OCEAN BLUE

✳ Have the children imagine that the room or playground is "the ocean blue" and that each one of them will be one of four types of boat: a rowboat, a motorboat, a sailboat, or a big ship (ocean liner).

✳ Have pictures or books of these boats to give the children something concrete to look at.

✳ Guide the children into trying out each type of boat. Tell them, "Together, let's be a *rowboat*." Using the arms, slowly pull back and push forward on the oars to a "1-2-3-4" count. Move around in a small space of the "lake."

✳ Next, "Let's be a *sailboat*." Raise the sail by pulling on a rope, then stretch arms out to either side like a sail, rocking side-to-side while sailing forward.

✳ "Let's be a *motorboat*." Turn the key to start it, and then move out from the shore with a "R-R-R-R-R-R" sound. Move around in a large part of the "ocean" or "lake."

✳ "Now here comes the *big ship, the ocean liner*." Put your arms out front, touching the hands together like a ship's prow. "Look out for me! Toot-Toot-Toot!"

✳ Next, the children choose whichever boat they wish to be. "Let's sail the ocean blue!"

✳ Remind them that it is a big ocean. Some of the boats stay closer to shore. So, watch out for each other.

✳ Continue to develop the Ocean Blue activity by adding various conditions: "Here comes a big wind. What happens to the boats now?" "Watch out, the waves are high!" "Now the ocean is calm again. Whew!"

Sensory Art

WATER PLAY

Provide opportunities for infants and toddlers to enjoy water play.

✳ Help young infants wash their face and hands with a washcloth. Make this into a game of peekaboo.

✳ Put one-half inch of water in a small plastic tub, and let them splash water and sail boats.

✳ Add food coloring to water, and make colored ice cubes. Place these in the water table.

✳ Put large seashells in the water table or sandbox.

✳ Toddlers love to paint *outdoors* with water. Provide several sizes of brushes, and let them paint the sidewalk and the building walls.

MAKE A SAILBOAT

Collect washed, empty plastic soda bottles, sand, colored construction paper, tape, scissors, and markers. This activity is more fun to do outdoors.

✳ You and the children add sand to one plastic soda bottle.

✳ Let the children add a little bit of sand at first to see if the bottle will float in a tub or wading pool with one to two inches of water.

✳ Keep adding sand until the bottle floats without tilting in the water.

✳ Put the top on tightly.

✳ Have the children cut out boat and sail shapes. Tape these on and around the bottle.

✳ Place the sailboat in the water.

✳ To extend this activity, turn on a small electric fan to create a wind. What happens to the sailboat now?

SALTWATER PAINTING

✳ With the children's help, mix warm water, salt, and food coloring into several small containers.

✳ The children, a few at a time, can paint pictures with the mixture on white paper. Try construction paper, newsprint, and computer paper. Will the results be the same or different?

✳ Let the pictures dry. The water evaporates, but the salt remains, creating beautiful pictures.

Creative Food Experiences

FROG FLOAT

You will need:

   1 bottle of lemon-lime soda or ginger ale

   lime sherbet

   chocolate chips

   paper cups

1. Wash hands.
2. Have each child fill a paper cup half-full with lemon-lime soda.
3. "Float" a scoop of lime sherbet in the soda.
4. Pour a handful of chocolate chips out for each child.
5. Place two chocolate chip "eyes" on the sherbet "frog."
6. Enjoy the treat!

FROG FLOAT

Wash hands.

Fill a cup half full with lemon-lime soda.

"Float" a scoop of lime sherbet in the soda.

Place 2 chocolate chip "eyes" on the sherbet "frog".

Enjoy the treat!

FISH SHAPES

You will need:

   4 envelopes flavored gelatin

   3 envelopes unflavored gelatin

   4 cups boiling juice or water

1. Wash hands.
2. Mix the 7 envelopes of gelatin together.
3. Add the boiling juice or water. An adult must do this.
4. Stir until the gelatin is dissolved.
5. Pour into a shallow pan.
6. Chill until firm.
7. Let each child use a fish-shaped cookie cutter to "catch the fish" in the pan of chilled gelatin.
8. You may have to make two "batches."
9. Serve and eat!

STARFISH SANDWICHES

You will need:

   wheat or white sandwich bread

   salmon spread or pimento cheese spread

   small jar of pimentos

   black olives

1. Wash hands.
2. You and the children make sandwiches using the salmon or pimento cheese spread.
3. With a star-shaped cookie cutter, press out a star-shaped sandwich.
4. Decorate the individual "starfish" with pimento eyes and olive mouths.
5. YUM!

TUNA CONES

You will need:

   6 1/2 ounce can of tuna (You may need more than one can, depending upon the number of children in your class.)

   1/3 to 1/2 cup of mayonnaise

2 tablespoons sweet pickle relish

1/4 teaspoon of salt (optional)

flat-bottomed ice cream cones, one for each child

pickle slices

1. Wash hands.
2. Mix tuna, mayonnaise, and sweet pickle relish in a bowl.
3. Scoop mixture into individual ice cream cones.
4. Top with pickle slices.

Math

COUNT THE SEASHELLS

* Collect seashells in a large, unbreakable jar. The jar should be smal enough to be filled in a reasonably short time.
* The seashells can be collected from yourself, other teachers, parents, family members, and the children.
* Have the children guess how many shells are in the jar when it is one-quarter full, one-half full, and full.
* Measure and mark the jar.
* Some children may want to use the seashells to see how far they can count. This is fine, as long as they put the shells back in the jar.

WHICH IS SMALLEST? LARGEST?

Make this a small group or individual activity.

* Place two or three dozen seashells of various types in the math center. Use some of the shells from the big jar mentioned in the Count the Seashells activity.
* Have the children place their seashells in order: smallest to largest, lightest to heaviest, shortest to longest.
* Ask them to think of other ways to sort and classify the shells.

Science

CREATING ICEBERGS

This is a demonstration that you and the children do together. You may want to conduct the demonstration with a small group, then repeat the activity with another small group later.

* Freeze a large bowl of water.
* Take the ice out of the bowl, and split it into two pieces.
* Float one lump of ice in a bowl of tap water.
* How much of the ice stays below the waterline?
* Now, float the second lump of ice in salt water.
* Do the children notice any differences? What are they?
* Discuss with the children that icebergs occur in oceans. Oceans have salt water.

IS THE SEA SALTY?

* Put rock salt, water, containers, strainers, and plastic spoons in the science center.
* Ask a few students at a time to pour water over rock salt that has been placed in a strainer.
* Put the dissolved salt into a plastic cup.
* Give each child a plastic spoon to dip into the water for tasting.
* Add the remaining salt water to the cup.
* Put the cup aside. Ask the children to check the cup periodically to see when all the water has evaporated.
* How much salt remains?
* Repeat the procedure to see if the result is the same. If the outcome is different, what occurred to cause the difference?

SALT WATER AND FRESH WATER

This experiment is easy for the children to do.

* Place two plastic drinking glasses, a plastic pitcher of tap water, table salt, food coloring, and an eyedropper for each color in the science center.
* Ask one or several children to fill one glass about half full of water.

✳ Into the other glass, pour one-half glass of water with two teaspoons salt added.

✳ Add a few drops of food coloring to the salt water.

✳ Pour the colored salt water into the half glass of fresh water.

✳ The colored salt water moves to the bottom of the glass, *below the fresh water!* Salt water is heavier than fresh water.

Social Studies

DON'T POLLUTE!

It is important for young children to understand the concept of taking care of our world and the community in which we live.

✳ We start by not throwing litter, or trash, on the floor in our classroom, on the playground, or at home.

✳ For older children, we expand to include keeping trash out of the ocean and lakes, and stop littering our beaches.

✳ Here are some tips from the Earthworks book, *50 Simple Things Kids Can Do to Save the Earth,* listed in the books section of this theme:

Do not throw litter on the beach, in the ocean, or in lakes. Plastic bags and other plastic garbage thrown into the ocean kill as many as a million sea creatures every year!

When you visit the beach, take along a large garbage bag. Try to fill it with trash, close it tight, then throw it in a garbage can. If there are no receptacles on the beach, take the bag with you, and throw it away at the first garbage can you see.

If you go fishing, never, never, throw a discarded fishing line into the water. Birds and sea creatures can get tangled in it and die.

✳ Primary-grade children can write reports on what they discover from reading books on environmental issues, ecology, and recycling.

MORE WATER THAN LAND

✳ Have a globe or map of the world available.

✳ Talk about how much more water than land there is in the world. Three-quarters of the world is covered by oceans and seas.

✳ Find the Atlantic, Pacific (the largest), Indian, and Arctic oceans on the globe. What states and cities are near the shorelines? Talk about islands.

✳ Have books and pictures to share with the children depicting different kinds of communities that are built around or near oceans and lakes.

✳ Talk about ocean-related occupations, such as: commercial fishermen; marine geologists, people who study rocks and the formation of the ocean floor; marine biologists, who study the animals and plants of the ocean; oceanographers, who explore and study the ocean; and captains and crews of commercial boats and cruise ships.

✳ If you live near an ocean or lake, ask someone whose occupation deals with the water to visit the class.

✳ Listen to the questions the children ask you about oceans and lakes. Let their interests guide you as you continue to develop curriculum.

Children's Books

Arnold, Caroline. (1994). *Sea Lion.* New York: Morrow.

Baldwin, Robert F. (1998). *This Is the Sea that Feeds Us.* Illustrated by Don Dyen. New York: Dawn Publishers.

Carle, Eric. (1988). *A House for Hermit Crab.* New York: Simon & Schuster.

Clements, Andrew. (1997). *Big Al.* (Reprint edition). New York: Aladdin.

Crews, Donald. (1995). *Sail Away.* New York: Greenwillow.

Crews, Donald. (1988). *Harbor.* New York: William Morrow.

Earthworks Group. (1994). *50 Simple Things Kids Can Do to Save the Earth.* Kansas City, MO: Andrews and McMeel.

Faulkner, Keith. (1997). *A 3-D Look at Oceans.* Illustrated by Robert Morton. New York: Little Simon.

Fleming, Denise. (1993). *In the Small, Small Pond.* New York: Henry Holt.

Gibbons, Gail. (1998). *Sea Turtles.* New York: Holiday House.

Gibbons, Gail. (1994). *Frogs.* New York: Holiday House.

Gibbons, Gail. (1991). *Whales.* New York: Holiday House.

Hardy, Ann. (1995). *Who Lives in the Oceans, Lakes, and Rivers?: A Baby Animal Sticker Book.* New York: Little Simon.

Heller, Ruth. (1992). *How to Hide an Octopus and Other Sea Creatures.* New York: Grossett/Putnam.

Hulme, Joy N. (1993). *Sea Squares.* (Reissue edition). New York: Hyperion Press.

Kalan, Robert. (1992). *Blue Sea.* Illustrated by Donald Crews. New York: Mulberry.

Koch, Michelle. (1993). *World Water Watch.* New York: Greenwillow.

Lasky, Kathryn. (1995). *Pond Year.* Illustrated by Mike Bostock. Cambridge, MA: Candlewick Press.

Lionni, Leo. (1995). *On My Beach There Are Many Pebbles.* New York: Mulberry.

Lionni, Leo. (1992). *Swimmy.* New York: Knopf.

MacDonald, Suse. (1994). *Sea Shapes.* New York: Gulliver Books.

O'Mara, Anna. (1998). *Oceans.* Chicago, IL: Children's Press.

Orr, Katherine. (1991). *My Grandpa and the Sea.* New York: First Avenue Editions.

Parker, Steve. (1989). *Seashore.* New York: Knopf.

Pfister, Marcus, and J. Alison James. (1996). *The Rainbow Fish.* (Board edition). New York: North South Books.

Ranger Rick's Naturescope Guides. (1997). *Diving into Oceans.* New York: Learning Triangle Press.

Zolotow, Charlotte. (1994). *The Seashore Book.* (Reissue edition). New York: HarperTrophy.

Parent Letter (School-age)

Dear Parents,

As we continue to study our Environment, we are beginning a new theme, Oceans and Lakes. We will provide opportunities for the children to learn:

- Water is necessary to all living things.
- *Ocean* water is salty.
- Most *lakes* have fresh water in them.
- Many plants and animals, especially fish, live in oceans and lakes.
- The four biggest oceans in the world are the Atlantic, Pacific, Indian, and Arctic.

We will be talking about:

- the oceans
- salt water
- fresh water
- safety on water
- environmental issues
- beaches
- ships and boats
- lake recreation
- fish and mammals

Things to do at home with your child to reinforce our classroom activities include:

- Talk about what you see and read in books, magazines, and newspapers relating to oceans and ocean life.
- If you have taken a vacation at or visited the seashore, look through the pictures and memorabilia from that trip.
- Visit an aquarium or pet store, and look at fish.
- Help your child start or add to a seashell collection.
- Talk about ways your family is helping to protect the environment.

Participate in these activities at school:

- Come visit us, and see how we have brought the ocean into our classroom.
  Date _____ Time _____
- Help us guess how many seashells are in our big jar.
  Date _____ Time _____
- If you know anyone who fishes for their occupation, marine life scientists, or someone who works on a boat or ship, please let us know. We are looking for someone whose work involves the water to visit our class.

Our wish list for this theme includes:

new sponges
empty, washed soda bottles
seashells
plastic pitcher

Thank you for your interest and participation.

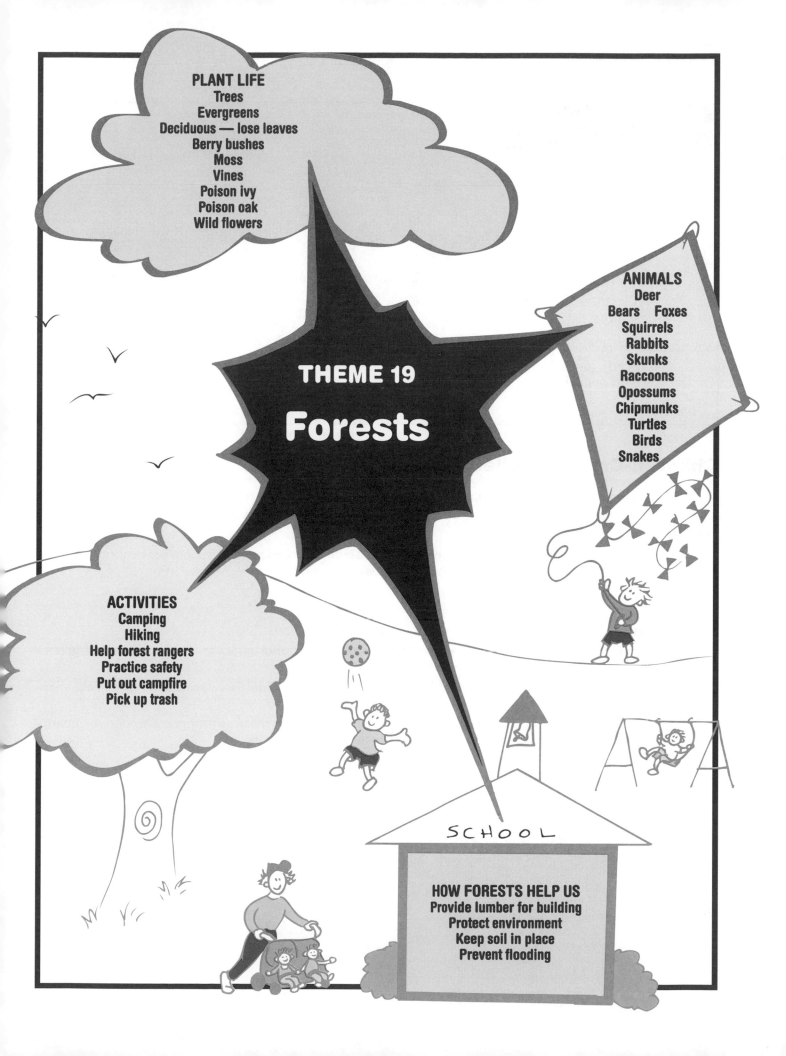

PLANT LIFE
Trees
Evergreens
Deciduous — lose leaves
Berry bushes
Moss
Vines
Poison ivy
Poison oak
Wild flowers

ANIMALS
Deer
Bears   Foxes
Squirrels
Rabbits
Skunks
Raccoons
Opossums
Chipmunks
Turtles
Birds
Snakes

THEME 19

Forests

ACTIVITIES
Camping
Hiking
Help forest rangers
Practice safety
Put out campfire
Pick up trash

SCHOOL

HOW FORESTS HELP US
Provide lumber for building
Protect environment
Keep soil in place
Prevent flooding

THEME GOALS

To provide opportunities for children to learn:

1. A forest is a home for plants, animals, and insects.
2. The tallest plants are trees, which provide shelter and food for many animals and insects.
3. Some trees are called evergreen because they do not lose their leaves in the winter.
4. Broadleaf, or deciduous, trees have leaves in the summer and lose their leaves in the winter.
5. Bushes, ferns, moss, and toadstools grow low on the forest's floor.
6. Many animals and birds, such as deer, bears, foxes, rabbits, raccoons, chipmunks, and owls, like to live in the forest.

Children-Created Bulletin Board

Make changes to this bulletin board while the Forest theme is emphasized. This bulletin board helps the children stay interested in the environment and how to protect it, and teaches them about the plants and animals of the forest.

✳ You and the children can create a three-dimensional bulletin board by taking paper sacks or brown butcher paper, and crushing it to create long limbs and vines.

✳ Make and glue leaves on the limbs.

✳ Hang the limbs around the bulletin board.

✳ Add a few real twigs and small branches to the bulletin board, too.

✳ Then, trace children's hands on dark green paper. Have the children cut these out to make an evergreen tree. Place the tree on one side of the board.

✳ Place a banner above the bulletin board that says: "A Forest Is a Home for Animals and Plants: Take Care of the Forest!"

✳ Ask the children to make animal tracks on strips of paper, and use these as the border around the board. An Animal Tracks activity is included in the math section of this theme.

✳ Continue adding to the board throughout the theme.

Vocabulary Starters

Let the children add additional words.

forest — a large area of land with many trees, plants, and animals.

woods — another name for forest.

tree — the tallest plant in the forest.

bark — the skin of a tree.

tracks — the footprints that animals make.

camouflage — the colorings or markings of forest animals that hide them among leaves, bark, and rocks.

Language Experiences

**POEM:
"I Was Walking in the Forest"**

✳ This is a poem with a strong beat. The rhythm can be accented by clapping hands or using rhythm instruments.

✳ Each verse also suggests actions that can be used to illustrate the words. With toddlers, use fewer verses.

✳ Have pictures of the animals to share with the children.

I was walking in the forest
And what did I see
But a wide-eyed owl
Sitting high in a tree.
"Who," he said, "Who, who, who
Who, my friend, are you, you, you?"
   I walked a little farther
   And what did I see
   But a big brown bear
   Getting honey from a tree.
   "Yum," he said, "Yum, yum, yum,
   I love honey in my tum, tum, tum."
I walked a little farther
And what did I see
But a raccoon mama
With her babies three.
"Come here, my babies, 1-2-3
Stay very close, very close to me."
   I walked a little farther
   And what did I see
   But an old woodpecker
   A-peckin' on a tree.
   He pecked, and he pecked, and he peck-peck-pecked
   And he said, "All this peckin' is a pain in the neck!"
I was walking in the forest
When what did I see
But a tall forest ranger
Who said to me,
"Be careful in the forest — don't harm trees
And be friends with the birds and animals, please."

Philip Jackman

Dramatic Play

TEDDY BEAR PICNIC

✳ For infants, place teddy bears and other stuffed animals on the floor around the edges of a blanket.

✳ Hold the younger infants in your lap, and talk about the stuffed animals. "Hello, little bear." "Say hello to Anna."

✳ The other babies can crawl to and interact with the animals.

✳ At snack time, plan a "teddy bear picnic" with the toddlers.

✳ Place a large blanket on the playground, and enjoy a picnic with the children and the stuffed animals.

PLAN A TEDDY BEAR PARTY

✳ Ask the children to bring their favorite stuffed animals to class, Beanie Babies included.

✳ Have the children plan a party for the teddy bears and all the stuffed animals.

✳ Encourage several children at a time to go to the dramatic play center to plan the party.

✳ Guide them in preparing a list of what they will need, writing invitations, and decorating for the party. Ask the children to draw or write the invitations any way they wish. Help them if they ask.

✳ Refreshments can be served at snack time.

✳ At the party, read Freeman's *Corduroy,* listed in the books section of this theme.

Puppet Play

FOREST FINGER PUPPETS

Make this puppet activity open-ended. Throughout the course of the Forest theme, the children may go to the manipulative or art center and make finger puppets anytime. This offers a visual way to demonstrate what they have learned about forest animals.

✳ Supply markers, crayons, oval-shaped pieces of paper, construction paper, scissors, and double-sided tape.

✳ Guide the children into drawing animal faces on the oval papers or cutting out other face shapes.

✳ Suggest they experiment using different kinds of lines, heavy or light.

✳ They can easily attach the puppets to their fingers with the double-sided tape.

✳ Encourage the children to make up dialogue between their finger puppets about life in the forest.

✳ With younger children, you might start the conversation with finger puppets of your own.

Music

SONG: "The Bear Lives in the Forest"

This song is based on the traditional one, "The Bear Went over the Mountain."

The bear lives in the forest.
The bear lives in the forest.
The bear lives in the forest.
He's happy as can be.
> *The opossum lives in the forest.*
> *The raccoon lives in the forest.*
> *The deer lives in the forest.*
> *They love to be free.*
What else lives in the forest?
What else lives in the forest?
What else lives in the forest?
Oh, please tell me.

SOUNDS OF THE FOREST

Introduce this activity to the children by reading an appropriate book about animals and the sounds they make. Duffy's *Forest Tracks,* listed in the books section of this theme, is one suggestion.

✳ Play a recorded musical selection that introduces children to the instruments of the orchestra. These selections suggest animal sounds: Prokofiev's *Peter and the Wolf* and Saint-Saëns's *Carnival of the Animals.*

✳ Place all of the rhythm instruments in the center of the floor during group time.

✳ Ask the children to choose one.

✳ As each child demonstrates the sound his instrument makes, ask, "Does the instrument sound like an animal in the forest?" "Does it sound like the wind in the trees?" "What does it sound like?"

✳ Have all the instruments play together to combine the sounds into one "forest symphony."

SONG: "Oh, the Forest Is a Lovely Place to Be"

Sing this song to the tune of the traditional "She'll Be Comin 'Round the Mountain."

Oh, the forest is a lovely place to be,
Oh, the forest is a lovely place to be.
It's got lots and lots of things to see,
Lots of fun for you and me.
The forest is a lovely place to be.
  But to keep it lovely you must be its friend,
  But to keep it lovely you must be its friend.
  So be careful when you camp out,
  Douse your fire, be sure it's stamped out.
  To keep it lovely you must be its friend.
Oh, the forest is a quiet place to be — sssh,
Oh, the forest is a quiet place to be — sssh.
Since most animals and birds are shy,
If you make noise they'll run or fly.
The forest is a quiet place to be — sssh.
  When you leave the forest, please leave it clean,
  When you leave the forest, please leave it clean.
  Remember: others go there too,
  Pick up your trash when you are through.
  When you leave the forest, leave it clean.

Philip Jackman

Movement

HOP LIKE A BUNNY, SCURRY LIKE A SQUIRREL

In this movement activity, each child picks a forest animal and tries to mimic its posture and movement. It is a good idea to have photos or illustrations of several animals to help the children visualize what they will act out.

✳ Have the children select from among creatures that have clearly contrasting styles of movement, such as bears (big, lumbering movements), deer (delicate, on tiptoes), rabbits (hopping, sniffing), owls (wide-eyed, head-swiveling), and snakes (watchful, slithering).

✳ For younger toddlers, concentrate on only two or three animals.

Sensory Art

BARK RUBBINGS

✳ Supply the children with thick drawing paper and crayons.

✳ Go for a walk to look for trees on the playground, around the school, and in the neighborhood.

✳ Have the children rub over the paper with a crayon until the pattern of the bark shows on the drawing paper.

✳ Working with a partner is helpful. One child holds the paper against the tree, while the other partner completes the tree rubbing.

FOREST SPECIAL EFFECTS

Place glue sticks, white drawing paper, tempera paint in various forest colors, brushes, and sponges in the art area. Make these available throughout the duration of the Forest theme.

✳ Suggest to the children that they use the glue sticks to draw something easy to outline, such as a tree, a flower, the sun, or a bird.

✳ Let the drawing dry.

✳ When the glue is dry, they color the paper with the paint. For best results, use one color.

✳ Let the paint dry.

✳ After the drawing is completely dry, dip the whole paper in water. Then watch what happens to the drawing.

✳ Hang with clothespins on a line placed over several layers of newspapers. Let the picture dry completely, and place the art on the bulletin board for all to see.

Creative Food Experiences

DEER SANDWICHES

You will need:

> slices of wheat bread
>
> peanut butter or plain hummus spread
>
> raisins
>
> pretzels
>
> gum drops

1. Wash hands.
2. Have the children cut pieces of bread into triangles with plastic knives.
3. Spread with peanut butter or hummus. Be aware of children's allergies.
4. Use raisins for eyes, pretzels for antlers, and gumdrops for noses.
5. Eat and enjoy!

FOREST TREE COOKIES

You will need:

> 1 cup margarine or soft shortening
>
> 1 1/2 cups of sugar
>
> 1 egg
>
> 1 teaspoon vanilla, almond, or lemon extract
>
> 2 tablespoons of milk
>
> 3 cups flour
>
> 1 teaspoon baking powder
>
> 1/2 teaspoon salt
>
> green food coloring

1. Wash hands.
2. Have children complete each of the cooking tasks, two or three children for each task.

FOREST TREE COOKIES

Wash hands.

Cream together 1 cup margarine, 1 1/2 cups sugar, 1 egg.

1 teaspoon vanilla, and 2 tablespoons of milk.

Add 3 cups flour, 1 teaspoon baking powder, and 1/2 teaspoon salt.

Add a few drops of green food color. Mix all ingredients together.

Chill. Roll out dough with a rolling pin and cut cookies with

tree-shaped cookie cutters. Bake at 375 degrees for 10 minutes.

---

3. Cream together the margarine, sugar, egg, vanilla, and milk.
4. Add flour, about a third at a time; baking powder; and salt.
5. Add a few drops of green food color.
6. Mix all ingredients together.
7. Chill. Then roll out dough with a rolling pin.
8. Cut cookies with tree-shaped cookie cutters.
9. Bake at 375 degrees for approximately 10 minutes.

As a time-saver, substitute ready-to-use cookie dough available at the grocery store.

Math

MATCH THE ANIMAL TRACKS

✳ Make a folder matching game of animal tracks.

✳ Use fewer, larger animal tracks for younger children.

✳ Open a file folder, and across it spread the animal tracks you have drawn and cut out.

✳ Glue them onto the folder.

✳ Print in lower case, beneath the track, the name of the animal that made it.

✳ Make a set of cards with duplicate animal tracks, omitting the name.

✳ Laminate the folder and each card.

✳ Label the front of the folder with two of the tracks and the words "Animal Tracks."

✳ Glue an envelope or locking plastic bag on the back of the folder. Place the card pieces in the bag or envelope.

✳ Place the folder game in the math center for the children.

DO YOU REMEMBER?

✳ Place objects that relate to this theme, such as acorns, leaves, pine cones, pictures of trees and animals, and pieces of wood on a tray.

✳ Start with a few items at a time. Gradually increase the number of objects displayed.

✳ Ask the child to study the objects on the tray closely.

✳ Then, cover the items with a cloth.

✳ Ask the child to name them.

✳ Uncover the tray and let the child see if she remembered them all.

✳ Play this like a game. It is self-correcting and non-threatening.

✳ Add more objects and pictures.

✳ Repeat the procedure.

✳ Do this as a one-on-one activity with all the children over several days.

✳ Try starting with the items, and then take some away. What's missing?

MATH WORD GAMES

✳ Have actual objects available for the children to count. After they have played the game several times, you can remove the objects.

✳ The first time younger children try these activities, let each choose a partner. It is encouraging to do this in pairs.

✳ For the first math word game, you need eleven pine cones.

Two children were gathering pine cones in the forest. The first one gathered four. The second one gathered three more than the first. How many did the second one gather?

✳ For the second math word game, you need seven acorns.

A squirrel was gathering acorns for the winter and was hurrying home with seven to store away. However, the squirrel dropped two along the way. How many are left?

✳ You need four pecans and six walnuts for this one.

A child was looking in the forest for nuts that had fallen from trees. He found four pecans and six walnuts. How many nuts did the child find?

✳ You need eleven leaves to start this math word game.

A deer was nibbling leaves from a branch. When she started there were eleven leaves on it, but when she finished, only three were left. How many did she eat?

✳ Present the math word games verbally to the younger children. Observe how they solve the problems. Let older children read the games. Observe how they solve the problems.

Science

LET'S STUDY TREES

For this project, gather pictures, books, magazines, and maps for the children to use.

✳ Talk about where the trees grow. For example, the tallest trees in the world are the redwoods, which grow along the Pacific coast of North America. Some of the oldest are the pine trees of the Rocky Mountains.

✳ Discuss the parts of the tree:

crown — the part of the tree above the trunk that is made up of leaves and branches.

trunk — the thick wood stem of the tree.

roots — the tree's anchor, which draws water and food from the soil.

timber — the name given to the wood of the tree.

✳ With the children's help, make a list of things that are made of wood, partly or completely.

✳ Walk around the school, and look for wooden things. Ask the children to walk around the house with their parents and identify things made of wood.

✳ Take several days to complete the list. Put it in the science center.

✳ Collect small blocks or pieces of timber. Check with local home improvement or hardware stores and carpenters for scraps.

✳ Label each type of wood with its name for identification.

✳ Put the pieces in the science center along with magnifying glasses. Ask the children to look for the patterns in the grain of the wood.

✳ Supply a spray bottle filled with water for the children to observe if any changes take place when the wood gets wet.

✳ Provide small tubs of water in which to float the wood pieces. Which sink? Which float?

✳ Leave these in the water and weigh them several days later. Which pieces have absorbed the water?

✳ Pound nails in some pieces. Which wood is the softest? Which is the hardest?

✳ As a culminating activity, have the children paint the wood pieces and make boats, which they can then take home.

Social Studies

DEAR WORLD

✳ Introduce the children to ways they can protect the environment by reading books about the subject.

✳ Invite visitors from local environmental organizations and a county conservation commission to talk to the children. Perhaps these individuals will take the children on a field trip with their parents.

✳ Celebrate Earth Day. Look at the earth and its surroundings. Clean up the grounds around the school and the neighborhood. If you live near a forest, lake, or wildflower area, take the children on a field trip.

✳ Read Lannis Temple's book *Dear World: How Children Around the World Feel about Our Environment*. Here are some excerpts:

> "I love nature. I like being out in the open. The thing I most like is walking in the forest. Then I hear the soft rustling of the treetops which sway gently in the wind. . . . The soft chirping of the birds makes me breathe deeply. Then I always lie down on the soft mat of moss which has grown over the forest floor, and begin to dream."
>
> Mirya Sauerland, Age 10
> Germany — The Black Forest

> "I like picking flowers outdoors to make necklaces because then I feel I am playing with the flowers. When it is no longer possible to make such things with wild flowers, the woods and forest will have been destroyed, and I feel uneasy about this. We know that paper is produced from timber and as we don't want the forest to be destroyed, we are recycling milk cartons."
>
> Yukiko Kitamura, Age 9
> Shikoku, Japan

✳ As a concluding activity for this project, ask the children to write or dictate to you their letters to the world. Display the letters on the bulletin board.

Children's Books

Brown, Margaret Wise. (1996). *Four Fur Feet*. Illustrated by Woodleigh Hubbard. New York: Hyperion Press.

Cherry, Lynne. (1990). *The Great Kapok Tree: A Tale of the Amazon Rain Forest*. San Diego, CA: Harcourt Brace.

Dorros, Arthur. (1997). *A Tree Is Growing*. Illustrated by S.D. Schindler. New York: Scholastic.

Duffy, Dee Dee. (1996). *Forest Tracks*. Illustrated by Janet Marshall. New York: Boyds Mills Press.

Freeman, Don. (1976). *Corduroy*. New York: Puffin.

Gise, Joanne. (1990). *A Picture Book of Forest Animals*. Illustrated by Roseanna Pistolesi. Mahwah, NJ: Troll.

Hines, Gary. (1993). *Flying Firefighters*. Illustrated by Anna G. Hines. New York: Clarion Books.

Hutchins, Pat. (1990). *Good-Night, Owl!* New York: Aladdin.

Jaspersohn, William. (1992). *How the Forests Grew*. Illustrated by Chuck Eckart. New York: Mulberry.

Lauber, Patricia. (1994). *Be a Friend to Trees.* Illustrated by Holly Keller. New York: HarperCollins.

Mazer, Anne. (1991). *The Salamander Room.* Illustrated by Steve Johnson. New York: Knopf.

McGee, Marni. (1994). *Forest Child.* Illustrated by A. Scott Banfill. New York: Simon & Schuster.

National Wildlife Foundation. (1998). *Trees Are Terrific (Ranger Rick's Naturescope).* New York: McGraw-Hill.

Pandell, Karen. (1994). *I Love You, Sun. I Love You, Moon.* Illustrated by Tomie De Paola. New York: Putnam.

Pfeffer, Wendy. (1997). *A Log's Life.* Illustrated by Stephanie Lurie. New York: Simon & Schuster.

Ross, Anna. (1992). *Grover's 10 Terrific Ways to Help Our Wonderful World.* New York: Random House and Children's Television Workshop.

Staub, Frank. (1998). *America's Forests.* Minneapolis, MN: Carolrhoda Books.

Stroud, Virginia A. (1996). *The Path of the Quiet Elk.* New York: Dial.

Taylor, Barbara, Kim Taylor, and Jane Burton. (1993). *Forest Life (Look Closer).* New York: Dk Publishers.

Temple, Lannis. (1993). *Dear World: How Children Around the World Feel about Our Environment.* New York: Random House.

Van Allsburg, Chris. (1990). *Just a Dream.* Boston, MA: Houghton Mifflin.

Vyner, Tim. (1995). *The Tree in the Forest.* New York: Barron's.

Waddell, Martin. (1996). *Owl Babies.* Cambridge, MA: Candlewick Press.

Wadsworth, Ginger, and Frank Staub. (1995). *Giant Sequoia Trees (Early Bird Nature Books).* New York: Lerner Publications.

Wildsmith, Brian. (1984). *Squirrels.* New York: Oxford University Press.

Yolen, Jane, and Laura Regan. (1997). *Welcome to the Green House.* New York: Putnam.

Yoshi. (1987). *Who's Hiding Here?* Saxonville, MA: Picture Book Studio.

Parent Letter (Preschool)

Dear Parents,

Our new theme is Forests. The children will learn:

- A forest is a home for plants, animals, and insects.
- The tallest plants are trees, which provide shelter and food for many animals and insects.
- Some trees are called evergreen because they do not lose their leaves in the winter.
- Broadleaf, or deciduous, trees have leaves in the summer and lose their leaves in the winter.
- Bushes, ferns, moss, and toadstools grow low on the forest's floor.
- Many animals and birds, such as deer, bears, foxes, rabbits, raccoons, chipmunks, and owls, like to live in the forest.

We will be talking about:

- plant life
- berry bushes
- animals
- protecting the forest
- trees
- moss and vines
- how forests help us
- forest rangers

Try some of these things to do at home with your child:

- Talk about ways to protect the environment that you can do every day.
- Go on a walk, and look at the trees. Collect nuts, acorns, and different kinds of leaves that have fallen to the ground. Talk about what you see.
- Go on a picnic with your family and be sure they all pick up their trash and put it in the garbage can.

Parent participation opportunities at school will be to:

- Come spend some time with us as we explore the forest. See what is going on in our classroom.

  Date _____ Time _____
- Come join us when we bake "forest trees" cookies.

  Date _____ Time _____
- Please tell us if you know of local environmentalist who could come and talk to our class.

Our wish list for this theme includes:

recordings of animal sounds

music relating to the forest

pine cones

pictures of animals

wire coat hangers

acorns

pictures of trees

nature magazines

Thanks for your interest and participation in our class activities.

SECTION V

Animals and More

It is important for children to participate actively in their own learning experiences and activities. The curriculum should adapt to their *individual* differences, abilities, and interests.

The thematic activities in this section suggest ways to help you provide appropriate learning experiences for the children in your classroom. Adjust these to individual, small group, or large group involvement. Children enjoy learning about living creatures, and these activities should encourage enthusiastic participation by the children.

The following themes are included in Section V — Animals and More:

Theme 20 — Zoo

Theme 21 — Farm

Theme 22 — Pets

Theme 23 — Insects and Spiders

Theme 24 — Fish

Theme 25 — Birds

Theme 26 — Circus

Theme 27 — Dinosaurs

TYPES OF WILD ANIMALS
Bear and cub
Elephant and calf
Lion and cub   /   Tiger and cub
Hippopotamus and calf
Rhinoceros and calf
Giraffe and calf
Zebra and foal
Monkey and baby
Gorilla and baby

THEME 20
Zoo

ACTIVITIES AT THE ZOO
Petting zoo
Tours
Small trains around zoo
Volunteers
Guides
Adopt-an-animal
Snacks
Picnic area

NATURAL HABITATS
Africa — lion
zebra   giraffe
elephant
rhinoceros
hippopotamus
Tropical forest — monkey and gorilla
Jungles or forests — tiger
Forests and cold climates — bears

SCHOOL

CARE OF ANIMALS
Zookeeper
Veterinarian
Food   Water

SHELTERS
Open and natural   Houses
Fenced areas   Cages

THEME GOALS

To provide opportunities for children to learn:

1. A zoo is a place where people can safely see wild animals.
2. Zoo animals from all over the world are kept in cages, houses, and fenced areas similar to their natural habitats.
3. Giraffes, bears, elephants, lions, tigers, zebras, monkeys, gorillas, hippopotamus, and rhinoceros are some zoo animals.
4. Baby animals usually are kept with their mothers. Sometimes they are placed in a zoo nursery for extra care.
5. Zookeepers and veterinarians take care of all the animals and keep them safe, fed, watered, exercised, and healthy.

Children-Created Bulletin Board

Make the zoo bulletin board interactive by suggesting ways for the children to add to it throughout the theme. The more the class explores the zoo theme, the more the board should reflect the children's exploration.

* Cover the surface with tan burlap to give texture to the bulletin board.
* String a nylon cord clothesline across the top. With clothespins, attach leaves that the children make, monkeys that are made to hang from the trees, and anything else the children wish to add.
* Crush brown paper bags to make the trunks of the trees.
* With the children's help, make a craft stick fence across the bottom of the bulletin board.
* Title the board "Welcome to Our Zoo."
* Place silhouettes of zoo animals on the board. Throughout the theme, the children can put their drawings and pictures on or beside the appropriate animal silhouettes.
* You may also put Velcro pieces on the silhouettes and on the backs of animal pictures. This way the children can match the correct animal picture to the silhouettes.
* As with all early childhood bulletin boards, the children frequently should have something new to discover or put on the board.

Vocabulary Starters

Let the children add additional words.

zoo — a place where we can go to see wild animals.

habitat — a natural place where animals live before they come to the zoo.

zoo nursery — a place for zoo babies needing special care.

zookeeper — a person who feeds and cares for the animals in the zoo.

veterinarian — a doctor for animals.

Language Experiences

STUFFED ANIMAL PLAY

✳ Hold the baby in your arms or lap.

✳ Introduce the child to a stuffed animal, such as a teddy bear or giraffe.

✳ Say the name and talk to the infant about the animal.

✳ Hold the animal in front of the baby's eyes.

✳ Slowly move the stuffed animal back and forth, so the child can follow the toy with her eyes.

✳ Stop the activity when the infant tires.

✳ Repeat with the same or a different stuffed animal.

GORILLA FUN

Read Rathmann's *Good Night, Gorilla* to the children (see books section in this theme). This limited-word picture book is delightful — you will probably be asked to read it many times.

✳ Make flannelboard characters of the people and animals in the book. This allows the children to participate in the retelling of the story.

✳ The book, flannelboard, and story pieces can be put in the language center for the children to enjoy whenever they wish.

✳ As a follow-up, the children can act out the story. This helps to develop memory and sequencing skills.

Dramatic Play

ZOO NURSERY

✳ Set up the dramatic play area as a zoo nursery.

✳ Provide doll beds, empty baby bottles, lots of small stuffed animals, baby blankets, aprons, and smocks.

✳ If possible, put several child-sized rocking chairs in the area too.

✳ To introduce the children to the zoo nursery, read Smith's *Inside the Zoo Nursery,* listed in the books section of this theme.

✳ This explains that baby animals cannot always be kept with their mothers. They go to the zoo nursery for special care by the zoo nursery keepers and the veterinarian.

✳ Suggest to the children that they take care of the baby stuffed animals in their own "zoo nursery."

Puppet Play

LET'S MAKE ZOO PUPPETS

✳ For toddlers, put paper sacks and crayons out.

✳ Demonstrate how to make a sack into a puppet by putting your hand inside.

✳ Leave the sacks on the table and let them explore playing with the sacks and coloring them.

✳ Put Styrofoam and paper cups, paper plates, paper sacks, construction paper, yarn, crayons, markers, gray paint, paper towel rolls, and craft sticks on a table.

✳ Invite the children to make animal puppets.

✳ A Styrofoam cup with a small circle cut in the side is a good beginning to an easy elephant puppet. The child sticks his finger into the cup and out the hole to make the elephant's nose.

✳ Fringe the outer rim of a paper plate all the way around and it becomes a lion's mane.

✳ Give the children time to experiment with the materials. They will make wonderful zoo puppets.

✳ Follow the puppetmaking with a parade of animal puppets.

✳ The children who did not want to make a puppet can play rhythm instruments to accompany the zoo parade.

Music

SONG: "Animals Marching in the Zoo"

Before introducing the song to the children, talk about the animals at the zoo. How do they think each animal moves? Ask them, "Which animals do you like the best?" "Which ones do you think you'll be when we sing the song?" Then, have fun! Sing to the traditional tune of "When Johnny Comes Marching Home Again."

The bears are marching in the zoo, hurrah, hurrah.
The elephants are marching too, hurrah, hurrah.
The lions and tigers and tall giraffes,
The rhinos and hippos, and baby calves,
The gorillas and monkeys marching in the zoo.

✳ For the second verse, sing "playing in the zoo."
✳ For the third verse, sing "eating in the zoo."
✳ For the fourth verse, sing "sleeping in the zoo."

Movement

ANIMAL ANTICS

This is a large muscle activity for outdoor play.

✳ Mark a starting point and an ending point on the grass.

✳ The children move from one point to another by following directions, such as:
— take two lion leaps;
— take four elephant steps;
— take three kangaroo hops, and;
— take five monkey jumps.

Sensory Art

STRIPES, SPOTS, AND PATTERNS

✳ Place wallpaper and fabric scraps (striped, spotted, and patterned), fake fur and leather scraps, cotton balls, yarn, scissors, glue, crayons, markers, construction paper, and paper plates on a table in the art area.

✳ Leave these materials throughout the zoo theme.

✳ Encourage the children to create with the materials. It will be interesting to see what things or animals the children make.

SQUIGGLE ART

This activity is designed to encourage creativity, develop flexible thinking, and stimulate brainstorming skills.

✳ Put a "squiggle" on a flip chart. This is just a random line marking made anywhere on the page.

✳ Have the children look at the line and talk about what they see.

✳ Ask one child to come up and draw her idea to complete the drawing. The drawing should contain the squiggle.

✳ Next, make another line on another sheet of paper on the flip chart.

✳ Ask another child to come up and draw an animal picture that includes the squiggle.

✳ Place a stack of white paper sheets, each marked with a different squiggle, crayons, markers, and pencils in the art area.

✳ Leave this for the children to experiment with squiggle art on their own.

Creative Food Experiences

TASTY SNACK

You will need:

> 1 banana for each child
> orange juice
> craft or popsicle sticks
> shredded coconut
> chopped peanuts

1. Wash hands
2. Place a small bowl of orange juice in front of each child.
3. Place several servings of shredded coconut and chopped peanuts on wax paper.
4. Have each child cut his banana into thick slices with a craft stick.
5. Each banana slice is then placed on a craft stick, dipped into the orange juice, and rolled in one or both of the toppings.
6. Enjoy!

ANIMAL MERRY-GO-ROUNDS:

You will need:

> 1 apple for every two children
> peanut butter
> animal crackers
> pretzel sticks

1. Wash hands.
2. Cut the apple in half ($\frac{1}{2}$ apple per child).
3. Spread peanut butter over the cut side of each apple half (peel is on the bottom).
4. Add animal crackers and pretzel sticks to represent the merry-go-round animals and poles.
5. The children also can separate the zoo animals from the other types of animals in the animal cracker box before they enjoy eating them.

ANIMAL MERRY-GO-ROUNDS

Wash hands.

Cut one apple in half.

Spread peanut butter over each apple half.

Add animal crackers and pretzel sticks to make the

merry-go-round animals and poles.

Look at your creation and then eat! Yum!

Math

LET'S BUILD A ZOO

✳ In the block area place stuffed animals, small animal toys, all sizes of blocks and Legos, berry baskets, boxes, grass, twigs, leaves, and hay.

✳ This will give the children a variety of materials to create a zoo and build areas for the animals.

✳ The bigger blocks, boxes, and stuffed animals usually prove to be the favorites for toddlers.

TALL, TALLER, TALLEST

Introduce this math activity by reading books and showing pictures of giraffes in their natural habitats and at the zoo.

✳ Ask the children to look closely at the pictures.

✳ Ask questions such as, "Which legs are the longest on a giraffe, the front ones or the back?" (The front ones are.) "What do you think giraffes eat?" (They eat leaves and twigs of trees.) "What about the neck and rest of the giraffe's body?" (The body is one continuous slope from horns to tail.)

✳ Younger children can draw pictures of the mother, father, and baby giraffes.

✳ Male giraffes are fifteen to twenty feet tall. Female giraffes are ten to fifteen feet tall. Newborn giraffes are more than six feet tall.

✳ As a class project, have the children use masking tape to mark off fifteen feet, ten feet, and six feet on the floor. This should help them visualize the height of giraffes.

✳ Supply tape measures, rulers, yardsticks, paper, and pencils.

Science

BABY ZOO ANIMALS

A study of the zoo gives children a unique opportunity to observe animals.

✳ Invite a zookeeper, veterinarian, or animal rehabilitator to visit the children in your class.

✳ If possible, ask the individual to bring a baby animal that lives in the zoo to visit the class. Some zoos provide this kind of service to schools and child care centers.

✳ Having someone who can answer the specific questions the children ask adds to the interest of this experience and helps the children learn. Someone who works with animals can explain firsthand about the habitats, characteristics, eating and sleeping habits of wild zoo animals.

Social Studies

WHAT DID WE SEE?

✳ In preparation for a field trip to the zoo, read Aliki's *My Visit to the Zoo* and Gibbons' *Zoo,* both of which are listed in the books section of this theme.

✳ As a follow-up to the field trip, talk about what you saw, including the zoo habitats, animals, zooworkers, what was happening, what the animals were doing, and other observations the children recall.

✳ With the younger children, read or reread Martin's *Brown Bear, Brown Bear, What Did You See?*

✳ Have the children dictate and illustrate a new book using animals that they saw at the zoo.

✳ Guide the older children to work with a partner to draw a map of the zoo. Ask them to label the areas with the names of the animals that live in each.

✳ Continue this activity for several days. Allow the children plenty of time to complete this project.

Children's Books

Aliki. (1997). *My Visit to the Zoo.* New York: HarperCollins.

Carle, Eric. (1997). *From Head to Toe.* New York: Harper-Collins.

Carle, Eric. (1987). *1,2,3 to the Zoo: A Counting Book.* New York: Putnam.

Deedrick, Tami. (1998). *Community Helpers, Zoo Keeper.* New York: Capstone Press.

Dun, Phoebe. (1984). *Zoo Animals.* (Board book). New York: Random House.

Ehlert, Lois. (1997). *Color Zoo.* New York: HarperCollins.

Ford, Miela. (1998). *Watch Us Play.* New York: Greenwillow.

Ford, Miela. (1995). *Bear Play.* New York: Greenwillow.

Gibbons, Gail. (1991). *Zoo.* New York: HarperTrophy.

Hill, Eric. (1996). *Baby Animals: A Lift-the-Flap-Book.* New York: Puffin.

Hoban, Tana. (1986). *Panda, Panda.* New York: Greenwillow.

Hoban, Tana. (1985). *A Children's Zoo.* New York: Greenwillow.

Kallen, Stuart A. (1997). *Field Trips: The Zoo.* Edina, MN: Abdo & Daughters.

Knowles, Sheena. (1998). *Edward the Emu.* (Reprint edition). Illustrated by Rod Clement. New York: HarperTrophy.

Martin, Bill Jr. (1997). *Polar Bear, Polar Bear, What Do You Hear?* (Board book). Illustrated by Eric Carle. New York: Henry Holt.

Martin, Bill Jr. (1983). *Brown Bear, Brown Bear, What Do You See?* Illustrated by Eric Carle. New York: Henry Holt.

Noble, Kate. (1994). *The Blue Elephant* (Zoo stories). Illustrated by Rachel Bass. New York: Silver Seahorse.

Ormerod, Jan. (1991). *When We Went to the Zoo.* New York: Lothrop Lee & Shepard.

Oxenbury, Helen. (1991). *Monkey See, Monkey Do.* (Board book). New York: Dial.

Paxton, Tom. (1996). *Going to the Zoo.* Illustrated by Karen Schmidt. New York: William Morrow.

Prelutsky, Jack, and Paul O. Zelinsky. (1983). *Zoo Doings: Animal Poems.* New York: William Morrow.

Rathman, Peggy. (1996). *Good Night, Gorilla.* New York: Putnam.

Rosen, Michael. (1989). *We're Going On a Bear Hunt.* New York: Macmillan.

Smith, Dale. (1997). *Nighttime at the Zoo.* New York: Golden Anchor.

Smith, Roland. (1993). *Inside the Zoo Nursery.* Photographs by William Munoz. New York: Cobblehill/Dutton.

Stamper, Judith. (1989). *Zoo Worker.* Illustrated by Kathleen Garry-McCord. Mahwah, NJ: Troll.

Tucker, Siam. (1995). *Animal Splash.* New York: Little Simon.

Waber, Bernard and Barbara. (1996). *A Lion Named Shirley Williamson.* New York: Houghton Mifflin.

Waddell, Martin. (1993). *Let's Go Home, Little Bear.* Illustrated by Barbara Firth. Cambridge, MA: Candlewick Press.

Weiss, Ellen. (1988). *A Visit to the Sesame Street Zoo.* Illustrated by Tom Leigh. New York: Random House and Children's Television Workshop.

Parent Letter (Preschool)

Dear Parents,

Here we go with another new theme for the children to explore. We are studying the Zoo and Zoo Animals. We will provide opportunities for the children to learn:

- A zoo is a place where people can safely see wild animals.
- Zoo animals from all over the world are kept in cages, houses, and fenced areas similar to their natural habitats.
- Giraffes, bears, elephants, lions, tigers, zebras, monkeys, gorillas, hippopotamus, and rhinoceros are zoo animals.
- Baby animals usually are kept with their mothers. Sometimes they are placed in a zoo nursery for extra care.
- Zookeepers and veterinarians take care of all the animals and keep them safe, fed, watered, exercised, and healthy.

We will be talking about:

- types of wild animals
- the names of the mothers and babies
- the animals' natural habitats
- how zookeepers and veterinarians care for the animals
- activities at the zoo

Here are some things to do at home with your child to support our classroom learning:

- Look at pictures of the zoo and zoo animals in magazines and books.
- Talk with your child about your visits to the zoo when you were a child.
- Go on a family trip to a zoo or a petting zoo. Take photographs for your child to have and to share with classmates.

Opportunities for you to participate at school include:

- Go with us on our field trip to the zoo.
      Date _____ Time _____
- Come visit our classroom and see the bulletin board and the block zoo the children have created.
      Date _____ Time _____
- Please tell us if you know a veterinarian who takes care of baby animals and would bring one to show the children.

The wish list for this theme includes:

pictures of wild animals

empty, clean baby bottles

Styrofoam cups

wallpaper and fabric scraps, preferably striped, patterned, and spotted

Thank you for your continued support.

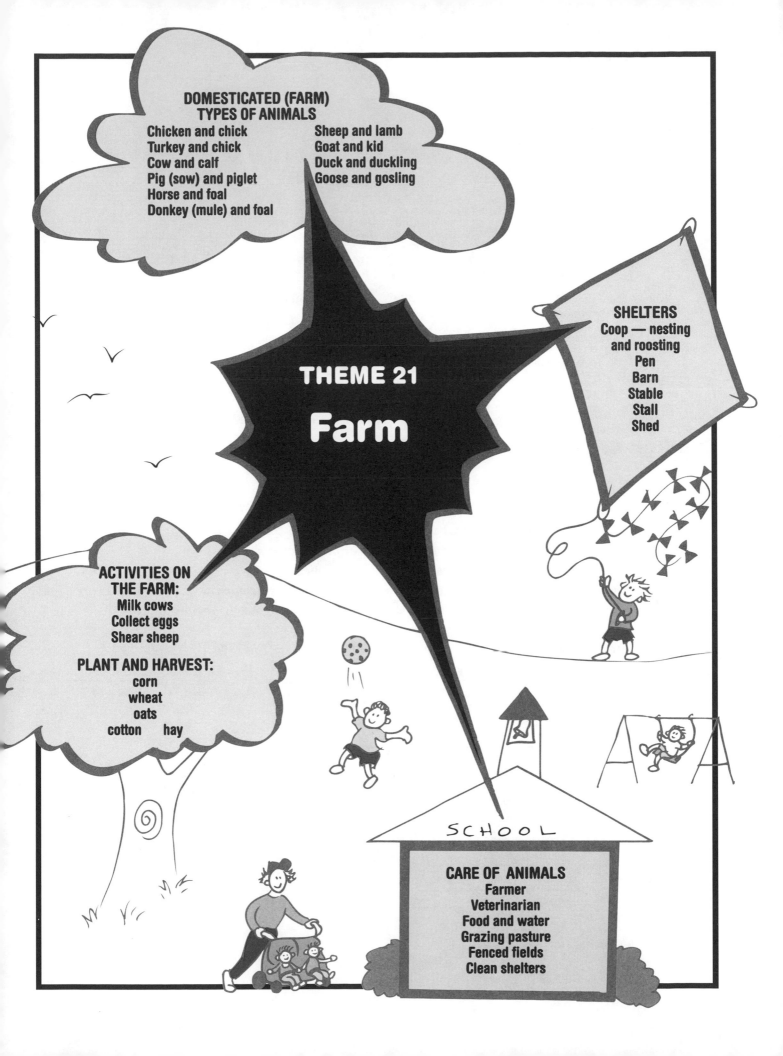

DOMESTICATED (FARM) TYPES OF ANIMALS

Chicken and chick
Turkey and chick
Cow and calf
Pig (sow) and piglet
Horse and foal
Donkey (mule) and foal

Sheep and lamb
Goat and kid
Duck and duckling
Goose and gosling

THEME 21

Farm

SHELTERS
Coop — nesting and roosting
Pen
Barn
Stable
Stall
Shed

ACTIVITIES ON THE FARM:
Milk cows
Collect eggs
Shear sheep

PLANT AND HARVEST:
corn
wheat
oats
cotton   hay

SCHOOL

CARE OF ANIMALS
Farmer
Veterinarian
Food and water
Grazing pasture
Fenced fields
Clean shelters

THEME GOALS

To provide opportunities for children to learn:

1. A farm is located outside a city.

2. A farm is land on which crops and animals are raised.

3. A farmer is the person who owns the farm and, along with family members and employees, works long hours to care for the animals and crops.

4. Chickens, turkeys, cows, pigs, horses, donkeys, sheep, goats, ducks, and geese are some of the farm animals.

5. Farm animals are sheltered in coops, pens, barns, stables, stalls, and sheds.

6. Much of the food we eat and the clothing we wear comes from the animals and crops raised on farms.

Children-Created Bulletin Board

This bulletin board focuses on the farm. It should express what the children know and want to find out about life on the farm. The bulletin board should change in appearance as the theme progresses.

* Cover the bulletin board with a light background.
* Ask the children to help you make a sun and some cotton ball clouds.
* Provide many pictures for the children to see actual farm life.
* Encourage some of the children to make a barn. Others can make a scarecrow standing in the corn field.
* Have mother farm animals with babies available for the children to match in appropriate pairs and put on the bulletin board.
* Activities throughout the theme will provide additional content to make the board interactive.

Vocabulary Starters

Let the children add additional words.

farm — a piece of land, usually with a house and barn, on which crops and animals are raised.

pasture — a field where farm animals can eat grass and other plants.

barn — a farm building where animals are protected and crops are stored.

veterinarian — a doctor for animals.

plant — to put seeds into the ground.

harvest — collecting crops when they are ripe.

crop — any type of food grown on a farm.

Language Experiences

NURSERY RHYMES
"Little Bo-Peep"

Little Bo-Peep has lost her sheep,
And can't tell where to find them;
Leave them alone, and they'll come home,
Wagging their tails behind them.

"Sing a Song of Sixpence"

Sing a song of sixpence,
A pocket full of rye;
Four and twenty blackbirds
Baked in a pie.
    When the pie was opened,
    The birds began to sing;
    Was not that a dainty dish,
    To set before the king?
The king was in his counting-house
Counting out his money;
The queen was in the parlor
Eating bread and honey.
    The maid was in the garden
    Hanging out the clothes,
    There came a little blackbird,
    That sat on her nose.

"Hey! Diddle, Diddle"

Hey! Diddle, diddle!
The cat and the fiddle.

The cow jumped over the moon;
The little dog laughed to see such sport,
And the dish ran away with the spoon.

"Little Boy Blue"

Little boy blue, come blow your horn,
The sheep's in the meadow,
The cow's in the corn.
Where's the boy that looks after the sheep?
He's under the haystack, fast asleep.
Will you wake him? No, not I;
For if I do, he'll be sure to cry.

"This Little Pig Went To Market"

This little pig went to market;
This little pig stayed at home;
This little pig ate roast beef;
This little pig had none;
This little pig said, "Wah, wah,
I can't find my way home."

"There Were Two Blackbirds"

There were two blackbirds sitting on a hill,
The one named Jack, the other named Jill.
Fly away Jack!
Fly away Jill!
Come again Jack!
Come again Jill!

WHAT WOULD I BE?

This activity encourages dictating and writing skills, and creativity.

✳ Ask the children to write about this idea: "If I could be a farm animal, which one would I be?"

✳ Have them write about what they would look like, what they would do all day, who their friends would be, and anything else they want to say.

✳ The children may also illustrate their words.

✳ Younger children can dictate their ideas for you to write down.

BOW-WOW! BOW-BOW! VOW-VOW! HUF-HUF!

Introduce this activity by asking the children to think about the sounds animals make.

✳ Ask them to talk about the animals they have actually seen and heard. "How do they sound?" "Do they all sound alike?"

✳ Read DeZutter's *Who Says a Dog Goes Bow-Wow?,* listed in the books section of this theme. This book offers an imaginative way to present different languages to children. As the author says, "Where people live and what language *they're* using determine what animals say to us humans."

✳ Have the children experiment with making the international sounds introduced in the book, such as how the rooster crows: cock-a-doodle-doo (English), kee-kee-ree-kee (Spanish, Italian), ku-ku-ru-ku (Turkish), and coco-rico (French).

✳ Ask the children to locate, on a globe or map, the countries where the languages are spoken.

✳ Set up art easels and put markers, crayons, all kinds of paper, scissors, and glue on the art table for children who want to create their own animals or books.

Dramatic Play

ON THE FARM

✳ Involve the class in a project to turn the dramatic play area into a farm.

✳ Read books, share pictures, watch videos, and talk about life on a farm.

✳ What would the children like to do if they lived on a farm? How many of them have been on a farm? Do any of their family members live on a farm?

✳ Write down all of their comments, suggestions, and ideas.

✳ Decide on props to complete the farm area. Some examples are a saddle for make-believe horse riding; a scarecrow for the corn- or wheatfield the children make; and a "cow to milk," based on the next dramatic play activity.

✳ The indoor dramatic play area can become the farm house and the barn.

✳ The outdoor playground area can become the pasture or planting fields.

✳ Once the children become involved in the process, this project could last for many days. Be flexible!

MILKING A PRETEND COW

Read Aliki's *Milk: From Cow to Carton,* listed in the books section of this theme. This book takes the children on a guided tour through the milking process and a trip to the dairy, and ends with the different foods made from milk. The story also connects with the creative food experiences section of this theme.

✳ To help the children understand more about cows, have them "milk a glove."

✳ Make a pinhole in each fingertip of a pair of latex gloves.

✳ Outside, hang a clothesline about three feet above the ground and away from the main "traffic areas" on the playground.

✳ Attach the prepared gloves about three feet apart to the clothesline with a spring-type clothespin.

✳ Place a pail below each glove and a low stool or chair beside each one.

✳ Fill the prepared gloves with water.

✳ Let the children take turns squeezing the fingertips of the glove as if milking, so that the water goes into the bucket.

✳ Be prepared to answer the children's questions. Otherwise, step back and become an observer.

Puppet Play

FARM PUPPETS

✳ Make a horse puppet by using a child-sized sock.

✳ Add yarn pieces to represent a mane.

✳ Add facial features. Refer to the Sock Puppet activity in Theme 2 for additional suggestions.

✳ Make a scarecrow hand puppet, based on the Scarecrow Puppet in Theme 12.

OLD MacDONALD FINGER PUPPETS

✳ Create, with the children, some rooster, horse, duck, cow, and pig finger puppets to act out "Old MacDonald Had a Farm."

✳ For this activity you will need one or more child-sized and adult-sized cloth gloves (such as garden gloves), scraps of colored felt, some Velcro (both hooked and soft sides), and some Velcro glue.

✳ To construct the finger puppets, glue a small square piece of soft-sided Velcro to each glove finger, and let dry thoroughly.

✳ Cut out each animal head (as suggested in the illustration) out of a felt scrap, keeping in the one-inch to two-inch size range. Make as many sets of animals as there are gloves.

✳ Using felt-tipped markers, draw animal features on each felt cut-out, and then glue a small square of hook-sided Velcro to the back.

✳ When ready to sing the song, the children can press each animal head into place on the glove fingers as the song names it.

✳ Store each glove and set of animals in a small plastic bag to protect them, and place in the dramatic play area to be used by the children whenever they wish.

Music

SONG: "My Kitty Just Says 'Meow' " by Jo Eklof

The bird in the tree says, "cheep cheep cheep. The dog says, "bow wow wow." The duck in the pond says, "quack quack quack." my kit-ty just says, "meow."

Additional verses:

"Cocka doodle doo," says the rooster. "Oink oink," says the sow. "He haw he haw," hear the donkey say. My kitty just says, "meow."

"Baa," says the fluffy lamb. "Moo," says the cow. "Buzz buzz buzz," says the honey bee. My kitty just says, "meow."

(See page 303 for enlargement.)

Movement

SIMON SAYS "GO TO THE FARM"

"Simon Says" is a familiar game played by many young children. Change it to be appropriate for your group of children.

✳ For toddlers, the pace should be slow with every action a "Simon Says" one. If the "Simon Says" concept seems too difficult, substitute a name with which the children are comfortable.

✳ It is helpful to model the actions along with the toddlers.

✳ For preschoolers and kindergartners, pick up the pace of the game.

✳ For all ages, use the farm animals to help "Simon." For example:

— Trot like a horse.
— Strut like a rooster.
— Run like a goat.
— Walk like a piglet.
— Chew like a cow.
— Scratch like a hen.
— Waddle like a duck.
— Move like a lamb.
— Fly like a goose.
— Kick like a donkey.

TOPPLE THE MILK CARTONS

✳ Collect at least ten quart-size, empty, and clean milk cartons.

✳ Collect several soft medium-size balls.

✳ Put a masking-tape line on the floor or a wide chalk line on the sidewalk.

✳ Place the line further away from the cartons for the older children.

✳ Set up the milk cartons.

✳ Standing at the line, each child can try to knock down the cartons with a ball.

✳ The older children can play while standing with their backs to the cartons and throwing the ball between their legs or throwing the ball with an overhand pitch.

✳ Let the children make up the rules. It is their game.

Sensory Art

MUD PLAY

Children like to play in the mud, and many do not have the opportunity to do so.

✳ Put some dirt and water in plastic tubs, along with plastic farm animals, including a lot of pigs.

✳ Let interested children mix the mud and play with it.

FARM FUN

✳ Put farm animal cookie cutters in the art center. The cookie cutters are available at many craft and discount stores.

✳ Add different colored tempera paint and paper.

✳ The children can discover that dipping the cookie cutters into the paint and pressing them onto the paper makes interesting animal designs.

✳ Place some horseshoes and brushes on the art table with the tempera paint and paper.

✳ The children can explore painting the horseshoes and then pressing paper on top of them to make other types of interesting prints.

✳ Add oatmeal to the tempera paint for still another addition to the sensory art experience.

IT'S CORN

✳ Put corn kernels, bowls, and tweezers on a table.

✳ Encourage the children to move the corn from one bowl to another with the tweezers.

✳ This is an activity that you can put out and leave, so the children can play with it whenever they want to.

✳ This promotes small muscle development and eye-hand coordination.

✳ To make this into a one-on-one activity with you and the child, ask her to count the number of pieces of corn she moves from one bowl to the next.

RECYCLABLES

✳ Have the children create farm animals from assorted recyclable materials.

✳ Furnish materials, such as feathers, Styrofoam, plastic lids, buttons, ribbons, paper, yarn, and fabric scraps, paper towel rolls, odds and ends of wrapping paper, and small plastic containers.

✳ After the children have made their "farm animals," ask them to label each one and place them on a display table that you have covered with recyclable burlap or gunnysacks.

Creative Food Experiences

ANIMAL CINNAMON TOAST

You will need:

bread (two slices per child)

margarine

3 tablespoons sugar

1 teaspoon cinnamon

1. Wash hands.

2. Children spread softened margarine on bread with plastic knives.

3. Mix cinnamon and sugar together. Sprinkle on bread.

4. Use animal cookie cutters to cut bread.

5. Put in toaster oven until margarine melts, approximately 1 minute. Enjoy!

ANIMAL CINNAMON TOAST

Wash hands.

Spread softened margarine on 2 slices of bread.

Mix 3 tablespoons sugar with 1 teaspoon cinnamon.

Sprinkle mixture on bread.

Use animal cookie cutters to cut bread.

Put in toaster oven until margarine melts. ENJOY!

COOKING EGGS

* Talk about how chickens lay eggs for us to eat.
* Give each child an uncooked egg to hold and gently explore.
* If an egg is dropped, simply let the child clean it up with a paper towel. This is part of the learning experience.
* Next, hard-boil an egg for each child. See the creative food experiences section of Theme 10 for a scrambled eggs activity.
* Give a whole cooked egg to each child.
* Ask the children to try cutting the egg in half with a plastic knife. This is a fun thing to do.
* If they succeed, then they can try to cut it in fourths.
* Some of the eggs will be eaten before the activity reaches this point. That's okay. It's the process that's important!

HAYSTACKS
Tasting Snack

(See creative food experiences for Theme 15.)

Important: Before preparing this snack, check to see that none of the children is allergic to milk products.

If so, use another food as the basis of this snack, such as popcorn (from corn grown on a farm) or wheat crackers (from wheat grown on a farm).

You will need:
  cow milk
  goat milk
  cottage cheese
  Swiss cheese
  chocolate milk
  buttermilk
  cheddar cheese
  Colby cheese

1. Wash hands.
2. Give each child a sample of the milk products.
3. Talk about each of the products. Did they know all of these come from cows?

Math

BARN AND ANIMAL PLAY

* Make a flannelboard barn with a door that opens and closes, and animal characters to use on the flannelboard.
* Make the animals in family sets, such as a rooster, hen, and chicks.
* Working with small groups, ask the children to place the animals "in or out" of the barn, put a cow "on top" of the barn, "by the side," "on the left side," "far away," etc.
* To extend this activity, read *Three Billy Goats Gruff*, listed in the books section of this theme.
* Make flannelboard characters to correspond with the story.
* Ask the children to help you tell the story with the flannelboard pieces.
* Emphasize math concepts in the story, such as how many goats, the number of legs each goat has, the total number of legs of all the goats, various sizes (small, medium, large), their order in crossing the bridge, and other concepts.

ADDING AND
SUBTRACTING EGGS

* Collect empty egg cartons and plastic eggs.
* Have each child start with a full carton of eggs.

✳ Take away some eggs, and ask the child to tell you how many are left. Observe how they determine their answer.

✳ Continue adding and subtracting the eggs in the carton.

✳ With older children, ask them to write a number sentence on a sentence strip to show what you did when you took out two eggs.

✳ Continue giving the children examples of addition and subtraction for them to write in number sentences. Observe how they determine their answers.

Science

WHERE'S MY MAMA?

✳ Read Gibbons' *Farming* and Chang's *Are You My Baby?*

✳ Talk about the hard work the farmer does to provide food for people to buy at the grocery store.

✳ In the spring, one of the tasks of the farmer is to care for the baby animals.

✳ Guide the children in learning the names of the baby animals and their parents:

Family	Father	Mother	Baby
chicken	rooster	hen	chick
cattle	bull	cow	calf
pigs (hogs)	boar	sow	piglet
horse	stallion	mare	foal
sheep	ram	ewe	lamb
goat	billy	nanny	kid
duck	drake	duck	duckling

✳ Have puzzles, pictures, and books available to demonstrate visually what you are talking about.

✳ Put plastic animal families in the manipulative and block centers for the children.

Social Studies

IT'S FARM DAY!

To bring closure to the farm theme, have a Farm Day. If possible, take the activities outdoors.

✳ Invite a veterinarian to bring a baby farm animal to share with the children.

✳ Have everyone dress like farmers with overalls, boots, hats, and jeans.

✳ Some of the activities can be: find the milk caps in the hay, shuck corn to be cooked and eaten later, bean bag toss at milk cartons, milk the cow, described in the dramatic play section of this theme, sit in the saddle to ride the "pretend horse" of your choice, and dance to recorded country music.

✳ Invite the children's family members to stay for a picnic supper when they pick up the children.

✳ Infants and young toddlers can participate as appropriate or observe what the older children are doing.

Children's Books

Aliki. (1992). *Milk: From Cow to Carton (Let's-Read-and-Find-Out Book.)* (Revised edition). New York: HarperCollins.

Ancona, George. (1997). *The American Family Farm: A Photo Essay.* (Reprint edition). Photographs by Joan Anderson. San Diego, CA: Harcourt Brace.

Asch, Frank. (1998). *Barnyard Lullaby.* New York: Simon & Schuster.

Boynton, Sandra. (1993). *Barnyard Dance!* (Board book). New York: Workman.

Brown, Margaret Wise, and Aida E. Marcuse. (1996). *Big Red Barn/El Gran Granero Rojo.* (Revised edition). Illustrated by Felicia Bond. New York: HarperCollins.

Burton, Jane. (1992). *Chick, Chick.* New York: Lodestar Books Dutton.

Carle, Eric. (1992). *Rooster's Off to See the World.* New York: Simon & Schuster.

Chang, Cindy. (1996). *Are You My Baby?* (Board book). Illustrated by Willabel L. Tong and Jill Dubin. New York: Random House.

Clayton, Gordon. (1993). *Calf (See How They Grow).* Photographs by Mary and Bill Ling. New York: Dk Publishing.

Crews, Donald. (1998). *Bigmama's.* (Reprint edition). New York: Mulberry.

Demi. (1993). *Little Baby Lamb.* New York: Grossett & Dunlap.

De Zutter, Hank. (1993). *Who Says a Dog Goes Bow-Wow?* Illustrated by Suse MacDonald. New York: Bantam Doubleday.

Dun, Phoebe. (1984). *Farm Animals.* (Board book). New York: Random House.

Ehlert, Lois, (1997). *Color Farm.* (Board edition.) New York: HarperCollins.

Fleming, Denise. (1994). *Barnyard Banter.* New York: Henry Holt.

Galdone, Paul, and Maria A. Fiol. (1996). *Three Billy Goats Gruff/Los Tres Chivitos Gruff.* New York: Lectorum.

Gibbons, Gail. (1990). *Farming.* New York: Holiday House.

Horenstein, Henry. (1994). *My Mom's a Vet.* Cambridge, MA: Candlewick.

Jones, Carol. (1998). *Old MacDonald Had a Farm.* Boston, MA: Houghton Mifflin.

Jordan, Sandra. (1996). *Down on Casey's Farm.* New York: Orchard Books.

London, Jonathan. (1995). *Like Butter on Pancakes.* Illustrated by G. Brian Karas. New York: Viking.

Martin, Bill, Jr. (1988). *Barn Dance.* New York: Henry Holt.

McDonnell, Flora. (1994). *I Love Animals.* Cambridge, MA: Candlewick.

Peters, Lisa W. (1995). *The Hayloft.* New York: Dial.

Rounds, Glen. (1994). *Three Billy Goats Gruff.* New York: Holiday House.

Tafuri, Nancy. (1995). *The Barn Party.* New York: Greenwillow.

Tresselt, Alvin, and Carolyn Ewing. (1991). *Wake Up, Farm.* New York: Lothrop Lee & Shepard.

Wallner, Alexandra. (1998). *The Farmer in the Dell.* New York: Holiday House.

Wormell, Mary. (1995). *Hilda Hen's Happy Birthday.* San Diego, CA: Harcourt Brace.

Parent Letter (Toddler)

Dear Parents,

We are now learning about animals and life on the Farm, as we begin our new theme. The children will learn:

- A farm is a piece of land located outside a city where crops and animals are raised.
- Many animals live on farms, such as chickens, turkeys, cows, pigs, horses, donkeys, sheep, goats, ducks, and geese.
- Farm animals are sheltered in coops, pens, barns, stables, stalls, and sheds.
- A farmer is the person who owns the farm and, along with family members and employees, works long hours to care for the animals and crops.
- Much of the food we eat and the clothing we wear comes from the animals and crops raised on farms.

We will be talking about:

- farm animals and their babies
- milking cows
- types of animal homes
- collecting eggs
- how farm animals are cared for
- sounds of animals
- activities on the farm
- foods from the farm

Try some of these things to do at home with your child:

- Go for a ride in the country. Talk about the farms and animals that you see.
- Read books about the farm.
- Play music, and sing songs about farm animals.

Parent participation opportunities at school will include:

- Come and join us for our tasting and cooking activities.
  Date _____ Time _____
- Come have fun with us on Farm Day.
  Date _____ Time _____

Our wish list for this theme includes:

animal cookie cutters

old, clean child-sized socks

paper towel rolls

empty, washed quart-size milk cartons

plastic lids

egg cartons

Thank you for sharing your child with us.

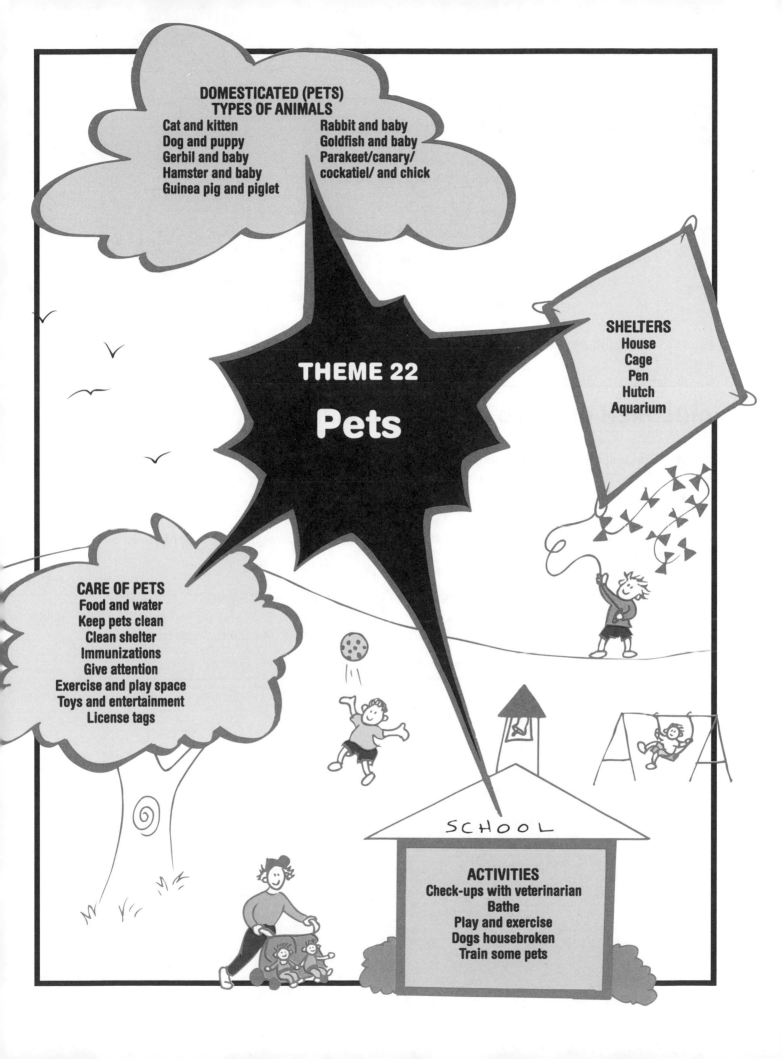

**DOMESTICATED (PETS)
TYPES OF ANIMALS**

Cat and kitten
Dog and puppy
Gerbil and baby
Hamster and baby
Guinea pig and piglet

Rabbit and baby
Goldfish and baby
Parakeet/canary/
cockatiel/ and chick

THEME 22

Pets

SHELTERS
House
Cage
Pen
Hutch
Aquarium

CARE OF PETS
Food and water
Keep pets clean
Clean shelter
Immunizations
Give attention
Exercise and play space
Toys and entertainment
License tags

SCHOOL

ACTIVITIES
Check-ups with veterinarian
Bathe
Play and exercise
Dogs housebroken
Train some pets

THEME GOALS

To provide opportunities for children to learn:

1. A pet is a tame animal that is taken care of and kept as a special friend.
2. Pets need food, water, shelter, and plenty of attention and love.
3. Pets need to be handled carefully and gently.
4. Pets also need exercise, a clean and safe home, and visits to the veterinarian.
5. Some common house pets are cats, dogs, gerbils, hamsters, guinea pigs, cockatiels, parakeets, and goldfish.
6. Families need to learn how to take care of a pet before getting one.

CHILDREN-CREATED BULLETIN BOARDS

This bulletin board gives the children an opportunity to share their pets with their classmates. Children who do not have a pet can choose an animal they would like to have as a pet.

✳ Title the bulletin board "Our Pets."
✳ Ask the children to bring a photo of the family pet to put on the board.
✳ Ask children who do not have a pet to cut out a picture of the animal they would like to have as a pet. Supply magazines for the children.
✳ The children can also draw a picture of a pet to put on the board.
✳ The bulletin board should reflect the children's interests and change throughout the theme.
✳ Put modeling clay in the art center, and leave it for the children to make clay pets whenever they would like.
✳ On a small table in front of the bulletin board, place the clay animals the children have made.

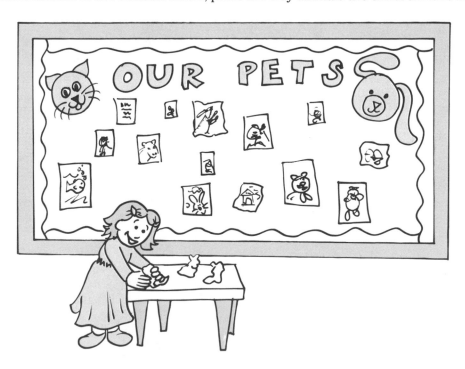

Vocabulary Starters

Let the children add additional words.

domesticated — animals that are not wild and are used to living around people.

fur — soft, thick hair that covers some animals.

feathers — the covering of birds.

scales — hard covering of fish and reptiles.

veterinarian — a doctor of animals.

Language Experiences

FINGERPLAY: "I Have a Pet"

I have a pet mouse
And her name is Rose.
She runs up my arm
And sits on my nose.
   (the fingers run up an arm and onto the nose)
I have a pet turtle
And his name is Bill.
He crawls a little bit
Then he just stands still.
   (the fingers on one hand "crawl" and stand still)
I have a pet canary
Her name is Miss Peep.
She flies around my head
And goes "cheep, cheep, cheep."
   (the fingers fly around the head)
I have a pet goldfish
His name is Joe.
He can't say a word
Just
   (make lips round and form three "O's" in time with the verse).

Philip Jackman

POEM: "Pet Guessing Game"

My name is Lulu,
And I'm black and white.
I wander around the house at night.
I like to play with a piece of string.
My paws are soft, but my claws can sting.
What am I? *(Cat)*
My name is Petey and my coat is brown,
I love to run and jump up and down.
I like to chew on a big old bone,
And I bark at the sound of a telephone.

What am I? *(Dog)*
My name is Poky and I'm hard on top.
My legs are so short I can't run or hop.
When I get scared and want to hide,
I can pull my head and my legs inside.
What am I? *(Turtle)*
My name is Cookie, I'm yellow and white.
I sing and sit on my perch all night.
I like to eat seeds with my little sharp beak,
If you cover my cage, you won't hear a squeak.
What am I? *(Cockatiel)*

Philip Jackman

Dramatic Play

THREE LITTLE KITTENS

Young children enjoy the story told in the familiar poem "Three Little Kittens." They also like to act out being the kittens in the retelling of the story.

✳ Have mittens for the children to put on and take off as they act out the story. See puppet play in this theme for easy mittens to make.

✳ With toddlers, use fewer verses to tell the story.

✳ Ask preschoolers what the three little kittens could have done to keep their mittens clean?

✳ Give them opportunities to retell the story in a different way.

✳ Brett's *The Mitten: A Ukrainian Folktale* and Tressellt's *The Mitten* (see the books section in this theme) tell another story about a mitten.

"Three Little Kittens"

Three little kittens
   Lost their mittens
And they began to cry,
   "Oh mother dear,
Come here, come here,
   Our mittens we have lost."
"Lost your mittens!
   My little kittens!
Then you shall have no pie."
   "Mee-ow, mee-ow
Now we shall have no pie.
   Mee-ow, mee-ow, mee-ow."
The three little kittens
   Found their mittens
And they began to cry,
   "Oh mother dear,
See here, see here,
   Our mittens we have found."

"Put on your mittens,
My little kittens,
Now you shall have some pie."
"Purr-r, purr-r, purr-r."
The three little kittens
Put on their mittens
And soon ate up the pie.
"Oh, mother dear,
Look here, look here,
Our mittens we have soiled."
"Soiled your mittens!
My little kittens!"
Then they began to cry,
"Mee-ow, mee-ow,"
Then they began to cry,
"Mee-ow, mee-ow, mee-ow."
The three little kittens
Washed their mittens
And hung them out to dry.
"Oh, mother dear,
See here, see here,
Our mittens we have washed."
"Washed your mittens?
My little kittens,
Now off you go to bed."
"Purr-r, purr-r, purr-r."

Puppet Play

PUPPETS FOR INFANTS

* Make this puppet for the older infants to enjoy.
* Use nontoxic, permanent markers to draw animal faces of pets on felt fabric.
* Cut out the faces.

✳ Measure the elastic around an infant's hand, then cut it, allowing an extra half inch at each end.

✳ Sew the strip together at the ends with a quarter-inch seam.

✳ Sew a face on the elastic covering the seam. Be sure the felt is securely sewn onto the elastic.

✳ Measure and sew other elastic strips for the other pet faces.

✳ Place a puppet on the infant's hand, and show the child how to make the puppet move and talk.

MITTENS FOR KITTENS

This activity can be related to the dramatic play activity in this theme.

✳ Put colored construction paper, various colors of yarn, pencils, crayons, markers, rulers, scissors, paper clips, and a paper punch on a table near the dramatic play center.

✳ In small groups, invite children to make a puppet at the table.

✳ Guide the children to draw around their hands on construction paper. Younger children may need some guidance from you to help them make their mitten puppets.

✳ Measuring with a ruler, help the children enlarge their hand drawings one to two inches (see illustration).

* Place this sheet over another, and fasten them together with a paper clip.

* Cut out the mittens, both sheets at once. For younger children, cutting one sheet at a time works better.

* Punch holes around the edges of each of the mittens, *not* the bottom. Weave a piece of yarn through the holes, and tie off the ends so that the two halves of the mittens are fastened together, as shown in the illustration.

* The children can draw faces on their mittens if they would like. This adds to the personality of the mitten puppet.

* The children put on their mitten puppets by inserting their hands in the open end.

Music

SONG: "How I Wish I Had a Little Dog" by Jo Eklof

Second verse:

How I wish I had a little doggie brown and white.
We'd romp around the yard all day. He's sleep near me at night.
We'd do many things together, life would seem just right.
How I wish I had a little dog. How I wish I had a little dog.

(See page 304 for enlargement.)

Movement

LET'S HAVE A PET PARTY

* Read Carle's *Have You Seen My Cat?*, Morley and Orbell's *Me and My Pet Fish*, Flanagan's *Buying a Pet from Ms. Chavez*, listed in the books section of this theme.

* Talk about the pets the children have or the pets they would like to have.

* Tell the children that they are going to have a "pet party!" Half of the group will get to act out being favorite pets, and the other half will be the pet owners.

* Suggest activities: the owner can have the pet do tricks, take the pet for a walk, pretend to feed the pet, and put the pet to "bed."

* After they have played for several minutes, suggest that the owners and pets switch roles.

* While the children are playing, encourage the positive aspects of pet care they demonstrate, such as: "Carmen, I like the way you are so gentle with your kitty"; "Jared, you are very patient teaching your puppy to do that trick"; or "Chris, when you pat your bunny like that, she knows you love her, doesn't she?"

Sensory Art

PETS OF CLAY

Introduce the children to making creative pets out of clay (ceramic clay, play dough, and plasticene). They can pull, tear, roll, cut, and create with clay. Clay offers a unique tactile and sensorimotor experience for the children.

* Purchase clay from a teacher resource store *and* make some in the class with the children.

* Have the children make their pets out of clay. They can make and remake the animals as often as they wish.

* Place the finished animals on a table near the bulletin board.

* Play dough recipes are given in the sensory art sections in Themes 6 and 10.

Creative Food Experiences

ROLL-AND-PAT "MOUSE" COOKIES

Read Numeroff's *If You Give a Mouse a Cookie* to the children. Everyone can then bake cookies.
You will need:

    1 cup Bisquick

    1 package instant pudding

    1/4 cup oil

    1 egg

    raisins, chocolate chips, or shredded coconut (optional)

You may need to double the recipe for more than ten children.

1. Wash hands.
2. Mix ingredients together.
3. Give each child a ball of dough on a piece of wax paper.
4. Use a hand to press the dough flat.
5. Decorate with raisins, chocolate chips, or coconut.
6. Bake 8 minutes at 350 degrees.
7. Yum!

Math

FEED THE DOG MATCH

* Take an ordinary file folder, open it, and draw ten dog houses inside the folder. (See the illustration.)
* Put a number on each dog house, not sequentially.
* Write "Feed the Dog" on the cover of the folder.
* Laminate the file folder.
* Draw ten small dog bones on a piece of tagboard.
* Place dots on each bone, from one to ten, to correspond with the dog house numbers.
* For younger children, you can put the numeral on the opposite side of the bone to make the activity self-correcting. (See the illustration.)
* Laminate the "bones," then cut them out.
* Place these pieces into a resealable plastic bag, and staple or glue to the back of the folder.
* Place the matching folder game in the math or manipulative center for the children to discover.

FIND THE GERBIL FOOD FOLDER GAME

* Draw a circular maze inside a file folder. (See the illustration.)
* Place "Start" at the beginning of the maze.
* At the "Stop" point, have an illustration of a gerbil's food box.
* On the cover of the file folder, write "Find the Gerbil Food."

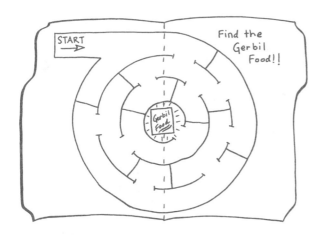

* Laminate the file folder.
* Provide a rub-off crayon or washable marker and a roll of paper towels for corrections and wipe-off when the folder is ready to be returned to the math center.
* The child playing the game begins at "Start," and marks a path to the gerbil food box.

Science

LET'S GET A PET

* Read Ziefert's *Let's Get a Pet*.
* Later, put this in the book center for the children to have as a reference.
* With the children's help, make a list of the animals that make the best pets. Put this on the bulletin board.
* Talk about what you should do *before* getting a pet.
* Make a list of these things to think about, such as:
  — Read about different kinds of pets.
  — Decide what kind of animal you want.
  — Decide how much money you have to spend to buy a pet.
  — Remember that some animals, such as dogs, can get big.
  — You have to clean up after some pets.
  — Some animals shed.
  — Some friends or family members might be allergic to pets.
  — Are you kind? Are you gentle?
  — Will you take the responsibility to take care of your pet?
  — Will you feed your pet and give it water?
  — Will you play with your pet?

* Put this list on the bulletin board.
* If possible, set up a pet center in the classroom. Check with your state's licensing department to learn which pets are acceptable in an early childhood classroom.
* Let the children take turns sharing responsibility for the class pet(s).

LET'S OBSERVE

* Observe a classroom pet. If you do not have a pet, perhaps you could borrow one for the day or bring a pet from home.
* In small groups, suggest to the children that they sit quietly and watch the animal.
* Younger children can tell you what they saw the animal doing. Write down what they describe.
* They can also draw pictures to show what they saw.
* Older children can keep a chart of the animal's activities and movements during the day. At the end of the observation time, they can report on what they observed.
* Discuss what the children learned about the classroom pet. What new questions do they have?

Social Studies

A VISIT TO A PET STORE

* Make arrangements to visit a pet store in your community.
* Go there first by yourself to arrange a special time for the field trip and to be sure the store is appropriate for young children to visit.
* It is important for someone to be available to show the children all the pets and to answer questions the children may have.
* Perhaps there will be one animal that the children can pet very gently.
* Follow up by sending thank-you notes from the class.
* Encourage the children to talk about the experience and to draw pictures and dictate stories about it.

Children's Books

Angelou, Maya. (1994). *My Painted House, My Friendly Chicken.* Photographed by Margaret Courtney-Clark. New York: Clarkson N. Potter, Inc.

Bauer, Marion Dane. (1997). *If You Were Born a Kitten.* Illustrated by Joellen M. Stammen. New York: Simon & Schuster.

Brett, Jan. (1996). *The Mitten: A Ukrainian Folktale.* New York: Putnam.

Buck, Nola. (1998). *Oh, Cats! (My First I Can Read Book).* Illustrated by Nadine B. Westcott. New York: HarperTrophy.

Cabrera, Jane. (1997). *Cats' Colors.* New York: Dial.

Carle, Eric. (1996). *Have You Seen My Cat?* New York: Little Simon.

Cole, Joanna. (1995). *My New Kitten.* Photographed by Margaret Miller. New York: William Morrow.

De Paola, Tomie. (1988). *The Kids' Cat Book.* (Reprint edition). New York: Holiday House.

Dr. Seuss. (1967). *Cat in the Hat: In English and Spanish.* New York: Random House.

Duke, Kate. (1998). *One Guinea Pig Is Not Enough.* New York: Dutton.

Flanagan, Alice K. (1998). *Buying a Pet from Ms. Chavez.* Chicago, IL: Children's Press.

Gibbons, Gail. (1998). *Cats.* New York: Holiday House.

Gibbons, Gail. (1996). *Dogs.* New York: Holiday House.

Hathon, Elizabeth. (1993). *Soft As a Kitten.* (Board book). New York: Grosset & Dunlap.

Keats, Ezra Jack. (1988). *Hi, Cat.* New York: Aladdin.

King-Smith, Dick. (1997). *Puppy Love.* Illustrated by Anita Jeram. Cambridge, MA: Candlewick Press.

Kuklin, Susan. (1988). *Taking My Cat to the Vet.* New York: Bradbury Press.

Kunhardt, Edith, and Dorothy Kunhardt. (1994). *Pat the Bunny and Friends.* (Board book). New York: Golden Press.

Landau, Elaine. (1998). *Your Pet Gerbil (True Books — Animals).* Chicago, IL: Children's Press.

McBratney, San. (1995). *Guess How Much I Love You.* Illustrated by Anita Jeram. Cambridge, MA: Candlewick Press.

Morley, Christine, and Carole Orbell. (1997). *Me and My Pet Fish (Me and My Pet Series).* Illustrated by Brita Granstrom. New York: World Book.

Numeroff, Laura Joffe. (1997). *If You Give a Mouse a Cookie.* Illustrated by Felicia Bond. New York: HarperTrophy.

Roth, Susan L. (1998). *Cinnamon's Day Out: A Gerbil Adventure.* New York: Dial.

Simon, Norma. (1986). *Cats Do, Dogs Don't.* Niles, IL: Albert Whitman.

Sun, Chyng-Feng. (1996). *Cat and Cat-Face.* Illustrated by Lesley Liu. Boston, MA: Houghton Mifflin.

Tressellet, Alvin. (1964). *The Mitten.* Illustrated by Yaroslava. New York: William Morrow.

Vagin, Vladimir, and Frank Asch. (1989). *Here Comes the Cat!* New York: Scholastic.

Voake, Charlotte. (1997). *Ginger.* Cambridge, MA: Candlewick Press.

Wolf, Jake. (1998). *Daddy, Could I Have an Elephant?* Illustrated by Marylin Hafner. New York: Puffin.

Ziefert, Harriet. (1993). *Let's Get a Pet.* Illustrated by Mavis Smith. New York: Viking.

Parent Letter (Preschool)

Dear Parents,

Our new theme is Pets. We will provide opportunities for the children to learn:

- A pet is a tame animal that is taken care of and kept as a special friend.
- Pets need food, water, shelter, and plenty of attention and love.
- Pets need to be handled carefully and gently.
- Pets also need exercise, a clean and safe home, and visits to the veterinarian.
- Some common house pets are cats, dogs, gerbils, hamsters, guinea pigs, cockatiels, parakeets, and goldfish.
- Families need to learn how to take care of a pet before getting one.

We will be talking about:

- domesticated types of animals, birds, and fish
- shelters for pets
- care of pets
- activities of pets

Things to do at home with your child to support and reinforce our classroom activities:

- If you are thinking about getting a pet, read and talk about what kind of animal the family wants, how much will it cost, who will be responsible for taking care of the pet, and other considerations.
- If you already have a pet, watch and talk about all the different things your pet does.
- Visit a pet store to see different kinds of pets.
- Check out books about pets from the library to read together at home.

Parent participation opportunities at school include:

- Come with us on our visit to the pet store.
  Date _____ Time _____
- Visit our class to see what's going on.
  Date _____ Time _____

Our wish list for this theme includes:

    magazines with pictures of animals

    file folders

    wide elastic strips

    yarn

                           Thank you for all of your help.

TYPES AND CHARACTERISTICS OF INSECTS

Three body parts
Four wings (some)
Six legs
(three pairs)
Two sensors
(antennae)
Egg, caterpillar
(larva), cocoon,

chrysalis,
pupa, butterfly
or moth
Bees
Flies
Grasshoppers
Ladybugs

Cockroaches
Wasps
Crickets
Beetles
Mosquitoes

THEME 23

Insects and Spiders

HABITATS OF INSECTS

Ants — colony
Bees — hive
Wasps — nests
Other insects:
water   trees
grass   ground
pollinating plants

TYPES AND CHARACTERISTICS OF SPIDERS

Two body parts
Eight legs (four pairs)
No antennae or wings
Spin webs to catch insect pests
Tarantula
Daddy longlegs
Others

SCHOOL

ACTIVITIES OF INSECTS

Ants — break down dead plant
material and add to soil
Butterflies — pollinate flowers
Bees — make honey
All insects — help us by feeding
on plant and animal waste and
are part of the food chain for
spiders, birds, frogs, and bats

THEME GOALS

To provide opportunities for children to learn:

1. There are many kinds of insects, and they are found all over the world.
2. Insects come in many sizes, shapes, and colors.
3. Insects have three body parts: head, thorax (middle section), and abdomen (usually the largest of the sections).
4. Insects wear their skeleton outside as a hard outer skin called the exoskeleton.
5. Insects have six legs (three pairs), two antennae, and if winged, four wings.
6. Insects help us by making honey, and pollinating flowers and fruits.
7. Spiders are not insects.
8. Insects and spiders come from eggs.
9. Spiders have eight legs (four pairs), two body parts, two feelers, and no wings or antennae.
10. A spider spins silk to get its food, build its shelter, protect its eggs, and to travel safely.
11. Spiders help us by eating insect pests.

Children-Created Bulletin Board

With the children's help, create this bulletin board from the point of view of an insect and a spider. As always, this board should be interactive, reflecting the children's input throughout the theme.

✳ Title this board "Look Everywhere for Insects and Spiders."
✳ On one side, create a spider's web using white thread or thin yarn. Children can make and add spiders to the web whenever they want to do so.
✳ Place grass at the bottom with insects the children have made "hiding" throughout.
✳ Make flowers out of wallpaper or gift-wrap to brighten the bulletin board. Put bees on and around the flowers.
✳ Place rocks made with burlap-covered cardboard or crumpled brown paper around the board. Attach some of them at one end so they may be lifted to reveal insects underneath.
✳ Label the items as they are placed on the board.
✳ Continue to add the children's creations as they work on this theme.

Vocabulary Starters

Let the children add additional words.

metamorphosis — life cycle of an insect from one stage to another, such as caterpillar to butterfly.

larva — caterpillar stage of a butterfly or moth's life.

cocoon — silky covering around the caterpillar as it sleeps and slowly changes.

chrysalis — hard covering that protects the pupa inside the cocoon.

pupa — stage of a butterfly, moth, or ant's life before it becomes an adult.

head, thorax, and abdomen — the three body parts of an insect.

antennae — two sensors on an insect that stick out from the head.

arachnids — class of eight-legged animals (*not* insects) that include spiders.

web — net that spiders weave from a spun thread.

Language Experiences

"I CAN'T" SAID THE ANT

✳ Read Cameron's *"I Can't" Said the Ant,* listed in the books section of this theme.

✳ This book is a favorite of young children. It offers opportunities for exploring letter-sound associations, rhyming words, and dramatizing the story.

✳ Some children will ask you to read the book again and again. Use flannelboard characters that the children can manipulate.

✳ Older children can read it themselves and then write their own story.

✳ They can work together or individually to create a classroom Big Book of their story.

✳ Encourage the children to think of other ways to retell the story, such as drawing or painting the story sequentially, discussing what clues they used to predict what would come next, and recalling their favorite rhyming lines.

✳ Here is an example of the delightful language:
— "What's all the clatter?" asked the platter.
— "Teapot fell," said the dinner bell.
— "Teapot broke," said the artichoke.
— "She went kerplop!" said the mop.

✳ *"I Can't" Said the Ant* also promotes working together cooperatively. Have the children talk about how the ants and other characters worked together to solve the problem.

LET'S CREATE A SPIDER'S WEB

✳ To introduce chapter books to the children, read White's *Charlotte's Web,* listed in the books section of this theme.

✳ As Charlotte starts to build her web, have the children start to build a web in one corner of the classroom using white yarn or twine.

✳ The class web can continue to grow along with Charlotte's.

✳ Guide the children into making spiders and putting them on the web with two-sided sticky tape.

✳ The children will think of additional insects to "get caught" in the web, as well as writing words in the web, just as Charlotte did.

Dramatic Play

ANTS AT A PICNIC

✳ Put several large picnic baskets in the dramatic play area. Add play food.

✳ Make a box tunnel by taking the ends out of boxes. Line the boxes up, and tape them together to form a tunnel.

✳ Use a cloth tunnel, if you already have one, to have more than one tunnel for the ants.

✳ The children can pretend to be ants taking the "food" from the picnic basket to their home through the tunnels.

✳ Continue to add items that the children want to use.

INSECTS HAVE SIX LEGS

✳ Brainstorm with the children to think of what they could make to add extra legs onto themselves. This helps them focus on the fact that insects have six legs.

✳ Walking on hands and knees is an easy way to create four legs.

✳ What can be done to make two more? One idea is to make long tube shapes from black material. Stuff the tubes with newspaper, and sew them onto a band for tying around the child's waist.

✳ Add antennae by using a headband and attaching pipe cleaners to the band.

✳ Ask a child to select an insect. Then, act out how they think the insect moves.

Puppet Play

PAPER BAG BEES

✳ Put pictures and books showing real bees around the area for the children to look at.

✳ For children who want to make puppets, have them color or paint paper lunch sacks yellow and black.

✳ When the paint has dried, have them stuff newspaper into the sacks.

✳ Tape on yellow construction paper for wings, but let the children use any color construction paper if they do not want to make the wings yellow.

✳ The children can "fly" the bees all over inside and outside as they play with their puppets.

✳ Later, if the children agree, take the puppets, attach string, and hang them around the bulletin board.

OTHER PAPER BAG PUPPETS

✳ Put paper sacks, construction paper, pipe cleaners, scissors, glue, crayons, and markers out on a table.

✳ Put pictures of insects, including caterpillars, around the area.

✳ For toddlers, precut small, medium, and large circles for them to glue as body parts on the paper sacks. Accept whatever they do with the circles.

✳ Model how you put your hand inside the sack to make the puppet move and "talk."

Music

SONG: "I Like to Look at Bugs"
by Jo Eklof

Additional verses:

Do they crawl and creep? Do they like to leap?

(See page 305 for enlargement.)

SONG:
"Shoo Fly"

This traditional song, "Shoo Fly," easily combines music and movement. It promotes coordination of action and words, and gives practice in following directions. Ask the children to form a circle and join hands. Then:

Sing: *Shoo fly, don't bother me.*
   Walk: four steps to the center.
Sing: *Shoo fly, don't bother me.*
   Walk: walk four steps back.
Sing: *Shoo fly, don't bother me.*
   Walk: four steps to the center.
Sing: *I belong to somebody.*
   Walk: four steps back.
Sing: *I feel, I feel, I feel like a morning star.*
   Walk: with joined hands, walk in a circle to the right.
Sing: *I feel, I feel, I feel like a morning star.*
   Walk: drop hands, walk in a circle to the left.
Repeat from the beginning up to:
Sing: *I feel, I feel, I feel like a morning star.*
   Walk: two children form an arch with their hands.
Sing: *I feel, I feel, I feel like a morning star.*
   Walk: one child leads the other children through the arch and begins another circle.

Sing: *Shoo fly, don't bother me. Shoo fly, don't bother me. I belong to somebody.*
Say: *"Shoo Fly!"* Use hand motions to get rid of the flies.

Movement

THE VERY HUNGRY CATERPILLAR

* Read Carle's *The Very Hungry Caterpillar* to the children.
* Ask the children to get their naptime blanket out of their cubbies. Or, you can ask parents to send an extra small blanket to school.
* Have the children wrap up inside of their blankets.
* After a short time, the children unwrap from their "cocoons" and become beautiful butterflies, using their blankets for wings.
* Put some music on so the "butterflies" can dance and move to the music.

LET'S MOVE LIKE INSECTS

* Play a record, cassette, or CD of Rimski-Korsakov's *Flight of the Bumblebee.*
* Play a portion first, so the children can hear the music.
* Have the children "fly like the bees" in rhythm to the music.
* Then change the music to a song they like.
* Ask them to jump like grasshoppers to the lively music.
* For children who want to do so, allow them, one at a time, to use a scooter board.
* Ask them to crawl like a bug: slowly, like a caterpillar, fast like a flea, etc.

Sensory Art

A GROUP CATERPILLAR

The children can do this activity over a period of time.

* Each day place a long piece of butcher paper on the art table with pie tins containing various colors of paint.

* Whenever a child wants to do so, he puts a hand, with fingers extended, into one of the paints and makes a handprint on the butcher paper. Ask the child to put the handprint next to another handprint with thumbs touching (see illustration).

* After eight or so children have made handprints, ask one of the children to draw a face on the caterpillar.

* Then display the caterpillar mural.

THREE-D INSECTS

* Collect large bottle caps, small container tops, thread spools, cardboard, construction paper, foil, felt and fabric scraps, pipe cleaners, yarn, string, Styrofoam spheres and squiggles, buttons, play dough, modeling clay, cotton balls, paper fasteners, garbage bag ties, twigs, and toothpicks.

* Place these items along with glue, crayons, markers, tempera paints, small brushes, scissors, single-hole paper punches, and staplers on a long table.

* Leave the materials out during the theme. This way the children can create unique "insects" as they explore the theme further.

* Take photos of the children making their bugs, and add these to the bulletin board.

Creative Food Experiences

CRUNCHY STRAWBERRIES

This cooking experience goes well with the story of *The Very Hungry Caterpillar*.

You will need:

    2 tablespoons strawberry yogurt per child

    2 whole strawberries per child

    1 teaspoon granola per child (optional)

    1 small plastic bowl per child

1. Wash hands.
2. Have each child cut up the strawberries with a plastic knife and place them in their bowl.
3. Spoon the yogurt on top.
4. Cover with granola, if desired.

SURPRISE MUFFINS

You will need:

    English muffins

    cream cheese

    red food coloring

    raisins

    lettuce leaves

1. Wash hands.
2. Give each child a lettuce leaf on a paper plate.
3. Place half of an English muffin on the lettuce.
4. Give each child a small amount of cream cheese.
5. Add a few drops of red food coloring to the cream cheese.

SURPRISE MUFFINS

Wash hands.

Place 1/2 of an English muffin on a leaf of lettuce.

Mix a few drops of red food coloring into a small amount of cream cheese. Spread the red cheese on the English muffin.

Add raisins on top of the cream cheese.

Surprise! It's a ladybug muffin!

6. Each child spreads the red cheese on her English muffin with a plastic knife.

7. Add raisins (dots) on top of the cream cheese.

8. Surprise! It's a ladybug muffin!

LET'S MAKE "DIRT CAKE"

You will need:

> 1 20-ounce package of chocolate sandwich cookies
>
> 1 8-ounce package of cream cheese
>
> 1/2 stick of margarine
>
> 1 cup powered sugar
>
> 3 1/2 cups milk
>
> 2 packages of instant chocolate pudding
>
> 1 12-ounce tub of whipped topping
>
> 1/4 cup mini-marshmallows
>
> gummy worms

1. Wash hands.

2. Place the chocolate cookies in a resealable plastic bag.

3. Have one or two of the children crush the chocolate cookies with a rolling pin.

4. Have one or two other children cream margarine, sugar, and cream cheese in a bowl.

5. Another child can mix the milk and pudding together. Let this sit until thick.

6. Stir the whipped topping into the cream cheese mixture, and add this to the milk and pudding mixture. Mix well.

7. Put one-third of the of the cookie crumbs in the bottom of a nine-by-nine-inch glass pan.

8. Add one-half the cream cheese mixture.

9. Repeat cookie crumbs and cream cheese mixture, adding some gummy worms and the mini-marshmallows.

10. Add extra crumbs on top, to look like dirt. Refrigerate over night.

11. Serve the next day as a special treat.

Math

GEOMETRIC DESIGNS

✻ Read McDermott's *Anansi the Spider,* listed in the books section of this theme.

✻ The bold, vivid colors and the geometric style of the illustrations can suggest to children a new way to look at math.

✻ Talk about all the shapes, sizes, and configurations of lines the children discover.

✻ Place all kinds of paper, crayons, markers, and paints in the math center.

✻ Encourage the children to experiment with their own designs and to create new ways to draw the insects they are studying.

MATH BOOK OF INSECTS

✻ Working with a small group of children at a time, encourage them to make a six-page booklet, including the cover.

✻ Punch holes on one side of each page. Later, the children can tie the pages together with yarn or staple the pages.

✻ Put books and pictures the children can use for reference in the math area.

✻ Ask them to write on the cover what they want to name their book: for example, "My Insect Book," "Ricardo's Insect Book," or "Insects."

✻ Ask the children to draw the three body parts of an insect on the second page (head, thorax/middle section, abdomen/large third section).

✻ On the third page, they draw the body parts again and add the six legs of the insect.

✻ On the fourth page, draw the three body parts, six legs, and add the two antennae.

✻ On the fifth page, draw the three body parts, six legs, two antennae, and four wings (some insects have wings).

✻ On the sixth page, ask the children write what they know about insects. The younger children can dictate to you what they want to say.

Science

SEE WHAT WE CAN FIND

✻ In a corner of the playground or in a special place you have prepared, let the children dig up several cupfuls of dirt.

✻ Dump the dirt onto a newspaper that has been spread on the sidewalk or on the floor.

✳ Ask the children to examine the dirt to see what they can find.

✳ Small sifters and magnifying glasses are useful tools to help search through a pile of dirt.

BUGS!

Make a bug jar! Spring is a wonderful time for the children to find and observe bugs. Provide magnifying glasses.

✳ In a plastic jar or bottle with a wide neck, place grass, twigs, leaves, and a wet cotton ball.

✳ Put all the bugs the children find in the bug jar.

✳ Attach some lightweight netting (found in fabric stores) to the top of the jar with a rubber band.

✳ Encourage the children to release the insects outside after they have completed their observations.

Social Studies

MIGRATING MONARCH BUTTERFLIES

✳ Read Heiligmam's *Caterpillar to Butterfly,* Gibbon's *Monarch Butterfly,* or Feltwell's *Butterflies and Moths,* listed in the books section of this theme.

✳ Discuss the fact that some butterflies travel or migrate every year to escape cold weather.

✳ In the fall, many thousands of Monarch butterflies fly from the northern United States and Canada south to southern California and Mexico, where they spend the winter. The Monarchs can cover whole trees.

✳ Have the children find these places on a globe or map.

✳ Ask the children where they would like to go if they could "migrate" for the winter.

✳ Point out the locations on the globe or map.

✳ Next, talk about how in late winter or early spring, adult Monarchs mate, lay eggs, and begin the journey north.

✳ The new eggs hatch, go through the metamorphosis cycle, and fly north as well.

✳ With the children, create a chart showing the life cycle of the Monarch butterfly.

✳ With the older children, extend the activity. Ask them how they think Monarch butterflies can

travel so far? Does the wind help the Monarchs when they fly?

✳ A simple demonstration is to have an electric fan blow pieces of paper.

✳ You can also blow up some medium-size balloons and hold the opening closed with your fingers.

✳ Everyone counts to three and the balloons are released. Discovery: when air is trapped, as with currents, it can become a power source and push objects.

✳ Wind currents help the Monarchs by letting them glide and pushing them on.

Children's Books

Cameron, Polly. (1961). *"I Can't" Said the Ant.* New York: Scholastic.

Cassie, Brian, and Jerry Pallotta. (1995). *The Butterfly Alphabet Book.* Illustrated by Mark Astrella. Watertown, MA: Charlesbridge.

Carle, Eric, (1997). *The Very Quiet Cricket.* (Board book). New York: Putnam.

Carle, Eric. (1996). *The Grouchy Ladybug.* New York: HarperCollins.

Carle, Eric. (1995). *The Very Busy Spider.* New York: Philomel.

Carle, Eric. (1994). *The Very Hungry Caterpillar.* (Board book). New York: Philomel.

Cole, Joanna, and Stephanie Calmenson. (1996). *Bug in a Rug: Reading Fun for Just-Beginners.* Illustrated by Alan Tiegreen. New York: William Morrow.

Climo, Shirley. (1995). *The Little Red Ant and the Great Big Crumb: A Mexican Fable.* Illustrated by Francisco X. Mora. New York: Clarion.

Cutts, David, and Diane Cutts. (1998). *I Can Read About Bees and Wasps.* Illustrated by Janice Kinnealy. New York: Troll.

Dorros, Arthur. (1988). *Ant Cities (Let's Read and Find Out Books).* New York: HarperTrophy.

Feltwell, John. (1997). *Butterflies and Moths (Eyewitness Explorers).* New York: Dk Publishers.

Fowler, Allan. (1998). *Inside an Ant Colony.* Chicago, IL: Children's Press.

Fowler, Allan, Robert Hillerich, and Fay Robinson. (1996). *Busy, Buzzy Bees.* Chicago, IL: Children's Press.

Fleming, Denise. (1995). *In the Tall, Tall Grass.* New York: Henry Holt.

Gibbons, Gail. (1991). *Monarch Butterfly.* New York: Holiday House.

Grifalconi, Ann. (1987). *Darkness and the Butterfly.* Boston, MA: Little, Brown.

Heiligmam, Deborah. (1996). *From Caterpillar to Butterfly.* Illustrated by Bari Weisman. New York: HarperTrophy.

Howe, James, and E. Young. (1987). *I Wish I Were A Butterfly.* San Diego, CA: Harcourt Brace.

Johnson, Sylvia A., and Isao Kishida. (1989). *Silkworms.* New York: First Avenue Editions.

Lambert, Jonathan. (1994). *Dottie the Ladybug Plays Hide and Seek*. (Baby Bug books). New York: Random House.

McDermott, Gerald. (1986). *Anansi the Spider*. New York: Henry Holt.

Mudd, Maria M. (1991). *The Butterfly*. Illustrated by Wendy Smith-Griswold. New York: Stewart, Tabori & Chang, Inc./Workman.

Polacco, Patricia. (1993). *The Bee Tree*. New York: Philomel.

Trapani, Iza. (1993). *The Itsy Bitsy Spider*. New York: Whispering Coyote Press.

Van Allsburg, Chris. (1988). *Two Bad Ants*. Boston, MA: Houghton Mifflin.

White, E.B. (1974). *Charlotte's Web*. New York: Harper.

Parent Letter (School-age)

Dear Parents,

We are now beginning our new theme Insects and Spiders. We will provide opportunities for the children to learn:

- There are many kinds of insects, and they are found all over the world.
- Insects come in many sizes, shapes, and colors.
- Insects have three body parts: head, thorax (middle section), and abdomen (usually the largest of the sections).
- Insects have six legs (three pairs), two antennae, and if winged, four wings.
- Insects help us by making honey and pollinating flowers and fruits.
- Spiders are not insects.
- Insects and spiders come from eggs.
- Spiders have eight legs (four pairs), two body parts, two feelers, and no wings or antennae.
- A spider spins silk to get its food, build its shelter, protect its eggs, and to travel safely.
- Spiders help us by eating insect pests.

We will be talking about:

- types and characteristics of insects
- habitats of insects
- activities of insects
- types and characteristics of spiders

Try one or more of these things to do at home with your child:

- Take a walk around your yard and neighborhood. Look for insects, spiders, and spider webs. Talk about what you find.
- Let your child tell you what he has learned about spiders and insects.
- Visit the public library, and check out books that will help your child further her interest in nature.

Join us for parent participation opportunities at school:

- Visit our classroom to see the spider web we've "spun," and all the activities that are taking place.
  Date _____ Time _____
- Come help us make and eat our "dirt cake."
  Date _____ Time _____

Our wish list for this theme is:

pipe cleaners	white twine and yarn
lunch-sized paper bags	old newspapers

Thank you for your interest and participation in our class.

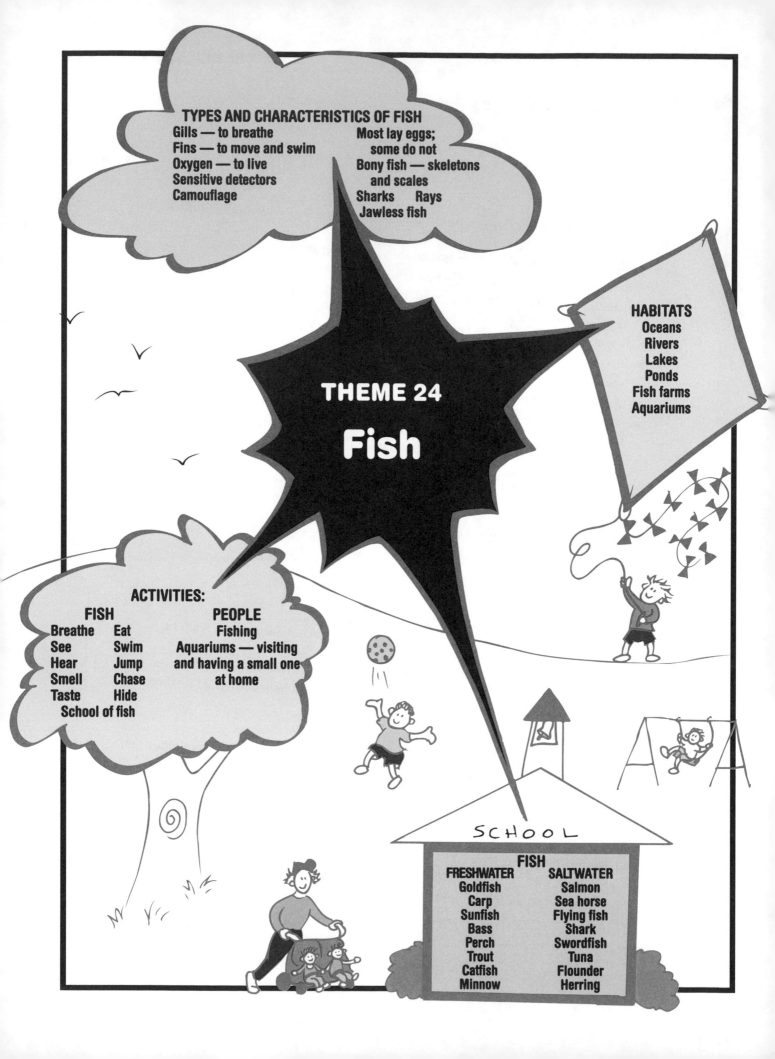

TYPES AND CHARACTERISTICS OF FISH

Gills — to breathe
Fins — to move and swim
Oxygen — to live
Sensitive detectors
Camouflage

Most lay eggs;
   some do not
Bony fish — skeletons
   and scales
Sharks   Rays
Jawless fish

THEME 24

Fish

HABITATS
Oceans
Rivers
Lakes
Ponds
Fish farms
Aquariums

ACTIVITIES:

FISH

Breathe   Eat
See   Swim
Hear   Jump
Smell   Chase
Taste   Hide
School of fish

PEOPLE
Fishing
Aquariums — visiting
and having a small one
at home

SCHOOL

FISH

FRESHWATER	SALTWATER
Goldfish	Salmon
Carp	Sea horse
Sunfish	Flying fish
Bass	Shark
Perch	Swordfish
Trout	Tuna
Catfish	Flounder
Minnow	Herring

THEME GOALS

To provide opportunities for children to learn:

1. Fish come in a large variety of shapes, sizes, patterns, and colors.
2. All fish have certain things in common that make them different from other creatures living in the oceans, lakes, rivers, and ponds of the world.
3. All fish live in the water, have gills for breathing oxygen in the water, fins for swimming, and scales for protection.
4. Fish rise or sink in the water by inflating or deflating a swim bladder, like a small balloon in their abdomens.
5. Fish depend on insects, other water-living animals, and plants for their food.
6. Fish provide food, entertainment, and sport for people.

Children-Created Bulletin Board

This bulletin board should invite the children to create an underwater wonderland filled with all kinds of fish drawings, creations, and stories. The board changes often as the children make it an important part of their thematic environment.

✳ Cover the bulletin board with a blue background.
✳ Title it "Our Aquarium."
✳ Have the children glue bright aquarium gravel along the bottom of the board.
✳ Ask the children to make a colorful school of fish to go all around the border of the board.
✳ Extend the bulletin board out to the side by placing colored fish netting (available at craft stores) around the board.
✳ Put clothespins on the netting for the children to add their stories, drawings, and anything else they choose.
✳ Put a big fish in the middle of the board labeled with the parts of the fish body: gills, fins, scales, mouth, and eyes.

Vocabulary Starters

Let the children add additional words.

aquarium — a building, tank, or other container where live fish and water plants are kept.

camouflage — colors or patterns on something (a fish, for example) that help it blend into its surroundings, making it difficult to see.

fins — parts of the fish that help it move and balance in the water.

gills — parts of a fish's body used for breathing.

school — a large group of fish swimming together, sometimes for protection.

bony fish — the biggest group, have skeletons made of bone and thin scales covering their bodies. Oysters, starfish, and jellyfish are not fish because they do not have a backbone.

Language Experiences

**POEM:
"Do You Know?"**

✳ With infants, move their hands and arms in rhythm to the words.

✳ Let the older children enjoy moving along with the motion of the words.

Do you know how the fish
Swim up and down the ocean?
If they don't have arms or legs
How do they make their motion?
   I'll tell you a secret
   If you promise not to tell.
   It is really very easy.
   You can do it very well.
Put your hands on your hips,
Put your elbows out wide,
And you wiggle and you waggle
From side-to-side.
   To do it like a fish
   You have to do it faster.
   So you wiggle waggle wiggle
   Waggle wiggle waggle faster.
You wiggle waggle wiggle
Waggle wiggle waggle faster.
You wiggle waggle wiggle
Waggle wiggle waggle faster.

Philip Jackman

THAT'S MY NAME

✳ To practice name recognition, you and the children make a fish for each child.

✳ Have each child write her name on it.

✳ Laminate the fish.

✳ Place a fish bowl on the floor or a table and put all the fish into the bowl.

✳ Have each of the children, one at a time, take a fish out of the bowl and hold it up.

✳ When each child recognizes her name, she gets the fish.

✳ At the end of the activity, put all the fish back into the fish bowl.

✳ This can be repeated many times and can be used as a transition activity as well.

Dramatic Play

AQUARIUM FUN

✳ Turn the dramatic play area into an aquarium.

✳ Set up a small table at the entrance to the area with a toy cash register, play money, or money and tickets the children make.

✳ With the children, make some tagboard fish to hang from the ceiling and a special tank filled with colorful felt fish. (See the sensory art section of this theme.)

✳ Put the water table or plastic tubs of water with "fish" and small aquarium nets in the area also.

✳ Place many kinds and sizes of seashells, starfish, pictures, and books of fish all around.

✳ Add additional items that the children suggest.

✳ If possible, visit an actual aquarium during the study of this theme.

Puppet Play

FISH PUPPETS

✳ Have the children bring some of their old socks from home.

✳ Guide them into making a "fish" sock puppet.

* Have yarn, thread, felt scraps, buttons, sequins, glue, and markers set up at the art table.
* Older children can sew on buttons using large, dull needles and thick thread.
* Have pictures of fish available for reference, especially those that show the varied colors and patterns of fish scales.
* Ready-made household hot mitts designed as fish also can be used to create another variety of hand puppets.

Music

"THIS IS THE WAY THE GOLDFISH SWIM"

The traditional tune to this activity is "This is the Way We Wash Our Clothes," or sometimes called, "Lazy Mary Will You Wake Up?" The children enjoy "swimming" along, "nibbling" with their fingers, and "gill breathing" with their elbows.

This is the way the goldfish swim —
  Back and forth, back and forth.
This is the way the goldfish swim —
  Back and forth in the water.
This is the way they move their gills —
  In and out, in and out.
This is the way they move their gills —
  When the goldfish are breathing.
This is the way they nibble their food,
  Nibble their food, nibble their food.
This is the way they nibble their food —
  When the goldfish are hungry.

This is the way the goldfish jump,
  Goldfish jump, goldfish jump.
This is the way the goldfish jump —
When the goldfish are playing.

Philip Jackman

Movement

SWIM LIKE A FISH

This movement activity is best to do after the children have had a chance to observe live fish in an aquarium and study how they move.

* Place six to eight chairs in any arrangement you choose in the middle of a cleared area, indoors or outdoors.
* Have each child decide what kind of fish he would like to be and then practice "swimming" about.
* Explain they are going to go exploring around the chairs, the way fish explore around rocks under water.
* Have each child take turns. Make appropriate comments, such as, "Evan's fish is swimming around all the rocks," "Look, Keesha's fish is zigzagging around the rocks," and, "See how Tamera goes fast, then slow."
* After each child has taken a turn, have all the children swim in and around each other and the chairs.
* You might also suggest changes in movement by asking them to explore way down low, way up high, and to hover motionless, as fish often do.
* To help create a "swimming mood," play an excerpt from appropriate music, such as Debussy's *La Mer (The Sea)*. Encourage the children to swim as the music makes them feel.

Sensory Art

CATCH THE FISH AND PUT IT BACK

* Take different colored pieces of foam board (available at craft stores), and cut dozens of little fish in all colors and shapes.
* Put these in the water table or a plastic tub with a small amount of water.
* The fish float, and the children enjoy catching the fish with small aquarium fish nets.

MAKE A FISH

✳ On a table, place a variety of sizes and colors of construction paper, tagboard, pencils, crayons, markers, and scissors.

✳ Leave these out for the children to draw, cut out, and color fish of their choosing. They can make them in all shapes, patterns, and sizes — the bigger the better. These fish will later be hung around the dramatic play area, which will become a giant aquarium.

✳ For older children, suggest they experiment with folding and cutting the paper to form fish. The illustration is just an example of one way to do this.

✳ Variety and creativity are important in this activity. Let the children experiment with the materials and apply their imaginations!

FOLD

FELT FISH AQUARIUM

✳ Use a small aquarium without a top.

✳ Tie thread across the top from corner to corner, and from side to side across the middle. The fish will hang from these.

✳ Place various colors of construction paper, felt, sequins, glitter, foil, beads, glue, yarn, thread, pipe cleaners, wire, and markers at the art table.

✳ Throughout the theme, the children can make small fish to put in the aquarium.

✳ For younger children, provide a few fish templates for them to trace around.

✳ Punch holes in the top of each fish, put thread through the holes, and attach to the thread across the top of the aquarium.

✳ Place this in the dramatic play area.

Creative Food Experiences

FISH IN THE CUP

You will need:

    packages of green or blue gelatin

    gummy fish

1. Wash hands.
2. With the children's help, make green or blue gelatin according to the directions on the box.
3. Put equal portions, enough for the class, into clear plastic cups.
4. After the gelatin has cooled in the refrigerator and is partially set, add some gummy fish to each cup.
5. Refrigerate until the treat is completely set.
6. Eat!

MAKE A FISH

You will need:

    wheat bread (2 slices per child)

    cheese

    raisins

    mini-marshmallows

1. Wash hands.
2. The children cut the bread slices with fish-shaped cookie cutters.
3. Grate some cheese or use prepackaged shredded cheese, and spread around bread for "fish scales."
4. Use raisins for eyes. Make a marshmallow mouth.
5. Put bread pieces on a cookie sheet, and bake in oven or toaster oven until cheese melts.

See Theme 18, Oceans and Lakes, for additional cooking recipes that work with this theme as well.

MAKE A FISH

Wash hands.

Cut 2 slices of bread with fish shape cookie cutters.

Spread shredded cheese around bread for "fish scales".

Use raisins for eyes and a mini-marshmallow for a mouth.

Put bread pieces on a cookie sheet.

Bake in toaster oven until cheese melts.

EAT!

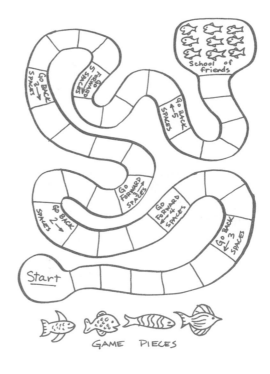

GAME PIECES

Math

FIND THE FISH SCHOOL OF FRIENDS

PRESCHOOL-K PRIMARY-GRADE

This is a board game in which one to four children move their "fish" around the board until they reach their "school of friends."

✳ To construct the game, you will need a large piece of posterboard or heavy cardboard, markers to draw the game (see the illustration), and scraps of cardboard on which to draw and then cut out the game pieces.

✳ In addition, you need one die for play with younger children, or a pair of dice for older children.

✳ Besides stimulating the children's interest in fish, this game emphasizes math skills.

✳ Keep the game pieces in a resealable plastic bag clipped to the game board.

✳ Place the game in the match or manipulative center so the children can play with it when they wish.

Science

SETTING UP AN AQUARIUM

PRIMARY-GRADE

✳ Setting up an aquarium in the classroom is a fascinating learning experience for the children. It integrates all content areas of the curriculum.

✳ Set up a budget and involve the children in how the money should be spent.

✳ To begin, provide the children with pictures and books on how an aquarium works, including the importance of keeping it clean, filtering and aerating the water, checking water temperature, and carefully feeding fish on a schedule.

✳ Decide on the size, make a list of what should be purchased, and how much everything will cost.

✳ Next, visit a pet store and consult with the personnel about purchasing the aquarium tank, pump and aerator, supplies and accessories, and the fish.

✳ Back in the classroom, the children, with your supervision, can fill the aquarium, add the parts, and place the fish in their new home.

✳ Once the aquarium is in operation, the children can make a schedule of how, when, and what their responsibilities will be.

✳ The children can observe the fish, and write their daily observations about each fish and its behavior in an aquarium journal or book. The journal can include the children's drawings of the aquarium and its fish.

Social Studies

THE WORLD OF FISH

* Read Lionni's *Fish Is Fish* or Pfister's *The Rainbow Fish* to the younger children. Older children can read the books themselves.

* Ask the children to tell you what happened in the book. "How do you think the fish felt?" "What made the fish happy?" "Would you tell me what happened in the book?"

* As you continue to discuss the stories with the children, guide them toward thinking about the concepts that are discussed in each of the books: sharing, feelings, giving, receiving, and helping others.

* Talk about how the children fulfill these actions every day in the world of the classroom and in their family world at home.

Children's Books

Ancona, George. (1991). *The Aquarium Book.* New York: Clarion.

Andres, Katherine. (1993). *Fish Story.* New York: Simon & Schuster.

Angelfish, Christopher. (1997). *The Fish Book.* Illustrated by Joseph Veno. New York: Golden Books.

Arnosky, Jim. (1993). *Crinkleroot's 25 Fish Every Child Should Know.* New York: Bradbury.

Coffelt, Nancy. (1994). *Tom's Fish.* New York: Gulliver Books.

Cohen, Caron Lee, and S. D. Schindler. (1998). *How Many Fish? (I Can Read Book).* Illustrated by Lillian Hoban. New York: HarperCollins.

Cole, Joanna. (1997). *Magic School Bus Goes Upstream: A Book About Salmon Migration.* Illustrated by Bruce Degen. New York: Scholastic.

Ehlert, Lois. (1992). *Fish Eyes: A Book You Can Count On.* San Diego, CA: Harcourt Brace.

Frieden, Sarajo. (1996). *The Care and Feeding of Fish: A Story with Pictures.* Boston, MA: Houghton Mifflin.

Krawczyk, Sabine. (Editor). (1998). *Fish (First Discovery Book).* New York: Scholastic.

Lionni, Leo. (1987). *Fish Is Fish.* (Reissue edition). New York: Knopf.

MacLeod, Heather. (1995). *The Fish.* Illustrated by Janice Skivington. Chicago, IL: Children's Press.

McKissack, Pat and Dena Schutzer. (1996). *A Million Fish . . . More or Less.* New York: Dragonfly.

Morley, Christine, and Carole Orbell. (1997). *Me and My Pet Fish.* Illustrated by Brita Granstrom. New York: World Book.

Pallotta, Jerry. (1991). *The Underwater Alphabet Book.* Illustrated by Edgar Stuart. Watertown, MA: Charlesbridge.

Palmer, Helen. (1989). *A Fish Out of Water.* New York: Random House.

Pfeffer, Wendy, and Holly Keller. (1996). *What's It Like to Be a Fish? (Let's-Read-and-Find-Out Science).* Illustrated by Wendy Keller. New York: HarperTrophy.

Pfister, Marcus. (1995). *Rainbow Fish to the Rescue.* New York: North-South Books.

Pfister, Marcus. (1992) *The Rainbow Fish.* New York: North-South Books.

Ryder, Joanne, and Carol Schwartz. (1993). *One Small Fish.* New York: Morrow Junior Books.

Snedden, Robert. (1993). *What Is a Fish?* Photographed by Oxford Scientific Films. Illustrated by Adrian Lascomb. San Francisco, CA: Sierra Club Books.

Toft, Kim Michelle. (1998). *One Less Fish.* Illustrated by Allan Sheather. Watertown, MA: Charlesbridge.

Wallwork, Amanda. (1998). *Find the Fish: That Looks Like This.* (Reprint edition). New York: Puffin.

Wildsmith, Brian. (1987). *Fishes.* New York: Oxford Univ. Press.

Wu, Norbert. (1997). *Fish Faces.* (Reprint edition). New York: Owlet.

Wylie, JoAnne, and David Wylie. (1983). *A Fishy Color Story.* Chicago, IL: Children's Press.

Parent Letter (Preschool)

Dear Parents,

The wonderful world of Fish is our new theme. The children will learn:

- Fish come in a large variety of shapes, sizes, patterns, and colors.
- All fish have certain things in common that make them different from other creatures living in the oceans, lakes, rivers, and ponds of the world.
- All fish live in the water, have gills for breathing oxygen in the water, fins for swimming, and scales for protection.
- Fish rise or sink in the water by inflating or deflating a swim bladder, like a small balloon in their abdomens.
- Fish depend on insects, other water-living animals, and plants for their food.
- Fish provide food, entertainment, and sport for people.

We will be talking about:

- types and characteristics of fish
- habitats of fish
- freshwater and saltwater fish
- activities of fish

Some things to do at home with your child are:

- Visit a pet store or aquarium with your child. Talk about and observe the fish.
- Read books about fish to your child.
- Talk about what we can do to stop polluting the oceans, rivers, lakes, and ponds.

Come in and participate at school:

- Go with us to visit the aquarium.
  Date _____ Time _____
- Come have lunch with us one day.
  Date _____ Time _____

Our wish list items for this theme are:

clean, old socks

beads and sequins

pictures and magazines of fish

yarn

fish food

Thank you for your special friendship and your help.

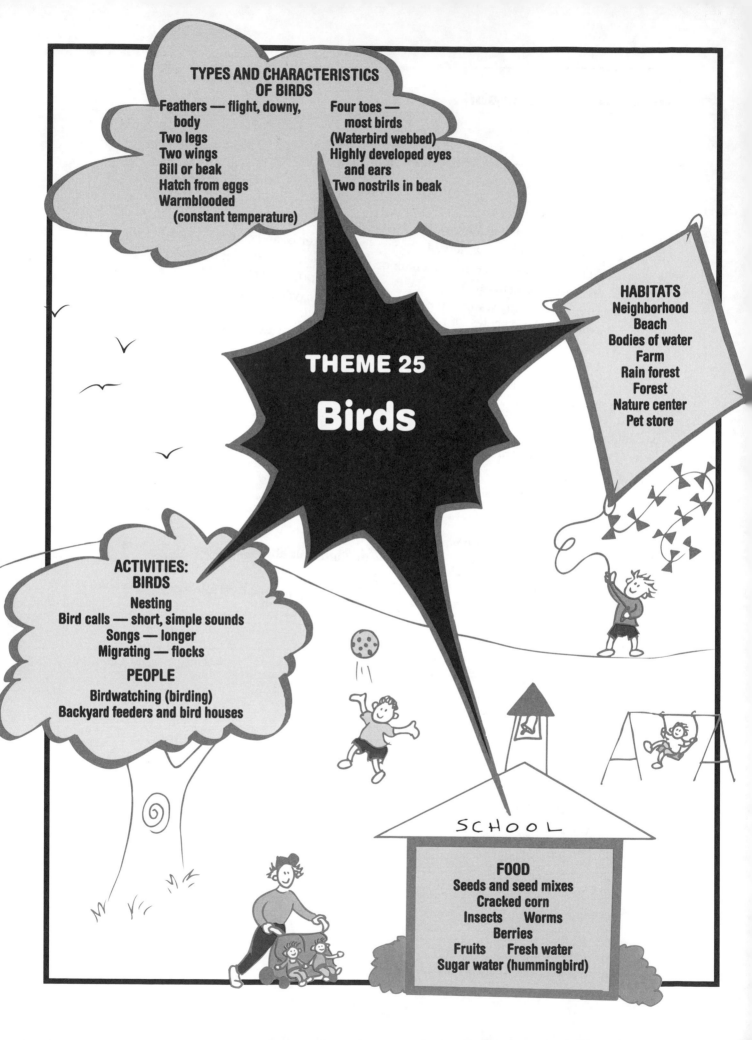

**TYPES AND CHARACTERISTICS
OF BIRDS**
Feathers — flight, downy,
body
Two legs
Two wings
Bill or beak
Hatch from eggs
Warmblooded
(constant temperature)

Four toes —
most birds
(Waterbird webbed)
Highly developed eyes
and ears
Two nostrils in beak

THEME 25

Birds

HABITATS
Neighborhood
Beach
Bodies of water
Farm
Rain forest
Forest
Nature center
Pet store

**ACTIVITIES:
BIRDS**
Nesting
Bird calls — short, simple sounds
Songs — longer
Migrating — flocks

PEOPLE
Birdwatching (birding)
Backyard feeders and bird houses

SCHOOL

FOOD
Seeds and seed mixes
Cracked corn
Insects   Worms
Berries
Fruits   Fresh water
Sugar water (hummingbird)

THEME GOALS

To provide opportunities for children to learn:

1. Birds are found everywhere in the world, from the city to the rain forest.
2. All birds have feathers: flight feathers, downy feathers, and body feathers.
3. All birds have wings, but not all of them can fly.
4. All birds hatch from eggs in nests.
5. Birds come in many sizes, shapes, and colors. They all have feet, and either a beak or bill.

Children-Created Bulletin Board

Each time the bulletin board is blank and ready to welcome a new theme, the children become interested. Keep their attention and curiosity alive by having them help you create the new bulletin board.

✳ Cover your board with all the pictures of birds you can find.
✳ With the children, divide the birds into categories, such as neighborhood birds, pet birds, beach and water birds, birds that do not fly, farm birds, and endangered birds.
✳ Label the largest bird (ostrich) and the smallest bird (hummingbird).
✳ Add to the board as the children draw pictures and write about the different kinds of birds.
✳ Glue on bird food and feathers to give it a textured effect.
✳ It is fun to see the birds "flying" all around the bulletin board.

Vocabulary Starters

Let the children add additional words.

ornithology — the study of birds.

aviary — a place or large building where birds are kept.

migration — the movement of birds, fish, and butter-flies from one place to another.

colony — a group of birds nesting near one another.

flock — a group of birds.

preening — birds cleaning and oiling their feathers.

molting — shedding feathers and growing others to replace them.

roost — a place where birds rest.

perch — a place where a bird sits.

sea birds — birds that cannot fly but can swim as well as a fish, such as penguins.

Language Experiences

FINGERPLAY: "What Do Birds Do?"

The tiny sparrow says chirp-chirp-chirp.
(make a sparrow beak with thumb and fingers; point beak up, open and close for each "chirp")
And eats some seeds with a peck-peck-peck.
(point beak down and peck seeds on the other hand)
Then flies away with a flap, flap, flap.
(cross hands in front, flap fingers on both hands)
The big blackbird says caw, caw, caw.
(make a blackbird beak with both hands and fingers cupped together; point beak up, open and close on each "caw")
And eats some berries with a chomp-chomp-chomp.
(point beak toward front and chomp three berries in a row)
Then flies away with a whoosh-whoosh-whoosh.
(flap arms and hands like large wings)

Philip Jackman

POEM: "Look! I See Birds!"

High, high, high in the sky,
See the eagle circle and fly.
Down, down, down on the ground,
See the pigeon walking around.
Glide, glide, glide on the pool,

See the swan quiet and cool.
Up, up, up in the tree,
See the owl staring at me.
Far, far, far and alone,
See the geese flying back home.

Philip Jackman

Language

POEM: "On Yonder Hill There Stands a Tree"

This is a traditional poem, author unknown, that the children enjoy learning and repeating.

✳ Start slowly. As they learn it, the children like to say it faster and faster.

✳ Ask the children to add additional lines.

On yonder hill there stands a tree:
Tree on the hill, and the hill stood still.
And on the tree there was a branch:
Branch on the tree, tree on the hill, and the hill stood still.
And on the branch there was a nest:
Nest on the branch, branch on the tree, tree on the hill, and the hill stood still.
And in the nest there was an egg:
Egg in the nest, nest on the branch, branch on the tree, tree on the hill, and the hill stood still.
And in the egg there was a bird:
Bird in the egg, egg in the nest, nest on the branch, branch on the tree, tree on the hill, and the hill stood still.
And on the bird there was a feather:
Feather on the bird, bird in the egg, egg in the nest, nest on the branch, branch on the tree, tree on the hill, and the hill stood still.

Dramatic Play

LET'S BUILD A NEST

This activity fits in nicely after the children have been learning about the characteristics of various types of birds, including the varied ways they build their nests.

✳ Turn the dramatic play area or a corner of the playground into a nest-building site.

✳ Collect a variety of materials, such as strips of assorted types of paper (butcher paper, newspaper, toilet paper, paper towels), cardboard, paper towel tubes, cloth scraps, string, yarn, small tree branches, twigs, craft sticks, glue, clay, and anything else that might be useful and safe for building a nest.

✳ By working together cooperatively and creatively, the children can problem-solve, divide up tasks, and figure out how to build the nest.

Puppet Play

IT'S A PUPPET BIRD!

✳ This is fun and easy for the older children to make at any time. It is also a great way to recycle old file folders.

✳ Supply file folders, pencils, markers, crayons, scissors, glue, feathers (available at teacher supply stores), and construction paper.

✳ Draw a simple bird outline on one side of a folder, with the fold at the bottom.

✳ Cut out the bird shape, cutting both halves of the folder at the same time.

✳ The wings can be bent out to either side.

✳ The children can complete their bird any way they wish.

✳ The birds are now ready to "fly," by simply holding the bottom of the puppets, and moving them up and down quickly until the wings move.

✳ A lot of dramatic play can emerge from these puppets.

Music

SONG: "Birds on the Rooftop"

(Adding) One lit-tle bird on the roof-top, chirp-ing, chirp-ing, flut-ter-ing its wings!
Two lit-tle birds their
(Sub-tracting) Ten
Nine

Soon it was joined by an-oth-er, and there were two lit-tle birds on the roof-top!
Soon they were three (etc.)
One flew a-way to the for-est, nine
One flew a-way to the corn-field, eight (etc.)

(Repeat as necessary to match number of birds desired.)

Reproduced by permission of B. Wolf - 1995
Copyright B. Wolf - 1993

(See page 306 for enlargement.)

LET'S LISTEN

✳ Introduce the children to the portion of Saint-Saëns *Carnival of the Animals* that relates to the theme of birds. Be familiar with the piece prior to sharing it with the students.

✳ Listen to the instruments that make the sounds of:
— "hens and roosters" (string section)
— "cuckoo" (clarinet)
— "birds" (flutes and violins)

✳ After the children have listened to the music once, ask them to imitate the birds through movement and in response to the music the next time you play it.

✳ Offer several follow-up activities, such as playing the rhythm instruments along with the recording, drawing special pictures while the music is playing, and playing the entire recording of *Carnival of the Animals* as background music throughout the following days.

Movement

SOAR LIKE A BIRD

✳ After spending some time observing birds outdoors and looking at pictures and books of different types of birds, talk about the various birds the children have seen.

✳ Find out which is each child's favorite bird. What does the child like most about it? Why?

✳ Ask the children to pantomime what their favorite birds look like in flight. Ask them to show how their wings move, how their heads move, how fast or slow they fly.

✳ Add music to their flying. A good selection could be the "Sunrise" part of Grofé's *Grand Canyon Suite* because it builds, flows, and soars. Skip the opening because it is very slow in building.

✳ You might give the children word pictures to help them get started. For example, ask them to imagine their bird waking up in a nest, stretching, looking around, then taking off. What does flying feel like? What do they see down below?

✳ Encourage students to use the whole space to "fly," but being careful to avoid other birds when flying, just as real birds avoid touching each other.

✳ After a time you might fade the music out slowly, suggesting that birds get tired and have to rest now and then.

✳ Have them imagine where they come to rest. Is it a nest, tree, housetop, or mountain top?

✳ Let each child conclude the activity at her own pace.

Sensory Art

FINGER AND HAND PAINTING

✳ Show the children pictures of red, blue, and multi-colored birds.

✳ Talk about the colors of the birds and show them the paint colors (they should be the same as the colors of the birds) you have put out.

✳ With smocks on and sleeves rolled up, older infants and toddlers can really get into finger and hand painting. Sometimes, the children use their whole bodies.

✳ They can paint on trays, tables, and paper.

✳ To make prints from the tray and table designs, slowly press white paper on top, and gently pull it up.

FEATHER PAINTING

✳ Set up the easels and the art table.

✳ Make several colors and thicknesses of tempera paint in flat shallow pans or trays, along with all kinds and shapes of paper, feathers, and feather dusters available for the children.

✳ Let them explore painting with these new kinds of "brushes."

WHY DO DUCKS STAY DRY?

This activity can be done by one to three children at a time.

✳ Have the children draw two pictures of a duck.

✳ Cut the ducks out of paper bags.

✳ Ask them to leave one duck plain and to rub vegetable oil on the other.

✳ Have them sprinkle or spray water on both ducks to observe what happens.

✳ How does the oil that ducks rub on their feathers while they are preening help them stay dry?

✳ This can lead to many more discoveries about ducks and how they survive in their environment.

Creative Food Experiences

NIBBLE A "NEST"

You will need:

> 2 large shredded wheat biscuits
>
> 1/4 cup coconut
>
> 1 tablespoon brown sugar
>
> 1/4 cup liquid margarine
>
> strawberry yogurt
>
> fruity jelly beans

Ingredients are for 6 servings. Double or triple the recipe, as needed for your class.

1. Wash hands.

2. With the children's help, use fingers to crumble shredded wheat biscuits in a bowl.

3. Stir in coconut, brown sugar, and margarine.

4. Line six muffin tins with foil.

5. Press the shredded wheat mixture into the bottoms and up the sides of the foil-lined cups.

6. Bake in 350-degree oven for about 10 minutes, or until crisp. Let cool.

7. Remove the "nests" from the cups by lifting up on the foil. Carefully peel the foil off.

8. Fill the "nest" with a spoonful of yogurt, and place jelly bean "eggs" on top.

9. Enjoy the treat!

NIBBLE A "NEST"

Wash hands.

Crumble 2 large shredded wheat biscuits into a mixing bowl.

Stir in 1/4 cup coconut, 1 tablespoon brown sugar,

and 1/4 cup liquid margarine. Line 6 muffin tins with foil.

Press the shredded wheat mixture onto the bottoms and

up the sides of the foil-lined cups. Bake in 350 degree oven

for 10 minutes or until crisp. Let cool.

Remove the "nests" from the cups. Carefully peel off foil.

Fill the "nest" with a spoonful of yogurt and place

jelly bean "eggs" on top. Enjoy the treat!

Math

IT'S FOR THE BIRDS

✳ Fill the sand/water table or plastic tubs with wild bird seed.

✳ Provide the children with measuring cups, measuring spoons, sifters, funnels, and many sizes of bowls.

✳ Add additional materials the children ask for to help them count, measure, pour, and stir.

BIRD PUZZLES

✳ Make some large cardboard or tagboard cards.

✳ Write a numeral on the bottom.

✳ At the top of the card, place the corresponding number of bird stickers. For younger children, make all the birds the same.

✳ Cut the cards in two. Use different types or configuration of cuts, such as a zig-zag, diamond, straight, curved, and diagonal.

✳ This will help the children put the puzzle card sets together correctly.

✳ As a follow-up activity for older children, let them make another set of card puzzles.

✳ Supply the materials. Let the students decide what the bird puzzles will look like and how they will make them.

Science

LOOK AT THE PICTURES

✳ Put pictures of birds in the sides of a photo cube. These can be photos you take or pictures from magazines.

✳ Point to each picture, and say the name of the bird to the children.

✳ Make several picture cubes, and leave them around the room for the children to play with.

✳ Take the children outside, and point out the birds you see.

✳ Repeat this activity to help the children learn about birds. Repetition is important for very young children.

WHAT'S IN A NEST?

✳ To tie in with the nest-building in the dramatic play area, place items that birds might like to use for a nest outside the windows.

✳ Let the suggestions come from the children. For example, yarn and ribbon pieces, scraps of paper, small twigs, dryer lint, grass, wads of wet tissue, mud, and broken craft sticks are some things birds use in their nests.

✳ Include all the items. It is important to include some things that the birds will not take.

✳ Watch the objects each day, and write down which things the birds like best.

BUILD A BIRD FEEDER TOGETHER

Make feeders at home and at school. This is a project that the children, their family members, and you can do together.

✳ A suggestion for a feeder is to make one from an empty, clean, one-half gallon milk carton. Simply cut away two adjoining sides of a carton, leaving two inches at the top and bottom.

✳ Punch two holes in the top of the carton. Thread some strong string through the holes and tie it, making a loop for hanging.

✳ Put wild bird feed, sunflowers seeds, or bread crumbs in the feeder.

✳ This will attract birds to the yard or playground. It will probably attract squirrels too, giving the children more to watch.

✳ Get several pairs of inexpensive binoculars, and keep them out at all times.

✳ Have a disposable camera for the children to take their own pictures.

✳ Invite someone from the local Audubon Society or a bird rehabilitator to talk to the families and the children at an early evening get-together.

✳ He or she can bring a bird, talk about local birds and their habits, and discuss rain forests, migrating birds, and endangered species.

✳ Everyone can share their experiences with bird watching.

✳ An activity like this that connects home and school can make everyone excited about learning.

Social Studies

A DUCKY FIELD TRIP

✳ Plan a field trip to a local pond, lake, or park that is a duck habitat.

✳ This will give the children a chance to observe ducks in their natural environment. They can see other birds too.

✳ Bring binoculars, cameras, paper and pencils, a tape recorder and blank tapes, and a bird field guide or other reference book.

✳ Remind the children that this is an *observation* field trip. Nothing should be done to disturb the waterfowl or nesting wildlife.

✳ Observe the different behaviors of ducks. Try to identify preening, waddling, swimming, flying, diving, and dabbling (head down and tail up in shallow water to feed).

✳ Are there any ducklings to observe? What type of behaviors do they exhibit?

✳ Drawing pictures and writing about their experience are good follow-up activities to this interesting field trip.

Children's Books

Arnosky, Jim. (1993). *Crinkleroot's 25 Birds Every Child Should Know.* New York: Bradbury.

Cannon, Janell. (1993). *Stellaluna.* San Diego, CA: Harcourt Brace.

Cherry, Lynne. (1997). *Flute's Journey: The Life of a Wood Thrush.* New York: Gulliver Books.

Eastman, P. D. (1988). *Are You My Mother?* New York: Random House.

Ehlert, Lois, and Gloria Dee Aragon Andujar. (1997). *Cuckoo = Cucu: A Mexican Folktale = UN Cuento.* San Diego, CA: Harcourt Brace.

Ehlert, Lois. (1993). *Feathers for Lunch.* San Diego, CA: Harcourt Brace.

Gibbons, Gail. (1998). *Soaring with the Wind: The Bald Eagle.* New York: William Morow.

Green, Jen. (1998). *Birds: Explore the Amazing World of Birds.* New York: Smithmark Publishing.

Hirschi, Ron. (1987). *What Is a Bird?* New York: Walker & Company.

Hutchins, Pat. (1990). *Good-Night Owl!* (Reprint edition). New York: Aladdin.

Landau, Elaine. (1992). *State Birds.* New York: Franklin Watts.

Lerner, Carol. (1996). *Backyard Birds of Summer.* New York: William Morrow.

McCloskey, Robert. (1976). *Make Way for Ducklings.* New York: Viking.

Muntean, Michaela. (1998). *Big Bird's Baby Book.* New York: Golden Books/Children's Television Workshop.

National Wildlife Federation. (1997). *Birds, Birds, Birds! (Ranger Rick's Naturescope Guides).* (Revised edition). New York: McGraw Hill.

Neitzel, Shirley. (1997). *The House I'll Build for the Wrens.* Illustrated by Nancy Winslow Parker. New York: Greenwillow.

Pallotta, Jerry, and Edgar Steward. (1990). *The Bird Alphabet Book.* Watertown, MA: Charlesbridge.

Parsons, Alexandra. (1990). *Amazing Birds.* Photographed by Jerry Young. New York: Knopf.

Rockwell, Anne F., and Harlow Rockwell. (1996). *My Spring Robin.* Illustrated by Lizzie Rockwell. New York: Demco Media.

Rockwell, Anne F. (1992). *Our Yard Is Full of Birds.* New York: HarperCollins.

Sill, John, and Cathryn P. Sill. (1997). *About Birds: A Guide for Children.* New York: Peachtree Publishers.

Tafuri, Nancy. (1984). *Have You Seen My Duckling?* New York: Greenwillow.

Waddell, Martin. (1996). *Owl Babies.* Illustrated by Patrick Benson. Cambridge, MA: Candlewick Press.

Wildsmith, Brian. (1992). *The Owl and the Woodpecker.* New York: Oxford University Press/Franklin Watts.

Wildsmith, Brian. (1987). *The Apple Bird.* New York: Oxford University Press/Franklin Watts.

Wildsmith, Brian (1980). *Birds.* New York: Oxford University Press/Franklin Watts.

Parent Letter (School-age)

Dear Parents,

Please join us as we begin our new theme, Birds. We will provide opportunities for the children to learn:

- Birds are found everywhere in the world, from the city to the rain forest.
- All birds have feathers: flight feathers, downy feathers, and body feathers.
- All birds have wings, but not all of them can fly.
- All birds hatch from eggs in nests.
- Birds come in many sizes, shapes, and colors, have feet, and either a beak or bill.

We will be talking about:

- types and characteristics of birds
- habitats of birds
- food birds eat
- activities of birds
- activities of people (birdwatching or birding)

Some things to do at home with your child are to:

- Build a backyard bird feeder.
- Watch birds around your house and in the neighborhood.
- Read books and magazines about birds.
- Learn about birds that are endangered species.

Opportunities for you to participate at school include:

- Join us for the family meeting, share the bird feeder you and your child made, and hear our guest speaker from the Audubon Society.
  Date _____ Time _____
- Go with us on our field trip to a duck habitat.
  Date _____ Time _____

Here is our wish list for this theme:

newspapers	string
paper towel tubes	cardboard scraps
foil	sifters
funnels	ribbon scraps
empty, clean half-gallon milk cartons	

Thank you for being part of our class family.

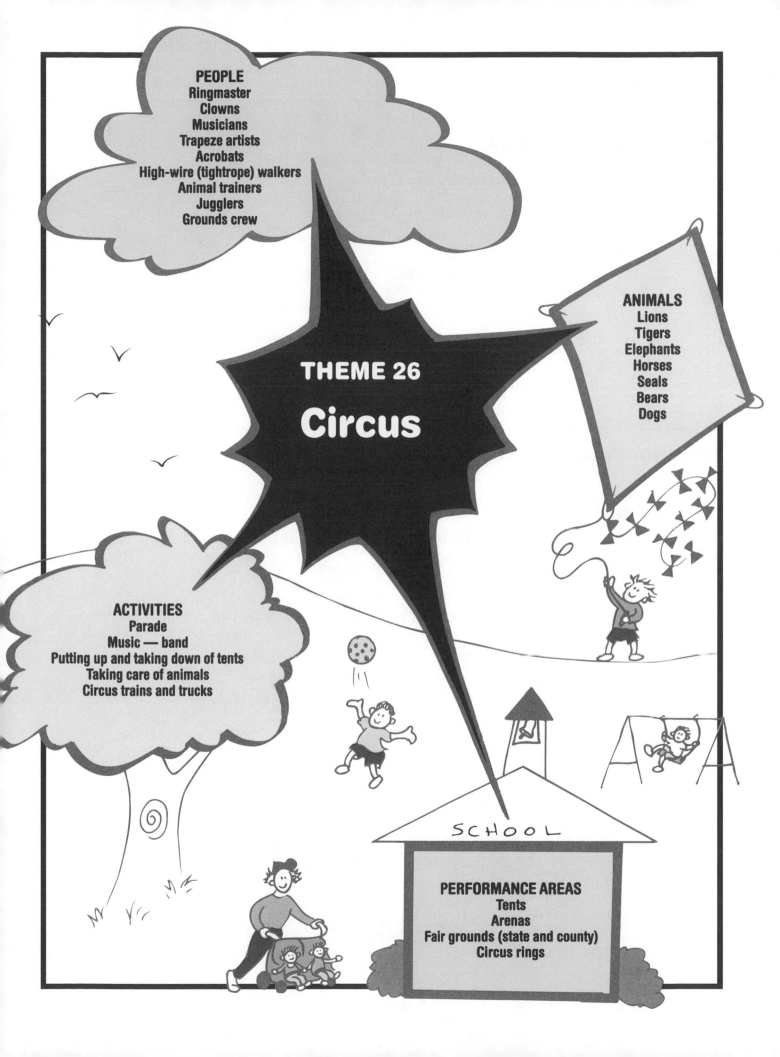

PEOPLE
Ringmaster
Clowns
Musicians
Trapeze artists
Acrobats
High-wire (tightrope) walkers
Animal trainers
Jugglers
Grounds crew

THEME 26
Circus

ANIMALS
Lions
Tigers
Elephants
Horses
Seals
Bears
Dogs

ACTIVITIES
Parade
Music — band
Putting up and taking down of tents
Taking care of animals
Circus trains and trucks

SCHOOL

PERFORMANCE AREAS
Tents
Arenas
Fair grounds (state and county)
Circus rings

THEME GOALS

To provide opportunities for children to learn:

1. The circus is family entertainment that takes place in big tents or arenas.
2. Many thrilling performers can be seen at the circus, such as trapeze artists and high-wire walkers.
3. Clowns are an important part of the circus because they make us laugh and keep the action moving.
4. Circus animals do special tricks.
5. The animal trainer teaches the animals how to do tricks and takes care of them.
6. Circus musicians play lively music from the beginning of the show to the end.
7. The ringmaster announces all the circus acts.

Children-Created Bulletin Board

This bulletin board should reflect the children's enthusiasm about going to the circus. It should be bright, colorful, and ever-changing.

✴ With the children's help, glue sawdust or confetti on a butcher paper background.
✴ Place balloons or streamers all around the board.
✴ Divide the board into three or four rings.
✴ Within the rings, place items the children suggest or create.
✴ Attach a strip of burlap along the bottom of the board as an extension on which to place the children's writing and drawings.
✴ Title the bulletin board "It Is Circus Time!"

Vocabulary Starters

Let the children add additional words.

circus — traveling show of animals, clowns, acrobats, and others.

circus backyard — small village of trucks and trailers surrounding the tent or arena. This is where the circus family lives.

ringmaster — person in charge of the circus performance.

trapeze — a high swing used for aerial circus acts.

acrobat — a person who performs tumbling and balancing acts.

juggler — a person who is able to keep many objects in the air at the same time.

Language Experiences

MAKE A CIRCUS BOOK

* Make a circus book for younger children. Mount pictures of animals, clowns, and circus performers on posterboard squares, and put them in resealable plastic bags.

* Stack the bags on top of each other with the resealable section at the top.

* Punch holes along one side of the plastic bags, and tie them together with yarn. This makes flipping through the book easy for children. It also is easy for you to change the pictures as you find others.

* Talk about the pictures with the children.

* Leave the circus book out for the older infants and toddlers to play with and "read."

POEM: "Toodles the Clown"

With a drum-drum-drum and rooty-toot-toot
The circus has come to town.
Say, who's that man in that funny suit?
I think it's Toodles the Clown.
    He's got a green hat and a big red nose
    And a polka-dot bow tie.
    His shoes have holes — I can see his toes —
    And he's carrying a pie.
Look out! Look out! And don't fall down,
Or you'll surely drop your pie!
Oh, my! Oh, my! He fell on the ground
And his pie got pushed in his eye!
    "Help, help!" He says, "Come help me please.
    I can't see with pie on my face."
    Now he's up on his elbow, he's up on his knees
    Now he wobbles all over the place.
He staggers and stumbles and finally stands,
But he's OK, I think,
'Cause he sneaks us a smile as he licks his hands,
Then gives us a great big wink.
    Be sure you remember the next time you hear
    That the circus is coming to town
    To look for the clown with the big red nose.
    He's Toodles — Toodles the Clown!

Philip Jackman

Dramatic Play

CIRCUS PLAY

It's fun time in the dramatic play area when you bring in the circus prop box!

* Have clown costumes, ballet shoes, ballet costumes, wigs, hats, small umbrellas, and stuffed animals. The children can bring their stuffed animals, too.

* Place hula hoops on the floor to create the rings at the circus. These mark a well-defined space that can be put anywhere.

* Put masking tape in a straight line on the floor to be used as a tightrope.

* Place a few sturdy boxes around for the Ringmaster and performing acts.

* Mix face cream with a small amount of powdered tempera or food coloring for clown makeup.

✳ You can also add some soap to liquid tempera paint and use a small brush to put on the makeup. Don't forget the mirrors!

✳ Put mats on the floor for the tumbling acts.

✳ Outside have a circus parade. Decorate the tricycles and wagons with crepe paper.

✳ Here comes the band! Play recorded lively marching music along with the children playing the rhythm instruments.

Puppet Play

MARIONETTES

Marionettes, controlled by strings, take muscle control and coordination that usually is developed in older preschoolers, kindergartners, and primary-grade children.

✳ A fun way for the children to begin is to tightly tie yarn or strings to the head and arms of stuffed animals. (Moving the legs in addition is more complicated.)

✳ Attach the other ends of the yarn or string to a dowel rod, ruler, stick, or paper towel tube.

✳ The children can pull the strings, and start talking to each other.

✳ If the older children want to try another type of marionette, the first question should be, "What do you want it to do?"

✳ It's important to think through and plan each step in the creation of a marionette. The "airplane control" is the easiest design to manipulate (see illustration).

✳ Start with one string to the head and a string to each hand. Strings to the legs can be added later.

✳ The children need time to experiment with their marionettes and to work through the frustration of the puppet not working the first time. It is the process that's important for young children.

✳ The children should hang the marionettes up when they are done playing. This eliminates tangled strings.

Music

"THIS IS THE WAY THE CIRCUS GOES"

✳ This a rhythmical beat poem that can be said or sung. The tune is a traditional song, "This Is the Way We Wash Our Clothes." The dashes in the song indicate pauses allowing for the up and down movement.

✳ Add rhythm instruments and body movements to vary the activity.

This is the way the trapeze man
Swings up — and down — up — and down.
This is the way the trapeze woman
Swings up — and down — at the circus.
  This is the way the acrobat
  Jumps up — and down — up — and down.
  This is the way the acrobat
  Jumps up — and down — at the circus.
This is the way the horses gallop
Round and round, round and round.
This is the way the horses gallop
Round and round at the circus.
  This is the way the clowns go round
  Clowns go round — and fall on the ground.
  This is the way the clowns go round
  And fall on the ground at the circus.

Philip Jackman

Movement

BE A CLOWN

✳ It is fun for the children to act silly! Ask them if they have ever seen a clown? Where? When?

✳ Talk about clowns and what they do.

✳ Let the children decide if they want to pretend to be clowns one at a time, with a partner, or everyone together.

✳ Ask the children to do the following, first in pantomime (without words), then with words:
— Walk in a silly way
— Do silly tricks
— Make silly faces
— Sing a silly song
— Do a silly dance

✳ Ask the children to show you what else they can do in acting like a clown.

Sensory Art

WASH THE ANIMALS

✳ Young children enjoy water play. For the older infants and toddlers, fill a plastic tub or the sand/water table with soap and water.

✳ Put some small plastic animals in the water.

✳ Let the children wash the animals.

✳ Have plenty of paper towels for the drying area.

✳ This activity works best if two to four children play together.

DRAW A CLOWN

✳ The "draw a clown" activity, based on the "draw a child" activity, is a favorite of young children.

✳ For toddlers, draw around each child lying on a large piece of paper.

✳ Older children can choose a partner, and they can draw around each other.

✳ Have plenty of fabric scraps, yarn, ribbon, construction paper, markers, crayons, paints, glue, and scissors available for the children.

✳ Then, each child can color and draw a clown face, add hair, and decorate the rest of the clown.

CIRCUS PUTTY

✳ Make an entertaining, stretchy, puttylike material.

✳ Use equal amounts of white school glue and liquid laundry starch, approximately $\frac{1}{4}$ cup of each per child.

✳ Pour glue and starch into a small bowl for each child.

✳ Let them mix it with their fingers. Closely supervise the young toddlers.

✳ The putty will be very sticky until *well* mixed.

✳ If it is too sticky, add more starch in very small amounts, and mix until you get a smooth, rubbery consistency.

✳ Store the mixture in an airtight container or plastic bag. The putty does not need to be refrigerated.

CIRCUS CRAYON ETCHING

The children can do this creative activity after they have talked about the circus, looked at pictures and books, and investigated the many features of the circus. Younger children will enjoy exploring this activity, while older ones should be encouraged to investigate detailed images and patterns.

✳ Put paper, crayons, craft sticks, paper clips, and wax paper on a table.

✳ Guide the children in using their crayons to cover the paper with many bright colors in assorted shapes. They need to press down hard to leave a thick layer of colors.

✳ After filling the paper, then color heavily over the whole paper using black crayons.

✳ Ask them to think about a circus design they would like to draw.

✳ Using the craft stick or paper clip, scrape or scratch through the layer of black crayon in whatever circus designs they choose.

✳ The light colors will show through when the black is scraped away.

✳ Polish the picture using wax paper to give it a shine.

✳ Leave the materials out for the children to use again whenever they wish.

Creative Food Experiences

TODDLER PRESCHOOL-K

BIG TOP SNACK

You will need:

6 cups popped popcorn

1 cup candy-coated milk chocolate pieces

1 cup raisins

1 cup peanuts (optional)

1 to 2 cups animal crackers

1. Wash hands.
2. Place all ingredients into a big paper bag, one-gallon resealable plastic bag, or container.
3. Shake everything up!
4. Pour into individual bowls, and enjoy!

CIRCUS TRAINS

PRESCHOOL-K

You will need:

celery sticks

peanut butter

carrots

animal crackers

1. Wash hands.
2. Cut the carrots into circles.
3. Use toothpicks to stick the carrot "rounds" onto a piece of celery. These are the "wheels."
4. Spread the peanut butter on the inside of the celery.
5. Stand the animal crackers in the peanut butter.
6. This is the animal car on the circus train.
7. Look at the train, then EAT!

CIRCUS TRAINS

Wash hands.

Cut a carrot into circles.

Use toothpicks to stick the carrot "wheels" onto

a piece of celery. Spread some peanut butter inside the celery.

Stand some animal crackers in the peanut butter.

Look at your Circus Train Animal Car, then eat!

Math

PRESCHOOL-K PRIMARY-GRADE

LET'S BUILD A CIRCUS

✳ Expand the block center so that the children can build a circus and circus grounds.

✳ In addition to the blocks, provide craft sticks, toothpicks, dowel rods, wooden clothespins, clay, fabric, string, yarn, plastic animals and people, cardboard boxes, and small, interlocking block pieces.

✳ Ask the children for ideas of what else they need to set up the circus.

✳ Leave the area open for expansion for the duration of the theme.

Science

PRIMARY-GRADE

BALANCING ACTS

Most circus performers — and that includes animals as well as people — have developed a sharp sense of balance. If they did not have it, they could not walk on a tightrope, fly on a trapeze, do acrobatics, juggle, or balance large objects. This balancing activity explores some of the principles of balance that circus performers understand.

* On a floor (not on carpet), put down a six-to-eight-foot-long piece of masking tape.

* Ask the children, one at a time, to try to "tightrope-walk" its length with their arms at their sides, and observe how easy or hard it is to do.

* Next, have them walk the tape, but this time with their arms held out to either side, observing how easy or hard it is.

* Ask the children to compare the two methods, and tell you which one makes balancing easier.

* Talk about their answers. (Balancing is easier with the arms extended. Why is this?)

* Have them walk the tape with only *one* arm extended. What happens? (They have to lean to the opposite side. Why? To balance the weight of the extended arm.)

* This experiment demonstrates that the more a person distributes his body weight outward from the center of balance, the *longer* it takes a person to fall sideways. This gives the person more time to shift weight and regain balance. This is why high-wire artists at the circus walk with long poles.

* To make this experience a little more challenging for the older children, place a six-foot length of one-inch by three-inch lumber on its wide side on the floor.

* When they balance on this, it is more like being on a tightrope.

Social Studies

TUMBLING TIME

Since much of what we see in the circus are various forms of tumbling and gymnastics, you could introduce the children to these skills by inviting a qualified gymnastics or physical education instructor to visit the class.

* In making arrangements for a class visitor, be sure to explain to the person that the children are studying the circus so they can tie in their presentation to this theme.

* Ask the visiting instructor to demonstrate some simple tumbling and gymnastics exercises.

* Be sure safe procedures are used and that you know exactly what the children will be asked to do.

* Place some mats on the floor so the children can practice some easy rolls and cartwheels, if *they* want to do so.

* Give the children plenty of time to ask questions.

Children's Books

Bernat, Eva. (1990). *The Wonder Shoes*. New York: Farrar Straus & Giroux.

Birdwell, Norman. (1990). *Clifford at the Circus*. New York: Scholastic.

Bourguignon, Laurence. (1996). *A Friend for Tiger*. New York: Bridgewater Books.

Brett, Jan. (1996). *Berlioz the Bear*. New York: Paper Star.

Bulloch, Ivan, and Diane James. (1997). *A Clown (I Want to Be Series)*. New York: World Book.

Chwast, Seymour. (1996). *The Twelve Circus Rings*. San Diego, CA: Harcourt Brace.

Dr. Seuss. (1994). *If I Ran the Circus*. (Reprint issue). New York: Random Library.

Dr. Seuss. (1966). *Horton Hatches the Egg*. New York: Random House.

Ehlert, Lois. (1992). *Circus*. New York: HarperCollins.

Hill, Eric. (1994). *Spot Goes to the Circus*. (Reprint edition). New York: Puffin.

Hopp, Lisa. (1997). *Circus of Colors (Poke and Look)*. Illustrated by Chiara Bordoni. New York: Grosset & Dunlap.

Johnson, Crockett. (1981). *Harold's Circus*. New York: HarperCollins.

Johnson, Neil. (1995). *Big-Top Circus*. New York: Dial.

Kastner, Jill, and Virginia Duncan. (1997). *Barnyard Big Top*. New York: Simon & Schuster.

Murphy, Stuart J. (1998). *Circus Shapes*. Illustrated by Edward Miller. New York: HarperCollins.

Paxton, Tom. (1997). *Engelbert Joins the Circus*. Illustrated by Roberta Wilson. New York: William Morrow and Company.

Prelutsky, Jack. (1989). *Circus*. Illustrated by Arnold Lobel. New York: Aladdin.

Sampson, Michael. (1997). *Star of the Circus*. Illustrated by Mary Beth Sampson and Jose Aruego. New York: Henry Holt.

Schumaker, Ward. (1997). *Sing a Song of Circus*. San Diego, CA: Harcourt Brace.

Xiong, Blia, and Cathy Spagnoli. (1989). *Nine-In-One GRR! GRR!: A Folktale from the Hmong People of Laos*. Illustrated by Nancy Hom. San Francisco, CA: Children's Book Press.

Parent Letter (Toddler)

Dear Parents,

We are beginning our new theme, The Circus. We will provide opportunities for the children to learn:

- The circus is family entertainment that takes place in big tents or arenas.
- Many thrilling performers can be seen at the circus, such as trapeze artists and high-wire walkers.
- Clowns are an important part of the circus because they make us laugh and keep the action moving.
- Circus animals do special tricks.
- The animal trainer teaches the animals how to do tricks and takes care of them.
- Circus musicians play lively music from the beginning of the show to the end.
- The ringmaster announces all the circus acts.

We will be talking about:

- people in the circus
- animals in the circus
- performance areas of the circus
- activities and performance acts at the circus

Here are some things to do at home with your child:

- Read books about the circus and circus life.
- Read books about clowns, and talk about what you see.
- Visit the zoo to see elephants, lions, and tigers.
- Enjoy eating popcorn and cotton candy together.
- Take your child to the circus when one comes to town.

Parent participation opportunities at school will include:

- Come visit us and see what "circus activities" we are doing.
  Date _____ Time _____
- Come read a book to my friends and me.
  Date _____ Time _____
- Come have lunch with my friends and me.
  Date _____ Time _____

Our wish list items for this theme are:

pictures of circus animals

pictures of clowns

paper towel tubes

string

Thank you for your special friendship.

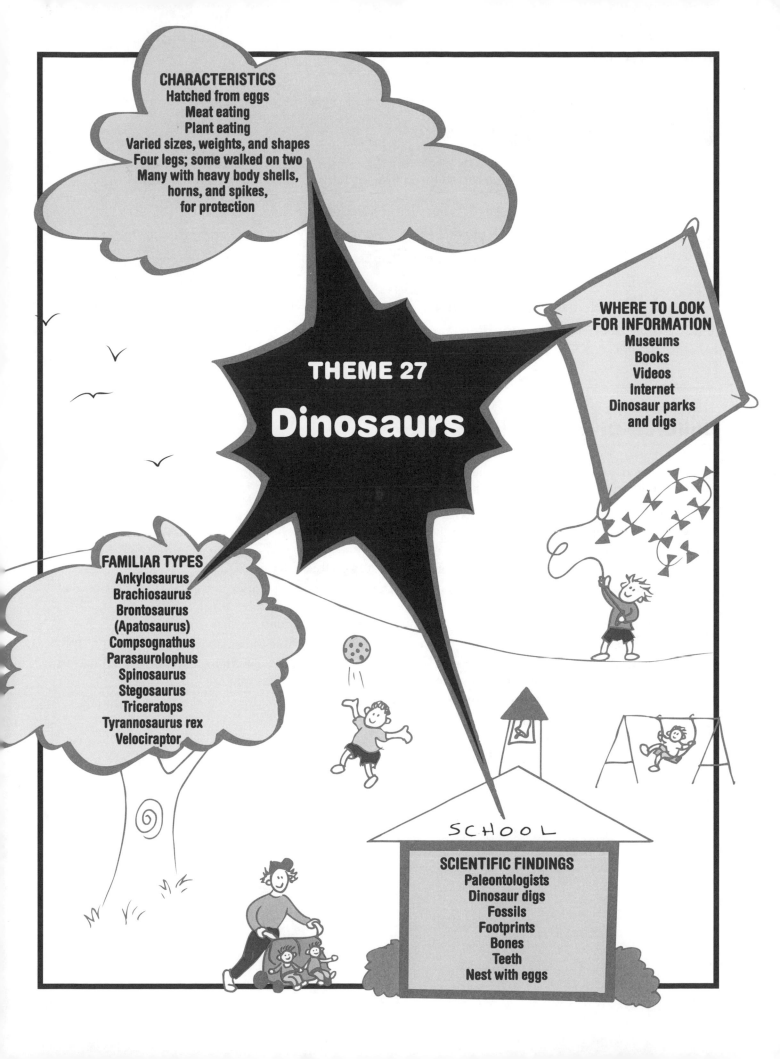

CHARACTERISTICS
Hatched from eggs
Meat eating
Plant eating
Varied sizes, weights, and shapes
Four legs; some walked on two
Many with heavy body shells,
horns, and spikes,
for protection

THEME 27

Dinosaurs

**WHERE TO LOOK
FOR INFORMATION**
Museums
Books
Videos
Internet
Dinosaur parks
and digs

FAMILIAR TYPES
Ankylosaurus
Brachiosaurus
Brontosaurus
(Apatosaurus)
Compsognathus
Parasaurolophus
Spinosaurus
Stegosaurus
Triceratops
Tyrannosaurus rex
Velociraptor

SCHOOL

SCIENTIFIC FINDINGS
Paleontologists
Dinosaur digs
Fossils
Footprints
Bones
Teeth
Nest with eggs

THEME GOALS

To provide opportunities for children to learn:

1. Dinosaurs lived long ago, before there were any people.
2. Some dinosaurs were big and some were small, with varying body shapes.
3. Some dinosaurs ate plants, some ate meat, and some ate both.
4. Dinosaurs hatched from eggs.
5. No one really knows why they died out (became extinct).
6. Scientists who study dinosaurs look for fossils of dinosaur footprints, bones, teeth, and eggs.

Children-Created Bulletin Board

Young children are fascinated by dinosaurs. This bulletin board, as with all boards in an early childhood classroom, should reflect the interests and participation of the children.

* Start with a completely blank bulletin board.
* Let the children suggest the color of the background and what should be added first.
* "Where are the dinosaurs?" is usually the first question asked. This presents an opportunity for the children to draw and place their images of the dinosaurs on the bulletin board.
* Throughout the theme their conceptions will change, and new art work can be placed on the board as well.
* At some point, resource pictures of dinosaurs also should be added.
* Trees, plants, sun, rocks, and mountains can be created for a three-dimensional effect.
* To make the mountains, the children dampen brown paper bags, crush them, and then paint them. The children can add the "mountains" to the bulletin board after they are dry.
* Tree trunks can be made from corrugated paper.
* Glue on dry leaves and dry grass.
* Foil makes a great lake.
* As the theme progresses, the bulletin board should change.

Vocabulary Starters

Let the children add additional words.

dinosaur — "terrible lizard," a prehistoric reptile with upright legs.

extinct — a type of animal or plant that has disappeared and no longer exists.

fossil — rocklike remains of prehistoric animals and plants.

paleontologist — a scientist who digs up dinosaur fossils and brings them to museums.

Language Experiences

FINGERPLAY:
Five Big Dinosaurs

Five BIG dinosaurs practicing a roar,
    (hold up five fingers)
One went away and then there were four.
    (hold up four fingers)
Four BIG dinosaurs munching on a tree,
One went away and then there were three.
    (hold up three fingers)
Three BIG dinosaurs didn't know what to do,
One went away and then there were two.
    (hold up two fingers)
Two BIG dinosaurs enjoying the sun,
One went away and then there was one.
    (hold up one finger)
One BIG dinosaur as lonesome as could be,
It went away and none were left to see.
    (hold up no fingers)

                                 Author Unknown

WHAT IF . . . ?

* Ask questions of the children that will lead to imaginative thinking, abstract imagery, and language development. The answers can also give you insight into how much the children know about dinosaurs: "What can you tell me about dinosaurs?" "What would the world be like if dinosaurs were still alive?" "Would we keep them as pets?" "What would you teach it to do?"

* Write down what they say, and put it in the form of a Big Book.

* Have the children illustrate their words.

* As an extension of this activity, ask the older children to write a letter to their parents and neighbors convincing them it would beneficial for the students if they could keep a dinosaur as a pet.

* The children can share their letters with each other if they wish.

DINOSAUR RIDDLES

Children enjoy making up riddles and jokes. Their sense of humor is delightful.

* Write down riddles the children dictate on sentence strips, and post them around the room. Older children can write their own.

✳ Have blank sentence strips available in the language center.

✳ Here are a few examples of children's humor:

What do you call Tyrannosaurus rex when it wears a cowboy hat and boots? — Tyrannosaurus tex!

What kind of dinosaur can you ride in a rodeo? — A bronco-saurus!

Which dinosaurs were the best police officers? — Tricera-cops!

What did dinosaurs have that no other animals had? — Baby dinosaurs!

What should you do if you find a dinosaur in your bed? — Find somewhere else to sleep!

Dramatic Play

PREHISTORIC TIMES

✳ In the dramatic play area and the book center, have plenty of books, pictures, and items for the children. Also provide plastic dinosaur figures, clay, dinosaur model sets, and other related objects.

✳ Read Pfister's *Dazzle the Dinosaur* (see books section in this theme).

✳ Provide an extra large cardboard shape of Dazzle (stegosaurus).

✳ Have the children glue on wads of newspaper to fill out the body, and then completely cover the shape with sheets of newspaper to create a pantable surface.

✳ Lay Dazzle flat, and paint. Then sprinkle sand all over to add texture.

✳ It is fun to cover the plates on the dinosaur's back with glitter or foil.

✳ When the dinosaur stands up, the children enjoy measuring themselves against "Dazzle." This offers a concrete way for the children to visualize the size of the dinosaurs. The sensory art section of this theme offers more ideas for creating dinosaurs, and the science section has more information about them.

Puppet Play

DINOSAUR SHADOW PUPPETS

✳ Provide the children with tagboard, posterboard, transparent or masking tape, and craft sticks.

✳ They can use books and other materials containing pictures of dinosaurs, particularly side views, for reference.

✳ The children draw their own creative outlines of several dinosaurs on tagboard and cut them out.

✳ Tape a craft stick so that it projects down from the bottom of each dinosaur. This serves as a handle for the puppeteer.

✳ For a quick, easy screen, tape a white sheet over an open doorway, and place a light behind it.

✳ For a more durable shadow puppet screen, construct one from a large piece of posterboard or cardboard. Cut a large rectangular hole in the middle, then fasten a piece of white fabric, such as a sheet, on the back side of it. Cut the fabric slightly larger than the hole.

✳ Bend back two "wings" on either side of the screen to serve as supports, as shown in the illustration.

✳ Place the screen on a table, and set up a bright light behind it.

✳ Some of the children can have fun throwing shadows of dinosaurs on the screen, making them move however they wish, while others can watch from the front.

✳ Create opportunities for the children to make up plays, enjoy the puppets, watch others with their puppets, and experiment with different kinds puppets in shadow play.

Music

SONG: "I Wish That I Could See a Dinosaur" by Jo Eklof

Second verse:

But I will never see a dinosaur, for dinosaurs aren't living any more.
So I'll have to read and look at their pictures in a book,
For I will never see a dinosaur, but I wish that I could see a dinosaur.

(See page 307 for enlargement.)

Movement

DINOSAUR STOMP

This activity combines music and movement.

✳ Have paper sacks available for the children to tie on their feet and stomp around like the dinosaurs to music.

✳ Add rhythmic beats, first as clapping, then as stomping steps.

✳ Young children really enjoy saying dinosaur names. They like the sounds and the rhythm of the names.

✳ Repeat the names with the children several times.

✳ Clap the syllables as you say the names.

✳ Stomp the syllables as you say the names.

✳ Use rhythm instruments to emphasize the syllables as you say the names.

✳ Here are some of the most familiar dinosaur names:

　　Ankylosaurus — ang-ḱa-low-śawr-us
　　Brachiosaurus — b́rak-e-o-śawr-us
　　Brontosaurus — b́ron-tow-śawr-us (also called Apatosaurus — a-ṕat-ow-śawr-us)
　　Compsognathus — comp-śog-na-thus
　　Parasaurolophus — pear-a-śawr-o-ĺofus
　　Spinosaurus — spy-no-śawr-us
　　Stegosaurus — śteg-o-śawr-us
　　Triceratops — try-śer-a-tops
　　Tyrannosaurus rex — tie-ŕan-o-śawr-us
　　Velociraptor — ve-lah-si-ŕap-tor

Sensory Art

DINOSAUR LACING CARDS

Older toddlers and young preschoolers enjoy this activity. It promotes hand-eye coordination and small muscle development.

✳ Draw several different dinosaur shapes on cardboard or posterboard.

✳ Punch large holes just inside the edges of each dinosaur.

✳ You will need ten- to fifteen-inch-long cotton shoe laces.

✳ Tie one end of the lace to the dinosaur.

✳ Modeling how to push the string through the holes can be helpful if the children have not done this kind of activity before.

LOOK FOR THE FOSSILS

✳ Collect a variety of bones, such as chicken or turkey bones. Have enough for each child to have more than one to use in the sensory activities.

✳ *Boil and clean* the bones thoroughly, *or soak them overnight* in a household bleach solution ($\frac{3}{4}$ cup of bleach to 1 gallon of water).

✳ Here are several activities the children enjoy. One is to cook up a batch of play dough (see Theme 6 and Theme 11 for recipes).

✳ The children take a bone, place it inside a lump of dough, and cover it completely.

✳ Put the dough-wrapped bones on a cookie sheet and slowly bake the dough in the oven until it is "rock" hard.

✳ Now it's time for the children to become paleontologists. How can the children break the "rocks" without destroying the bones and the imprints inside?

✳ Let them experiment with a variety of instruments and brushes. Give the children plenty of time to complete this process. The activity works best done in small groups. If a lot of children want to do it at the same time, spread out onto two or three tables.

✳ For younger children, hide the bones in the sand table or outside in the sandbox.

✳ The children can be paleontologists and find miniature "dinosaur" bones.

Creative Food Experiences

UNUSUAL BISCUITS

✳ Read Hoff's *Danny and the Dinosaur* to the children, listed in the books section of this theme.

✳ Talk about dinosaurs, explaining that they are animals that lived a long time ago.

✳ Put dinosaur cookie cutters (available at kitchenware stores and some teacher's resource stores) out along with canned biscuit dough.

✳ Let the children make dinosaur biscuits. Some may not want to use the cookie cutters. That's okay. It is fun to shape the dough with your hands.

✳ Bake the biscuits. Be sure to mark the placement of each child's biscuit on a chart, so each child gets to eat her own biscuit.

✳ Enjoy them at snack time.

DINOSAUR NESTS

You will need:

    chocolate chips

    jelly beans

    chow mein noodles

1. Wash hands.
2. Melt the chocolate chips.

3. Let the children serve themselves $\frac{1}{4}$ to $\frac{1}{2}$ cup of chow mein noodles on a paper plate labeled with each child's name.

4. Pour spoonfuls of chocolate onto the noodles until they are covered.

5. As the chocolate cools, the children place jelly bean "eggs" into the nest with a spoon.

6. Let the chocolate cool until it hardens.

7. Eat and enjoy.

DINOSAUR NESTS

Wash hands.

Melt some chocolate chips. Pour spoonfuls of melted chocolate onto 1/4 to 1/2 cup of chow mein noodles.

As the chocolate is cooling, place jelly bean "eggs" into the dinosaur "nest" with a spoon.

Let the chocolate cool until it hardens. Eat and enjoy!

COOKIE FIND

This activity is not only fun, it also helps develop small muscle skills and hand-eye coordination.

✳ Give the children several chocolate chip cookies and toothpicks.

✳ Ask the children if they would like to carefully dig out each chocolate chip while trying not to damage the chip.

✳ After all the chips are removed (or before for some children), they eat the cookies and chips!

Math

HOW LONG WAS A DINOSAUR?

✳ With the children's help, cut pieces of yarn into one-foot lengths.

✳ Have the children line up the pieces of yarn along the floor to measure the length of a dinosaur; for example, twelve pieces of yarn for a twelve-foot dinosaur.

✳ How many dinosaurs would fit into the classroom? How many could play on the playground?

✳ Perhaps the children could continue measuring when they go home. "How many dinosaurs would fit in your room at home?" "In your backyard?"

✳ What about dinosaur tracks? How many of the children's footprints would fit inside a dinosaur track?

✳ Consult reference books and dinosaur resources on the internet for information.

TOOTHPICK SKELETON

This activity can be done in small groups or individually. It encourages sharing ideas and working together to solve a problem.

✳ Ask the children to estimate how many toothpicks (representing bones) it will take to create a dinosaur skeleton on a nine-by-twelve-inch piece of construction paper?

✳ Give each child the number of toothpicks he estimated.

✳ After the toothpicks are glued in place to form the skeleton, ask the children to figure out the number of toothpicks they overestimated. Did they underestimate? How many more do they need to complete the dinosaur skeleton?

Science

LET'S MAKE A BOXOSAURUS

This is a problem-solving, creative thinking, and scientific investigating type of activity. Allow plenty of time over many days for this project, until the children say it is completed. This process is fascinating to observe.

✳ Collect many sizes of cardboard boxes, paper plates, paint, fabric scraps, yarn, glue, scissors, and anything else the children might need.

✳ After the children have seen books, pictures, and reference materials, encourage them, as a class, to make a dinosaur out of boxes.

✳ *They* need to decide how tall and how long the "boxosaurus" should be. Does it have a long tail? Short or long front legs? Is it a plant eater or meat eater? What color is it?

WHICH DINOSAUR IS WHICH?

✳ To help the children see the differences in the dinosaurs, place many pictures of both plant- and meat-eating dinosaurs around the classroom and in activity centers.

✳ Here is some additional information that might be helpful:

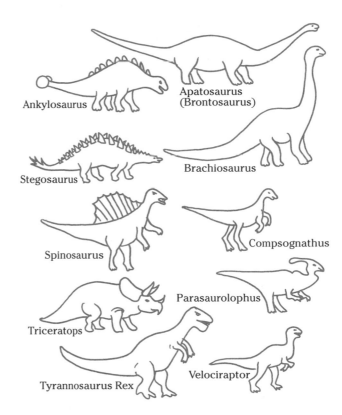

Plant Eaters

Ankylosaurus (ang-ḱa-low-śawr-us) — A huge, armored dinosaur, twenty-five to thirty feet long, six feet wide, four feet tall, and weighing five tons. It had four short legs, a short neck, and a wide skull with a tiny brain.

Brachiosaurus (b́rak-e-o-śawr-us) — One of the tallest and largest dinosaurs found, eighty-five feet long, forty to fifty feet tall, weighing fifty to eighty tons. It had a long neck, small head, thick tail, front legs longer than its hind legs, and nostrils on top of its head. It was probably one of the slowest of the dinosaurs.

Brontosaurus (b́ron-tow-śawr-us)/**Apatosaurus** (a-pat-ow-sawr-us) — In some reference materials, both names are used. This was one of the largest land animals that ever existed at seventy to ninety-five feet long, fifteen feet tall, and weighing thirty-five to fifty tons. It had a long neck, long whiplike tail, a very tiny brain, hind legs larger than the front legs, and nostrils on top of its head.

Parasaurolophus (pear-a-śawr-o-Íofus) — A long-crested (six feet), duck-billed dinosaur, thirty-three feet long, sixteen feet tall, weighing about three to four tons. Its nostrils, located at the end of its snout, went up through the crest and back down. It had a notch in its back, right where the crest would touch the back when its head leaned backwards.

Stegosaurus (śteg-o-śawr-us) — This dinosaur was twenty-five to thirty feet long, nine to eleven feet tall, weighing about one ton. It had a very small brain — about the size of a walnut — and carried its head close to the ground, probably no more than three feet high. It also had approximately seventeen bony plates embedded in its back, a heavy spiked tail, and rear legs longer and straighter than its front legs.

Triceratops (try-śer-a-tops) — This dinosaur looked somewhat like the rhinoceros does today, but much bigger. It was about thirty feet long, ten feet tall, and weighed six to twelve tons. Triceratops walked on four sturdy legs and had three horns on its face, along with a large bony plate projecting from the back of its skull. This dinosaur had one of the largest skulls of any land animal ever discovered; its head was nearly one-third as long as its body.

Meat Eaters

Compsognathus (comp-śog-na-thus) — This was a birdlike dinosaur that walked on two long, thin legs. It was from twenty-eight inches to four feet long, weighed about six and one-half pounds, and was about the size of a chicken. It was a very fast, agile dinosaur with a small pointed head, short arms with two clawed fingers on each hand, and three-toed feet.

Spinosaurus (śpy-no-śawr-us) — Called a "spiny lizard" because it had a series of large spines up to six feet long coming out if its back, this dinosaur was about forty to fifty feet long and weighed four tons or more. It walked on two legs and had arms smaller that its legs.

Tyrannosaurus rex (tie-ŕan-o-śawr-us) — This dinosaur was huge, about forty feet long, fifteen to twenty feet tall, weighing five to seven tons, and couldn't run very fast. It walked on two powerful legs with claws, had tiny two-fingered arms, and had a slim pointed tail for balance and quick turning while running.

Velociraptor (ve-lah-so-ŕap-tor) — This was a fierce, fast dinosaur about six feet long and three feet tall that walked on two legs. It had about thirty very sharp, curved teeth; long thin arms with three-fingered clawed hands; and four-toed clawed feet. It was very intelligent and may have hunted in packs.

✳ Many internet sites offer a wealth of information on dinosaurs. You may want to investigate some of them.

Social Studies

MEET A SCIENTIST

✳ Plan a field trip to a museum. Arrange beforehand for someone familiar with dinosaurs, fossils, and how fossils are found and collected to talk to the children.

✳ Ask the museum staff to show the children around the museum and, if possible, show actual dinosaur bones or fossils.

✳ You may want to discuss with the children what a museum is and what to expect when they get there. Share McGowan's book *Discover Dinosaurs: A Royal Ontario Museum Book,* listed in the books section of this theme.

* If you cannot visit a museum, invite a college or high school science instructor to talk to the children about dinosaurs and tell them how scientists use fossils to learn more about dinosaurs.
* Ask the visitor to bring some fossils to show the children.
* If possible, have them help you set up a "dig" on a part of the playground.
* Follow up by asking the children to draw pictures or write stories about what they learned.
* They can also write thank-you notes to the individual who helped them at the museum or visited their class.

Children's Books

Aliki. (1988). *Digging Up Dinosaurs.* New York: Ty Crowell.

Aliki. (1985). *Dinosaurs Are Different.* New York: Ty Crowell.

Berenstain, Michael. (1997). *Baby Dinosaurs.* New York: Good Times.

Barton, Byron. (1994). *Dinosaurs, Dinosaurs.* New York: HarperTrophy.

Barton, Byron. (1990). *Bones, Bones, Dinosaur Bones.* New York: Ty Crowell.

Dodson, Peter, and Wayne D. Barlowe. (1995). *An Alphabet of Dinosaurs.* New York: Scholastic.

Hennessy, B.G. (1990). *The Dinosaur Who Lived in My Backyard.* (Reprint edition). Illustrated by Susan Davis.

Hoff, Syd. (1998). *Danny and the Dinosaur Go to Camp.* (Reissue Edition). New York: HarperTrophy.

Hoff, Syd. (1993). *Danny and the Dinosaur.* (Reissue edition). New York: HarperTrophy.

Joyce, William. (1998). *Dinosaur Bob.* New York: HarperCollins.

McGowan, Chris. (1992). *Discover Dinosaurs: A Royal Ontario Museum Book.* New York: Addison-Wesley.

Pallotta, Jerry. (1990). *The Dinosaur Alphabet Book.* Illustrated by Ralph Masiello. Watertown, MA: Charlesbridge.

Petty, Kate. (1997). *Dinosaurs Laid Eggs (I Didn't Know That).* Illustrated by James Field, Mike Lacy, and Jo Moore. New York: Millbrook Press.

Pfister, Marcus. (1994). *Dazzle the Dinosaur.* New York: North-South Books.

Prelutsky, Jack. (1992). *Tyrannosaurus Was a Beast: Dinosaur Poems.* Illustrated by Arnold Lobel. New York: Mulberry.

Pringle, Laurence. (1995). *Dinosaur!: Strange and Wonderful.* Illustrated by Carol Heyer. New York: Boyds Mill Press.

Sattler, Helen Roney. (1984). *Baby Dinosaurs.* New York: Lothrop, Lee & Shepard.

Parent Letter (Preschool)

Dear Parents,

We are very excited about beginning our new theme, Dinosaurs. We will provide opportunities for the children to learn:

- Dinosaurs lived long ago, before there were any people.
- Some dinosaurs were big and some were small, with varying body shapes.
- Some dinosaurs ate plants, some ate meat, and some ate both.
- Dinosaurs hatched from eggs.
- No one really knows why they died out (became extinct).
- Scientists who study dinosaurs look for fossils of dinosaur footprints, bones, teeth, and eggs.

We will be talking about:

- characteristics of dinosaurs
- ten of the most familiar types of dinosaurs
- scientific findings of the paleontologists
- where to find information about dinosaurs

Try doing some of these things at home with your child:

- Read books and talk about dinosaurs.
- Take your child to a museum.
- Visit a store that has all kinds of rocks to look at.
- Try to answer your child's dinosaur riddles?

Parent participation opportunities at school will be to:

- Come visit us and see what we have added to our room.
  Date _____ Time _____
- Go with us on our field trip to the museum.
  Date _____ Time _____

The wish list for this theme is:

foil

toothpicks

large pieces of white fabric or a sheet

cardboard boxes (varied sizes)

Thank you for your interest and participation in our study of dinosaurs.

SECTION VI

Transportation

*E*arly *childhood curriculum builds upon what children already know and are able to do.* It is important to strengthen their knowledge and encourage learning of new concepts and skills.

With this in mind, the thematic activities in this theme suggest ways to continue expanding the experiences of children. The content also takes into consideration the children's ages, stages of development, and individual differences in prior experiences and community involvement. Mix and match the activities to meet the needs of the children in your classroom.

The following themes are included in Section VI — Transportation:

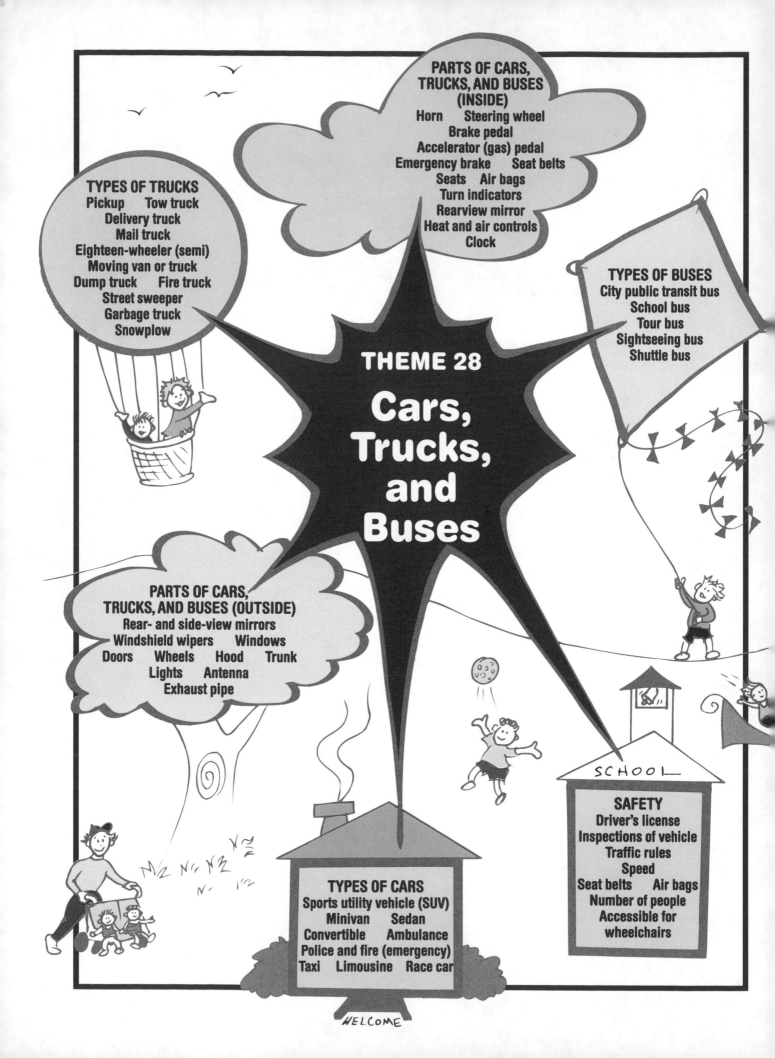

PARTS OF CARS, TRUCKS, AND BUSES (INSIDE)
Horn   Steering wheel
Brake pedal
Accelerator (gas) pedal
Emergency brake   Seat belts
Seats   Air bags
Turn indicators
Rearview mirror
Heat and air controls
Clock

TYPES OF TRUCKS
Pickup   Tow truck
Delivery truck
Mail truck
Eighteen-wheeler (semi)
Moving van or truck
Dump truck   Fire truck
Street sweeper
Garbage truck
Snowplow

TYPES OF BUSES
City public transit bus
School bus
Tour bus
Sightseeing bus
Shuttle bus

THEME 28
Cars, Trucks, and Buses

PARTS OF CARS, TRUCKS, AND BUSES (OUTSIDE)
Rear- and side-view mirrors
Windshield wipers   Windows
Doors   Wheels   Hood   Trunk
Lights   Antenna
Exhaust pipe

SCHOOL

SAFETY
Driver's license
Inspections of vehicle
Traffic rules
Speed
Seat belts   Air bags
Number of people
Accessible for
wheelchairs

TYPES OF CARS
Sports utility vehicle (SUV)
Minivan   Sedan
Convertible   Ambulance
Police and fire (emergency)
Taxi   Limousine   Race car

WELCOME

THEME GOALS

To provide opportunities for children to learn:

1. Cars, trucks, and buses are forms of transportation that move people and things from place to place.

2. There are many kinds, colors, and sizes of cars, trucks, and buses.

3. A driver's license is required to operate these vehicles.

4. All vehicles need to be inspected, repaired, and kept clean.

5. Many occupations involve car, truck, and bus transportation.

Children-Created Bulletin Board

This bulletin board gives the children an opportunity to share what they know and what they want to know about cars, trucks, and buses. Throughout the theme, the board changes as children become more aware of and learn new information about these methods of transportation.

✳ Let the children create a border for the bulletin board by "tire track painting" with toy cars and trucks dipped in paint and rolled on strips of paper.

✳ Title the board, "Transportation: Cars, Trucks, Buses and Wheels."

✳ At the beginning of this theme, have the children draw or cut out pictures of land transportation vehicles and put them on the bulletin board to make a collage.

✳ Provide pictures of tricycles, bicycles, and wagons too. These are the wheeled vehicles with which they have had experiences.

✳ Throughout the theme, more of the children's ideas, safety rules, drawings, and stories will be added to the collage background.

Vocabulary Starters

Let the children add additional words.

driver — a person who operates a vehicle.

fuel — material, such as gasoline or diesel fuel, used to produce power that moves a vehicle.

mechanic — a person who repairs (fixes) a vehicle.

eighteen-wheeler — a large truck with eight wheels on the trailer and ten on the tractor, or cab unit.

cab — the driver's area of a truck.

Language Experiences

SAFETY RULES

To introduce this theme, it is helpful to talk about safety rules. Write down each rule that the children suggest.

✳ Older children can write their own rules on sentence strips.

✳ Make one safety list for riding in a car and another for riding in a bus.

✳ Examples from children for riding safely in the car:

Buckle up your seat belt.

Little children should ride in the back seat.

Do not bother the driver.

Red means **stop**; yellow means **slow down** and **be ready to stop**; green means **go**.

✳ Safety suggestions from children for riding the bus:

Use the handrail when getting on and off the bus.

No dogs on the bus.

Be quiet on the bus.

Be nice.

Do not stand on your seat.

✳ Encourage each child to draw a picture that illustrates her safety rule.

✳ Put the lists and pictures on the bulletin board.

Dramatic Play

BUS RIDE

✳ Collect items for a prop box, such as a bus driver's cap, coins, tickets, steering wheel made from cardboard or a Styrofoam plate, bicycle horn, and a cassette tape of traffic sounds. Tape the sounds yourself, including sirens and honking horns.

✳ Arrange chairs to form a line for seats on a bus.

✳ Tie one end of heavy ribbon pieces onto the chairs for seat belts.

✳ Put Velcro on the other ends of the ribbons so the seat belts will fasten.

✳ Encourage the children to take turns being the bus driver and the passengers.

✳ Model safe ways to get on and off the bus.

PLAYGROUND GAS STATION AND CARWASH

✳ Ask the children to tell you about when they went with a family member to a service station or carwash.

✳ Let them help you set up a gas station and carwash on the playground.

✳ Attach an old hose to a post or tree for use as a gas hose. Use other hoses for air and water. Label each.

✳ Place a "toolbox" in the area. This can be a prop box filled with an air pump, safety glasses, all kinds of tools, flashlights, car diagnostic papers and service diagrams collected from car dealers and service stations, receipt books, car magazines, tool catalogs, and car advertisements from the newspaper.

✳ The children can drive their trikes, wagons, or cardboard-box cars to the station to get fuel, or to be repaired or washed.

✳ Set up the carwash with a couple of buckets of soapy water, smocks, sponges, spray bottles, some rags or old towels for drying, and a cash register for the attendant.

✳ Add toy trucks and cars, Big Wheels, and trikes.

✳ Allow plenty of time for the children to explore and enjoy this outdoor dramatic play area.

LET'S MAKE A CAR!
LET'S MAKE A BUS!

✳ Cardboard boxes can provide hours of fun and learning experiences for young children. Provide a collection of large, medium, and small boxes, cutting tools, construction paper, paint, crayons, brushes, tape, glue, brads, yarn, ribbon, and plenty of space for creating.

✳ Large boxes are available from furniture and appliance stores. Medium boxes are found in grocery stores, offices, and homes. Ask parents to save small, sturdy boxes such as those that come with shoes, stationery, and bank checks.

✳ Offer suggestions and encouragement, but avoid giving patterns or models to copy.

✳ Let the children drive their "cars, trucks, or buses." (See the sensory art section of this theme for ways to make driver's licenses.)

✳ Expand the dramatic play area by opening up a "fast food drive-through window."

Puppet Play

COMMUNITY TRUCK
AND DRIVER PUPPETS

✳ Have pictures and books of trucks available for the children.

✳ Read Behrens' *I Can Be a Truck Driver,* Barton's *Trucks,* and Becker's *You Can Name 100 Trucks!* (See the books section of this theme.)

✳ Talk about all the different kinds of trucks.

✳ Discuss how both women and men drive trucks.

✳ Do any of the children's family members drive trucks?

✳ Guide the children into making truck and driver puppets. Examples are tow truck, tractor-trailer truck, dump truck, and trash truck.

✳ Use cardboard or tagboard for the base, and provide craft sticks, dowel rods, straws, crayons, markers, paint, felt and fabric scraps, scissors, glue, and yarn.

✳ Younger children can create stick puppets using a truck picture or stencil to draw a truck on a piece of paper and attach it to a straw.

✳ Older children can make a set of truck and driver puppets if they wish to do so.

Music

"DO YOU WANT TO TAKE A TRIP?"

This song, to the traditional tune "She'll Be Comin' Round the Mountain," talks about the major types of land transportation in a way that emphasizes *response singing* and has fun with sound effects. Use the rhythm instruments to accompany the song, and add a "bicycle horn" and a "train whistle."

Do you want to take a trip?
  Response: *Yes we do! Uh-huh!*
Do you want to take a trip?
  Response: *Yes we do! Uh-huh!*
Do you want to take a trip,
A zippety-dippity-trip?
Do you want to take a trip?
  Response: *Yes we do! Uh-huh!*
    Do you want to drive a car?
      Response: *Yes we do! Beep-beep!*
    Do you want to drive a car?
      Response: *Yes we do! Beep-beep!*
    If you want to drive a car
    You can drive it pretty far.
    Do you want to drive a car?
      Response: *Yes we do! Beep-beep!*
Do you want to ride a bus?
  Response: *Yes we do! Honk, honk!*
Do you want to ride a bus?
  Response: *Yes we do! Honk, honk!*
If you want to ride a bus
I don't want to hear you fuss.
    Do you want to ride a bus?
      Response: *Yes we do! Honk, honk!*
    Do you want to take a truck?
      Response: *Yes we do! Zoom-zoom!*
    Do you want to take a truck?
      Response: *Yes we do! Zoom-zoom!*
    If you want to take a truck

Just be careful — don't get stuck!
Do you want to take a truck?
    Response: *Yes we do! Zoom-zoom!*
Do you want to take a train?
    Response: *Yes we do! Toot-toot!*
Do you want to take a train?
    Response: *Yes we do! Toot-toot!*
Do you want to take a train
And go see your Auntie Jane?
Do you want to take a train?
    Response: *Yes we do! Toot-toot!*

Philip Jackman

Movement

LET'S PLAY RED LIGHT–GREEN LIGHT

This is a traditional game that continues to be played by young children.

✳ One person is the traffic light with a green circle and a red circle. It is easy to add a yellow circle for "slow down."

✳ All children who want to play start out in a line facing the traffic light player.

✳ When the green light is shown, everyone moves forward.

✳ When the yellow light is shown, then everyone slows down.

✳ When the red light is shown, everyone stops!

✳ If a child moves instead of stopping, that child goes back to the starting line and begins again.

✳ Continue until the whole group reaches the traffic light or the children decide to stop.

✳ For a change, use Walk and Do Not Walk symbols instead of red, yellow, and green.

START YOUR ENGINES

✳ Have the children sit in a circle and number-off, one through four.

✳ Let the children in each number group decide on the name of their car (Jaguar, Chevrolet, Porsche, etc.).

✳ The game leader, chosen by the entire group, calls a car name, and those cars get up and run around the outside of the circle.

✳ The first person back to his spot wins that round.

✳ *But,* there is a *surprise* to this game: The cars can have something wrong with them. The leader decides. For example, "flat tire" (hop around the circle on one foot); "run out of gas" (crab walk around the circle); or "no muffler" (make noises while slowly running around the circle).

✳ The children can think up things that could go wrong before the game starts.

Sensory Art

SAND AND WATER TABLE PLAY

✳ Children enjoy playing with small cars and trucks. To make the activity multisensory, put sand, salt, cornmeal, or gravel in the sand table or in large plastic tubs. Add fresh salt and cornmeal often if these materials are chosen.

✳ Add the cars and trucks.

✳ Continue to add objects, such as paper towel rolls (tunnels), blocks (ramps), and small traffic safety signs, such as Stop and Yield.

Here is another entertaining sensory activity using the sand and water table or plastic tubs.

✳ Clean out the table or tubs. Put in a small amount of water.

✳ Add bubble wrap and plastic toy cars to the sensory table.

✳ The children drive their cars over the bubble wrap to make popping noises. The water just adds extra sensory fun.

LICENSE PLATE RUBBINGS

✳ Collect old license plates. Put tape around the edges for safety. If possible, have some from other states to show the children.

✳ Talk about the purpose of license plates.

✳ Explain that each state has a different design and that each plate within that state is different.

✳ Put the old license plates, paper, and crayons in the art center so the children can make rubbings.

✳ Ask the children to look for license plates when they are riding in their family vehicle or on the bus, and keep a list to share with classmates.

PERSONAL DRIVER'S LICENSE

✳ Put tagboard, crayons, markers, pencils, a small bathroom scale, tape measure, and yardstick in the art center.

✳ Show the children your driver's license and ask the parents to do the same.

✳ The children can make their driver's licenses based on real ones, or design new ones.

✳ Take a picture of each child to be used on the license. They can also draw pictures of themselves.

✳ Have the children figure out how much they weigh and how tall they are. This information is put on the driver's license.

✳ Put the licenses on the bulletin board, if the children wish to do so.

Creative Food Experiences

STOPLIGHT COOKIES

You will need:

    packaged sugar cookie dough in a roll (enough for each child to have three cookies)

    white icing

    red, yellow, and green food coloring

1. Wash hands.
2. Bake sugar cookies according to instructions on package.
3. Divide white icing into three equal portions.
4. Add red food coloring to one bowl of icing, yellow food coloring to another bowl of icing, and green food coloring to the third bowl of icing.
5. Each child spreads icing on her cookies with a plastic knife to make Stoplight Cookies. Yum!

TRUCK STOP PANCAKES

You will need:

    2 eggs

    4 tablespoons sugar

    2 cups all-purpose flour

    2 tablespoons baking powder

    1 teaspoon salt

    2 1/4 cups milk

    4 tablespoons oil

    1 teaspoon vanilla **or** cinnamon for added flavor

1. Wash hands.
2. Start with 2 cups of milk and mix with other ingredients.
3. For thicker pancakes, use less milk; for thinner ones, add more milk.
4. Spray skillet with fat-free cooking spray.
5. Cook pancakes on medium heat, not high, or the sugar will scorch your pancakes.
6. Turn when bubbles have formed and edges are cooked enough. Turn only once.
7. Recipe serves 4 to 6. Enjoy!

TRUCK STOP PANCAKES

Wash hands.

Mix 2 cups milk, 2 eggs, 4 tablespoons sugar,

2 cups all-purpose flour, 2 tablespoons baking powder,

1 teaspoon salt, 4 tablespoons oil, and

1 teaspoon vanilla or cinnamon.

Spray skillet with fat free cooking spray. Cook pancakes on

medium heat. Turn when bubbles have formed and edges are

cooked enough. Turn only once. ENJOY!

Math

RACE CAR TRACK

This game is best when played by small groups of children. Use an old sheet to make this math game.

✳ With the children's help, draw a large oval shape on the sheet.

✳ Draw four lines inside and parallel to the oval shape to form lanes. Mark these lanes into small spaces, similar to the way lanes are drawn in board games.

✳ In the open area inside the lanes, draw a large rectangular grid to create small squares. Randomly number each square with a number from 1 to 10.

✳ Each child chooses a small car and puts it in a lane space marked "Start." Then, in turn, each child stands outside the sheet and tosses a large washer or other round disk onto the numbered squares.

✳ The child advances his car the number of spaces indicated. If the washer does not land on a numbered square, the child loses a turn.

✳ Continue playing until all cars have reached the finish line, or the children choose to stop the game.

Science

WHEELS

✳ Have pictures and books available for the children.

✳ Have toy cars, trucks, and buses, along with trikes, wagons, and tires for the children to inspect.

✳ Use these to help the children visualize the different kinds of wheels there are.

✳ Explain that there would be no wagons, trikes, bicycles, skates, or cars if we did not have wheels.

✳ Discuss the many different materials used in making wheels.

✳ Go for a walk around the neighborhood and look for wheels.

✳ Show pictures and talk about the different "wheels at work." Ask the children to name some of these in their community, such as ambulances, fire trucks, garbage trucks, mail trucks, pickup trucks, cement mixers, dump trucks, and eighteen-wheelers.

✳ Add different kinds of wheels to the block center.

DRIVING IN TRAFFIC

Go for a drive without ever leaving the classroom. With the children's help, lay out some short streets by laying down masking tape on the floor in a zigzag pattern, as described.

✳ With the tape, mark a starting place with an "X."

✳ Then, start *forward* with the masking tape for four feet. Each street segment is four feet long.

✳ Turn ninety degrees *right* for four feet, then *left,* then *left* again, then *right, right* again, then *left, left* again, then *right* for four feet, ending with "Stop" marked on the floor.

✳ The children who want to play sit in a circle around the "streets," with two children at a time acting as "driver" and "police officer."

✳ The driver follows the tape from "X" to each turn, at which point she must signal with the appropriate hand before turning, say either "left" or "right," and then make the turn.

✳ The police officer follows behind the driver. If the driver does not make the correct signal and say left or right before turning, the officer issues a warning ticket. Let the children design the warning tickets.

✳ Then the driver continues to the Stop sign, and her turn is over.

✳ Let the children take turns being driver and officer until all who wish to do so have participated.

✳ For younger children, let them "drive" along the streets, one child at a time. If they can identify left from right, let them do so. Otherwise, it is fun for them to just drive.

✳ Ask questions to the group about the activity. "Why do drivers need to make signals in traffic?" "Do real drivers put their hand out before turning?" (Yes, if they are on a bicycle or if their turn indicator signal is not working.) "How do real drivers signal a turn?" "Why do we need to have police officers watching drivers?" "Do you know what happens if a driver is given a real ticket for a violation, like not signaling?"

Social Studies

WHAT DOES A MECHANIC DO?

PRESCHOOL-K PRIMARY-GRADE

✳ To introduce this activity, read Flanagan's *Mr. Yee Fixes Cars,* Delafosse's *Cars and Trucks and Other Vehicles,* Leslie's *Let's Look Inside the Red Car: A Lift-the-Flap-Book* or Radford's *Harry at the Garage,* listed in the books section of this theme.

✳ Invite a car, truck, or bus mechanic to visit the class, or take a field trip to a garage and visit with a mechanic there.

✳ Ask the mechanic to show and talk about the tools he uses to repair vehicles, and to demonstrate how the tools are used and what they do.

✳ The children always enjoy seeing the mechanic take a ride on the "creeper," a piece of equipment used to slide under vehicles.

✳ Perhaps the mechanic can show the children what an engine looks like or what the car or truck looks like when raised on "the rack."

✳ After the visit, the children can write thank-you notes, and draw or write about what they learned.

Children's Books

Barton, Byron. (1998). *Trucks.* New York: HarperCollins.

Becker, Jim. (1994). *You Can Name 100 Trucks!* Illustrated by Randy Cherning. New York: Cartwheel Books.

Behrens, June. (1985). *I Can Be a Truck Driver.* Chicago, IL: Childrens Press.

Bingham, Caroline, and Deni Brown. (1995). *Fire Truck: And Other Emergency Machines.* New York: Dk Publishers.

Crews, Donald. (1997). *Truck.* Tupelo, MS: Tupelo Books.

Crews, Donald. (1993). *School Bus: For the Buses, the Riders, and the Watchers.* New York: Mulberry Books.

Deesing, Jim. (editor). (1997). *Busy Trucks: A Pop-Up Book.* Illustrated by Richard Stergulz. New York: Random House.

Delafosse, Claude. (editor). (1996). *Cars and Trucks and Other Vehicles.* New York: Cartwheel Books.

Dingus, Bill N. (1998). *Jeffery the Jeep.* Illustrated by Carol B. Murray. New York: Overmountain Press.

Eick, Jean. (1998). *Bulldozers.* New York: Raintree/Steck-Vaughn.

Flanagan, Romie. (1998). *Mr. Yee Fixes Cars.* Chicago, IL: Childrens Press.

Hoban, Tana. (1997). *Construction Zone.* New York: Greenwillow.

Kirk, Daniel. (1997). *Trash Trucks.* New York: Putnam.

Leslie, Amanda. (1997). *Let's Look Inside the Red Car: A Lift-the-Flap Book.* (Reissue edition). Cambridge, MA: Candlewick Press.

Leslie, Amanda. (1997). *Let's Look Inside the Yellow Truck: A Lift-the-Flap Book.* (Reissue edition). Cambridge, MA: Candlewick Press.

Osinski, Christine. (1998). *Riding the School Bus with Mrs. Kramer.* Illustrated by Alice K. Flanagan. Chicago, IL: Childrens Press.

Oxlade, Chris. (1997). *Car (Take It Apart).* Illustrated by Mike Grey. New York: Silver Burdett.

Pienkowski, Jan. (1997). *Trucks and Other Working Wheels.* Illustrated by Renee Jablow and Helen Balmer. New York: Dutton.

Piers, Helen. (1996). *Is There Room on the Bus?: An Around-the-World Counting Story.* Illustrated by Hannah Giffard. New York: Simon & Schuster.

Pomerantz, Charlotte. (1997). *How Many Trucks Can a Tow Truck Tow?* Illustrated by R.W. Alley. New York: Random House.

Pritchard, Louise. (1998). *Cars, Trucks, and Buses.* New York: Dk Publishers.

Radford, Derek. (1997). *Harry at the Garage.* Cambridge, MA: Candlewick Press.

Raffi. (1998). *The Wheels on the Bus (Songs to Read).* Illustrated by Sylvie K. Wickstrom. New York: Crown.

Rockwell, Anne F. (1992). *Cars.* New York: Dutton.

Royston, Angela. (1991). *Diggers and Dump Trucks.* New York: Little Simon.

Scarry, Richard. (1997). *Cars and Trucks and Things That Go.* New York: Golden Press.

Siebert, Diane. (1987). *Truck Song.* Illustrated by Byron Barton. New York: HarperTrophy.

Wilson-Max, Ken. (1997). *Big Red Fire Truck.* New York: Cartwheel Books.

Wilson-Max, Ken. (1997). *Little Green Tow Truck.* New York: Cartwheel Books.

Wilson-Max, Ken. (1996). *Big Yellow Taxi.* New York: Scholastic.

Ziefert, Harriet, and Andrea Baruffi. (1992). *Where Is Mommy's Truck?* New York: HarperCollins.

Parent Letter (Toddler)

Dear Parents,

We are starting to study transportation, and our theme is Cars, Trucks, and Buses. We will provide opportunities for the children to learn:

- Cars, trucks, and buses are forms of transportation that move people and things from place to place.
- There are many kinds, colors, and sizes of cars, trucks, and buses.
- A driver's license is required to operate these vehicles.
- All vehicles need to be inspected, repaired, and kept clean.
- Many occupations involve car, truck, and bus transportation.

We will be talking about:

- types of cars
- types of trucks
- types of buses
- parts of cars, trucks, and buses (inside)
- parts of cars, trucks, and buses (outside)
- safety

Try some of these hings to do at home with your child:

- Take your child with you when you go to the service station, go through the car wash, or have your car repaired.
- Talk to your child about the family car. For example, the type of car, the parts of the car, how you take care of the car, and the importance of wearing seat belts.
- When you and your child are in the car, look for stop signs, yield signs, traffic lights, and different types of cars, trucks, and buses.

Some opportunities for you to participate at school will include:

- Come join us when we cook Truck Stop Pancakes and stay to help us eat them.
  Date _____ Time _____
- Go with us on our field trip to the mechanic's garage.
  Date _____ Time _____

Our wish list for this theme includes:

all sizes of cardboard boxes

out-of-date (expired) license plates

paper towel tubes

car, truck, and bus magazines

Thank you for sharing your child with us.

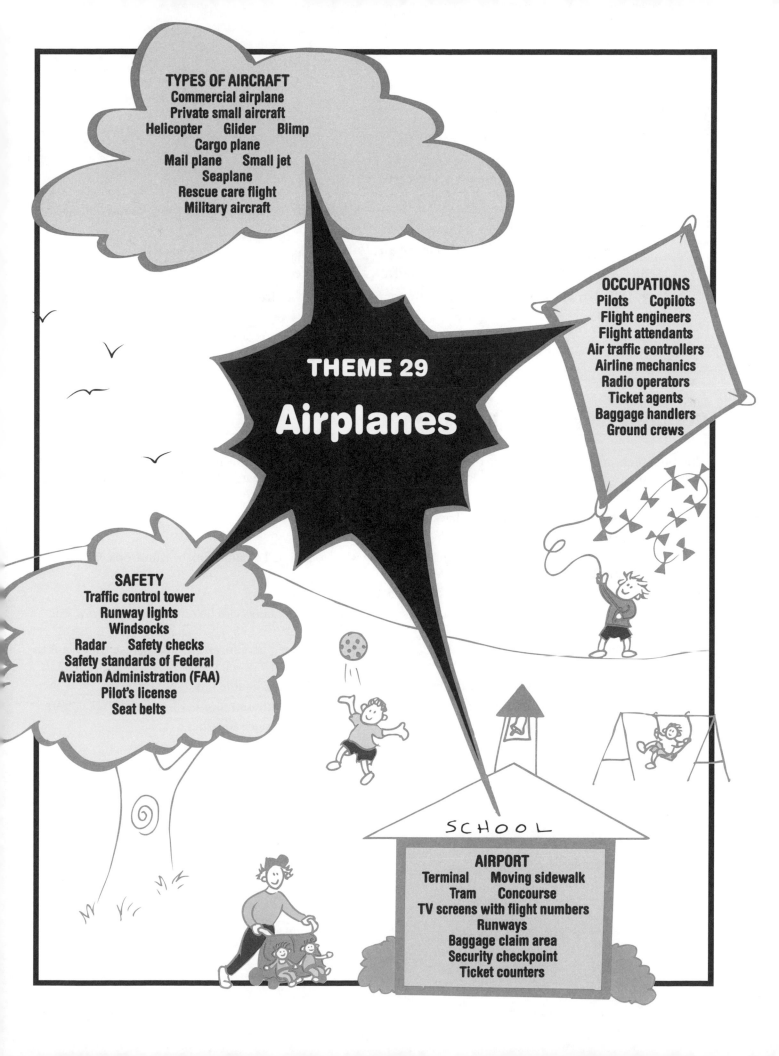

TYPES OF AIRCRAFT
Commercial airplane
Private small aircraft
Helicopter   Glider   Blimp
Cargo plane
Mail plane   Small jet
Seaplane
Rescue care flight
Military aircraft

THEME 29
Airplanes

OCCUPATIONS
Pilots   Copilots
Flight engineers
Flight attendants
Air traffic controllers
Airline mechanics
Radio operators
Ticket agents
Baggage handlers
Ground crews

SAFETY
Traffic control tower
Runway lights
Windsocks
Radar   Safety checks
Safety standards of Federal
Aviation Administration (FAA)
Pilot's license
Seat belts

SCHOOL

AIRPORT
Terminal   Moving sidewalk
Tram   Concourse
TV screens with flight numbers
Runways
Baggage claim area
Security checkpoint
Ticket counters

THEME GOALS

To provide opportunities for children to learn:

1. Airplanes are a form of transportation with wings. Airplanes move people and things from place to place.

2. There are many kinds and sizes of airplanes.

3. A pilot's license is required to operate an airplane.

4. All airplanes have to be carefully inspected and repaired to keep them operating safely.

5. There are many occupations that involve airplane transportation.

Children-Created Bulletin Board

This bulletin board is an interactive discovery area that will keep changing during the time airplanes are being studied. Encourage the children to think of things to put on the bulletin board and to discover what you have added.

* Cover the board with a light blue background.
* Title the board, "Transportation: Going On An Airplane."
* The top part of the board could represent the sky with cotton ball clouds, sun, or raindrops. Change the weather as the actual weather changes.
* The bottom half of the board can be the airport.
* Encourage the children to place planes all over the board. The planes can be ones that they draw, cut out, or make from craft sticks.
* As the theme progresses, the children can add the control tower, people, and anything else they want to contribute.
* Cut a large front and back cover for a suitcase-shaped book with a handle out of posterboard.
* Attach this book below the bulletin board. Ask the children to paint or color the front and back covers.
* Using the cover for a pattern, cut pages for the book. Staple the pages together.
* Cover the staples by binding the book along the edge with clear mailing tape or duct tape.
* Let the children fill the pages with pictures, drawings, or written stories that fit inside the suitcase.
* Ask the children to number the pages.

Vocabulary Starters

Let the children add additional words.

airplane or aircraft — a vehicle that travels in the air.

airline — a company that owns and operates airplanes.

airport — the place at which airplanes take off and land.

terminal — the building at the airport where people buy tickets and wait for airplanes.

windsock — a sleevelike tube that indicates wind direction for the pilot.

FAA — Federal Aviation Administration, which sets safety standards for airlines.

Language Experiences

FINGERPLAY:
My Little Airplane

This fingerplay may be recited as a poem or sung to the traditional tune of "I'm a Little Teapot."

✳ With infants and young toddlers, you should demonstrate the hand motions. They do not have the muscle control needed yet, but they enjoy watching the motions and will try do them with you.

My little airplane sits on the ground.
   (put one hand flat on floor or table)
I turn the propeller round and round.
   (with other hand, turn the propeller at tips of fingers)
I go down the runway, then up in the sky
   (move hand forward, then hand zooms straight up)
And loop-the-loop — just look at me fly!
   (hand does one or more loops over the head)
In a big circle I go round and round,
   (make a horizontal circle over the head)
Then tip the plane over and dive to the ground.
   (fingers point down, then hand zooms down)
I circle near the ground and get ready to land,
   (circle hand horizontally near floor or table)
Then come to a stop as nice as I can.
   (hand moves forward, then comes to a stop)

Philip Jackman

POEM:
"That's My Air-r-r-r-r-plane"

This poem has a strong jazz beat and calls for lots of body movement and hand clapping. Each line has two strong beats. However, on the last line of each verse, "Air-r-r-r-r-plane" is dragged out for four beats.

Let me tell you 'bout an airplane,
   It's silver and blue.
It flies up high
   And down low too.

It has a smart pilot
    and a wonderful crew.
That's my air-r-r-r-plane.
We're going down to Houston,
    Then, what do you say,
We'll fly to Seattle,
    Then on to L.A.
We're having lots of fun
    Just flyin' around
In our air-r-r-r-plane.
Do you want to fly too?
    Well, hop right on.
We're headin' on up
    To Saskatchewan.
We'll visit cousin Bob
    Then we'll jump back on
Our big air-r-r-r-plane.
Look down there!
    We're comin' back home.
Man, I love to ramble
    And I love to roam,
But I've run out of tickets
    And I've run out of poem
'Bout my air-r-r-r-plane.

Philip Jackman

Dramatic Play

AIRPLANE TRIP

This activity encourages planning together as a family does, sequencing, problem-solving, sharing, taking turns, and creativity.

✳ Expand the home living/dramatic play center to three times its usual size. You can close another center to make room for this.

✳ Make one portion of the expanded area for the "planning stage" of the trip. The children can make lists of what to take and what they are going to do.

✳ Place maps or road atlases, travel brochures, and travel posters here.

✳ Take another part of the area and make it the "getting ready to go on a trip" space.

✳ In this section place suitcases, clothes to pack, shoes, toy or discarded cameras, sunglasses, hats, scarves, backpacks, envelopes, picture postcards, and airplane tickets and passports the children have made.

✳ For younger children's luggage, use small suitcases, camera cases, briefcases, or backpacks.

✳ In another area put chairs in rows with two or three chairs side by side to form seats in an airplane. To make seat belts, tie one end of the ribbons to the chairs and place Velcro on the other ends to connect.

✳ The children take their seats, fasten their seat belts, put their luggage under their seats, and prepare for takeoff.

Puppet Play

PILOT, COPILOT, AND FLIGHT ATTENDANT PUPPETS

✳ With the children's help, cut cardboard circles eight to ten inches in diameter, or use large paper plates.

✳ For infants and young toddlers, draw large simple facial features on the cardboard circles.

✳ Attach a stick, such as a paint stirring stick or tongue depressor, to make a puppet.

✳ Play peekaboo by placing the face in front of an adult's or baby's face.

✳ Older children can create a set of pilot, copilot, and flight attendant stick puppet faces themselves.

✳ Have construction paper, crayons, markers, scissors, and glue available for the children to add hats and uniforms to their puppets.

✳ The children can play with their puppets in the dramatic play area or in other learning centers.

Music

SONG: "I LOVE TO GO UP IN AN AIRPLANE"

Flying in an airliner is a great adventure for a small child and may be quite frightening at first. These original lyrics, sung to the folk tune "My Bonnie Lies Over the Ocean," try to create a friendly, reassuring feeling for young children.

I love to go up in an airplane,
I love to go up in the sky.
I love to go up in an airplane,
I feel like a bird when I fly.
Up, up, up, up, up in an airplane I'll fly, I'll fly,
Up, up, up, up, up in an airplane I'll fly.
　The airplane has powerful engines,
　They all make a great roaring sound.
　The wings lift us up like a feather,
　Oh, look, we are up off the ground!
　Up, up, up, up, up in our airplane we fly, we fly,
　Up, up, up, up, up in our airplane we fly.
The pilot's in charge of the airplane,
And knows how to make it fly high.
For helpers we have flight attendants,
They'll take care of us as we fly.
Up, up, up, up, up like a bird in the sky, the sky,
Up, up, up, up, up like a bird in the sky.

Philip Jackman

Movement

LANDING AT THE AIRPORT GAME

This simple game can be adapted to different age levels. It is based on the idea that to land an airplane safely, you must put it down on the center of the runway and follow it straight to the terminal. The game is best when played with small groups of children.

✳ Clear an area on the floor on which you can, using masking tape, lay out a "runway" that is two feet wide and six to twelve feet long.

✳ To get the children used to the concept of flying and landing, ask them to hold out their arms and pretend to be planes flying, circling in, and landing on the masking tape runway.

✳ They have to watch out for the other planes and line up to land one at a time.

✳ Then, show them a ball, approximately two to five inches in diameter, that represents an "airplane."

✳ To help the child aim the airplane (ball), put another piece of tape down the center of the runway.

✳ At the end of the runway, place a small open box, which represents the terminal, on its side, with the open side facing the pilot (child) trying to land.

✳ Each pilot rolls the airplane down the runway and tries to reach the terminal.

✳ If the ball fails to go into the box, the pilot must go to the end of the line while other pilots try to land.

✳ Play continues until all airplanes have arrived safely to the terminal or the children choose to stop playing.

Sensory Art

AIRPLANE EASEL PAINTING

This type of sensory art develops eye-hand coordination, and provides a creative and imaginative self-expression activity.

✳ An airplane is a big transportation vehicle.

✳ Painting airplanes on a large piece of newsprint or newspaper attached to an easel can help young children learn to express the concepts of form, shape, and size.

✳ Place two easels close together so that children can socialize and share their ideas about their paintings.

LOOK AND SEE

✳ Collect several pictures from magazines, travel brochures, and newspapers that show airplanes and other types of transportation.

✳ Cut a one-inch hole shaped like a circle or square in several pieces of construction paper.

✳ Tape or clip one piece of construction paper over each picture so that the one-inch opening shows only a portion of the picture.

✳ Discuss with the children what it could be. Let them make guesses.

✳ Then lift the construction paper to show what the picture is.

✳ Show another covered picture and play again.

✳ Have the children make some surprise pictures. They can play the guessing game with each other.

Creative Food Experiences

AIRPLANE PRETZEL COOKIES

You will need:

    1 1/2 sticks butter or margarine

    1/2 cup sugar

    1 teaspoon vanilla

    1 3/4 cup enriched all-purpose flour

    2 tablespoons milk

    1 egg

1. Wash hands.
2. Combine butter or margarine, sugar, and vanilla. Beat until blended.
3. Add flour and milk. Chill dough.
4. Divide dough into four parts.
5. Divide each part into eight pieces, and place each piece on individual wax paper pieces. Each child gets two pieces.
6. Roll each piece into a long strand about the width of a pencil.

7. Twist dough into an airplane-shaped pretzel.
8. Beat egg slightly, brush tops of pretzels, and sprinkle with sugar.
9. Bake 8 to 10 minutes at 350 degrees on a greased cookie sheet. Eat!

See Theme 17 for a different pretzel recipe.

Math

AIRPLANE-COLOR MATCHING GAME

The object of this matching game is to match each of four types of airplane to each of three colors.

✳ You will need a standard file folder, a piece of tagboard for a "pocket," three sheets of construction paper, and sturdy game pieces made of cardboard or tagboard.

✳ On the right side of the open folder, draw a grid (see illustration).

✳ At the top, glue three squares of three different colors.

✳ Down the left side, draw four different types of airplanes. The illustration shows two types of propeller-driven airplanes and two types of jets with varying numbers of engines.

✳ In the middle of the left half of the folder, glue or tape a pocket made from a piece of tagboard.

✳ Cut out three squares from each color of construction paper, with each square the same size as the blank grid squares. Draw each type of airplane on each color.

✳ Laminate the folder and all game pieces. Be sure to laminate the pocket *before* attaching it to the folder.

AIRPLANE PRETZEL COOKIES

Wash hands.

Combine 1 1/2 sticks butter, 1/2 cup sugar,

and 1 teaspoon vanilla. Beat until blended.

Add 1 3/4 cup flour and 2 tablespoons milk. Chill dough.

Divide dough into 4 parts. Then divide each part into

8 pieces. Roll each piece into a long strand and twist dough

into an airplane shaped pretzel. Beat 1 egg slightly, brush

tops of pretzels and sprinkle with sugar. Bake 8 to 10 minutes

at 350 degrees on a greased cookie sheet. EAT!

Science

MAKE A PARACHUTE

You may use a parachute for outdoor fun, and the children may have seen them used at air shows or on television. In this activity the children make their own parachute, only with the "jumper" attached to it.

✳ Provide plenty of tissue paper squares, about the size of a paper napkin, string, ruler, scissors, wooden clothespins, crayons, and markers for the children.

✳ After the children draw designs on their tissue paper, they measure and cut four pieces of string twelve inches in length.

✳ Then, tie a piece of string to each of the four corners of the tissue paper. Tie the loose ends together.

✳ The children may want to decorate the clothespin "jumper" before clipping it to the knotted strings.

✳ Then, it's time to "launch" the parachutes! Give the parachute, with "jumper" attached, a toss into the air. The parachute should billow open and float the "jumper" to the floor or ground. It may take a few tries for the children to accomplish this.

✳ As the children try out their parachutes, ask them questions about what is happening, such as, "Why doesn't the parachute jumper come down faster?" "If she didn't have a parachute, would she come down faster?"

✳ Questions like these deal with the interplay between gravity and the wind resistance of falling objects, important issues in aviation.

Social Studies

AIRPORTS AND AIRPLANES

✳ Arrange a field trip to visit an airport. Most airports and airlines welcome children and teachers and have orientations and tours to accommodate all ages.

✳ If the children do not get a chance to have all their questions answered, invite a pilot, copilot, or flight attendant to visit the class.

✳ This offers time for questions to be answered and personal stories to be shared.

✳ As a follow-up to the visits, talk about safety rules. You and the children develop a list of safety rules for airplane travel. Many airlines offer educational packets for teachers.

✳ Suggestions to get the children started:

Put everything you will need in carry-on luggage.

Bring safe, soft toys to play with.

Electronic games may interfere with an aircraft's navigational system.

Stay in your seat.

Pay attention to what the pilot and flight attendant say. They are there to help us.

✳ Put the list and pictures that the children have drawn on the bulletin board.

✳ With the children, build an airport with runways, windsocks, a terminal, and streets. Place small airplanes and cars in their proper places at the gates and parking lots. Add people.

✳ This type of activity will let you know what the children have learned and what else they want to know.

Children's Books

Barton, Byron. (1998). *Planes.* New York: HarperCollins.

Bellville, Cheryl. (1992). *The Airplane Book.* Minneapolis, MN: Carolrhoda Books.

Benjamin, Cynthia. (1997). *Working Hard with the Rescue Helicopter.* Illustrated by Steven J. Petruccio. New York: Cartwheel.

Benjamin, Cynthia. (1994). *I Am a Pilot.* Illustrated by Miriam Sagastis. New York: Barrons.

Berger, Melvin. (1996). *How Do Airplanes Fly?* Illustrated by Paul Babb. New York: Hambleton-Hill.

Blackburn, Ken, and Jeff Lammers. (1996). *Kids' Paper Airplane Book.* New York: Workman.

Bursik, Rose. (1994). *Amelia's Fantastic Flight.* New York: Henry Holt.

Cooper, Jason. (1992). *Airports: Great Places to Visit.* Vero Beach, FL: Rourke Books.

Evans, Frank. (1994). *All Aboard Airplanes.* Illustrated by George Guzzi. New York: Price Stern Sloan.

Felix, Monique. (1995). *The Plane.* New York: Creative Education.

Felix, Monique. (1995). *The Wind.* New York: Creative Education.

Kalman, Bobbie. (1995). *Wings, Wheels, and Sails.* New York: Crabtree.

Martchenko, Michael. (1988). *Angela's Airplane.* Illustrated by Robert N. Munsch. New York: Firefly Books.

Maynard, Christopher, and Deni Brown. (1995). *Airplane and Other Airport Machines.* New York: Dk Publishers.

Pallotta, Jerry, and Fred Stillwell. (1997). *The Airplane Alphabet Book.* Illustrated by Rob Bolster. Watertown, MA: Charlesbridge.

Petersen, David. (1983). *Helicopters.* Chicago, IL: Childrens Press.

Petty, Kate. (1998). *Some Planes Hover (I Didn't Know That).* Illustrated by Ross Walton and Jo Moore. New York: Copper Beech Books.

Robison, Fay (1997). *Pilots Fly Planes.* New York: The Child's World.

Rockwell, Anne F. (1998). *I Fly.* Illustrated by Annette Cable. New York: Dragonfly.

Siebert, Diane. (1995). *Plane Song.* Illustrated by Vincent Nasta. New York: HarperTrophy.

Stott, Dorothy. (1995). *Up, Up in a Plane!* New York: Grosset & Dunlap.

Tucker, Sian. (1993). *The Little Plane.* (Board book). New York: Little Simon.

Wilson-Max, Ken. (1995). *Little Red Plane.* New York: Cartwheel.

Parent Letter (School-age)

Dear Parents,

We are studying transportation, and we are beginning our theme on Airplanes. The children will learn:

- Airplanes are a form of transportation with wings. Airplanes move people and things from place to place.
- There are many kinds and sizes of airplanes.
- A pilot's license is required to operate an airplane. All airplanes have to be carefully inspected and repaired to keep them operating safely.
- There are many occupations that involve airplane transportation.

We will be talking about:

- types of aircraft
- occupations
- airports and airport regulations
- safety

Here are some things to do at home with your child:

- Point things out to your child, and talk about them when you take someone to or pick someone up from the airport.
- Read books about aviation, aircraft, and careers in airplane transportation.
- Talk to your child about all the planning it takes to prepare for a trip on an airplane.

Some opportunities for you to participate at school include:

- Going with us on our field trip to the airport.
  Date _____ Time _____
- Let us know if any family member or friend is a pilot, copilot, flight attendant, or works in any capacity for an airline or airport. We would like to invite this person to visit the classroom and talk with the children.

Wish list items for this theme are:

maps
used/cancelled airplane tickets
small suitcases
file folders
clothespins

Thank you for your continued support.

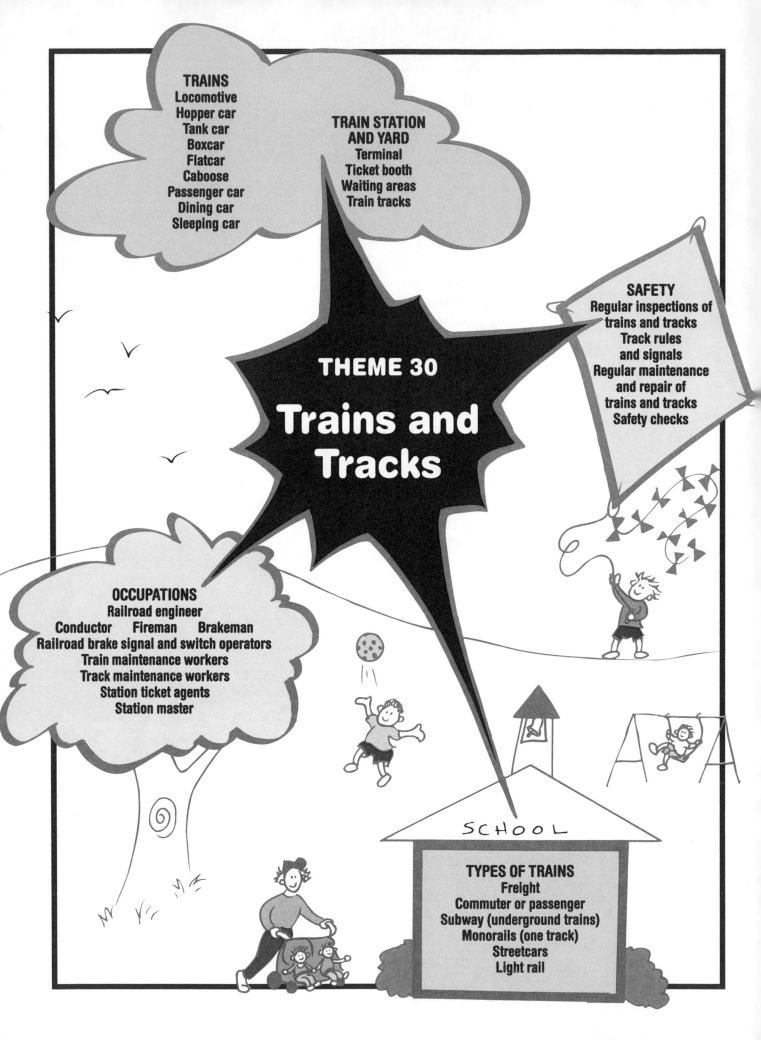

TRAINS
Locomotive
Hopper car
Tank car
Boxcar
Flatcar
Caboose
Passenger car
Dining car
Sleeping car

TRAIN STATION AND YARD
Terminal
Ticket booth
Waiting areas
Train tracks

SAFETY
Regular inspections of trains and tracks
Track rules and signals
Regular maintenance and repair of trains and tracks
Safety checks

THEME 30
Trains and Tracks

OCCUPATIONS
Railroad engineer
Conductor   Fireman   Brakeman
Railroad brake signal and switch operators
Train maintenance workers
Track maintenance workers
Station ticket agents
Station master

SCHOOL

TYPES OF TRAINS
Freight
Commuter or passenger
Subway (underground trains)
Monorails (one track)
Streetcars
Light rail

THEME GOALS

To provide opportunities for children to learn:

1. Trains are a form of transportation that move people and things from place to place on tracks.

2. There are different kinds of trains.

3. Some trains run on tracks above ground, and some run on tracks below ground.

4. All trains have to be inspected and repaired to operate safely.

5. Many occupations involve train transportation.

Children-Created Bulletin Board

This bulletin board offers you and the children an opportunity to explore the world of trains. This should be a cooperative project in which each child is involved in adding to and changing the bulletin board throughout the theme.

* You and the children make a train with one car for each child and you, plus a locomotive and caboose.
* Extend the train and tracks, made from craft sticks, outside the border of the bulletin board.
* Have the train moving from left to right to be consistent with how we read.
* Encourage the children to cut out, draw, or paint a picture, or write something to put in their train car.
* The bulletin board should keep changing throughout the theme. The children will come up with additions as they continue to explore and discover trains and tracks.

Vocabulary Starters

Let the children add additional words.

train engineer — a person responsible for safely driving the train.

fireman — a person who assists in safe operation of the train and is the assistant engineer.

brakeman — a person who operates and repairs the brake systems of trains.

conductor — a person responsible for general safety of passengers, crew, and freight aboard the train.

train or rail yard — an area where trains are put together, safety checked, fueled, and switched to the right track.

throttle — the lever that controls the speed of the train.

Language Experiences

ACTION POEM: "Choo-Choo Train"

When sharing this poem with infants, it is helpful for you to move the babies' arms and hands as you sing.

Here's the choo-choo train.
   (bend arms at elbows)
Puffing down the track.
   (rotate forearms in rhythm)
Now it's going forward,
Now it's going back.
Now the bell is ringing.
   (pull bell with closed fist)
Ding, ding, ding.
Now the whistle blows.
   (hold hands around the mouth)
Wooo-wooo-wooo!
It makes a lot of noise
Everywhere it goes!
   (cover ears with hands)

Author unknown

ACTION POEM: "Here Comes The Freight Train"

Here comes the freight train
   (move arms back and forth)
Chugging down the track,
   (make "chugging" sounds)
Zooming by the crossroads,
   (one hand "zooms" across chest)

Wheels go "clackety clack."
   (hands roll over one another)
Soon it's at the station,
   (pull back the "brake" motion)
Loading up the cars,
   (bend down and pick up "crates")
Some have bikes or roller skates,
Some hold candy bars.
When the cars are hitched on,
   (children get in train formation by putting hands on waist of child in front of him)
The brakeman says okay,
The engineer blows "toot-toot"
And we're on our way!

Author unknown

CLOTHESLINE STORY

This activity helps develop communication skills, sequencing skills, and left-to-right progression.

✳ Read Piper's *The Little Engine That Could* to the children, listed in the books section of this theme.

✳ With toddlers, retell the story with flannelboard characters. They love interacting with the engine that keeps saying "I think I can — I think I can."

✳ With older children, retell the story using the characters the children have drawn and cut out. Laminate these figures.

✳ When everyone is ready to tell the story, ask two children to hold a nylon cord, approximately thirty-six inches long, to form a clothesline.

✳ As the story is being told, other children pin the characters on the clothesline with the clothespins, beginning on the left and proceeding to the right.

✳ Make the materials available to the children so that they can read the story and put the characters on the clothesline whenever they choose.

Dramatic Play

RIDE THE RAILS

✳ Visit an appliance store, electronic equipment store, or check with parents to get a large packing carton to make into a train car.

✳ Put the box in the dramatic play area.

✳ With the children's help, tape a second, smaller box to the front of the big box to represent the engine.

✳ Some of the children can paint and decorate the train car and engine.

✳ Other children can color paper plates to tape along the sides of the box to make the wheels. Older children can punch small holes in the box, insert large brads, and attach the paper plates to keep them firmly on the box.

✳ A paper towel tube can be taped inside the front of the large box for the throttle.

✳ If the children want to add additional boxes to make the train longer, collect other boxes and tape them to the big box. The children will decide what else is needed.

✳ To keep the train from interfering with other classroom activities, outline train tracks on the floor with masking tape. The train should stay on the tracks.

✳ Put travel posters all around the room.

✳ Add a train whistle sound recording or a bell to create a more realistic train effect.

✳ The children can take along a snack to eat as they travel down the tracks (see the creative food experiences section of this theme).

✳ Enjoy riding the rails!

Puppet Play

PUPPET TRAVEL

✳ Select one of your favorite puppet characters. It can be made out of a sock, sack, paper plates, kitchen gadgets, and other objects. Refer to puppet play sections in other themes for suggestions.

✳ Introduce the puppet as a character who is going on a trip and needs the children to help.

✳ In a large bag place small toy vehicles, such as train cars, airplanes, helicopters, cars, trucks, boats, and buses.

✳ The puppet tells the children that he is going to visit a grandmother in (let the children help you think up where), and he does not have a way to get there.

✳ Ask a child to reach in the bag and select a vehicle that will help the puppet get to his destination. The children keep selecting objects from the bag until the bag is empty.

✳ In order for the puppet to make a decision, the toy vehicles have to be sorted according to which ones are for travel by air, land, or water. The children sort them.

✳ Finally, the puppet makes a decision. He will go by train because that is what the children are studying.

✳ Make the puppet and all the toys available for the children to play with again.

Music

WE'RE GOING TO TAKE A TRAIN RIDE

✳ Let's take a train ride! The song starts very slowly, just the way a train starts, then gets faster and faster, finally slowing down until it stops.

✳ The lyrics are original, and the tune is the traditional song "Skip to My Lou," which is rhythmic and easily remembered.

✳ The song also suggests trainlike movements, with the children starting slowly, speeding up, and finally slowing to a stop.

Get on the train, hear the whistle blow.
Get on the train, hear the whistle blow.
Get on the train, hear the whistle blow.
We're going to take a train ride.
The train starts to move, it's going kind of slow.
The train starts to move, it's going kind of slow.
The train starts to move, it's going kind of slow.
We're starting to take a train ride.
The wheels are turning, we're picking up speed.
The wheels are turning, we're picking up speed.
The wheels are turning, we're picking up speed.
We're moving along on our train ride.
Look at us go, we're going pretty fast.
Look at us go, we're going pretty fast.
Look at us go, we're going pretty fast.
We have lots of fun on our train ride.
The wheels are slowing, we'll be there soon.
The wheels are slowing, we'll be there soon.
The wheels are slowing, we'll be there soon.
We'll soon be finished with our train ride.
Here comes the station, the whistle goes "toot."
Here comes the station, the whistle goes "toot."
Here comes the station, the whistle goes "toot."
We're almost finished with our train ride.
The train is stopping, we're almost there.
The train is stopping, we're almost there.
The train is stopping, we're almost there.
We've come to the end of our train ride.

Philip Jackman

Movement

LOOSE CABOOSE

This is a fun game to play outside.

✳ One of the children is the "loose caboose."

✳ The rest of the children divide into trains with three cars each.

✳ The first player in the train is the engine.

✳ The other players can choose what they want to be, such as a locomotive, hopper car, flatcar, boxcar, or tank car.

✳ The object is for the loose caboose to try to attach to a train.

✳ When all are aboard, the "trains" chug around the train yard making sound effects.

✳ The trains dodge and turn to keep away from the caboose.

✳ When the caboose attaches to a train, the engine of that train becomes the new loose caboose.

Sensory Art

SHOE BOX TRAINS

✳ With younger children, have the children color the shoe boxes.

✳ Add two wheels on each side of the shoe box. Make the wheels with corrugated cardboard circles and attach them with brads.

✳ String the boxes together.

✳ Add a string with a large bead tied securely on the end so the children can pull their train.

✳ Older children can make a flatcar by using the bottom of the shoe box and attaching wheels to it.

✳ They can put small cars, blocks, or anything they choose to fill up the flatcar.

I SPY A TRAIN

✳ Read and look closely at Micklethwait's *I Spy a Freight Train: Transportation in Art,* listed in the books section of this theme.

✳ As the author says, "You don't need to have any knowledge of art to introduce a child to a painting. . . . All that is important is there in front of you in the picture, waiting to be discovered."

✳ Gather books of paintings from the library, and postcards of paintings from a local art store or museum.

✳ Make these into a display that invites the children to look for details in each painting.

✳ For this theme, include many paintings representing transportation, especially trains. For example, Mary Cassatt's *In the Omnibus (The Tramway),* Vincent Van Gogh's *The Langlois Drawbridge,* Ernst Thoms's *Train,* and Claude Monet's *Gare Saint-Lazare, Arrival of a Train.*

✳ If possible, follow up this activity with a visit to the art museum or gallery with the children.

Creative Food Experiences

NUTRITIOUS SNACK FOR BABY

Before you prepare this snack, check with the parents to be sure the baby is not allergic to any of the ingredients. This can be used by parents when travelling with their infant.

You will need:

 2 teaspoons low-fat plain yogurt

 3 teaspoons any fruit baby food

 2 teaspoons rice cereal (you can substitute barley or oatmeal cereal)

Then, mix well and serve!

TRAIN TAKE-ALONG SNACK MIX

You will need:

 1 1/2 tablespoons of butter or margarine

 2 1/2 tablespoons of honey

 1 cup of Cheerios

 1 cup of Crispix cereal

 1/2 cup of peanuts (optional)

 1/2 cup of thin stick pretzels, broken in half

 1/2 cup of raisins

 1 cup of chocolate mini-baking bits

1. Wash hands.

2. Let the children measure and put ingredients in individual bowels, ready for you to pour into a hot skillet.

3. In large skillet, over low heat, melt butter.

4. Add honey until blended. Add cereal, nuts, pretzels, raisins, stirring until all pieces are evenly coated.

5. Continue cooking over low heat about 10 minutes, stirring often.

6. Remove from heat and immediately place on wax paper or a cookie sheet to cool.

7. Add chocolate mini-baking bits.

8. Store in tightly covered container.

TRAIN TAKE-ALONG SNACK MIX

Wash hands.

Melt 1 1/2 tablespoons butter -- add 2 1/2 tablespoons honey

until blended. Add 1 cup Cheerios, 1 cup Crispix cereal,

1/2 cup peanuts (optional), 1/2 cup broken stick pretzels, and

1/2 cup raisins stirring until all pieces are evenly coated.

Continue cooking over low heat about 10 minutes, stirring

often. Remove from heat and immediately place on wax paper

or cookie sheet to cool. Add 1 cup chocolate covered mini

baking bits. YUMMY!

Math

WHAT'S MISSING?

PRESCHOOL-K

This is an activity for small groups of children or one-on-one with the teacher.

✳ Make individual freight train car drawings on index cards and laminate the cards. For examples of these cars, see illustration.

✳ You can also play the same game by using small toy train cars.

✳ Place some of the cards or toy trains on a tray.

✳ For younger children, use fewer items.

✳ Ask the children playing the game to look at each item and name it.

✳ Have them close their eyes while you take an object away.

✳ Ask them to guess which item is missing.

✳ Continue this and take several of the train cars away.

✳ Make the game available for the children in the math center.

LOCOMOTIVE: The engine that pulls the train. The engineer, who drives the train, rides near the front

HOPPER CAR: It carries the type of freight that has to be poured into it, such as coal, sand or wheat. It is open on top.

FLATCAR: It carries very large or long things, like logs, steel beams, or machinery. Loads have to be tied down.

BOXCAR: It carries all kinds of smaller things, like boxes of hardware, toys, paper products, and food.

TANK CAR: It carries liquid freight, such as oil, gasoline, and chemicals.

CABOOSE: It is the last car on a Freight Train. Inside it are offices and beds for the train crew.

Science

MAKE A MINIATURE RAILROAD

PRESCHOOL-K   PRIMARY-GRADE

All you need to make a classroom railroad is a smooth, flat, rigid surface, some regular craft sticks, a marble, and a bottle of rubber cement. This kind of activity helps children develop skills relating to cause and effect, and how to work together to solve a problem.

✳ At one end of your flat surface, which can be cardboard, plywood, or foam core, the children start "laying tracks." It is helpful for you to guide the younger children. They run two parallel lines of craft sticks end-to-end, separated by the width of a craft stick.

✳ Put rubber cement at each end of each stick to hold it in place.

✳ As the children lay the track, they should gently curve it first in one direction, then in another, in an "S" pattern until they reach the far edge of the cardboard, plywood, or foam board.

✳ When the track is done, slightly elevate the edge where they began.

✳ Place the marble between the two tracks, and start it rolling downhill.

✳ If the surface is not tilted enough, the marble may stop rolling. Tilt it too much, and the "train" jumps the track.

✳ They need to experiment to get just the right tilt.

✳ If the sticks are angled too sharply on the curves, the train may keep stopping. They may need to redesign the curve to make it less angular.

✳ Talk about how this experiment in making a railroad presents the same problems real railroads have: Trains must be careful not to go too fast on curves, or they will jump the tracks; the people who lay the tracks must not make curves so sharp that trains have difficulty in going around them.

Social Studies

TRAINS IN OUR COMMUNITY

✳ Call the local train information center in your community to check on the times trains arrive at your train station.

✳ Take the children on a field trip to see the trains.

✳ Many train stations have a tour and orientation sessions for children. If you live in a city with subways, the children probably already are familiar with trains and tracks.

✳ Discuss the safety equipment located at train crossings within a city and its outlying areas. **Signal arms** are found at train crossings on very busy roads. These are lowered to block the road so cars cannot cross the tracks when a train passes by. **Blinking lights** are seen where train crossings and crowded roads intersect. The lights blink on and off to warn cars that a train is coming. **Warning signs** are placed at train crossings on roads that are not heavily traveled. The signs tell drivers to stop and look both ways to see if a train is coming before crossing the tracks.

✳ You can also invite a community or family member who is a train enthusiast to show the children some of their electric trains. These miniature train cars help children identify the individual cars and learn even more about trains.

Children's Books

Awdry, W. (1994). *New Tracks for Thomas.* Illustrated by Owain Bell. New York: Random House.

Aylesworth, Jim. (1995). *Country Crossing.* Illustrated by Ted Rand. New York: Aladdin.

Barton, Byron. (1998) *Trains.* New York: HarperCollins.

Burton, Virginia Lee. (1997). *Maybelle the Cable Car.* Boston, MA: Houghton Mifflin.

Crampton, Gertrude. (1997). *Tootle.* Illustrated by Tibor Gergely. New York: Golden Books.

Crebbin, June. (1996). *The Train Ride.* Illustrated by Stephen Lambert. Cambridge, MA: Candlewick Press.

Crews, Donald. (1992). *Freight Train.* New York: Mulberry.

Demarest, Chris L. (1997). *All Aboard!* San Diego, CA: Harcourt Brace.

Galef, David. (1996). *Tracks.* Illustrated by Tedd Arnold. New York: Morrow.

Gibbons, Gail. (1988). *Trains.* New York: Holiday House.

Jeunesse, Gallimard. (1998). *Trains (First Discovery Book).* Illustrated by James Prunier and Wendy Barish. New York: Scholastic.

Johnston, Tony. (1996). *How Many Miles to Jacksonville?* Illustrated by Bart Forbes. New York: Putnam.

Magee, Doug. (1994). *All Aboard ABC.* New York: Puffin.

McMillan, Bruce. (1995). *Grandfather's Trolley.* Cambridge, MA: Candlewick Press.

Merriam, Eve. (1994). *Train Leaves the Station.* Illustrated by Dale Gottlieb. New York: Henry Holt.

Micklethwait, Lucy. (1996). *I Spy a Freight Train: Transportation in Art.* New York: Greenwillow.

Mills, Claudia. (1998). *Gus and Grandpa Ride the Train.* Illustrated by Catherine Stock. New York: Ferrar Straus & Giroux.

Petty, Kate. (1997). *Some Trains Run on Water: And Other Amazing Facts About Rail Transport (I Didn't Know That).* Illustrated by Ross Walton and Jo Moore. New York: Millbrook Press.

Pinkney, Gloria Jean. (1994). *The Sunday Outing.* New York: Dial.

Piper, Watty. (1978). *The Little Engine That Could.* Illustrated by George and Doris Hauman. New York: Grosset & Dunlap.

Quattlebaum, Mary. (1997). *Underground Train.* Illustrated by Cat Bowman Smith. New York: Bantam.

Royston, Angela. (1992). *Eye Openers — Trains.* New York: Little Simon.

Scarry, Richard. (1995). *Richard Scarry's Longest Book Ever/8 Feet of Lift-the-Flap Fun!* New York: Little Simon.

Suen, Anastasia. (1998). *Window Music.* Illustrated by Wade Zahares. New York: Viking.

Torres, Leyla. (1997). *Gorrion Del Metro/Subway Sparrow.* New York: Farrar Straus & Giroux.

Voake, Charlotte. (1998). *Here Comes the Train.* Cambridge, MA: Candlewick Press.

Welply, Michael, and Dawn Bentley. (1998). *Choo-Choo Charlie: The Littletown Train.* New York: Piggy Toes Press.

Wilson-Max, Ken. (1996). *Big Blue Engine.* New York: Cartwheel.

Parent Letter (Preschool)

Dear Parents,

We will be starting our new theme, Trains and Tracks, this week. We will provide opportunities for the children to learn:

- Trains are a form of transportation that move people and things from place to place on tracks.
- There are different kinds of trains.
- Some trains run on tracks above ground, and some run on tracks below ground.
- All trains have to be inspected and repaired to operate safely.
- Many occupations involve train transportation.

We will be talking about:

- types of trains
- occupations
- train station and yard
- safety

Here are some things to do at home with your child:

- Talk about the train tracks and trains you see around your community. Ask your child what she sees, which type of train is her favorite, and why.
- Talk about the blinking lights, warning signs, and signal arms at each train crossing in the community. This is a perfect time to talk about car safety too.
- Visit the library and check out books to read to your child about trains and tracks.

Parent participation opportunities at school will include:

- Let us know of a family member or friend who is an electric train enthusiast. We would like to invite this person to visit the class, show some of the trains, and talk to the children.
- Come visit our classroom and see all the activities we are doing as we learn about trains and tracks.
  Date _____ Time _____

Our wish list for this theme includes:

clothespins
shoe boxes
cardboard boxes
marbles
paper towel tubes

Thank you for everything you do.

"Name Song"

_____ , that's my name; that's what peo- ple call me.
(your) (you).

_____ , _____ ! That's a ver- y fine name, in- deed!

"It's So Good to Be with Friends"

Jo Eklof

It's so good to be with friends in

an - y kind of wea - ther. We could go for a walk or

sit and talk. We love to be to - geth - er.

Additional verses:

It's fun in the snow with friends in cold and snowy weather.
We could shiver and play all through the day. We love to be together.

It's fun to swim with friends in warm and sunny weather.
We could splash and play all through the day. We love to be together.

"I Am a Member of My Family"

Jo Eklof

Additional verses:

We love each other..........
We're kind to each other..........
We laugh with each other..........
We take care of each other..........
We play with each other..........
We smile at each other..........
We hug each other..........
We cheer up each other..........

"I Have Two Ears"

Jo Eklof

I have two ears to hear, hear, hear. I have a brain to think. I have two eyes to look, look, look. I have two lids to blink. I have a nose to sniff, sniff, sniff. I have some hands to touch. I have a mouth to give a smile and say, "I love you so much!

"Brr, It's Cold Today!"

Jo Eklof

Put on your hat. Put on your gloves Brr, it's cold to -
day. Be sure that you dress up warm - ly when you go out to
play. Put on your coat. Put on your boots. It
looks like win - ter will stay. Oh, it's cold. Yes, it's cold.
Brr, it's cold to - day. Yes! Brr, it's cold to - day!

"When I Wear Red"

Jo Eklof

When I wear red, I nod my head, and
this is what I say, "I nod my head when
I wear red, and I'm wear-ing red to-day.

Additional verses:

Have children make up what to action to do with other colors, for instance, "When I wear green, I always lean."

"The Frog Song"

Jo Eklof

Late last night while you and I were in our beds a - sleep, the frogs came out and sang this song, "rib - bit rib - bit rib - bit rib - bit rib - bit ba - reep!"

"My Kitty Just Says 'Meow'"

Jo Eklof

The bird in the tree says, "cheep cheep cheep. The

dog says, "bow wow wow." The duck in the pond says,

"quack quack quack." my kit - ty just says, "meow."

Additional verses:

"Cocka doodle doo," says the rooster. "Oink oink," says the sow.
"He haw he haw," hear the donkey say. My kitty just says, "meow."

"Baa," says the fluffy lamb. "Moo," says the cow.
"Buzz buzz buzz," says the honey bee. My kitty just says, "meow."

"How I Wish I Had a Little Dog"

Jo Eklof

Second verse:

How I wish I had a little doggie brown and white.
We'd romp around the yard all day. He's sleep near me at night.
We'd do many things together, life would seem just right.
How I wish I had a little dog. How I wish I had a little dog.

"I Like to Look at Bugs"

Jo Eklof

When the sun comes out and the win-ter goes a -way, I

like to go out on a nice warm day. I like to run and I

like to play and I like to look at bugs. (Do they

jig-gle and jump? Yes, they jig-gle and jump. Do they wig-gle and bump? Yes, they

wig-gle and bump.) I like to look at bugs.

Additional verses:

Do they crawl and creep? Do they like to leap?

Do they hop and fly? Way up in the sky?

"Birds on the Rooftop"

(Adding) One lit-tle bird   on the roof-top,   chirp-ing, chirp-ing, flut-ter-ing its wings!
Two lit-tle birds   their
(Sub-   Ten
tracting) Nine

Soon it   was joined by an- oth-er, and there were two lit-tle birds on the roof-top!
Soon they were   three (etc.)
One flew a- way   to the for-est,   nine
One flew a- way   to the corn-field,   eight (etc.)

(Repeat as necessary to match
number of birds desired.)

"I Wish That I Could See a Dinasaur"

Jo Eklof

I wish that I could see a din - o - saur.

I'd like to see him move and hear him ro -

ar. I'd like to count each scale, look him o - ver head to

tail. I wish that I could see a din - o - saur, but

but I wish that I could see a din - o - saur.

Second verse:

But I will never see a dinosaur, for dinosaurs aren't living any more.
So I'll have to read and look at their pictures in a book,
For I will never see a dinosaur, but I wish that I could see a dinosaur.